NEW
VENTURE
MECHANICS

NEW VENTURE MECHANICS

Karl H. Vesper

University of Washington

 Prentice Hall, Englewood Cliffs, New Jersey 07632

Library of Congress Cataloging-in-Publication Data

Vesper, Karl H.
    New venture mechanics / Karl H. Vesper.
        p.   cm.
    Includes bibliographical references and index.
    ISBN 0-13-620790-1
    1. New business enterprises.   2. Entrepreneurship.   I. Title.
HD62.5.V46   1993
        658.1'1 — dc20   91-43340
                                                              CIP

Acquisitions editor: Alison Reeves
Editorial/production supervision and
    interior design: Mary McDonald
Copy editor: Linda Pawelchak
Cover design: Patricia Kelly
Prepress buyer: Trudy Pisciotti
Manufacturing buyer: Bob Anderson

 © 1993 by Prentice-Hall, Inc.
A Simon & Schuster Company
Englewood Cliffs, New Jersey 07632

Printed in the United States of America

10 9 8 7 6 5 4 3 2

ISBN 0-13-620790-1

Prentice-Hall International (UK) Limited, *London*
Prentice-Hall of Australia Pty. Limited, *Sydney*
Prentice-Hall Canada Inc., *Toronto*
Prentice-Hall Hispanoamericana, S.A., *Mexico*
Prentice-Hall of India Private Limited, *New Delhi*
Prentice-Hall of Japan, Inc., *Tokyo*
Simon & Schuster Asia Pte. Ltd., *Singapore*
Editora Prentice-Hall do Brasil, Ltda., *Rio de Janeiro*

To Joan,
the One of All

CONTENTS

Preface   xi

SECTION I   DEVELOPING CONCEPTS

1. **Seizing Business Opportunities**   1

   Introduction   1
   Opportunity Occurrence   2
   Detecting Opportunity Clues   5
   Assessing Possibilities   9
   Looking Ahead—A Software Start-up   12
   Developing Concepts   14
   Marshalling Resources   17
   Start-up Actions   20
   Planning   24
   Moving On   27
   Planning Questions   28
   Possible Milestones for a Planning Time Line   29

2. **Idea Refinement**   30

    Introduction   30
    Feasibility Analysis   31
    Design Stages   32
    Market Fitting   47
    Planning Questions   62
    Possible Milestones for a Planning Time Line   63

3. **Defensive Measures in Design**   68

    Introduction   68
    Curbing Liability   69
    Forestalling Imitation   81
    Planning Questions   102
    Possible Milestones for a Planning Time Line   103

SECTION II   MARSHALLING RESOURCES

4. **Teaming**   104

    Introduction   104
    Solo Takeoff   104
    External Team   111
    Sharing Ownership   115
    Planning Questions   135
    Possible Milestones for a Planning Time Line   136

5. **Inside Equity Capital**   137

    Introduction   137
    Cash Requirements   141
    Internal Seed Capital Sources   152
    Bank Borrowing   160
    Financing Growth—Retaining Equity   168
    Planning Questions   171
    Possible Milestones for a Planning Time Line   172

6. **Outside Equity Capital**   173

    Introduction   173
    Private Placements   177

Formal Venture Capital   185
Going Public   197
Combination Deals   203
Planning Questions   204
Possible Milestones for a Planning Time Line   205

SECTION III START-UP ACTIONS

7. Lining Up Sales   206

Introduction   206
Responding to Prospective Customers   206
Advertising   213
Opening an Outlet   218
Personal Selling   223
Engaging Others to Sell   235
Combining Sales Elements   237
Planning Questions   238
Possible Milestones for a Planning Time Line   239

8. Starting Operations   241

Introduction   241
Premises   245
Equipment   254
Dealing with Suppliers   259
Hiring   262
Producing   266
Planning Questions   271
Possible Milestones for a Planning Time Line   273

9. Start-up Paperwork   274

Introduction   274
Paper Hurdles   276
Other Legal Aspects   289
Insurance   294
Accounting   296
Records   304
Planning Questions   307
Possible Milestones for a Planning Time Line   308

SECTION IV   PLANNING

10. **Venture Plans   310**

Introduction   310
Taking Incremental Action   315
Selective Planning   319
Formal Written Plans   330
Planning Questions   341
Possible Milestones for a Planning Time Line   342

Appendix A: Other Business Plan Outlines   344

Appendix B: Business Plan Example   346

Author Index   363

Entrepreneur Index   367

Enterprise Index   371

Subject Index   375

PREFACE

New Venture Mechanics covers the "nuts and bolts" topics of entrepreneurship, using numerous examples from real life entrepreneurial adventures to illustrate them. Usually, such topics in themselves are neither very difficult nor, unfortunately, very interesting. But it may be important to know about them. The purpose of the examples is partly to clarify the topics and partly to give them life so that the reader will retain an awareness of them.

There are some similarities between this text and an earlier book of mine, *New Venture Strategies*. Overlap occurs in the first chapter of *New Venture Mechanics*, which briefly summarizes the strategies that are covered in much greater detail in the other book. There is also an examination of how venture opportunities arise and how they may be discovered, but that topic too is given more attention in the earlier book.

New Venture Mechanics gives much more attention to how venture ideas are refined, developed, protected, and implemented than did *New Venture Strategies*. It concentrates on implementation of strategy, as opposed to its formulation.

In that respect it has similarities to other entrepreneurship books on the market. Core topics such as venture capital, legal forms of business, and creation of venture plans are common fare to such books. Using examples and including the most up-to-date research data on these topics are ways this book distinguishes itself from other texts that treat those "standard" topics.

In this book, some ideas discussed, and the emphasis placed upon other topics, are markedly different. For example, with the concept of venture idea refinement, there seems to be an implicit assumption in much entrepreneurship literature that the stages of idea conception and idea implementation follow in order—idea discovery is completed and then idea implementation begins and is carried through according to plan, creating the venture.

In fact, idea discovery is often only the starting point of a hunting process through which the idea is shaped, modified, refined, and implemented through iteration. This progressive refinement process is the focus of an entire chapter in this book. It examines idea refinement both from a design and engineering perspective and from a market fitting perspective. It is not unusual for an entrepreneurship book to pay some attention to the latter, usually under the heading of "market research." However, a discussion of refining the technology of the product or service to fit the market often tends to be left out, apparently on the rationale that the subject is the domain of engineering and science schools and therefore not appropriate in a business school setting. In fact, technology is as much an integral part of business as is accounting, finance, personnel, or production, and that is the way this book treats it.

Another topic treated differently from what is found in other books concerns idea protection, which is typically limited to "legal aspects" such as patents, trademarks, and copyrights. In this book, too, those methods of protection are covered, but within a broader perspective that includes strategic protection not just through legal formalities but also through secrecy or by being a "fast mover," approaches that are often cheaper and more effective.

The chapters on capitalization treat topics common to most entrepreneurship books, notably excepting *New Venture Strategies*. But most books treat capitalization alternatives either in a rather random order or by separating them between debt and equity. This book arranges the alternatives in a manner that tends more to fit the entrepreneur's perspective, by grouping them first as to whether they require sharing ownership or not and then by likelihood of use. In that way, these chapters become a natural extension of the issue of whether to team up or go solo. This issue, a common topic of most entrepreneurship books, is treated in this text also, but as an introduction to issues of financing.

It seems ironic that more attention is not given in entrepreneurship books to questions of how to generate sales, beginning with the first customer order, in a new enterprise. *New Venture Strategies*, while elaborating very little on the topic, nevertheless gives it more treatment than many start-up books. This book, *New Venture Mechanics*, expands it to a full chapter, and begins by discussing a way many entrepreneurs get their first orders that is not even treated in marketing textbooks, namely responding to customer-initiated requests. It goes on to examine, channel by channel, the alternatives for gaining new venture sales.

The topics of finding and equipping a location for production, staffing it, and setting up needed paperwork for government approvals, taxes, insurance, and the like are similar to those in most other start-up books, although they complement rather than duplicate anything in *New Venture Strategies*. These, however, tend to be basically drab topics. Using examples from real-life ventures to illustrate them will make them more vivid, enjoyable, and memorable.

The subject of preparing formal venture plans is not, by itself, unusual in a start-up book. It was not developed in *New Venture Strategies*, however, and so its treatment in this text casts it as a complement to that book. The way of presenting it, moreover, also contrasts in more ways than one to the treatment it is given in other books.

It is simple to give a "laundry list" of topics to cover in a venture plan and to suggest one or more possible plan outlines. But not all ventures need formal plans. Indeed, most start without them. Plans do not guarantee success. Most plans are probably never even implemented. Those venture situations in which plans are needed may call for systematic planning only on particularly crucial aspects, not all aspects of the venture. Which aspects of the plan should be worked on first can vary from one venture to another. And yet to complete a plan may require review of the whole venture, not just some parts or one part at a time.

To cope with these ambiguities, *New Venture Mechanics* does the following. First, the reader can, if he or she wishes, start with any chapter, depending on what aspects of a particular venture have the highest priority. Second, at the end of each chapter is a list of questions for developing aspects of the plan that draw upon topics covered in that chapter. Third, a chapter on pulling the whole plan together, or whatever parts of it are worth writing up, appears at the end of the book. A reader can turn to that chapter whenever he or she feels ready to formalize answers to planning questions in any of the earlier chapters.

The chapter on planning itself suggests that planning can be carried to whatever depth is most appropriate, either for the sake of instruction and learning or for the sake of an actual venture. Examples excerpted from a variety of prior business plans are included for guidance, although it is pointed out that each plan should be tailored to the needs of the venture it depicts, not to any general format.

Each of the topical chapters leading up to the plan also includes a list of possible milestones pertaining to the chapter topic. These can be applied directly, when appropriately selected to fit the individual venture, to a venture plan. Typically, too few plans include specific milestones. Those in this book may contribute directly to plan improvement as well as learning.

The variety of topics to be considered in planning a venture spans virtually the entire scope of business, since a venture aims to become a complete business. Most entrepreneurship books, consequently, tend to contain a very large number of chapters, one for each topic. A problem with this approach is that the topics can become hard to organize in memory. Instead, they simply turn into a grab bag of topical scraps, unlinked and hard to make sense of.

This book makes more sense of those topics by combining them coherently into ten chapters. For a "we read one chapter per class meeting" course that may be too little subdivision. But for a course with the philosophy that a venture is whole cloth and the full range of topics should be scanned and rescanned from the outset, it is preferable.

I would like to thank Dr. W. Ed McMullan of the University of Calgary for his exceptional encouragement in this work, many former students from whose endeavors I also learned and derived examples, and my family for their support and forbearance.

Karl H. Vesper

NEW
VENTURE
MECHANICS

Chapter 1

SEIZING
BUSINESS
OPPORTUNITIES

INTRODUCTION

The goal of an entrepreneur is to gain a profitable proprietary advantage in a marketplace. Discovering such an opportunity happens in a variety of ways and often comes as a surprise. According to an *Inc.* magazine survey of 500 fastest growing ventures, 47 percent of business opportunity discoveries arise out of some work activity. Fifteen percent come from making improvements on what someone else has done. Eleven percent of discoveries follow noticing an unfilled niche in the consumer marketplace. Other sources include systematic searching, brainstorming, hobbies, and a fairly large "other" category (16 percent) that could include events such as chance encounters, discoveries in the normal course of living, or an invitation from a potential partner or a customer.[1] Sorting individual cases into separate categories based on how ideas were discovered is a complicated task that deals with overlapping definitions and shades of gray as well as unfathomable mysteries.

The opportunity to create a venture may have been produced by recent events or may have waited a long time for discovery. It may be well suited to the person who discovers it or may better fit someone with different capabilities. It may lead to a venture of long life and high growth or to one of limited success.

[1]John Case, "The Origins of Entrepreneurship," *Inc.* (June 1989), p. 54.

Deciding what can be made of a potential venture opportunity and how to do so is a job in which the entrepreneur may benefit from studying what has worked for others. The chapters to follow aim to serve that study, starting briefly with the nature of entrepreneurial opportunity and then expanding upon what may be involved in exploiting it.

OPPORTUNITY OCCURRENCE

Opportunity is defined as "a set of favorable circumstances for the purpose."[2] It arises from the existence of a gap between the actual state of affairs and a potentially improved state coupled with the possibility of bridging that gap. An opportunity can be considered viable when the benefits of bridging the gap or making the transformation from the present state to the improved state outweigh the costs of doing so. If there is a way to capture as a profit the difference between benefits and costs, then the opportunity can be regarded as a *business opportunity*. If the business opportunity is such that only a new, as opposed to an established, enterprise can capture that profit, then the opportunity can be considered a *new venture opportunity*.

There are always, it seems from hindsight at least, numerous possibilities for improvements in products and services available for entrepreneurial exploitation. Theoretically there should not be, because existing enterprises should take care of them. Established companies usually try to meet present customer needs and to anticipate future ones. But they don't always succeed, and hence they leave openings for entrepreneurs.

What is it that leaves a start-up opportunity "up for grabs" by entrepreneurs rather than its being seized by an established company? Answers fall into the following three categories:

1. Nobody in the company that should have exploited the opportunity thought of it, or
2. Somebody thought of it, but the company declined to go after it, or
3. The company did decide to go after it but did not do so effectively.

These situations represent three types of failures with which the entrepreneur must also contend. When an opportunity arises, there is usually more than one person who could take advantage of it. *How* to be the one who does *in contrast to the one who does not* is a subject that has been little studied. It may help, however, to consider some forms venture opportunities may take and the kinds of clues that may signal their presence.

The elements that combine to make an opportunity may have all been present well before discovery or may only have come together recently. An oppor-

---

[2]*Webster's New World Dictionary*: Opportunity: 1. A combination of circumstances favorable for the purpose, a fit time. 2. A good chance or occasion, as to advance oneself.

tunity may lie quietly awaiting discovery, like the message in a code, the pattern in a jumble of puzzle pieces, a winning hand in a set of cards, or a story waiting to be written. Business profits could be latent in a vein of ore in the ground, the tailings of an old mine, the talent of a painter, or a lost treasure, as well as in a product or service not yet invented that could be profitably produced as soon as someone thinks of it.

Opportunities that could have been exploited earlier if only someone had spotted and acted upon them might be described as *ready*. Examples have included

- Hot-air corn poppers
- Aseptic packaging of U.S. foods
- Just-in-time inventory control
- Fiberglass skis
- Telephone information numbers paid for by advertisers who put commercials along with the answers
- Credit cards

Who could have taken advantage of such opportunities and used them to start new companies? Possibly many people. But some were in better positions than others to do so. What makes a position better might be the possession of particular technical or market knowledge acquired from personal experience through work or hobbies in fields closely related to the opportunity.

For example, Howard Head drew upon his engineering training and his work experience as an aeronautical engineer when he undertook to design a better ski made from laminated plastic and metal. But there was more to it than that. Many others had training and experience similar to his and also skied. Head undertook to improve his skis because he was dissatisfied with their performance. Some of those other engineers may also have been dissatisfied but may not have felt sufficiently motivated to do something about it. Or if they tried, possibly they did not have quite as much ingenuity or persistence as Head. Certainly, he demonstrated extraordinary innovativeness when, after his ski enterprise fell victim to another innovation, the K-2 ski made of fiberglass rather than metal, Head sold his ski company and went on to develop another innovation, the Prince tennis racket, that made him another fortune.

Another start-up company, Farallon Industries, began with a two-person recreational submarine, which was not profitable, and then rapidly added a string of other products, which did pull the company through. Among those other products were gauges, such as pressure sensors, depth meters, and compasses that were illuminated so they could be seen underwater in the dark. One of the founders, Norman H. Moore, commented as follows:

■ *It should no more have been possible for a new, upstart company to come out with the first illuminated underwater gauges in late 1972 than for me to fly to the moon on a broomstick. This should have been done long ago. The devices represent nothing that is either revolutionary or technologically difficult. It is just a matter of taking good engineering and innovation to a consumer field that hasn't had much.*[3]

How a "more ordinary" person with similar training, experience, and motivation could reach for enhanced innovativeness as well is not known, although it is believed by scholars of creativity that trying, training, and tools such as brainstorming can help.

Alternatively, the needed expertise and talent for exploiting an opportunity could come through the recruitment of a partner who possesses it. Unfortunately, it is easier to see how such recruitment could be done *after* discovery of the opportunity than before.

In contrast to *ready* opportunities that may have lain dormant awaiting discovery are *future* opportunities that cannot be exploited until something else happens to make them possible. Examples of these would include

- Microcomputers, for which microchip technology was prerequisite
- Popular software products, for which microcomputers were prerequisite
- Biotechnology start-ups, for which gene-splicing technology was prerequisite
- Discount stock brokers, for which securities deregulation was prerequisite
- Service industries such as fast food chains, for which life-style changes were required
- Residential development of Arizona, for which economical home air conditioning was needed
- Shopping centers, which required first that enough potential customers have cars

For such opportunities as these, timing is a crucial element. They cannot be exploited until *prerequisite events* occur. Categories into which such events can be grouped include the following:

- *Technological discoveries.* Start-ups in biotechnology, microcomputers, and electronics followed.
- *Demographic changes.* Medical and nursing organizations have sprung up to serve an aging population.
- *Life-style and taste changes.* Start-ups have capitalized on new clothing trends, desire for fast food, and public interest in professional sports.
- *Economic dislocations,* such as booms or failures. The oil boycott spawned new drilling firms. Steel industry collapse was accompanied by mini-mill start-ups.
- *Calamities* such as wars and natural disasters. Henry Kaiser's business expanded to shipbuilding in World War II. Mt. St. Helen's eruption spawned new tourism firms.
- *Rule changes by government.* Environmental legislation created opportunities for new consulting firms and cleanup machinery firms. The Small Business Innovation Research Program underwrote new product innovation firms. Deregulation spawned new airlines and trucking companies.
- *Resource discoveries.* North Slope oil production spawned new construction firms in Alaska. When the price of gold rose, new companies in Colorado and Nevada started to reprocess the tailings of old mines.

[3]Norman H. Moore, "Farallon Industries: A Case History." P. 42 in Donald M. Dible (ed.), *Winning the Money Game* (Santa Clara, CA: Entrepreneur Press, 1975).

   It is fairly easy to trace many opportunities for start-ups back to such events as these. But going the other way can be hard. Some of these developments become apparent only after their effects, including the exploitation of start-up opportunities they created, are past. When hindsight does reveal them, it will also show that much of the opportunity exploitation has been done by preexisting companies in lines of business related to the nature of the technology or market where each opportunity arises, and not by start-ups. For some types of opportunity-generating events, such as war or production of new medicines, pesticides, and other chemicals, virtually all the business opportunities at the raw material level are seized by preexisting companies. Start-ups then may participate farther downstream in application and distribution.

   One technique to help foresee prerequisite events and the opportunities they may produce is the sketching of "implication trees," "impact wheels," or "consequence chains." A presumed event, such as global warming, is written down in the center of a page. From this initial event, several impacts or consequences can be projected as spokes radiating out from the initial event. Any of those impacts can be viewed as the center of another collection of impacts that radiates out from it, and each of those as the center of yet another such collection, and so forth. By mapping these chains on a piece of paper, blackboard, or flipchart, a wide range of potential future events and their implications can be envisaged. Each of those can be used to trigger ideas about potential new product and service opportunities. Intriguing as such exercises may be, however, it is hard to find viable new business ideas that were discovered by using them.

DETECTING OPPORTUNITY CLUES

The path to discovery of a new business opportunity must at some point include observation of clues that indicate the possible matching of a market with the production of a specific product or service. The source of opportunity is ultimately the customer for whatever the new venture will sell. Needs may exist under a variety of circumstances, some of which display obvious clues, as in the following examples:

■ **Patterns of demand** *in an existing line of business suggest a shortage of supply of some particular product or service. Phil Carrol and Dave Steele were on their way from Calgary, Alberta, to Vernon, British Columbia, to go skiing with a third friend, a carpenter named Rob Jensen, when they passed through a small town lined with houseboats on the Shuswap River. Thinking "what a howl to have a week on one of these," they stopped to inquire about rentals. Two things struck them. One was how shoddy many of the houseboats seemed. The other was that it was January 1982 and all of them were booked through the coming August.*
     Carrol and Steele had worked together on student enterprises prior to their recent graduation from the University of Calgary. The latest had been a ranch party attracting over twelve hundred students, the largest ever held at the university. They had also considered other enterprises — lawn maintenance, a "permastamp" venture, and "twenty different businesses in all." Now Carrol said to Steele, "What a fantastic business to be

in." Jensen said, "I can build boats." Steele said, "If you can build them, we can rent them."

The business was begun and soon developed into not only boat and marina rentals but also, thanks to tax depreciation technicalities, boat sales as well. Within three years, rental bookings were over $2 million and sales over $8 million per year.[4]

■ **Present prices relative to quality *in some field reveal the potential to provide customers with a better deal.*** Rudolph Wurlitzer was surprised at the high prices of musical instruments when he browsed through a Cincinnati music store in 1865. The explanation given by the store owner was that the instruments were all imported and had to pass through a European sales agent, an exporter, an American importer and a local jobber, each of whom added to the cost. Wurlitzer believed he could do it cheaper.

He had adopted a personal policy of setting aside one-fourth of his earnings since coming to America thirteen years earlier so he could one day start his own business. Now from humble positions as a porter and later a bank cashier, he possessed $700 which he sent to relatives in Germany along with a shopping list of musical instruments. When they arrived, he set up as a part-time wholesaler while keeping his bank job. Four years later, the venture had grown to the point where he quit the bank, and a year after that he started manufacturing. A big government order for band instruments during the Civil War, followed by innovations in low pricing, mail-order selling, and product design helped build success.[5]

■ **Advertisements by the customer *express the desire for a particular product or service.*** The federal government, for instance, advertises regularly in the Commerce Business Daily to solicit bids from existing or potential suppliers. State and local governments also regularly disseminate requests for bids. Private companies typically do not advertise publicly but do maintain lists of bidders, which anyone can request to be on, to whom they send news of opportunities.

■ **A problem is widely obvious *but nobody has figured out what product or service might solve it.*** Gail Borden had been a schoolteacher, newspaper editor, real estate salesman, customs collector and surveyor, and inveterate inventor. One of his less successful ideas was a "terraqueous wagon" or amphibious vehicle powered by sails. Another, inspired by his wife's death from yellow fever, was a refrigerated building for Galvestonians to live in during the summer to "freeze out disease." When no tenants applied, he used the building as a food plant for another invention, the "meat biscuit." It too was a commercial failure, but it earned him a Gold Medal at the 1851 London Crystal Palace Exposition.

On the voyage home he saw four children die from contaminated milk. Upon his return he began to experiment with ways of removing water from milk so it would keep better. Straight evaporation imparted a burnt taste. During a visit to friends at a Shaker colony in New Lebanon, New York, he noticed the use of vacuum pans to condense maple sugar at lowered temperature. In 1856 he received a patent for applying a similar process to condense milk. The first business he set up failed when local dairies refused him credit. A second business with a wealthy backer took hold and army purchases of condensed milk during the Civil War helped propel it to success.[6]

---

[4]Alan Gould, *The New Entrepreneurs* (Toronto: Seal Books, 1986), p. 308.
[5]Joseph J. Fucini, and Suzy Fucini, *Entrepreneurs* (Boston: G. K. Hall, 1985).
[6]Fucini and Fucini, *Entrepreneurs*.

■ **Personal request by customers *to an entrepreneur who has developed a product or service for one situation reveals further opportunity.* Elisha Otis, a bedstead factory mechanic, was asked by his employer to help move the factory to a new multistory building. In particular he was asked to design a safe elevator for lifting machinery to upper floors. The solution he devised involved suspending the elevator with a leaf spring that would expand to jam against the shaft walls if the rope pulling up on the spring broke.**

    After the move was satisfactorily completed, Otis quit to go prospecting for gold in California. But before he could leave, another company asked him to build such an elevator. Then yet another company made the same request, and instead of mining Otis built an elevator company.[7]

One injunction that would seem to follow from these examples is to look for ways to solve problems that others who can afford to pay for solutions might care about. Beyond finding solutions, it may help to ask who else might be interested in them. That will still leave, however, the important question of whether there can be a worthwhile profit in making the solution more broadly available. Note that it must also be possible to deliver results and to receive payment. More college students might like to have Ferraris, but unfortunately they cannot afford to pay for them; hence they do not comprise a viable market yet.

Probing the Future

Clues to venture opportunities are also discovered by trial and error. An entrepreneur can enter a line of business on the assumption that opportunity is there. He or she can open a store, advertise a service, or make and offer some specimens of a new product and then let the market announce whether there was an opportunity present for that venture or not. Reaching into the unknown future to find a market can take several directions:

- The *entrepreneur clearly sees* the likelihood or even the certainty of customers from a vantage point of working for a company in or adjacent to that market. When the company declines to pursue that market, the entrepreneur does so.
- The *entrepreneur guesses* that customers will want the product or service after they see it but has no way of being sure and hence must gamble. The "Pet Rock" idea of two advertising men during the 1970s was such an idea that paid off. Illuminated road curbing with lights inside to make it easy to see at night did not.
- The *entrepreneur,* having devised a product or service to fulfill a personal need or desire, *finds that others want it too.* The example of Elisha Otis's elevator fits this case. Another was the microcomputer devised as a hobby project by Steve Wozniak, whose friends then asked for duplicates, leading to the formation of Apple Computer.
- The *entrepreneur* develops a product for one application and later *discovers the product has a different application* that gives it a market. Development of the CP/M operating system for microcomputers was done before microcomputers even existed and not as the basis for starting a company. Much earlier, long before the idea of digital computing occurred, Boolean algebra, the basis for computer languages, was invented in pursuit of proof that God exists. The electric train was invented as a store

[7]Fucini and Fucini, *Entrepreneurs.*

window display, not a toy for children, and the basis for the flashlight was invented as an "electric flowerpot."

- **Precedent gives the entrepreneur reason to expect that there will be customers.** James Dole could see that people in Hawaii liked to eat pineapple and thought consumers would buy it on the mainland too if it could be delivered unspoiled. He solved the spoilage problem by canning, and sales rose to 32,000 cases within three years. More recently, some employees at Apple Computer thought that enough people would like to buy full-page display monitors for their computers if a company were formed to produce them. They left Apple to found Radius Corporation and found they were right.

- The *entrepreneur foresees a coming future need* and sets up in advance to meet it. An example would be housing contractors who build in advance of expected population movements. But other service and product examples among entrepreneurial start-ups are relatively rare. More often, established companies anticipate future markets based on past experience, present trends, and expected developments in their fields of expertise.

Other clues must be added to those from the customer to prove that a viable business opportunity is truly present. The entrepreneur must be able to discern elements of a competitive advantage in his or her capabilities to exploit the opportunity.

Systematic Searching

Most entrepreneurs find opportunities without explicitly looking for them. Hence, one personal strategic option for the would-be entrepreneur can simply be to wait and hope for a happy event, while, at the same time, preparing to take advantage of the event, if and when it occurs.

Alternatively, there is the option of actively searching for new business ideas. Books offer lists of "creative thinking" techniques, lists of information sources, and examples coupled with arguments that, after all, "these entrepreneurs found winning ideas, so surely you can too."

It is fairly easy to find entrepreneurs who entered business through the purchase of a *going* concern that was found through systematic searching. Not so easy to find are examples of entrepreneurs who found opportunities to start up *new* businesses through such a deliberate search. It is almost impossible to find venture opportunities through brainstorming or other creative-thinking exercises. The following four examples show how some form of deliberate search led to venture opportunity discovery.

■ *An engineer interviewed purchasing agents to learn what they had trouble obtaining. From one he learned of market need for an electronic delay line, which he then formed a company to make.*

■ *A team of MBA students at the University of Denver searched together for venture ideas through nightly discussions. Each eventually found one to pursue as a student project. One became the basis of a telephone information service that the team formed jointly. Within two years they were handling 24,000 calls per day, rising at a rate of 12 percent per week.*

■ *An engineer adopted a personal policy of calling at least one person each workday to say he was seeking a venture. Within a year he had a partner, and after one more they had found and licensed a product around which they created a successful start-up.*

■ *Masaru Ibuka, an electronics engineer who initiated what would eventually become Sony Corp., began looking for product ideas with a small team meeting in a bombed-out Tokyo department store. Ideas as "far out" as miniature golf courses and bean cakes were considered. Novel rice cooker and bread cooker ideas were tried unsuccessfully. Eventually, the company started making shortwave adapters for home radios. Later, it seized on the idea of tape recorders, and eventually Sony emerged.*[8]

It does not necessarily follow that because few entrepreneurs to date can be found who used formalistic methods to find successful venture ideas that the same will be true in the future. Searching techniques might produce more results if more people try them. And maybe other searching techniques that are more highly effective will be developed. Searching can take two routes to venture discovery. One is to find a venture opportunity or venture idea. The other is to find someone else who has found the opportunity or idea and could use the assistance of a partner with complementary capabilities.

Ways to "tune in" to signals that might indicate emerging venture opportunities are not hard to find. Consider the following:

- Be alert to what people, including yourself, but particularly those people you know who can afford to pay, would like to have that they do not now have. Consider how it could be provided.
- Frequently ask, whether out loud or inwardly, how could a product or service be made, provided, or performed better?
- Take note of changes in technology and consider both how else they might be applied and what impact they may have on what potential customers might like.
- Notice signs that other new businesses in certain areas or fields of activity seem to be catching on, possibly indicating the spread of some new opportunity.

Merely detecting opportunity signals is not enough, however. There is also the need to analyze them to discover patterns that, like in a good hand of cards, may make up winning combinations. Crystallizing the concept for a venture requires supposing at least one way a potential business opportunity can be exploited, or possibly several ways of doing so.

ASSESSING POSSIBILITIES

Whether an apparent opportunity is viable or not is a function of both the nature of the opportunity and of the entrepreneur's capabilities and desires. Both must be considered not only in absolute terms but, more importantly, relative to whoever else might seriously consider competing with the start-up.

[8]Akio Morita, *Made in Japan* (New York: Dutton, 1986), p. 44.

Venture Needs

In assessing the business concept, consider the following questions:

- How much better is the value that the venture will offer the customer in its product or service compared to what competitors offer? What is the source of that greater value, and can it be further augmented, either right away or downstream?
- What features, skills, or contacts can the venture use to discover and/or convince enough customers of that better value?
- What can the venture draw upon to be able to deliver what it must—where will it obtain adequate resources, talent, and facilities at an operating efficiency high enough to yield a profit on sales?
- How will the venture derive enough staying power in order to get up to speed, and how likely will it be to have it?

Although they have been described here as if they were static or occurred at a single point in time, in fact the answers to these questions must be dynamic and shift with time through initiatives of the entrepreneur.

Personal Capabilities

To shape and guide the business advantage of a venture, not just to design it at the outset, but to redesign it as time progresses and problems arise, the entrepreneur will need to draw upon the following capabilities:

- *Technical competence.* Who in the business will be able to perform its service or put out its product in a quality/price ratio as high or higher than that of competitors?
- *Business competence.* The closer the competition on technical advantage, the more important it will be to set up and operate the business in an effective and cost-efficient manner. Where will the talent come from to do this?
- *Contacts who can help.* Which functions will the entrepreneur be most competent to perform personally and for which ones will other people, either within the business or on contracts from outside, be needed? Who will those helpers be or through what network(s) will they be sought?
- *Resources* such as capital and time to subsist during start-up. Does the entrepreneur(s) have them personally, or through what personal contacts will they be sought?[9]

Preferences

Beyond personal capabilities, it can be important for a would-be entrepreneur to consider personal needs, wants, and likes both in seeking out business opportunities and in deciding which ones to pursue. Some possible areas to consider include

- Kind of industry
- Activities involved in performing the work
- Required hours and fit with family

---

[9]Karl H. Vesper, *New Venture Strategies* (rev. ed.) (Englewood Cliffs, NJ: Prentice Hall, 1990), Appendix B.

- Required investment
- Presence of entry hurdles such as licensing
- Geographical constraints
- Ambiance preferences
- Kinds of customers
- Type of product or service produced
- Nature and number of employees required
- Time required to break even
- Level of risk and how much could be lost
- Profit and growth potential
- Match with personal capabilities
- Match with learnable and/or recruitable capabilities

Different preference dimensions may be important for each person, and those preference dimensions may shift as different potential opportunities come to mind and the dimensions are reconsidered. The point of the dimensions is to help guide the searching and screening process but, importantly, not to stymie it. One thing to avoid is being too mechanically systematic in applying them. That can waste time and create discouragement. It may be sufficient simply to consider what the list might contain, then let it slide to a subconscious level to do its work there without interfering in the search for possibilities. If a given potential opportunity seems to emerge as a strong contender, then the list can be reconsidered consciously as a cross-check on both whether to pursue the opportunity further and how to try shaping it to fit.

Experimentation

Highly promising venture opportunities are sometimes discovered not by great foresight but rather as "sidestreet" discoveries. After starting with a prosaic venture, the entrepreneur later discovers tangential directions of much greater promise, as happened in the next examples.

- *Gerhard Mennen's enterprise was a drugstore. Not content with this, he looked for proprietary product ideas. His foot remedy, Sure Corn Killer, did not succeed, but a later product, Borated Infant Talcum Powder, did and others followed.[10]*

- *Henry Steinway, a successful piano maker in partnership with his three sons in Germany, found his business stifled, first by governmental tariffs and then by a revolution. Emigrating with his family to the United States, he started over by making the same type of instruments. A year after start-up, Steinway introduced a radical new design with crossed strings and a cast iron frame that won a series of prestigious awards and tilted the company's sales trajectory sharply upward.[11]*

- *Dwight Baldwin's venture was a piano store that sold, among others, Steinway products. When Steinway withdrew Baldwin's distributorship, Baldwin's bookkeeper, Lucien Wulsin, who had bought a one-sixth interest in the store, responded by leading the*

[10]Fucini and Fucini, *Entrepreneurs.*
[11]Fucini and Fucini, *Entrepreneurs.*

company into the manufacture of its own brand, which subsequently became the company's main line of business.[12]

■   *Masaru Ibuka, previously mentioned, began making shortwave adapters and heating pads to get his business going, but his main goal was creating products on a technical leading edge. He chose wire recorders but could not obtain wire. Then he saw a U.S.-made tape recorder, appreciated the superiority of tape over wire, and set about learning to make tape and designing Sony's first recorder.*[13]

These examples suggest that one way to find a major business opportunity can be to initiate a prosaic enterprise and see where it leads. Starting a business can be like entering an avenue down whose sidestreets lie opportunities that can only be seen after traveling a ways. Or, to view this "sidestreet effect" in another way, entry into business shifts an entrepreneur's vantage point to where he or she may intercept new opportunity signals. The odds of finding an opportunity that will lead to high growth through any of these approaches, however, are slim because history has shown that the vast majority of businesses are destined never to grow larger than four or five employees at most.[14]

LOOKING AHEAD—A SOFTWARE START-UP

Creating a company, even a small one, requires synthesizing a complex new set of human relationships and habit patterns. Some of this complexity can be anticipated by listing a few functional areas of the business and aspects of each that must somehow be brought into operation:

> *Sales*—Not only must customers be contacted and persuaded to make the first purchases, but some kind of pitch, advertising, channels, and pricing systems that yield sales automatically, repeatedly, and in large total dollar amounts steadily over time must be set in motion.
>
> *Production*—It is not enough to create an operating prototype or to make the first few deliveries of the product or service. A system must be devised that keeps producing steadily as needed, with suitable quality and cost to stay ahead of competitors. This may require interaction with many vendors and employees, all of whom must be dependable.
>
> *Purchasing*—Connections must be arranged for obtaining suitable quantities of whatever materials are needed—materials that are of appropriate quality and price and are available when needed.
>
> *Personnel*—If one person is to do everything, then he or she must have the know-how and aptitude for all of it. With company growth, others must be added to carry pieces of the load dependably, cooperatively, and economically. Methods must be

[12]Fucini and Fucini, *Entrepreneurs.*
[13]Morita, *Made in Japan.*
[14]David L. Birch, "Live Fast, Die Young," *Inc.* (August 1988), p. 23.

set up by the entrepreneur for recruiting, training, and managing, so that all functions of the firm will be performed correctly.

Finance—Setting-up will require obtaining capital, probably through both equity and bank debt. With time, either extremely poor performance or extremely good performance will likely generate a need for more capital, which the entrepreneur must arrange, preferably without having to drop other important tasks of the business to do so.

Legal—Protection of any unique ideas and the arrangement of contracts with suppliers, employees, customers, capital sources, and tax collectors may require legal help. The entrepreneur must arrange for competent help and be able to pay for it.

Records—Clearing red tape with city hall will be a minor matter for many types of new firms, a major one for others. Setting up effective accounting records and reporting systems will be important for most. Professional help must be selected and paid for by the entrepreneur.

This list can easily be extended by looking at management textbooks or by examining examples, as will be done in later chapters here. Research, engineering, shareholder relations, governmental interaction, outlet location, service handling, retirement plans, partnership or corporate provisions, charity solicitations, memberships in associations—the list can be endless, and yet creating a new company requires somehow taking care of it all.

For an overview of what to anticipate in venture creation, it may be helpful to consider a specific start-up that illustrates some topics to be considered more extensively in later chapters. Further details on some techniques used in developing this particular venture are described in a book by Bruce Milne, its lead entrepreneur.

■ *In January 1980 Bruce Milne and two fellow employees of a minicomputer sales company set up a new company of their own to develop and sell software for accounting firms that operated on microcomputers. Discovery of the business opportunity had come from Bruce's prior experience in selling minicomputers to accountants, first for Burroughs Corporation and then for a Digital Equipment Corporation (DEC) dealer. Most minicomputer installations involved custom development of new software, which seemed to Bruce to be an inefficient procedure compared to what the development of more standard software might be able to provide. He had suggested that his employer develop more standard software, possibly through acquisition of other software companies, to go with the minicomputers it sold, but the idea had not been acted upon.*

He had also noticed the advent and rapidly increasing power of microcomputers together with the growth of standard software to go with them. He suggested to a programmer in his office that they might consider becoming involved part-time in the microcomputer industry. The two visited a San Francisco Bay area microcomputer manufacturer and a nearby company reputed to be the leading vendor of microcomputer accounting software at the time. The two concluded they could develop a much better product, although it would have to be a full-time enterprise to move fast enough to stay ahead of growing competition.

Recruiting a third partner from work, pooling their savings, and pulling in three outside investors, they established a new corporation, Dataword, to capitalize on the business idea. The three partners at first sold minicomputers and took in consulting work to support themselves while the programmer developed the new microcomputer software package. Nine months later, in September 1980, they introduced the package, bundled with an Altos microcomputer. It offered accounting firms most of the same accounting capabilities they had with minicomputer systems, but at around one-third to one-half the cost.

As regional sales began Bruce raised additional capital for expanding operations nationally through additional equity investment. A series of limited partnerships was used to fund development of additional products, such as accounting systems for attorneys. One of the founders withdrew, but growth continued as the company worked out joint marketing arrangements with "Big Eight" accounting firms, all of which eventually adopted the software for themselves and their clients. Ultimately, Accountants' Microsystems, Inc. (AMI, the new name of the company, adopted because its original name, Dataword, conflicted with that of another company's product) was sold to a public firm. Bruce left the company to pursue other ventures, some of which he had initiated on the side as AMI developed.[15]

The advantages of using this example for illustrating the mechanics of start-up are that it is in a field where many start-ups occur and it includes many elements of business: product design, development, production, distribution, and servicing as well as resale of other companies' products. No example can fully illustrate all facets of start-up, but more can be seen in this one than in most other examples. It shows some aspects of the topics discussed in the chapters to follow, although they will be developed around a variety of other start-up examples. The four broad categories into which these topics are grouped are developing concepts, marshaling resources, start-up actions, and planning.[16]

DEVELOPING CONCEPTS

Seizing Opportunities (Chapter 1)

This chapter explores how new venture opportunities arise and how they may be discerned. In Bruce Milne's case opportunity was produced by a combination of advances in microcomputer technology, existence of a market for better accounting software, and slowness on the part of existing companies, including the one Bruce was working with, to take advantage of it.

Idea Refinement (Chapter 2)

The development of a business concept is often an evolutionary process that may begin even before discovery of the opportunity and then may develop and change over time. Three early types of activities in this process are (1) preliminary planning and cash flow assessment, (2) prototyping, either abstractly or physically, and (3) tuning the idea to match with the marketplace.

Shaping and refinement of the concept may be linked both before and after the concept itself is recognized by the entrepreneur. Antecedents of Bruce Milne's

---

[15]Bruce Milne, *Power Planning: Structuring Your Software Company for Success* (Seattle, WA: Resolution Business Press, 1989).

[16]Quotations from Bruce Milne are from conversations and interviews with the author.

venture concept can readily be seen in such events as his prior employment by computer companies; the fact that he spent a summer between the first and second years of his Harvard MBA program studying computer distribution channels for Digital Equipment Corporation; and the fact that as a youth before college he had created many small, independent ventures of his own, fixing and reselling used Volkswagens, importing and selling Swiss watches in Mexico, and setting up and operating a swim school. As early as age eight, he had enjoyed operating his own little Christmas card retailing operation. The microcomputer business idea seemed to emerge as an obvious opportunity to a mind conditioned over years by such experiences, coupled with observation of current events in the rapidly emerging microcomputer industry as well as the accounting industry. Many people witnessed the current events, but without the antecedent experiences. Others did not pursue the opportunity Bruce saw. He and his partners did—the partners as a result of his initiative.

Beyond having the initial concept, however, there remained much further decision making and refining to be done. There was a debate among the partners as to whether the initial software package should concentrate on word processing or accounting capabilities, two functions that were offered in combination by the minicomputer systems they were currently selling. Once accounting was selected for focus, the programmer knew what to do in general, but there were still many technical decisions to be made about how the new program would be designed and implemented. Working these out took a year for the first version of the program, which still had to be further refined through successive improvements. Bruce recalled:

> ■ *Once we settled on the accountants market we did a mail survey to a list we got from the local accounting society to learn more about just what it needed. The three page questionnaire went to about 300 accounting firms asking what software they had, what they wanted, whose products they were aware of and what was good and bad about them, and whether they were considering buying. If they responded they were to get a summary of the study. About thirty of them responded and six of them became users of our software.*

However, there were still questions of whether the company was really on the right track. Should it simply stick to minicomputer sales for the longer term? Or should it terminate them sooner to concentrate on microcomputers? The many complications and service demands of the minicomputer installations started to become an increasing cash drain as the number of installations grew. Eventually, the partners had to take two installations back and wound up wishing they could have cut off the minicomputer business earlier, especially because they had had to guarantee the initial sales personally.

Planning in these early stages was informal. Even the first investors were recruited without the use of a formal written business plan. Bruce had only some sketchy financial forecasts plus what he could tell people about his vision of the company's future to persuade them to invest. In addition, of course, they also had their prior experience of dealing with Bruce personally, plus the growing number of microcomputer success stories beginning to emerge, on which to base their judgments.

In hindsight, the founders could see which decisions in shaping the business were most constructive, which ones might have been made earlier, and which should have been made differently. But in "real time," refinement of the venture and its product was largely a step-by-step process of working out problems based upon both strategic and short-term goals but no detailed long-range plan.

Protection (Chapter 3)

Two potential dangers to consider early in the development of a new venture concept are, first, the risk that someone will claim injury as a result of buying from the company and, second, the risk that competitors will copy the company's idea and thereby undercut its margin. Fortunately, the first of these two risks, that of product liability lawsuits, did not seem to be much of a problem for Bruce and his partners' product. If it had, there would have been reason to look for ways of redesigning it to minimize that risk and possibly to take out liability insurance for protection, as many companies do. But there appeared to be no need for such precautions in this case.

To deal with the second of these risks, that of imitation, such defensive legal options as patents, copyrights, and trademarks may be applicable. Much of the investment in creating and refining a new company's product can be lost if competitors are immediately able to imitate it. The development is protected initially by competitors' lack of knowledge about just what is being developed and for exactly what application and market. Then, when a product is first introduced, it has the advantage of being new and being first. It may take a while for competitors to appreciate the opportunity the new product is seizing and a bit longer for them to react. But if they see a truly attractive opportunity getting away, some of them will begin to move on it. The most direct method of encroachment will likely be imitation, which may take a while to accomplish; but during that time a competitor will also be able to devise ways of going one better on the start-up in terms of product refinements, pricing, or other marketing variables.

Bruce's programming partner, Brian Duthie, provided a combination of better design concept and superior programming capability compared to the products of other companies that did attempt to compete. Advantages, Bruce recalled, included a unique data-packing algorithm and a powerful report writer. So this too was an early protection for concepts of the new company. Competitors could not see, let alone foresee, what new software Brian was inventing until it had matured through the many months of the developmental process and emerged in the marketplace. (In hindsight, Bruce observed that an advisory board made up of users might have been helpful in guiding product design.)

Right from the outset, Bruce Milne and his partners sought to obtain legal protection through trademarks on the company name and products and copyrights on the software. Bruce recalled:

■ *We registered the name Dataword right away but the attorney made the mistake of registering it only at the state level. Later I put a tiny advertisement with the name in the* Journal of Accountancy *and we got a call from the attorney of a* Fortune 500 *company saying that they already owned the name and we were not entitled to advertise it nationally. So we dropped it.*

Later, we started an offshoot company to develop new software and called it Micro-Software Development Corporation. We started getting phone calls from people asking for Microsoft. Another attorney called us on that one and we abandoned that name too. Those experiences caused us to be careful about both how we chose names and how we applied for legal protection on the names we did use and the software we wrote. Initially, we also copyprotected the software disks themselves, but that form of protection later became out of fashion in the industry, so we stopped trying to use it.

Once use of its product began to spread, the company began to develop further protective shielding by using its reputation with customers. Eventually, this led to endorsement by the "Big Eight" accounting firm of Coopers and Lybrand in particular, which allowed its name to be used in conjunction with Accountants' Microsystems products.

The company also used the continued refinement of existing products and the development of new ones to strengthen its protection, an approach used to good effect by many companies and essential to those in high technology industries.

MARSHALLING RESOURCES

Teaming (Chapter 4)

Bruce had, as it turned out, a viable business idea plus considerable experience and knowledge about computers and their users. He also had both venturing and management experience. But he still had to have help to start the company. One indispensable talent was that possessed by his "resident genius" programmer, Brian Duthie. Without that talent, the company could not create the software it needed. Hence, Bruce and Brian teamed up as partners. Whether they also needed as a third founder Laurie Chandler, Bruce's secretary, to manage the office and contribute expertise in the applications of word processing might have been more debatable. But Bruce and Brian thought they did, bringing the "internal team" of the venture to three members.

Key decisions in the teaming process concern what the legal arrangements among partners are to be. For this new software company, a corporate legal form, rather than a partnership, was chosen because it was simpler and less expensive to set up. It also offered the advantages of limiting legal liability, because debts of the corporation were not automatically those of the owners as they would be in a partnership, and easier entry and exit of partners through buying and selling of stock, rather than reformulating the partnership each time a partner came or left. Beyond choosing the corporate form, there were other decisions concerning allocation of ownership and provision for sharing ownership with other people who might be recruited in the future as well as how departures from the company would be handled.

They also had to form an "outside team," beginning with an attorney who would draw up the papers for incorporating. Why they should have a corporation instead of a partnership, what its terms should be, and what the procedures should be for setting it up were things the three could have figured out on their own. But using a lawyer was faster and less likely to introduce mistakes and omissions in the process. Their initial choice of a lawyer, the friend of a friend, could have been better. They later changed to another. Other members of the outside team included the venture's accountant and its banker.

A network of business contacts also could be viewed as an extension of the outside team. These included Bruce's friend John Torode, who developed an early microcomputer, perhaps the first to employ two disk drives, an essential element for the systems later sold by Bruce's company. The network also included contacts for obtaining suppliers and for obtaining customers — crucial elements for the company to commence business.

Inside Equity Capital (Chapter 5)

The financing of new companies can be discussed in terms of the stage in the company's development at which the financing is needed, the source of the financing, and whether it is debt or equity funding. However, these categories are not always clear. For instance, debt is sometimes convertible into equity. Leasing is in some ways a form of debt and in other ways it is not because, for one thing, there is no interest charge associated with it. Customer advances are another variation on debt because the company must make good on them.

There may be two stages in the financing process: one that allows founders of the company to retain all ownership internally, and one that involves sharing ownership outside the company. Different capital sources tend to predominate at the different stages in company development. At the seed stage, personal savings and savings of relatives and friends — "friendly money" — are most often used. In some lines of business, such as construction, advances from customers may also play an early role, and modest amounts of trade credit may be available. Leasing may help reduce cash needed for start-up equipment. Bank borrowing, if it occurs at the early stage, will likely involve personal guarantees by the entrepreneur and possibly the pledging of personal assets. These allow internal retention of ownership.

In the start-up of Dataword, Bruce Milne and his two cofounders began with their personal savings and friendly money. Bruce borrowed $20,000 from his mother and Laurie $5,000 from her father. Bruce used support from his wife's job to forgo salary and thereby reduce the start-up's cash needs. He also recruited $10,000 each from three business acquaintances — two former competitors and a former sales prospect — with whom he had developed personal friendships. The company used no bank borrowing initially. Later, it did some bank borrowing and also developed trade credit.

Bruce's plan was to get started with these funds plus income that would be generated initially from consulting and from sales of minicomputer systems and third-party software. After this initial phase he expected the company to introduce its first product and then raise more capital to support expanding sales of that product. He recalled:

■ *At the start we did a little minicomputer consulting, a little software writing, sold some word processors with a little data processing, and I did some expert witness work for a computer company down in the Bay Area, anything that would bring in cash to support the business. And we all kept our salaries down to conserve it. My income for the first two years combined was under $25,000.*

Bank borrowing also helped as soon as company sales began. Bruce went to the bank where he had his personal checking account and applied for a line of credit, which, to his pleasant surprise, the bank granted.

■ *Here we were with this little rinkidink company, and they gave us a $75,000 line of credit. I guess they had read some complimentary articles about us in the local paper and were impressed. They started to finance 80 percent on our receivables and I decided banks were OK. The banker and I got along well.*

Suppliers were less generous, he found. Computers were initially bought one at a time on ten-day terms.

■ *I remember thinking at the time that I didn't like being billed with reminder invoices every ten days, but in retrospect I can see it was smart. People in the software business come and go quickly, since many of them are broke to begin with.*

As the new company demonstrated it could pay the bills, better purchasing arrangements became possible. First, it became qualified to buy direct from manufacturers, and then it joined a buying group of other dealers that bought in sufficient volume to bargain for lower purchasing costs. For the first six to nine months, however, payment terms remained ten days.

Typically, the seed financing from friendly money, bank loans, and supplier credit is a relatively small amount used for early product development or possibly the first stages of start-up. If the company remains small or if it is low in capital intensity and high in margin, then this first small capital infusion may be all it will ever need from outside. Some companies, however, need larger amounts of capital, either for start-up, expansion, or both, that usually must be obtained from other sources such as private placements, finance companies, venture capital firms, and public offerings through sharing equity with outsiders.

Outside Equity Capital (Chapter 6)

Like most start-ups, Dataword did not need a great amount of money at the first stage to get started. Personal savings, friendly money, frugality, and sideline income were enough to underwrite product development and a selling seminar.

But then more capital was needed to realize the vision of going national with the product; to expand sales; and to support inventory, receivables, and servicing work. Margins on software alone were very high, but software was only part of what the company sold. It also had to carry computer hardware as part of the systems it was offering to the accounting market. Selling costs tended to be high because each purchase required a major commitment by the customer and was not likely to be bought through dealers, let alone mail order.

Bruce had seen insolvency rapidly creeping up on Dataword as the summer of 1980 advanced and complications arose in selling and servicing minicomputer systems to support Brian's development work on the new software. Setting up the sales seminar for September had added a final major drain on the company's vanishing assets. Then when the seminar produced sales orders, there was suddenly an even bigger need for cash to buy inventory and support installation work.

Dataword was essentially out of money by the time it landed its first sales at the September 1980 selling seminar. There were many possibilities for raising more capital. Even though the original sources had been pushed to the limit, other possible sources included informal investors, venture capital firms, corporate venture capital, merging with a corporate partner, and public stock offerings.

Bruce thought his best alternative for additional capital was recruitment of more private investors. The idea of recruiting such investors by setting up "R&D Partnerships" was one he had come upon through reading some of the literature from potential accountant customers. An advantageous feature of these partnerships was that they offered certain tax advantages under the law at that time.

Bruce formed a separate corporation, Accountants' Microsystems, Inc., to own and distribute the company's proprietary software and organized first one and then several successive R&D partnerships to finance it. This raised $50,000 in late 1980, another $250,000 in 1981, and $350,000 in late 1982. These were used for product development. To fund the growth of the rest of the company, its marketing, sales, and support, he raised another $200,000 in early 1981. Additionally, he raised $500,000 in 1982 through a debt offering to a private investor and finally another $8.5 million in late 1983 through professional venture capital. He recalled:

■ *Each time we sold more interest we had to clear it through the existing shareholders, so there was a lot of legal work involved. We also had to make sure our financials were in order and work up extensive business plans to raise the money.*

START-UP ACTIONS

Developing Sales (Chapter 7)

In Bruce's company, sales began before the company had to recruit outside equity, and thanks to the success of the sales, outside equity was cheaper to obtain and required less sacrifice of ownership.

Start-up sales may be divided into *first sales* and *follow-on sales*. Most often, the first sales are made personally by the lead entrepreneur on a "push" basis. Once a flow of sales has been started, the follow-on pattern may be different, involving more links in the channel, more customer orders arriving without solicitation, and less participation by the lead entrepreneur. Any number of combinations of different links and patterns may be possible, including different patterns in different geographical areas and for different products or services offered by the company as it matures and expands.

In the case of Dataword, at least three sales development phases can be seen. The first followed the pattern of the jobs Bruce and Brian previously held — selling minicomputers and other companies' software direct to end users. There were a couple of sales leads that came to them just as they were leaving their employer that they were able to continue with during the start-up to gain their first minicomputer sales in the new venture. Occasional consulting jobs during Dataword's start-up by all three founders were also developed out of direct customer contacts.

The second stage involved the introduction of the company's newly developed microcomputer software package. This was a change in offering, from a nonproprietary product with custom installation to a proprietary product, the software, bundled with a nonproprietary product, the Altos computer, and noncustom installation. The selling of this new offering was still direct to end users, but through a different mechanism — mail advertisement plus a seminar — rather than one-on-one sales calls to customers.

Use of a sales seminar was a technique Bruce had become experienced with in his prior work with DEC. It consisted of performing a mail survey of potential customers, followed by selecting a limited number of the most promising ones for a personal invitation to attend a seminar where the company's new product would be demonstrated.

Numerous customer contacts through both mail and personal phoning took place before and after the seminar. "The smart sale," Bruce commented, "is one that contacts the customer repeatedly and through varied forms. You aim to get six or seven contacts, even if they are only for a minute each. That way, when it comes time to ask people to sign the order, they will have a high enough level of comfort with you." Further strength was added to the seminar by obtaining Continued Professional Education (CPE) accreditation through the American Institute of Certified Public Accountants (AICPA). Accountants need some forty hours of instruction in such programs per year to maintain their professional standing.

The third sales development stage for this venture was geographical expansion. Accreditation of the seminar was extended to progressively more states while expanded national distribution through advertising, phone calls, and opening sales offices was developed.

■ *We would sometimes make dealers out of accountants we knew. For professional reasons they would often have to set up companies separate from their accounting practices. We would give them 35 percent to 40 percent discounts, while distributors we didn't use got 50 percent to 70 percent and OEMs [Original Equipment Makers] got 70 percent to 80 percent. We had a video professionally produced that covered all the seminar information, and we showed them how to do the seminars as well.*

One of the things we did right was follow-up in the sales process. Those leads from the seminar and other ones we did later were worth a fortune. We wrote a multi-terminal system for logging everything that came in, to set up a customer data base and tickler file to be contacted on mailings, press releases, product update newsletters and the like. With that we could build sales through constant contact, sending brochures, seminar invitations, and videotapes on the products. We sold 3,000 videotapes a year at $49 each through telemarketing. Some of the accountants even used the tapes for CPE credits, although I don't think they were supposed to.

Through a modem we would send prospect data to all our sales representatives, who in turn would contact the dealers. We would have telemarketing calling leads back to see how well the dealers were following up. Repetition, following up, and incredible attention to detail is what works.

Starting Operations (Chapter 8)

From the first steps of forming the company at the beginning of 1980 through what Bruce characterized as "heavy R&D" culminating in release of the first Dataword product in September 1980, there had to be a major emphasis on "staying alive" through consulting and minicomputer sales work. From mid-1980 on, the company, he said, was continually running out of money. An important part of making ends meet was to minimize expenses, not only in the first stages of getting started, but also as the company grew. Initially, operations began in Bruce's den. As Brian and Laurie joined the venture, they too began working out of their respective homes as well as Bruce's. The arrangement, Bruce recalled, was less than satisfactory, although it saved cash:

■ *Sometimes I'd be out selling during the day. But other times I'd need to work at home and maybe be talking to customers there. My wife would come home. Our privacy would be interrupted. It seemed like I was always scrambling to find some place to meet people.*

The trio moved to a 400–square foot office in a nearby executive office park. They rented an additional 100 square feet when the first employee, a programmer who was chosen in part because he was willing to work for a low wage, was recruited through a classified advertisement offering an opportunity with an exciting new software company:

■ *It's true that you get what you're paying for and companies are really only as good as their employees. But what you find in a start-up is that you're running alone and suddenly you need somebody but have no time to look. So you don't go through any kind of formal hiring process. Someone's in-law has moved to the area and is a warm body willing to work cheap, so you sign the person on. The reality is that you don't have the time or cash to do more.*

Right away it was very crowded. We had a couple of phone lines, a couple of our machines that we used for doing our own word processing, and our supplies, plus the four of us and then another lady we hired to do typing and reception work. The criterion for selecting her also was that she would accept low pay, like the programmer. We were watching the small amount of money we had slip away faster and faster as we continued R&D to ready our software for the market.

Supplier relationships grew out of prior contacts in the business. The new company needed mainly computers and peripherals, which it sold together with its own software. Servicing of the computers the company sold, another highly important function, was handled first through loaning out demonstrators to customers whose machines needed attention, and later by hiring free-lance service people. As the industry matured, other channels for providing service became available; but when Bruce's company was starting, those other channels had not yet been established.

The way another start-up might handle the tasks of obtaining facilities, setting up shop, hiring needed help, making arrangements with suppliers, and providing service could be very different, even for another software firm. Behind each step in the process of setting up operations may be numerous decisions about whom to make the arrangements with, whom to reject, what the arrangements should be, how to pay, how to obtain satisfaction, and how to prevent extension of the arrangements beyond where they should go. Underlying such details are basic questions of how to obtain the needed quantity and quality of output from the venture within the time available and on the most economical basis, topics that will be explored further in Chapter 8.

Start-Up Paperwork (Chapter 9)

Many steps in setting up shop call for records. Contracts, warranties, government forms, correspondence, literature on alternatives will be needed, will accumulate, and will have to be winnowed over time. Financial records are particularly crucial, not only for managing the company's cash, but also for preparing statements needed in raising money and paying taxes. At first, it is simple, as Bruce Milne found:

■ *We didn't even have an accountant at the beginning. Then toward the end of 1980 we needed one. We used our checkbook at first, and then went to a pegboard system. We let the bank handle our payroll records. Up to the end of our first year we slid by somehow with our quarterly tax reports, but by the end of the year we needed help with our tax filing. Since our product was sold to the accounting community anyway it wasn't hard for us to pick an accountant we thought could do the right job for us. They also helped us get our statements ready when we needed to go after financing.*

One mistake we made was typical of software companies. We used our own software, which was OK because we learned more about our own products. And we had great reporting systems. But there's a natural tendency to overanalyze the process and try to write the perfect software programs for our own situation instead of just getting the job done. It wasted a lot of expensive time.

For some types of paperwork, such as forms, Bruce imitated examples he had seen in his prior work at Burroughs and DEC. Others, such as job descriptions and a policy manual, he wrote himself as needs arose. These, and records such as competitor and supplier data and transaction documents, all went into one filing cabinet initially, using whatever system the most recent secretary preferred. Bruce commented:

■ *Filing becomes a problem, because you get behind on it. Other activities are more important than going through and purging it, so it fills up with junk. Things like supplier information are always changing, so new stuff is being added, and after a while it becomes hard to find things and you waste a lot of time looking.*

Companies differ in paperwork requirements, some being considerably more complex than what a software start-up requires. For instance, if government contracts are involved, there may be requirements ranging from affirmative action to national security regulations. Some lines of work involving potentially hazardous substances or noisy machines may require permissions to operate. Zoning laws impose restrictions in many areas. Other enterprises like Dataword involve relatively little in the way of regulatory requirements. But there are still needs for records on taxes, customers, suppliers, and employees. Insurance is a small factor in some lines of work (Bruce's start-up needed only "errors and omissions" and "property" insurance initially) and a major one in others where there is potential for employees or customers to be injured in connection with the company's activities. For Bruce's software start-up, these problems were minor. In other start-ups, as will be discussed in Chapter 9, they may not be.

PLANNING

Planning takes place throughout a company's development and can take different forms depending on the purposes it is intended to serve. Sometimes planning takes the form of mentally thinking ahead and at other times of preparing a formal written document. Most often, the purpose of a written plan is to raise capital, but there are other purposes as well. In a very routine enterprise, it may serve as a rule book. In a very novel venture, it may help in testing feasibility. For many types of ventures, it may aid the process of fine-tuning details to maximize success. Different benefits can come both from the process of planning and from a written planning document.

Venture Plans (Chapter 10)

Like most entrepreneurs, and contrary to the advice of many publications and lectures on entrepreneurship, Bruce Milne did not develop much of a formal written plan either before or at the inception of his venture. He had a feel from experience about how much money could be generated from computer sales, and he could mentally estimate about how much money per month would be needed to start the company and support Brian's software development work. A few calculations gave an approximate figure for the cost of the sales seminar. Bruce figured that once he could see how much money was coming in from the preliminary sales effort, he would be in a position to make better forecasts and to develop a plan for raising capital. He commented as follows:

■ *Essentially, we knew we had so much in the bank and we couldn't spend more than that. Whenever we ran out of cash we would try to raise some or we'd stop taking salaries. My experience has been that even when start-ups have a cash flow forecast they tend not to follow it. The reality is that they react to the environment they have created for themselves.*

The first two investors essentially "bought in" on the general prospect that the company would develop proprietary software, with some financial support from minicomputer sales and servicing. Once that software was developed, there would be a high potential for profit. They acted on faith in the general business idea and the capabilities of the founders to become competitive in the computer business, rather than detailed financial forecasts and supportive descriptive documentation.

As the time approached for raising larger amounts of money through limited partnerships and people less well known to Bruce, there was clear need for a written business plan. Investors in such circumstances usually want to see details about why their money is needed, how it will be used, how it is projected to earn, and how high a rate of return. This calls for a more detailed sales forecast and breakdown of expenses, monthly for the first two years and then annually for perhaps another three to make a five-year plan.

In hindsight, Bruce wished he had developed more extensive forecasts earlier and sought greater capitalization at the start. He found himself continually running out of money and having to spend his time seeking funds rather than being able to concentrate on building the business. Thus, his experience became an argument for earlier formal planning.

The most common purpose of writing out a business plan is, as in Bruce's case, to prepare a loan proposal or a prospectus for raising money. A plan need not be written, though, to be useful. Mental planning is usually a vital part of venture creation.

Pros of Planning.　Planning, whether mental or in writing, can be used for designing, negotiating, testing, and learning about the venture. It can be performed solo or in collaboration with others, and its payoffs may include the following:

- To test all or pieces of the venture concept and make "go/no go" decisions about them
- To find ways of refining aspects of the product or service and the start-up process so they work better
- To look for ways to improve upon the design goals and concept of the venture itself
- To look for other venture opportunities
- To anticipate needs that may require advance preparatory time
- To anticipate and head off potential problems in the start-up
- To prethink future decisions so they can be made faster and better later
- To get started on long lead time parts of the task in a timely fashion
- To get the benefit of others' thinking
- To reach a common understanding of cooperative tasks
- To learn about venturing by thinking through what may be involved in it

This process of planning may produce nothing concrete and yet still be valuable. It may also directly produce a venture. Or it may produce something in between—a product in the form of a written plan. This document itself can serve some useful purposes:

- As a prospectus for recruiting (1) partners, (2) capital, (3) employees, (4) credit, and (5) customers
- As a check on (1) the completeness of information and (2) the logic used in thinking about the venture
- For obtaining feedback from others to improve the venture's conception
- As a guide for team cooperation, a common "sheet of music for the choir to sing from," benchmarks for checking progress later
- As a contract for holding people to commitments
- To describe standard operating procedures, for controlling quality and costs in any routine functions
- As a performance-checking device to assess progress against expectations
- As a "portfolio specimen" to show what the entrepreneur can do

Writing out the plan as part of thinking it through can further reinforce learning. According to Atari founder, Nolan Bushnell, "Every time you prepare a business plan, you become a better entrepreneur."[17]

Cons of Planning.   With so many potential reasons in favor of planning, why don't entrepreneurs do more of it and why do so few entrepreneurs prepare formal written plans at all? Reasons for minimizing planning efforts in trying to create a venture include the following:

- Time cost of gathering more information, rather than reprocessing what is already known, and of having to redo the plan as conditions change and new information makes old obsolete
- Danger of reinforcing misleading fantasies about how things will develop, thereby producing poor decisions
- Risk of becoming discouraged by envisioning so many complexities that it all seems impossible
- Drugery of abstract activity with no real-world feedback or results until action is taken
- Discouragement from review by others who are better equipped to discover weaknesses than to add reinforcements and reveal directions for further opportunity
- Pain of being wrong, a likely experience in planning

The fact that such arguments sometimes prevail and that many entrepreneurs do not start with formal written plans does not mean that such plans are not a good idea for a given venture. For the reasons noted earlier, formal planning may be helpful for even a humble enterprise or essential for a more ambitious one. However, whether to plan need not be an all-or-nothing choice. It can be done selectively, as will be further discussed in Chapter 10.

As an aid to thinking through prospective ventures, planning questions are listed at the end of this and other chapters. The answers to these questions can

---

[17]Nolan Bushnell, quoted in Jeffry A. Timmons, *New Venture Creation* (Homewood, IL: Irwin, 1990), p. 331.

become the basis of a venture plan, either one that remains in the entrepreneur's mind or one that is written out more formally—the topic of the final chapter of this book. One element such a plan should contain is a time line giving target dates for the accomplishment of anticipated milestones. Some possible milestones are suggested at the conclusion of this and each succeeding chapter.

MOVING ON

The fact that topics appear in a particular order in the following chapters does not mean that some other order might not be more suitable for a particular entrepreneur or venture. Hence, the reader is invited to skip around in whatever pattern seems most helpful. The last chapter on venture plans is intended to help integrate the topics again, either as an ending or possibly as a beginning. What sequence will be best for a given reader may depend on

- *What the reader already knows* about how to start the business. Prior work experience may have made the reader familiar with how to perform venture tasks. There may be no need to refine the product or service further. If the need to generate start-up sales is the most pressing problem, perhaps the reader should begin with Chapter 6.
- *The nature of the venture.* If a major developmental effort will be needed on the product or service, the venturer may first need to join forces and develop a business plan to seek major growth capital from the start. Creation of a formal business plan will require anticipation of all aspects of the business. Hence, review of topics in all the other chapters may be helpful.
- *The business concept.* Some business concepts call for careful action to obtain legal protection in the form of patents and copyrights. In such cases, it can be crucial to begin as early as possible to take proper steps in documentation to establish ownership of the ideas. Chapter 3 on protecting ideas should then be given top priority for early reading.
- *Growth prospects of the business.* If the business is destined to remain small, then some sources of capital, such as formal venture capital firms and growth-oriented individual investors, will not apply. But if high growth is an objective, then, except for a start-up having unusually low capital intensity and extraordinarily high margins, Chapter 9 will be of early interest. Either way, however, Chapter 5 on inside capital should probably be read first, because the forms of seed capital it describes will probably be employed prior to the growth capital.
- *Capabilities and limitations of the entrepreneur.* Often one entrepreneur can start a business without partners, particularly if the venture is relatively simple and/or the entrepreneur has strong prior experience plus enough savings to finance it personally. If not, or if the entrepreneur is not that confident, then Chapter 4 on teaming may be important to read. It should help both with assessing personal capabilities and with suggesting how they can be complemented to increase the chance of success.

Thus, a case can be made for any of several different starting points. If the reader is not sure which will be best, then continuing with Chapter 2 may be advisable. It explores ways of checking out the feasibility of a venture idea and at the same time reshaping it to make it stronger as a prelude to more serious commitment of time and money.

PLANNING QUESTIONS

The following questions are intended to stimulate thought about what should be considered in moving ahead with a venture. Which questions best apply can vary among entrepreneurs and ventures, as can the order in which they should be considered, the priority that should be placed on them, and which of them should be answered in a written plan.

Opportunity

- What clues indicate there could be a market opportunity for what this venture will offer?
- What forces or changes gave rise to the opportunity?
- How can those factors external to the venture that cause its opportunity to exist be expected to change in the future and why?
- Are these factors likely to be temporary or of long duration?

Assessment

- What features of the company's product or service can be unique?
- What is the evidence that potential customers will care enough about those features to buy from a new and unproven company?
- How well do the interests and capabilities of the prospective founder(s) fit this prospective venture?
- What other businesses or entrepreneurs may have spotted the same opportunity and may be preparing to exploit it?
- What are their relative advantages and disadvantages for doing so?
- What are the pros and cons of recruiting them as partners?

Exploitation

- How can the new company make the most of its advantages and competitors' disadvantages?
- How will the venture's capability to capitalize on that opportunity compare in the future with the capability of other existing or potentially formable companies?
- What can the founders do to strengthen that capability?
- How will that link to customers' future desires?
- What other opportunities might spring from the same source(s) as this one?
- What implications might they have for this venture?
- What, if anything, can the venture do to influence those factors?
- What other alternatives to the venture's product or service do customers have available now or will they have in the future?
- What different ways can the venture's line of business be defined?
- Could any outside experts help verify and/or improve on the venture's products and/or processes?
- What information sources will management use to track further advances, trends, threats, and opportunities in its industry and market?
- What kind of margin is possible in this business and why?
- What magnitude of investment is required to obtain a sustainable entry and what must it be spent on?
- What are some possible ways of testing this idea cheaply before plunging ahead?

POSSIBLE MILESTONES FOR A PLANNING
TIME LINE

The most suitable milestones for a time line for a particular venture must be a function of the individual case. Those that follow are intended to help stimulate thought.

- Apparently profitable product or service opportunity identified
- Target market tentatively defined; appropriate thinking-through begun
- Initial action taken
- Venturing decision made

Chapter 2

IDEA REFINEMENT

INTRODUCTION

Discovering a promising idea for a product or service is an essential starting point in a new enterprise. But it is just the beginning. The inventor of the Weed Eater, George C. Ballas, commented on the need for follow-through:

■ *Millions of people have "an idea," but unless they do something with it, their ideas aren't worth a dime. There are a lot of quacks and kooks out there who claim they invented the Weed Eater, and I don't doubt that there are some people who genuinely thought of this idea—but what did they do with it? Nothing. What do they deserve? Nothing.*[1]

What is called for is action that refines the product or service concept so that it works properly, fits customers' desires, and can be sold at a profitable price. It costs time and money to carry through the design process, so there is a continuous need to judge whether further refinement is worthwhile. Refinement also requires creative thought, which can be impeded by worrying about whether the process is worthwhile. The best compromise may be to recognize that feasibility analysis may be called for but to use it to help find ways of making the venture *more* workable, rather than as the basis of a go/no go decision.

[1]George C. Ballas and David Hollas, *The Making of an Entrepreneur* (Englewood Cliffs, NJ: Prentice Hall, 1980), p. 13.

FEASIBILITY ANALYSIS

Feasibility analysis comprises at least four other "abilities": (1) workability, (2) marketability, (3) produceability and (4) profitability. Each of these, in turn, depends to some extent on the others. Other concerns include the capacity of the entrepreneur or venture to carry through development and market introduction. With some pieces missing, the venture may survive. But for each venture, there is a minimum that must be present.

■ *Gene Amdahl successfully led a major computer development at IBM, then left to start his own computer company, Amdahl Corporation. That too he successfully started, with nearly $20 million in start-up capital from several corporate investors. A subsequent venture, Trilogy Corporation, failed to deliver because, according to* Fortune, *it was simply not able to get all the required pieces of new technology working together in time.*[2]

What Can Go Wrong

Feasibility analysis may help guard against the following causes of venture failure:

- The concept around which the venture is developed is either unworkable or does not fit the market. Money and effort spent on introducing it is wasted.
- Although the concept is workable, the effort applied to refining it and tuning it to customers is insufficient or misdirected. Performance, styling, packaging, instructions, and/or service procedures are in some way inadequate. Before long, competitors offer the market something better and sales for the venture dry up.
- The product or service of the venture is as good or better than that of competitors, but inadequate attention to designing it for economical production causes high costs and losses consume the venture's cash.
- Failure to anticipate ways in which the product or service can misperform leads to product liability lawsuits that kill the venture (see Chapter 3).
- Failure to appreciate the wide array of talents and resources needed to keep the company up with competitors produces a weak start-up that is soon overtaken and surpassed.
- The venture succeeds, but not nearly as grandly as it could have if more attention had been given to other opportunities that were present in addition to the one exploited.

Between conceiving the idea and making it work physically, much further invention, trial, error, and refinement may be needed. Moving ahead too slowly risks the loss of the concept and/or the market opportunity to a competitor. Moving ahead too quickly or carelessly can waste money and time on unworkable ideas. Which steps should be taken first depend on the enterprise.

Sometimes careful analysis can help, as indicated by the following examples from *Venture*.

[2]Myron Magnet, "Gene Amdahl Fights to Save a Wreck," *Fortune*, September 1, 1986, p. 66.

■ *Sumner A. Milender's one venture investment failure to date was with Air Designs, a company founded by a Buckminster Fuller protege to manufacture chutes that could be used as fire escapes. The ex-tanner wisely counseled the founders that it could take a decade to get regulatory approval for a fire escape device; he suggested that they develop the product for materials handling instead. He had already found the company a test site when he discovered that Otis Elevator was producing a similar product. "Obviously, we hadn't checked into patents thoroughly enough," he sighs.*

■ *When Jim Mann invested in Right Products, he wasn't canny enough about the market. The Connecticut company packaged hardware products for supermarkets. It showed promising figures, but had done only one four month test. Unfortunately, sales plunged after the fifth month. After two years the company folded. "At least it dropped dead on the spot," Mann reflected. "It's annoying when they die by inches."*

■ *The founders of Metamorphic Systems had hoped to produce hardware to make the Apple compatible with the IBM PC. After a venture capital investment of $800,000 technical product development work finally created an add-on device that cost almost as much as a new PC.*[3]

These examples illustrate situations in which more analytic checking and testing before spending large amounts on development or implementation could have minimized losses. Checklists have been proposed as one way of assessing whether continuation is justified.[4]

The feasibility of a service that can begin without much money or help, such as a small store or a restaurant, may best be checked simply by renting space, obtaining equipment on lease or loan, buying minimal inventory, and opening for business. If traffic builds up before cash runs out, the test supports viability. If sales are too slow, the test may reveal something better to try next.

For a service requiring more capital or for a new product, a better first test may be pencil and paper sketches, calculations, and a market survey. If the product is one for which a prototype or jury rig to test operating principles can be made cheaply, that may be the best first step.

DESIGN STAGES

Serious design work begins at different points for different ventures. Raising capital may come before or after feasibility testing. Prototyping is sometimes done in advance of the venture by a future customer. The development process can be divided into many different steps, as illustrated by one possible product design sequence depicted in Exhibit 2–1.

[3]William Bryant Logan, "Finding Your Angel," *Venture* (March 1986), p. 38.

[4]For example, Gerald G. Udell, Kenneth G. Baker, and Michael F. O'Neill, *Guide to Invention and Innovation Evaluation* (Eugene: University of Oregon, College of Business, 1977). Also, Karl H. Vesper, *New Venture Strategies* (Englewood Cliffs, NJ: Prentice Hall, 1990), chaps. 2 and 6.

A first task in laying out details of the development sequence for a new product or service could be to cross out those steps in Exhibit 2–1 that are not applicable and add others that fit the individual case. Next, single out for top priority the areas of greatest vulnerability. Third, work out a schedule of time, materials, and people responsible for carrying through the development.

Role of Precedents

Early concept development in most new ventures is based on historical precedent. A person starting another construction firm or a boat yard seldom relies on pilot projects and trials. Instead, similar prior or concurrent enterprises and personal experience are the guides. The entrepreneur can, in such ventures, hypothesize how the company will look and perform, who the customers will likely be, and what resources and setup will be required for the operation. A substantially accurate financial forecast and plan of action can be written by extrapolation from past experience, with correction for minor variations in prospective circumstances.

New products for ventures can sometimes be made most economically by using standard off-the-shelf components. New boats costing hundreds of thousands of dollars, for instance, may be almost entirely created adapting prior specifications and existing equipment. The following venture used standard technology in production but added better quality control:

■ *An engineer working for a company building nuclear reactors was sent to visit the supplier for its control rods, because of a late delivery. At the supplier, he was struck by the amount of careless handling in what seemed to him a fairly straightforward process for fabricating the rods. Returning home, he set up shop in his basement to make rods himself during evenings and weekends. Eventually, he left his job to become a full-time producer of rods, not only for his former employer but for other companies as well.*

Many companies begin with a product or process similar to ones that are already successful. Small refinements and technological advances can be added with little risk of malfunction. Thus, there may be little need for esoteric technical analysis or pilot runs.

■ *When Georgena Terry set out to create a company to make bicycles for women there was no need for reinvention. Starting with a conventional bicycle she changed the frame geometry to make the handlebars narrower and closer to the rider for easier reach. A smaller front wheel increased stability for smaller riders. Still basically a bicycle with changes designed to fit a special market it achieved sales of $660,000 the first year rising to an estimated $1.8 million and profitability the second.[5]*

The most used source of precedents is the entrepreneur's own experience, followed by the experience of others. From a study of 160 entrepreneurs, Birley concluded that "The choice of networks is key in understanding the nature of the

---

[5]"A Bicycle Built for Women," *Venture* (April 1987), p. 15.

EXHIBIT 2–1 New Product Development Steps to Consider

A. *Preliminary Investigation and Feasibility Analysis*
  1. Abstract sketches of scheme
  2. Preliminary estimation of market needs
  3. Listing of performance requirements
  4. Examination of prior art—patent scan
  5. Conception of alternative schemes
  6. Tentative specifications
  7. Time and cost estimates for development
  8. Estimated production costs
  9. Estimate of financial rate of return
B. *Development Exploration*
  1. More analysis of alternatives
     a. Computations
     b. Schematics
     c. Choices of components and materials
     d. Preliminary layout drawings
  2. Jury rig/breadboard tests—test of principles
  3. Mockup, preliminary user analysis, styling
  4. Consultation with outside experts
  5. Patent search and listing of possible claims
  6. List and compare competitors
  7. Consideration of production alternatives
  8. Evaluation of likely technical success
  9. Evaluation of likely market success
C. *Development Model Design*
  1. Examine potential liability
  2. Examine prospective service needs
  3. Layout and detail drawings
  4. Recheck with market, potential customers
  5. Check with possible suppliers
  6. Recheck patents, possible infringements
  7. Recheck costs
  8. Examine possible compromises
  9. Schedule spending, work on financing
D. *Development Model Construction*
  1. Purchase materials
  2. Hire help needed for styling and treatment of other human factors such as safety, ease of use, comfort, and convenience
  3. Manufacture and shop test
  4. Analyze results, modify design
  5. List possible production model changes
  6. Reestimate production costs
E. *Development Model Test*
  1. Establish test specifications
  2. List test procedures
  3. Install instrumentation
  4. Collect and analyze test data
  5. Reconsider market fit
  6. List most worrisome aspects in priority order
  7. Reassess likelihood of commercial success

(continued)

F. *Production Model Design*
1. Assess adequacy of specifications and design
2. Analyze costs
3. Analyze alternative production methods
4. Explore possible economies in design and production
5. Prepare detail drawings and bills of material
6. Develop user and service instruction
7. Recheck patents
8. Recheck market fit, competitiveness
9. List tooling alternatives and costs
10. Predict manufacturing difficulties

G. *Production Model Construction*
1. Temporary tool design and fabrication
2. Purchase materials
3. List production instructions
4. Manufacture and shop-test production model
5. Beta test with potential customers (utilization in advance of an offering to the market by a potential future customer)
6. Modify as advisable

H. *Production Model Test*
1. Design test according to specifications
2. Set up, test, and record results
3. Obtain customer reactions
4. Obtain outside expert assessment
5. Assess against likely competitive developments
6. Modify based on experience
7. Design future improvement program
8. Test customer and service instructions

subsequent firm. . . . An efficient network is one where, no matter where the entrepreneur enters the network, his needs are diagnosed and he is passed round the system until he gathers the necessary information and advice."[6]

Abstract Design

When the cost of physical models is high, or there are many decisions to be made in creating one, the most practical starting point for design may be to perform some sort of abstract analysis first.

Thinking Through.   Cheapest and in some ways easiest to begin with is simply thinking through the design, as the following inventor did:

■ *Before he went into the army, Bob Carver had been earning his way through graduate school in physics by repairing TV sets for local retailers in Seattle. In boring periods during active duty, he had time to think, and during one thought session, he became intrigued with a new electronic amplifier circuit design idea. He recalled from fixing one*

[6]Sue Birley, "The Role of Networks in the Entrepreneurial Process," p. 335 in John A. Hornaday, Edward B. Shils, Jeffry A. Timmons, and Karl H. Vesper, *Frontiers of Entrepreneurship Research, 1985* (Wellesley, MA: Babson Center for Entrepreneurial Studies, 1985).

particular brand of TV sets that some used a certain "bat-wing" shaped transistor in the circuit, which he knew was also used in automotive electronic ignition systems. It had caught his attention because this seemed an unusual combination of applications for the same electronic part.

Thinking further, he realized that the transistor was probably used for ignitions because it could carry large amounts of electrical power, much more than most transistors. Extending this reasoning, he saw that the transistor might work in hi-fi amplifiers of very high power. He began to think through design of an amplifier using this part that would be both more powerful and cheaper to construct than existing amplifiers. In his mind, he later recalled, he designed the entire circuit. "I did it following a system which I understand Einstein used—pursuing each piece of the design in my mind until it hit a problem, stopping to work out that problem, and then moving on to the next problem."

When released from the service, he moved back to Seattle, set up shop in his living room with a soldering iron and parts, and assembled the amplifier circuit he had designed in his mind. It delivered three times the power of anything else on the market and could be sold profitably for the same price. Through the stores for whom he had previously worked he got orders, and soon had a booming business. His company, Phase Linear, eventually was sold to a large Japanese manufacturing firm. Bob Carver then went on to start another hi-fi manufacturing firm, Carver Corporation, which hi-fi magazines shortly credited with yet another "breakthrough amplifier design." By 1990 Carver Corporation was publicly traded.

A study of entrepreneurs reported that over fifty out of 400 respondents said they had used mental visualization in start-ups for such things as physical designs, clarification of needs for capital and other resources, planning of action sequences, devising ways to save money, anticipating staffing and procedural needs, and practicing tactical moves in such things as negotiations. Such activity, some said, served also to maintain and renew enthusiasm and confidence. Most who visualized said it was helpful; some said it was vital; and only two of the fifty said that such dreams led them to make mistakes.[7]

Pencil-and-Paper Analysis.   Pencil and paper are inexpensive tools for taking visualization one step further. One entrepreneur, who had developed several successful new types of restaurants, explained how he did this.

■ *Most people, when they think about a new restaurant, seem to envisage one without people in it. They just think about how it will be laid out, the nice features it will have, what the menu will be, and maybe what color they will put on the walls. Or maybe an architect will make some sterile-looking mechanical drawings. I always think of mine as being full of customers and with people lined up waiting to get in the door, and then I think out the reasons why they are doing that. To raise capital for my last restaurant, I hired a regular first class artist to make beautiful pictures showing all the activity going on, the way I saw it in my mind. When I showed the pictures to my lawyer, my banker and some investors, they all went for it in a big way, and I had no trouble raising money to get it started.*

[7]Edward H. Rockey, "Envisioning New Business: How Entrepreneurs Perceive the Benefits of Visualization." P. 344 in Robert Ronstadt, John A. Hornaday, Rein Peterson, and Karl H. Vesper, *Frontiers of Entrepreneurship Research, 1986* (Wellesley, MA: Babson Center for Entrepreneurial Studies, 1986).

In manufacturing industries, product development usually begins with sketches, before anything is physically made. In the following example, the creation of the Tucker automobile, a designer, Alex Tremulis, prepared some suggested sketches and showed them to the entrepreneur, as described by Pearson:

■ *Tucker suggested some changes and then told Tremulis to get going, he was in a hurry. So Tremulis took the drawings home and started work on new sketches that same night. He used most of the measurements on the full-scale layouts we had done in the plant, and from them started new drawings that were scaled accurately. Six days later he called Tucker and said the sketches were ready. When could he come to look at them?*

Tremulis recalled, "It was about seven o'clock New Year's Eve when he got to our office in the Field Building, on his way to a party. He looked at the pictures and told me: 'That's it.'"

"The job was finished in five working days, and I think it was the fastest styling job that was ever done. I'm sure it was the fastest job ever done of making a full-size metal prototype of a production car directly from drawings without a clay model. Beginning New Year's Eve, the model was ready for paint in one hundred days."[8]

The power of well-drawn pictures to simulate an enterprise can be great, not only to sell a good idea but also to reveal flaws in a bad one. More often, however, pencil and paper are used to analyze the quantitative aspects of a proposed venture, and again, the effect can be powerful in either direction. The following venture was killed by such analysis:

■ *An inventor conceived an idea for a new parking garage. It would be automated, so that when a customer drove up to park, he or she would leave the car on an entry platform that would lift the car to whichever level had an empty spot and then place it there. Sketches made of the scheme were incorporated into a prospectus along with pro forma financial forecasts. With this prospectus, the inventor approached a venture capitalist, who in turn invited a business school graduate student to look it over. Working from the forecast, the student calculated that the rate of speed with which the garage could accept cars and shuffle them for parking and later for return to customers was such that several hours would be required to fill and empty the garage. The only way the forecasts could be achieved would be if the motorists came single file to the garage every few minutes throughout the day. If they came several at a time during rush hour or after work, some would have to wait hours.*

Here the pencil-and-paper model saved a great amount of time and money for all concerned. In hindsight, perhaps, the flaw should have been immediately obvious. But it was not foreseen, possibly because the designers were preoccupied with other problems, such as zoning, mechanisms for moving cars, costs, management of the garage, and myriad other details. The paper description helped to work these out and, also, to reveal a fatal problem.

Theoretical mathematical analysis, another pencil-and-paper tool, is also necessary for some types of new products, such as bridges, airplanes, pressure vessels, and computers. An extreme example would be space shots, where cut-and-try methods would be both prohibitively expensive and inadequate.

---

[8]Charles T. Pearson, *The Indomitable Tin Goose* (New York: Pocket Books, 1960), p. 88.

■ *When Frank Whittle proposed to the British government that it build a gas turbine he was turned down. Intuitively, it was obvious that lighting an explosion amid rotating fan blades would be useless. The expanding gas might try to push some blades one way and others another. But how could it produce thrust? Besides, to get an explosion the gas would have to be compressed by a piston, as in autos. Otherwise, not enough compression would take place; the gas would just flow around the fan blades, not compress. No less an authority than Louis Marks, Harvard engineering professor and editor of the* Mechanical Engineers' Handbook, *was said to have proclaimed it impossible.*

Whittle produced calculations, based on theoretical analysis of gas dynamics, which he had studied in engineering school, showing that Marks was wrong. When his government turned him down, he raised capital to form a new company, Power Jets, Limited. With this company he built an engine and proved it would work. He also had a plane built, installed the engine and flew it over the head of Winston Churchill, very low, very fast.

At that point the British government changed its mind and took over Whittle's project. Whittle was so enraged by the takeover that he turned his back on jet engines and never worked on them again. Britain failed to keep up in jet development with Germany, where another student, Hans Von Ohain, had also invented a turbojet. The German engine powered a jet fighter that proved very effective against allied bombing raids, although it was too late to change the final outcome of World War II.

Such major mechanical projects are more often done by established companies than by new ones. New companies are more likely to use mathematical analysis to refine their first products in such fields as electronics and computers.

Computer Models. Computer modeling is used by major companies such as those of the auto and aerospace industries, but not much yet for start-ups, except those involved with computer products themselves. The future will likely see more use of computer modeling in start-up product design. Exotic new ideas on the horizon may enhance model making for companies at all stages of development. One possibility is "stereolithography," a technique for forming plastic physical models through interaction between computer-directed light rays and plastic solidification triggered by intersections of the light rays to make "instant" three-dimensional forms.

Physical Models

Beyond the use of pencil and paper, the creation of a new product or service design in physical form can help to

- Make sure it really works
- See what it will look like and alternative forms it may take
- Learn ways of improving it
- Gather and refine cost data
- Reduce it to practice for obtaining patent protection (see Chapter 3)
- Demonstrate it for potential customers and thereby test the market
- Demonstrate it for potential partners, investors, or employees for recruiting purposes

Mockups. A *mockup* is a physical form to show what a concept will *look* like. A product mockup might be made of wood, clay, or plastic. A service might be shown through a wood, plaster, clay, or cardboard model of facilities used for rendering the service, such as an architect's model of the building that will house the business. Mockups are usually relatively cheap and quick to make, but they look very much like the real thing. Auto manufacturers, for example, often create new car designs first in clay, wood, or plaster that are realistic enough to use in photographs for early advertisements.

Jury Rigs.   The purpose of a *jury rig* (called a *breadboard* if the concept is an electrical one) is to demonstrate the workability of a concept often by concentrating on some particularly crucial aspect of the design. What the jury rig looks like is of no importance, so long as it can be made to perform the function it is designed to test. It can be enormously informative about the venture concept, what is required to accomplish it, and how it can be improved.

■ *George Ballas had succeeded in both real estate and dance studio businesses but had never worked in manufacturing. His concept of the Weed Eater began in 1953. Watching the brushes in an automatic car wash spinning their bristles into the creases and cracks of cars passing through, it occurred to him that a similar action might trim away grass around the edges of trees and along walls lining a lawn. He did nothing about it, however, until 18 years later in the summer of 1971 when he was struggling in his yard with weeds. He recalled, "in a fit of anger over my weeds, I dashed over to the garbage can, and grabbed the first clean tin can I could find, which turned out to be a popcorn can. I grabbed a Phillips head screw driver and started punching holes in it. Then I grabbed some insulated radio wire, pushed the wire through the holes, and tied a knot at each end inside the can. I removed the blade from my standard edger and attached this contraption. It only worked for a couple of seconds before flying off, but it worked long enough for me to see that it could work."*

Later, he observed that had he possessed more knowledge of model making, he might have been able to move quicker on his venture. He said, "If I had known that I could take an idea to a machine shop and have a machinist build a prototype from it, I would have developed the Weed Eater years ago."

Prototypes.   Going a step further, *both* appearance and operating features may be combined to make a *working prototype* for testing and experimentation, as well as realistically demonstrating the proposed product to potential buyers and users. "The idea is only 10 percent of the proposition. Showing that it can work is 90 percent," according to a senior professional at Arthur D. Little Enterprises, which selects for backing about ten to fifteen inventions out of a thousand each year.[10]

One way to get a working prototype is to make it yourself, as did the following entrepreneur:

■ *When Walter Meyer, an aerospace engineer, was laid off by Boeing in early 1975 at age 59, he anticipated difficulty in finding another job because of his age. Instead of seeking a job, he decided to try an enterprise of his own. Several years earlier he had designed a finlike apparatus that could be attached to inner tubes, enabling riders to propel themselves through the water; he made a few, but they did not sell. Now, he had another idea,*

[9]Ballas and Hollas, *The Making of an Entrepreneur*, p. 16.
[10]Andrew Feinberg, "Getting a Prototype Made," *Venture* (October, 1984), p. 41.

a combination radiant heating unit and oven, which could be installed in a fireplace and used in case of power failure. Meyer envisioned a two-chambered tin box. The lower chamber would be the firebox, and the upper an oven. Smoke and hot air generated in the firebox would flow up and around the oven and then escape up the chimney. The firebox front would have two glass doors, to give a view of the flames, and transmit radiant heat into the room.

In his garage he bent sheet steel to form what he decided to call a "fireplace range." He installed it in his front room, crumpled some newspapers, threw them into it, and lit a flame. Somewhat to his surprise, he found that it worked not only as an oven, but also as a source of more heat than he expected. Experimenting with placement of vents, he found he could keep the glass doors relatively cool and soot-free by cutting a vent hole directly above them.

As he continued experimenting with the prototype, Meyer began seeing ways to make it cheaper, easier to install, and more attractive in appearance. Taking it to fireplace shops yielded still more improvement suggestions. Within a few weeks he had installed several in homes of friends, and friends of friends. A local newspaper article on him and his product brought in more orders. A few weeks later, he arranged with job shops to make some of the parts and rented space to make other parts and do the assembly. Meyer Engineering company was now in operation.

There were several advantages in Meyer's approach. The physical prototype not only let him experiment with and refine it, but also to try the idea out on other people, which in turn generated additional ideas for improvement and gave some indication of its market potential and price range. Being able to work out physical details and manufacture the prototypes by himself saved money and probably time. It was made possible in part because the device was relatively simple and did not require special tooling or expensive shop machinery, and in part because he possessed the necessary fabrication skills.

An entrepreneur lacking such skills can still try to recruit or purchase them. For the Weed Eater, George Ballas got help from a machinist, Tom Geist, who had bought real estate from him but wanted to back out of the deal. In an attempt to save the sale, Ballas invited Geist to lunch and during the conversation learned of his prototyping capability. Ballas recalled their collaboration, which in three months produced a working model and patent application:

■ *Sometimes Tom Geist and I would rent a machine shop starting at five o'clock in the evening, and we would sit there all night making different Weed Eater heads, and then we would test them the next day.*

We didn't use any drawings in building our prototypes. Normally you'd have to have drawings to take to a machinist. As you may know, that normally takes weeks or months to prepare. I would suggest to Tom that we make a cutting head so big. We would brainstorm on it for a few minutes; then he'd start cutting! We would build a head in several hours, whereas it would normally take a couple of months. We would then take it out and try it. If it didn't work, we would go right back and build another head. . . . The fellow we rented the machine shop from, John Collis, got involved in a casual way, but for all practical purposes it was just Tom and me.[11]

[11]Ballas and Hollas, *The Making of an Entrepreneur*, p. 16.

If he had not met this machinist, Ballas could have located others by asking for referrals from patent lawyers and inventors, or by looking under "machine shops" or "manufacturing model makers" in the *Yellow Pages* or *Thomas Register*. One experienced inventor suggested that deciding what material the product would be made from should come first, approaching suppliers for help. This, he said, would likely be cheaper than a job shop. Drawings also help save money.[12]

Many job shop owners, experienced in prototyping and product development work, are very clever at helping to solve design problems and suggesting better ways to manufacture. Curiously, perhaps, they rarely develop new products of their own, possibly because they are so busy working for inventors and other manufacturers that they have no time to look for unidentified market needs.

Most model makers encounter inventors who want prototype work done in exchange for a "piece of the action," but they know from experience that most inventions don't pay off, and so they usually prefer to work for cash in advance. They also prefer to work from comprehensive and unambiguous machine drawings so there will be no dispute afterward about whether the work was done correctly. But if the inventor is willing to pay in advance and to chance the machinist's judgment, he or she may find it possible to work on a more informal and collaborative basis from rough sketches and hand waving.

An inventor should visit several shops to get schedule and dollar estimates and to size up the owners for personal compatibility. Cleanliness, level of activity, reputation with other shops, and examples of prior jobs can give clues as to which shop is best. Machine shop owners are accustomed to being evaluated and should not be offended by it. Valuable additional ideas for bettering the design and the venture concept may also be discovered without charge from such visits.

But even with assistance from professionals, the construction of a prototype that works can be illusive, notwithstanding a prior demonstration of its operating principles by jury rig. The following excerpt describes some prototyping experiences in the development of a machine to mechanize the Xerox process:

■ *Carlson, the inventor of xerography, filed his first patent in 1937, calling his discovery electrophotography. His first successful image was made in 1938. Over the next nine years he tried to sell his idea to more than twenty companies, including RCA, Remington Rand, General Electric, Kodak, and IBM. They all turned him down, wondering why anyone would need a machine to do something you could do with carbon paper.*

Although Carlson was often frustrated by the lack of interest in his invention, he never quit. Sometimes he put his idea and equipment on the shelf for a few months, but soon the enthusiasm would return. He scraped together a few hundred dollars in 1939, a large sum during the Depression, and had a prototype of an automatic copier built by a model shop in New York. It didn't work. Another model maker got it working briefly, but soon the war diverted expert machinists to more urgent tasks. Carlson went back to demonstrating his process with manual plates.[13]

[12]Feinberg, "Getting a Prototype Made," p. 41.
[13]Gary Jacobson and John Hillkirk, *Xerox, American Samurai* (New York: Macmillan, 1986) p. 54.

Some of the drama that can accompany the creation of a first working model was illustrated by development of the Tucker, a new automobile in the late 1940s. A corporation was formed and capital was raised. Parts of other cars plus a helicopter engine were adapted to save time and money. The engine had to be modified by the addition of water-jacketed cylinders to change it from air to water cooling. Pearson described the experience as follows:

■   *Before the first casting for the blocks had cooled Leabu hauled them from the foundry in a pickup and set them in a jig mill, and when they were ready he brought them back to put in cylinder liners. They already had the liners, a standard size of alloyed steel from Thompson Products. After weeks of hard, almost continuous work the end of the job was almost in sight, and they decided not to stop until they finished it.*

They turned Mrs. Tucker's kitchen into a heat treat department with Mrs. Tucker furnishing the oven, though she didn't know it at the time. They set up a progressive assembly line starting on the back steps, and popped the first two blocks into the oven of the electric stove. It took about three hours to get them up to between 500 and 600 degrees, which was as high as the oven would go. As soon as they were heated through they were set on burners on top of the stove to keep them hot, and two more blocks were stuck in the oven and the blocks outside moved up a step.

Equipment for installing the liners was all ready and consisted chiefly of two large cans, one of the kind fruit comes in for restaurants. The larger of the two cans was set on the floor and the smaller one placed inside of it. Then the sleeves were placed one at a time in the smaller inside can, covered with naptha to keep them from frosting so they would slide into the blocks easily. To cool them, liquid oxygen was poured into the space between the cans from a thermos-like jug.

One at a time the blocks were set on the kitchen floor on bricks, to keep them level and not burn holes in the linoleum. Then one of the men, wearing asbestos gloves, took a liner and slid it into the cylinder opening in the block. Heat had expanded the hole in the block and cold contracted the liner, but it had to be put in fast before it started to expand again.

While the liner expanded it made a shrill humming sound until it was locked in place, and if it went in crooked the only way to get it out was to break it with a hammer, knock out the pieces and start over. On the first block they only lost one liner.

Within eleven hours after the first blocks were put in the oven, the first engine was together and ready for a test. In a garage space in the front of the building the engine was set on a makeshift stand, with a garden hose connected to the water inlet on the block and a five-gallon can of gasoline hung overhead, connected to the carburetor with a length of rubber tubing. A flexible tube running under the garage door carried off the exhaust. It was still winter in Ypsilanti.

After a few moments the engine took off. It was a climax, but everybody was too tired to celebrate. They let it run about five minutes, yanked off the gasoline and water connections and the flexible exhaust tube, and threw the engine in the back of a pickup. Offutt and Leabu took off for Chicago, and Tucker had an engine. With the engine were patterns and temporary tooling for making at least another hundred.[14]

Although makeshift, the procedures these prototypers used were not amateurish. These venturers knew their machinery, and they drew upon expert suppliers for necessary parts and machine work. At the same time, their shortcut

[14]Pearson, *The Indomitable Tin Goose*, p. 134

procedures and facilities saved vast amounts of time and money compared to those used in prototyping by established automakers.

Contract Development. If the product is highly technical, requiring esoteric engineering and fabrication capabilities, then contracting with an established organization for the entire development may be best, as was done in the next example:

■ *As an account supervisor for McCann-Erickson in London, Roger Percy was frustrated by poor information about people's immediate responses to TV advertisements. "The fastest way we could get information," he said, "was to park a van with a TV set in it at a shopping center, recruit six housewives to sit in it and play a string of commercials for them. They always told us how great the commercials were and how they wanted to run right out and buy the products. When people know what you're looking for in market research, they tend to give it to you. This caused me to ride one brand from 24 percent of the U.K. market down to 8 percent. We could get better information with more expensive studies, but they took six months, and by then it was too late."*

He wondered if it would be possible to equip home TVs with a device that selected viewers could push buttons on indicating their responses, which would be directly fed to a computer in real time. Returning to the United States, he asked technical experts. He learned that the idea was not new, but also that technology had recently advanced to where it might be possible. Not experienced in the technology himself, he searched for others who were and could help with the design. "There were just two difficulties," he said. "First, a lot of people thought they could do the job when they actually could not. And second, everybody wanted a third of the pie to do it."

Finally, his search led him to Stanford Research Institute. He worked out terms there, raised money from family and friends, and signed a development contract. "They built the machine," he recalled, "and it didn't work. I was out of business.

"But then the lead engineer called and asked if they could go on working for free. He said the seven engineers he had working on it were coming in on weekends, working on it at home and were so intrigued they couldn't leave it alone. Whereas they usually were assigned a tiny part of some big system, here they had the whole job and wanted to finish it. They stayed on until it worked and still let us have all the rights. I'll always be grateful to S.R.I." With the new device he started his own market research company, which was shortly operating in the black and growing rapidly.

Hiring engineers out of his own pocket was only one of several ways for Percy to obtain the design help he needed. Another would have been to recruit partners. But he would have had to share control and coordinate all major decisions with working partners at a cost in time and energy. He might also have had to negotiate some sort of royalty terms with whoever did the design, thereby reducing both immediate cash outlays and risk. But it would also have reduced his subsequent profits.

Debugging

Throughout the development process, thought must be given to what can go wrong with the new product or service. Precedents are not enough. The DeHavilland Comet airliner failed from fatigue fracture of its metal skin. The Lockheed Electra failed because of an undiscovered vibration mode. Crash of a DC-10 revealed that its entire control system was vulnerable to failure due to design weakness in a single location. Every design has its weakest point, and a new venture too can crash from one failure.

■   *Bill Bennett had quit his job as buyer for the Jewel supermarket chain to buy a small company that manufactured cottage cheese. As a way to build sales he made a deal with a French company to become the first manufacturer and distributor of its product, Yoplait Yogurt, in the United States. Yoplait had commissioned market research which concluded that Americans would not like its tapered package but would like its taste.*

Bennett decided to keep the package anyway, but make it half again as large and print the label in both French and English. He also decided to eliminate taste enhancers and stabilizers from the formula to make the yogurt "all natural." His decisions were based, he said, "on what was in my head and my heart, based on observing the marketplace for years.... I'm cautious about research. You can't be blind to it, but you can't be its prisoner either.... I was so convinced I had the right product that I was sure it would sell itself once someone tasted it."

Needing cash to develop production and sales, he prepared a presentation that included taste testing, which he used on potential investors and retailers alike. It worked. He raised $1.5 million by selling a 51 percent interest in his company, and store sales began. Initial reception by the market was encouraging.

But then leakage problems began, and grew with sales, both on store shelves and in customers' refrigerators. The leaks seemed sporadic and mystified both Bennett and the French. Eventually, it was found that changes in the food formula and package size together had weakened its seal. The cure was to change from wax to plastic package coating, but it came too late. Bennett's investors lost confidence and sold the company to General Mills, which made the shift to plastic and saw sales rise over three years to $450 million per year. "The cup problem," Bennett said, "was a bad break."[15]

More complex prototypes and ventures require more people to help out, but even then there can be many bugs and frustrations, as illustrated by the following case. It concerns a venture formed by Bert Bunnell to produce a medical device, called a "Puffer," for aiding the breathing of babies with respiratory problems. Bunnell had developed his concept through a combination of analysis and prototyping with several employers, each of whom in turn dropped it although both prototypes and market prospects grew progressively stronger. Finally, he had obtained the rights and struck a deal for support to take over development in his own enterprise. But the product still needed final debugging, as recounted by McMullan:

■   *Day by day, Bert would ask about progress on the Puffer. He wanted badly to know when Chris and Jack would finish it but not what problems they were having because he was preoccupied with writing a plan to raise money from venture capitalists. He wanted the technical work completed so he could get clinical studies underway. Yet the design was riddled with problems. For instance, arrangement of the hardware made it physically*

---

[15]Susan E. Currier, "Creating a New Product: Two Paths to the Same Marketplace," *Inc.* (October 1980), p. 95.

impossible to tell when the slave processor received a command. That took two weeks to correct. Meanwhile, it was becoming apparent that much of the code needed rewriting. Wiring added to the confusion because of loose connections. Before long Chris and Jack were totally frustrated.[16]

This case not only illustrates that debugging can be a major task, it also highlights the severity of problems that can arise from running out of start-up capital. Here the entrepreneur was being forced to neglect development of his product in order to search for capital. This neglect aggravated the capital need as delays consumed more of the company's dwindling cash.

Styling and Packaging

While feasibility analysis and design are underway, thought should also be directed to the presentation of the product or service. This includes styling, human factors, packaging, and a host of other variables concerned with how customers will perceive the product.

In the specialized area of styling and packaging, assistance by a professional industrial designer or packaging consultant may be worth considering. These professionals will give suggestions about how to make the product better looking, easier and safer to use and service, and perhaps even more versatile. It may be more economical to visit several custom packaging companies and obtain their suggestions. Experts can help with designing the product for packing, shipping, stacking, reducing theft, appealing to children, and aiding waste disposal.

Artistic help in creating a logo, graphics for the package, display racks, price tags, letterheads, emblems, and especially brochures is available from industrial designers, commercial artists, and advertising agencies. Young people just getting started in such professions are typically much less expensive to hire. They may be just as good as or better than a high-priced consultant with an established reputation, but because they lack experience the quality of their output may be less predictable. When inventors and entrepreneurs design their own artwork, it usually looks amateurish. That may not matter for some businesses, but for others it may be a great handicap. The package and graphics, like the product, can first be tested at relatively low cost in mockup or prototype form.

Production Design

The next design stage, taking the product or service from prototype to regular production form, can be equally or even more challenging. Alejandro Zaffaroni, who founded a major new drug company with the extraordinary seed capital amount of $52 million, commented as follows:

[16]W. Ed McMullan, *The First Five Years: A High Tech Company* (Calgary: Center for Venture Development, University of Calgary, 1981), p. 40.

It doesn't take too long to get a group of gifted individuals together and invent and invent — and you can go on inventing forever. There's always an opportunity to make a better switch or something. Now, to go from the idea to prototype in some cases is a major hurdle. But to go from the prototype to the product — that is the mountain. That always comes the hardest.[17]

Production design requires that the product or service be produceable from standard materials; operate on a reliable routine basis; be produced by the most economical workers, sometimes relatively unskilled workers; be suitable for whatever additional servicing may be required; and be reliably of expected quality for the customer. (Chapter 8 will discuss the task of designing and setting up production.) But production design also deals with the configuration and specifications of the product itself. In the following case, the inventors succeeded in creating a product that worked well in both prototype and production form, but unfortunately due to its design, it was too costly to produce.

■ *The Kramer brothers of Seattle became intrigued with photographic slide projectors and undertook to develop one that would allow any two slides out of a carousel tray to be shown superimposed on the screen. One slide could slowly be faded in or out over another to create a more elegant presentation. Working in a home shop, they produced a box that held two lenses, one for each slide, and designed a mechanism for pulling slides on command from any in the tray.*

After much tinkering, fitting, adjusting, and refining, they finally worked the product out. It would not only superimpose and fade slides as selected, but it could also be programmed to play music and operate the slides automatically under control of a tape cassette. Customers bought the machine, found it reliable, and liked its performance. But although they paid several thousand dollars per machine, the company, Source Technology, lost several thousand more on each one and eventually failed, several million dollars in the red.

Subsequently, the Kramers discovered there were many ways to cut product costs. By mounting components on a spine, as video recorders do, rather than different walls inside a box as they had done, the framing was much cheaper and alignment of parts much easier to control. By using a beam splitter, they found there would be need for only one lens instead of two, and so forth.

With new knowledge about how to design for cheaper production, they attempted again to raise capital to restart the company. But no investors were willing to gamble on a prior failure. Attempts were also made to sell the venture to other companies, but without success. Many customers who bought the first machines still loved them. But when the supply of inventory taken over by the bank was sold, it was no longer available.

In hindsight, these entrepreneurs could see that although their design was good for operation, it fell far short on production design. The technology to do it right was available, but they did not find it in time. An earlier search for more expert design review and assistance could have changed the outcome.

[17]Gene Bylinsky, *The Innovation Millionaires* (New York: Scribners, 1976), p. 127.

MARKET FITTING

At the same time that the product is designed to work well and be produceable, it must also be shaped to fit the market. This, in turn, requires information and understanding about what customers want and what they are willing to pay for it. Many times the customers themselves do not know until the company helps them discover it.

Technology Push versus Market Pull

The term *technology push* implies gambling that customers will want a new product or service if it can be created. *Market pull* works back from what customers are asking for and seeks to provide it. Either approach can work in a venture, and both should be considered.

Historically, scholars claim, market pull seems to have paid off more often than technology push. Marquis observed that "Recognition of demand is a more frequent factor in successful innovation than recognition of technical potential."[18] Among the 567 innovations he studied, market demand accounted for 45 percent of the successes as an initiation force, and production need, another form of market pull, for another 30 percent, whereas recognition of technical feasibility accounted for only 21 percent.

An example of technology push would be the Xerox process. Chester Carlson conceived the idea, then went looking for support to develop it and get it to market. It took years of rejection before he got backing, more years to develop a salable machine, and still more for the market itself to develop. Another example is the pocket calculator. Bill Hewlett wanted one. His company's market research studies indicated that nowhere near enough people would buy it to justify production. He had it developed anyway. The studies turned out wrong and his product succeeded.

In the next example, the entrepreneur entered business as a middleman in the push process by helping the market become aware of newly developed technology.

■ *Joseph Sugarman, an advertising man for an Illinois gubernatorial candidate, had briefly tried a new desk top electronic calculator in 1971 and been impressed with its performance, although at $600 it cost more than he could afford. Some time later, he read in Business Week that there might soon be pocket-sized electronic calculators selling for as little as $240. By phone he located the manufacturer, Craig Corporation in California, and asked the sales manager if he could, by mounting a direct mail campaign, be first to sell the new product.*

[18]Donald G. Marquis, "The Anatomy of Successful Innovations." P. 14, in *Corporate Strategy and Product Innovation*, ed. Robert B. Rothberg (New York: Free Press, 1976).

Buying a sample unit for $141, Sugarman showed it to some friends to raise money for a direct mailing. He spent $12,000 to rent ten mailing lists, prepare brochures, and send them to 50,000 accountants, engineers, and others whom he thought might be interested at $240 per calculator. It would take, he figured, a two-tenths of 1 percent response rate to break even. Soon letters began arriving, with checks and order forms enclosed, but not enough of them. This was his first venture using other people's money, and it looked like only half would be recovered.

He analyzed his sales results, breaking them out by list. Some lists were doing poorly, including those to engineers and accountants. But others were doing very well, notably the ones to presidents of million-dollar corporations. It had not even been his idea to include this list and he did so somewhat against his own judgment, but at a friend's suggestion. If he had used only those lists, he would have doubled his investment in one mailing.

Now he felt he knew how to profit with the product, but more money was needed. Calling Craig, he learned that his cost on a next round would drop from $140 per calculator to $103. He convened his investors and asked them to stay in for another round. "The $6,000 left would just cover about 25,000 mailing pieces," he recalled, "and yet if I was going to score big, I had to roll my campaign out fast and big to beat the competition.

"I was thirty-three years old, just barely able to pay my mortgage, and had a wife and child to support. I knew that each time in my life that I had felt I had a sure winner, something came up at the last minute and grasped success from me just as I felt it was within reach. I knew that if I invested the huge sums of money I needed to make this program a success, and lost, it might be a blow I wouldn't recover from for years."

He asked suppliers to extend credit for a mailing to 400,000 names, at a total cost of around $100,000. The mailing went out in early January 1972, and Sugarman waited for a response. After ten days, "the response started to trickle in, then pour in, then it literally started to gush in. There were more responses . . . than I could possibly imagine."[19]

Here the technology and the market were both new. In the next example, the technology and market were both very old, but new circumstances led entrepreneurs to believe there would nevertheless be opportunity from an increase in market demand or pull.

■ *During the "energy crisis" in 1980, a successful Massachusetts furniture retailer and one of his business associates were discussing the energy crisis and the markets it might create. It occurred to them that people who lowered thermostats in their homes might become good customers for wool sweaters to wear around the house. Neither was experienced in the sweater business, so they sought out someone who was. They contacted the president of a major U.S. sweater company and raised the possibility of the three of them forming a company to import sweaters from the Orient for sale in the United States.*

The sweater company was a division of a large conglomerate, and management of the conglomerate had been giving relatively little support or recognition for the division's profitable performance. Hence, the division president welcomed a chance to leave and contribute his efforts and expertise to the new company in return for a third ownership. The other two put up the money, and contact was made with a Hong Kong supplier. One

[19]Joseph Sugarman, *Success Forces* (Chicago: Contemporary Books, 1980).

sales trip around the United States with samples produced $2 million in orders. Ship-
ments from Hong Kong began to arrive, and the company was in business. Within a year
it had become very profitable and part was sold off to a larger company, leaving the three
founders with a handsome return on their investment as well as a viable new company.

Although Sugarman's venture was pushed by new technology and this one was not, both push and pull can be seen in both enterprises. Sugarman's venture could not be foreseen as market pull inasmuch as he did not know if the market was there when he mounted his first campaign to sell, but he supposed it was. He used the precedent of electronic calculators as the basis for anticipating a demand for the much smaller and much cheaper pocket version. In this way it could be argued that both market pull and technology push were involved in his enterprise.

The sweater venture was certainly not technology push, but it had to offer something different from existing products already on the market. These entre-preneurs felt it was styling that they had to offer. Based on that they had to gamble by making a substantial commitment to suppliers, obtaining samples, and going on the road to sell sweaters before they could be sure sales would come. Thus, market pull was not certain at the outset, but there was at least some "styling push" in their product. Thus, again both push and pull elements were present in some form.

It is important that both push and pull be considered wherever possible in developing a venture. Sooner or later competition will attack on both fronts. The venturer should anticipate this by incorporating an analysis of the market as part of the concept refinement process.

Market Buzz Words

Market analysis must consider attributes of the product or service relative to both the customer and the competition. The litany of marketing includes consid-eration of the venture's *unique selling proposition* that helps provide *differentiation* for *positioning* that the venture offers relative to its competitors. Such *buzz words* capture concepts of importance to start-ups as well as going concerns.[20] It is most crucial to remember that it is the customer's perception of the benefits, quality, and value of the venture's product or service that is most important, not that of the entrepreneur.

Normally, for a start-up, *market segmentation* and *target customers* should be narrowly and sharply defined as part of a *niche strategy*. The view that it is best to seek a large market share is supported by both conventional wisdom and statistical evidence. Companies with large shares relative to competitors tend to enjoy higher profits as a percent of both sales and investment. To pursue such strategic advantage requires clear market information. The information can be used for

---

[20]Richard A. Drossler, "How to Plan Marketing Strategy." P. 111, in Donald M. Dible, *Winning the Money Game* (Santa Clara, CA: Entrepreneur Press, 1975).

feasibility analysis, product or service design, formulation of market strategy, and prediction of volume to anticipate production and financial needs.

Market Research

Two broad approaches to learning about the market are possible. First are five "armchair" approaches that the entrepreneur can perform personally and quietly without contacting potential customers. Second are four "contact" approaches that require making contact with other people to learn what customers may buy. The most certain approach is simply to go ahead with the venture. In the view of venture capitalists, according to Hills,[21] entrepreneurs tend to operate more by intuition in market assessment, and often appropriately so. But if the venture requires risking a lot of money, investment in market data before start-up may be the wiser course.

Solitary Approaches.   The easiest place to look for market information is in the entrepreneur's own experience—information that the entrepreneur either already has or can read in published or secondary sources.

Egocentric evaluation.   Probably the most common assessment approach is egocentric evaluation, wherein the inventor asks, "What might I like to have?," conceives an answer (maybe a combination corkscrew, compass, and whistle?), and then hypothesizes that perhaps a lot of other people might like such a product also. George Ballas, inventor of the Weed Eater, recalls that "people were the causes of all my discouragements." In answer to the question "What information did you use to determine whether there was a market for the Weed Eater?," he replied, "My own personal need. I knew I had a need that a lot of people had." In his case egocentric evaluation worked. In many cases it is not sufficient.

Market comparisons.   Making market comparisons with what competitors offer currently or guessing what they will offer in the future may yield ideas for design improvement. The existing products can be listed down one side of a page and the features across the top to make a grid, which is then filled in with comparative data, as is done in *Consumer Reports*. The product or service of the new company can then be measured relative to others, possibly yielding helpful ideas for improvements. It may be important to recognize, however, that it will be competing with the *future* products of those other companies, not just the present ones.

Along with the product features, it may be helpful to list respective sales or shares of the market. If the new company cannot expect to obtain a major share of some segment of the total market by careful tuning of its design, the venture may never achieve volume cost reductions sufficient to survive cost cutting by competitors.

---

[21]Gerald E. Hills, "Market Analysis and Marketing in New Ventures: Venture Capitalists' Perceptions." P. 43 in John A. Hornaday, Fred Tarpley, Jr., Jeffry A. Timmons, and Karl H. Vesper, *Frontiers of Entrepreneurship Research, 1984* (Wellesley, MA: Babson Center for Entrepreneurial Studies, 1984).

Market segmentation.   Market segmentation refers to grouping potential customers with significantly similar characteristics. It can be useful in estimating the number of potential customers, defining just what will most effectively appeal to them, and forecasting how much the venture should be able to sell them. Possible segmentation of potential motorcycle customers, for instance, might be as shown in Table 2-1.

For a particular product or service, the segmentation shown in Table 2-1 might be much finer. If the focus were on new riders, the racing categories would likely disappear. Those that remained might be further broken down into cycle weight, engine size, or cost. Street riders might be subdivided into those who prefer foreign cycles versus Harley-Davidson riders. Harley-Davidson riders might be subdivided into "traditionals" (beards, tattoos, and leathers), "second childhood" (older riders), police, and females. Clearly, there would be some overlap, but it would not be great. Some products, such as motor oil, might appeal to all segments. Others, such as modification parts or riding apparel, might vary greatly in appeal from one segment to another. If a venture is to attune to its chosen segment(s), it must define and understand them clearly.

Secondary market research data.   Market research involves both primary and secondary data. *Primary data* refers to new data gathered specifically for the new product or service. *Secondary data* refers to that information already available from existing sources, such as a chamber of commerce, newspaper advertising departments, trade associations, the familiar *Yellow Pages*, the U.S. Statistical Abstract, and Manufacturers' Directories. A listing of some secondary sources appears in Table 2-2. It is often easier to begin with secondary data by making a few phone calls and visiting the library.

Demographic analysis.   Published demographic data can help in estimating sales volume and also in designing the business. A new product or service may be ideal for a certain type of customer, but if there are very few of those customers, the total market may be correspondingly limited. One inventor, for instance, designed a glove that he claimed was ideal for tambourine players. Perhaps it was, but he did not find many people interested in buying it. Even if they needed it, tambourine players are few in number and therefore limit the potential market

TABLE 2-1   Possible Segmentation of Motorcycle Market

GROUP AGE	Street	Off Road	Dirt Racing	Paved Racing	Touring
18–22					
23–35					
36–40					
40+					

CYCLE TYPE (spanning header over Street, Off Road, Dirt Racing, Paved Racing, Touring)

TABLE 2–2 Some Sources of Secondary Market Research Data

LIBRARY

U.S. Government Publications

Statistical Abstract of the United States
Measuring Markets: A Guide to the Use of Federal and State Statistical Data
Census of Business (also of Retail Trade, Service Industries, Housing, Population)
County and City Data Book
State and Metropolitan Data Book
Monthly Urban Review
Survey of Current Business

Other Publications

Manufacturers' Directory (state and local)
Predicasts F&S Index
Encyclopedia of Associations
Encyclopedia of Business Information Sources
Industry magazines such as *Advertising Age, Catalog Showroom Business, Chain Store Age, Direct Marketing, Discount Merchandising, Drug Store News, Progressive Grocer, Restaurant Business, Stores, Supermarket News, Women's Wear Daily*

Other Sources

Market studies done by or for other companies
Chambers of commerce
Newspaper advertising sales offices
Mailing list companies
Port authorities
Private research companies, such as A.C. Nielson, Audits and Surveys, R.L. Polk (auto surveys)

---

severely. Telephone calls or visits to a few music stores, or possibly to a tambourine manufacturer, might have given an indication of the extent of the market.

Other sources of demographic information include newspaper advertising departments, chambers of commerce, trade associations, and government agencies such as the United States Department of Commerce. Phone calls can quickly narrow the search for helpful information. Demographics can be important in any line of business, but perhaps the most straightforward examples are in retailing and services, as the following may illustrate:

■ *After completing graduate school and working for someone else for a couple of years, a young Texas veterinarian decided he would like to move back to his home town and open his own clinic. Having little money, he first applied for work there at two clinics in different neighborhoods. Both required that he sign agreements not to set up a competing clinic nearby. He negotiated with each a radius to which this agreement would apply. Drawing these areas on a map showed where he would be free to set up his clinic.*

To choose the best site within those areas, he and an MBA entrepreneurship student formulated a list of demographic variables important to veterinary clinic sales. These included the number of people living within a two-mile radius, family status, age (homeowners aged 20–40 own most pets), income (some income ranges tend to have more pets and to buy more care for them), and, from the Yellow Pages, *the number of other veterinarians nearby.*

Inevitably, there were conflicts among the data. Low-income areas, for instance, had more pets but gave them less care. Areas with fewer veterinarians per capita and higher family incomes were growing slower, and so forth. Judgments and compromises had to be struck, not only on demographic aspects, but also on areas where suitable space and parking were available at acceptable rental rates. But decisions were at least based on data most likely to influence business performance.

Most start-ups do not use such formal demographic analysis, although successful chains virtually always do. Often, the entrepreneur simply looks for a vacant space, considers the lease terms and proximity to his or her home, and moves in. This is sufficient for some kinds of businesses: mail order selling, coffin manufacturing, telephone answering, job machining, and so forth. For others, particularly retailing, it is not enough. Consequently, a storefront may see many unsuitable businesses come and go. The key question in determining whether such an analysis should be performed is, "Does the customer care about location?" If the answer is yes, then the entrepreneur should apply a corresponding amount of attention to demographic analysis.

Contact Approaches for Primary Data.   A second general category of market information-gathering methods is one that reaches out to other individuals beyond the company founder.

Informal interviews.   Informally interviewing people who have had experience with similar markets or products can greatly help entrepreneurial judgment, both for improving the product or service and for estimating market size in developing plans. Two contrasting examples may be illustrative. In the first, the advice was taken; in the second, it was not. Both worked out well.

■ *When Bob Howard and a fellow MBA student at the University of Washington got the idea of starting a little business to produce powdered mix for making hot spiced wine, they first experimented with recipes until they were satisfied and then made up a batch in their kitchen. Putting some into a thermos, they visited supermarket managers, offering to let them taste it and soliciting reactions. The managers said the mix had promise if they would put it into packages priced at less than one dollar each. This was a change, for they had been planning on larger packages. But they took the grocers' advice; got a custom packaging company to make, package, and ship the product for them; and soon had a business going. When Bob finished school and graduated, he went into the venture full-time.*

■ *When John Humphrey and his partners were considering starting up a sales and management training company in Boston in 1972, they solicited the advice of fifteen business* *acquaintances. All said not to try it. But they did anyway, starting with only $987. Their company, The Forum, was earning $10 million a year by 1980.*

There are many differences between these examples that might explain the contrasting value of advice: the business lines, types of advisers, timing, information provided, and so on. Advice is not always right just because it comes from someone who should know. Most venture capitalists, including very successful ones, can recall many mistakes they made in judging ventures, despite their experience. But Howard's example illustrated that advisers may help with the design of the product or service in important ways. The cost of such helpful advice, which the entrepreneur is always free to reject, may be no more than the time required to ask for it.

Formal surveys. Conducting more formal surveys with structured interviews and questionnaires is a way to explore on a broad statistical basis what prospective customers care about. They are used extensively by large companies, but rarely by entrepreneurs. The principal differences between this approach and informal interviews are that a formal survey collects opinions or reactions from a larger number of people who are selected on some sort of systematic basis and it attempts to ask the same prepared questions of all of them in the same way. It may be done in person, over the phone, or through the mail. It may present samples for reaction or may simply ask abstract questions. Books on market research describe alternative ways of setting up the sampling, defining and pretesting questions, carrying out surveys, and interpreting the resulting data. The list in Table 2–3 illustrates some of the possibilities.

Although most entrepreneurs reason from prior experience about markets and do not undertake formal primary data-gathering efforts, some do. One was Michael Shane, who had started and later sold successful ventures in imported wigs and imported blue jeans. For his next venture, he was considering entry into the wholesaling of microcomputers in 1980, when the industry was still very young

TABLE 2–3   Market Data Gathering Methods

TO BE TESTED	RESPONDENTS	METHOD
Soup taste preference	Consumers	In-home trial
Chemical process byproduct salability	Paint manufacturers	Lab samples given
Carton filling machine innovation	Dairies	Mail questionnaire
New beer bottle design	Consumers	Test markets
How much to bid	None	Historic bid data
New casserole dish design	Consumers' reactions	Comparison
Washing machine prices	Consumers	Sales tests
Dealer sales push on film	Store clerks	Field interviews
Dealer reaction to inventory scheme	Dealers	Attitude scale
New brand name	Homemakers' reactions	Interviews

and its markets not yet well known. The target market he contemplated was comprised of microcomputer retailers. To learn about it, he commissioned a mail survey using the questionnaire at the end of the chapter. Based upon the results, he started his company, Leading Edge, whose unique selling proposition was that if the retailers would agree to pay him COD, thereby reducing his receivables and collection problems as a wholesaler, he would provide them with fast delivery, which would reduce their problems of maintaining and financing inventory. Leading Edge rose to become a major competitor in the industry. After a decade, it went through bankruptcy, but it continued in business. Shane went on to start another company.

The problems with this method, from the entrepreneur's point of view, are usually that a broad sampling design and analysis can be expensive and the entrepreneur may not know how to make such a survey. Time is typically limited, and he or she will need to allocate it to other activities. Some ways to curb costs include (1) performing at least some of the survey work personally, (2) seeking no more information than is most needed, (3) buying studies or parts of studies done for others, (4) buying opinions from appropriate experts, and (5) joining and obtaining information from appropriate trade associations. The following entrepreneur engaged a lower-cost source of assistance—college students:

■ *In November 1976, Steve Sutherland, a young man from Seattle, became intrigued with a new type of business he saw in Denver, ten-minute oil change shops. They seemed to him a better way for a driver to get a car lubricated. Rather than having to make an appointment in advance at a filling station, then waiting or leaving the car for an hour or more while attendants sporadically worked on it in between pumping gas, a customer at the quick-lubrication store could drive up for immediate concentrated attention, then be on the road again in ten minutes.*

He learned that franchises for such stores were available, and he spent several days investigating the possibility of becoming a franchisee. Ideas for improvements kept coming to mind. Clearly, his profit potential would be higher if he did not have to share revenues with a franchisor. So he decided to attempt an independent start-up.

Returning to Seattle, he began work on a business plan to serve both as a blueprint for start-up and as a prospectus for raising capital. For help, he contacted a professor at the University of Washington Business School, Dick Johnson, who found a team of students interested in it for a class project. They designed a questionnaire and interviewed consumers about the business design. They investigated such items as who would be more likely to use such a service (men or women), income level, neighborhoods, reasons for using the service. Also, what brands of oil were preferred; was there a single brand most would accept? How often would they use the service? How far would they drive to reach it? To what extent would they want to participate in or watch the servicing? What would they prefer to do while waiting?

In a 68-hour 7-day week, a 2-bay store could theoretically service 45,000 cars per year at 10 minutes each. Consumers seemed willing to drive up to $2\frac{1}{2}$ miles for servicing, and quite a few locations in Seattle had over 100,000 cars within such a radius. If each customer bought 3 lubrications per year, the estimated 1 million cars in the Seattle area would produce a theoretical demand of 3 million lubrications per year. At $10 each that would be $30 million in sales.

The most preferred oil brand appeared to be Pennzoil, and responses suggested that over 90 percent of customers would be satisfied if that were the only brand available. This could give the new company strong purchasing advantages with its supplier. Customers would be willing to help fill out the order form, which would save time. Through a carbon, the form would also provide a self-addressed reminder to return, which could be sent out later to bring the customer back for the next lubrication. It appeared that some customers would like to watch, many would be housewives, a waiting room would be appreciated, and cleanliness would be a competitive advantage, counteracting people's impressions of filling stations. To incorporate these features in the design, an architect was selected on the basis of his other architectural works in and around Seattle.

With the business plan completed in the summer of 1976, $100,000 in start-up capital was raised, in part from the professor and other faculty members at the University of Washington, and the company began. By the fall of 1977, the company's first store was doing well, its second had just opened, a third was under construction. Subsequently, Speedylube expanded its stores through franchising and ultimately its investors sold out to a larger company.

Here the survey of prospective customers was clearly only a part of the design process. Other crucial inputs were derived from professional advisers, such as the architect and suppliers, as well as from the creative intelligence of the founders. But the survey played an important part in shaping the concept, in order to get started with a desired service and to develop a lead over competitors who were likely to follow.

In contrast, the following start-up used much more extensive testing and market research with less satisfactory results:

■ *David Goldsmith and Robert Finnie had worked together as business consultants for large consumer product companies. In 1973 they raised $1 million from a former client, Sentry Insurance, to create a yogurt company. "We knew," Goldsmith said, "we were going to get involved in some very expensive product development and testing. We decided that if we could come up with innovative packaging, create some exotic flavors, and give yogurt a whole new fun feeling, we had a reason for being."*

Over the next eighteen months, they applied several approaches. Two focus groups of twelve each were impanelled in three different cities to learn consumer desires. The entrepreneurs watched behind one-way mirrors as a moderator started with a broad topic and then "focused" down to yogurt. Over sixty new product ideas resulted. Consultants were hired to help narrow them down; then food technologists prepared test batches for eight of them, which were tried in four different cities on a total of 200 consumers. A packaging consultant tested shapes and graphics on another 500 consumers. Three flavors were taste-tested at booths at five shopping centers on an additional 500 consumers. The product was then placed in thirty Binghampton, New York, supermarkets on a carefully tracked six-month test. Encouraging results, including a 30 percent expansion of the local yogurt market followed and provided information for a few more calculated changes.

Finally, after eighteen months and $200,000 spent on development, the product was "rolled out" in the northeastern United States. Initially, it did fairly well, obtaining a 7 percent market share in the New York metropolitan area, for instance. But then it faltered and fell to 2 percent. Goldsmith blamed the result on the failure of fruit flavors to catch on against plain yogurt, a proliferation of competing brands, and troubles with the food broker first used by the start-up. His response to criticism about too much market research was that "there are a lot of guys who have tried to make it in this business who aren't around anymore. We're still here, and it's because we did market research."[22]

[22]Currier, "Creating a New Product," p. 95.

Trade show display. A third contact approach for gathering design intelligence — one that would not have helped Speedylube, but would be appropriate with other start-ups, particularly when a product rather than a service is involved — is trade show display. A *trade show* is essentially a gathering at which professionals in a particular line of business — toys, machine tools or housewares, for example — meet to display their products to each other. It is not open to the public but rather is limited to manufacturers, wholesalers, retailers, manufacturers' representatives, and large customers, depending on the particular line of business. It serves as a forum in which participants can make deals for getting the products to market. Hence, the entrepreneur founding a new company within any part of the business process, from raw materials or labor to delivery to the final customer, will probably fit somewhere in one or more trade shows. By attending and possibly displaying the new company's concept at such shows, he or she can obtain reactions and ideas from professionals with experience in the business, and possibly obtain orders as well. Many new companies begin their selling efforts at trade shows (see Chapter 7).

Pilot selling. The fourth contact approach, pilot selling, can serve as the beginning of a permanent sales program or as a way of testing feasibility and refining the product or service concept prior to that permanent effort. This selling may follow naturally from informal interviews with prospective buyers. In Bob Howard's case, some of the grocers interviewed for reactions to the hot spiced wine mix went beyond giving advice about how to shape the product and said they were prepared to place orders and put it on the shelf as soon as it became available. In the next example, the first selling effort resulted in a total product change.

■ *Charity and Michael Cheiky met as undergraduate students at Hiram College in Ohio, she in math and psychology, he in physics and chemistry. Shortly after graduation, they founded a company in partnership with Dale Driesbach, a Hiram professor, to make calculators which taught statistical concepts. That product failed. But Michael, making use of newly mass-produced microprocessor chips, was ready with plans for a small, inexpensive computer. Charity took aim at the hobbyist market, advertising first in computer magazines. Almost from the start, orders rushed in. Ohio Scientific products attracted computer buffs by offering them generous "functionality and computing capacity for the price." Later, the company developed higher-priced computers for small businesses. In its first year, 1975, OSI sold $20,000 worth of computers. Sales in 1980 reached $20 million.[23]*

The similarity of Ohio Scientific to MITS, the Albuquerque company sometimes credited with launching the microcomputer wave earlier the same year is striking. MITS first failed with a kit for pocket calculators sold through mail order. Then it tried advertising a kit for microcomputers and was swamped with orders. Both companies were soon left behind as others surpassed them, but not before achieving spectacular sales growth. In each case, it was a failed market experiment that led them to try a different product that did succeed.

[23]Robert Runde, "Seven Who've Made It Big," *Money*, 10 (No. 1) (January 1981), p. 40.

Most pilot marketing experiments are more systematic, less dramatically hit and miss, and most are conducted by established companies with more experience in using them, often at multimillion-dollar cost. For smaller companies at the low-cost end, according to *Venture*, one consulting firm proposed consumer product testing in two markets, ten stores, over ninety days, for $30,000 or less. Another, Bud Johnson of Stamford Marketing Group in Stamford, Connecticut, pointed out that test marketing could be helpful for raising capital, as illustrated by one of his clients:

■ *Vicky Papson took his advice to heart, the magazine said, when she worked on the start-up of She's a Sport, Inc., to manufacture and distribute women's active wear. A year ago she tried to raise capital but found it was difficult without a test. "We decided to concentrate our efforts on setting up a test in our home market of Connecticut," Papson said. "As soon as I get six months of data from that test, I'll be able to go back to the investors with hard sales numbers. I initially wanted to raise $1.5 million for a national rollout, but just going through this test has shown that it's much more sensible to start with $500,000 and roll out region by region." Her test was expected to cost $25,000, mostly for advertising, public relations, and promotional displays.*

Bud Johnson, her consultant, continued, "You have to simulate the marketing tools you're going to use when you roll the product out. But if you're clever, you can do it for very little money, perhaps as little as $5,000 to $10,000, depending on how much advertising you plan to do." A radio ad, Venture *added, can have an impact similar to a television spot, for much less cost. Coupons can be distributed on-site at the test stores, eliminating costs of newspaper placement while still providing information on their effect on sales by comparison with the data from stores that did not receive coupons. For point-of-purchase displays, Johnson often uses local silk screeners who can produce five or six displays for about $1,000.[24]*

Pricing

Pricing begins with guesses about what production will cost, learning what other companies charge, and deciding what customers will be willing to pay. There are rules of thumb, such as aiming to sell for at least twice the cost of labor plus materials plus overhead to middlemen, or at least five times those amounts to end consumers. The rules depend on whether the company function is manufacturing, wholesaling, retailing, or selling services by the hour. Price can also be balanced against other variables, such as speed of delivery, quantity ordered, warranty and service terms, custom features, and promptness of payment. Usually there are norms to be aware of for whatever the company's function and industry are. Talking with others in the industry is the most likely way to learn them.

There are laws that regulate pricing. It is illegal, for instance, to fix prices among competitors (unless the government does it), to make sales contingent upon a buyer's not purchasing from competitors, to discriminate in such a way as to injure competitors, or to pay brokerage fees to buyers. Prices cannot be advertised

[24]Nancy Maldin, "Making the Most of Test Markets," *Venture* (August 1985), p. 25.

as lower than other prices that did not exist before, or as being at the wholesale level unless they really are.

There is also an abundance of general advice about pricing. Baty, for instance, suggests that entrepreneurs should price based on value to customers rather than cost; should use caution not to overestimate the impact price reductions will have on sales volume; should take care to anticipate future overhead increases and the costs of such things as warranties and amortization of development costs; and should consider a policy of "skimming the initial cream" of the market at a high price, erring on the side of being too high rather than too low.[25]

Research studies indicate that competing on price with a new product is a weak strategy. Generally, it seems better to start with higher quality at a justifiable premium price.[26] Calculations also easily show that a small cut in price means a much bigger cut in margin and hence requires a big increase in volume to keep profits level. Logic suggests that introducing a new brand at a lower price may simply set up an image of low quality. Thus, there are good arguments for pricing high if possible.

Supporting these views is the experience of Arthur P. Alexander, who successfully started a company with a high pricing strategy, which he described as follows:

■ *In our initial product line, we decided to price as high as the highest competitor's price. We justified this position by being able to offer something to the customer which he was not getting at the time from existing suppliers—service. In a word, we were being more responsive to the customer's needs. This pricing technique was so successful over the years that it became yet another facet of our corporate image—high prices. This was probably the single most important factor in shaping the format and image of our company. In effect, we said "We will operate under the philosophy of low volume–high margin." This is not a bad philosophy for a small company starting out.[27]*

But the rule of pricing high where possible does not always fit. Discount store successes have been based on low price with high volume. Pricing high can have the disadvantage of attracting competition and low pricing can help shut it out. An intriguing example of pricing low as a strategy for new product entry is *shareware*. This was microcomputer software for large volume markets such as word processing and database management that was introduced after other brand names in those applications had already become established. To get users, the developers of this new software offered free copies. Anyone who accepted a copy was supposed to try it and decide whether to continue using it. If the decision was to continue, then the user was asked on an "honor system" basis to send a modest "user fee" to the shareware company. There was no way of making users pay this fee, but there

[25]Gordon B. Baty, *Entrepreneurship for the Nineties* (Englewood Cliffs, NJ: Prentice Hall, 1990), p. 159.
[26]Robert D. Buzzell and Bradley Gale, *The PIMS Principles* (New York: Free Press, 1987), p. 70.
[27]William D. Putt, *How to Start Your Own Business* (Cambridge, MA: MIT Press, 1974), p. 194.

were "tie-ins." Paying the user fee entitled the user to free consultation by phone on any problems with the programs. And beyond the initial free program, there were subsequent upgrades that were not free. Thus, with time, the shareware companies managed to build up paying customers and succeeded in breaking in as start-ups by beginning with a low-price strategy.

Another example of pricing low as part of a start-up strategy was that of an entrepreneur interviewed by Collins and Moore, who commented as follows:

■ *I'd go to the purchasing agents and tell them, "Our bid is ridiculously low, and you know that it's ridiculously low. All I want is just a small part of your business to prove something to you. It's not to prove we can give you the parts for nothing. . . . You and I know we can't go on doing that. Not and stay in business—but I want to prove we can give you a better job with less grief to you, never miss delivery, and still save you money. We just want a crack at it. That's all."*

And I'd say, "We just ship one bad piece—one piece that isn't up to spec—and you get that shipment free. You get the entire lot and it doesn't cost you a dime." I was out to dig the ground out from under those slobs [competitors]. They were fat, and I was out to cut the ground right out from under them. And I did it, too.[28]

Both high and low pricing strategies have risks and advantages. It is important that the entrepreneur consider what the alternatives and their implications are. In hindsight, it seems easier to find examples of mistaken underpricing than of overpricing.

Profitability

Interwoven with pricing and feasibility are questions of profitability. To check profitability carefully requires detailed financial forecasting. Early on in designing the venture, however, it should be possible to "guestimate" a breakeven analysis. This requires estimating fixed expenses such as rent and variable costs such as labor, materials, and the price per unit of sales. Then breakeven sales volume can be estimated by simply dividing fixed expenses by the gross margin.

This formula, which is greatly simplified through assuming constancy of fixed expenses and linearity of variable costs, can be refined by allowing changes in the assumptions at several break points in sales. Illustration of such an approach appears in Figure 2–1. Still further refinement comes through plotting the figures of more detailed financial statement forecasts.

Then the questions become (1) how reliable are these forecasts, (2) how much must be invested to make them come true, and (3) is the projected profitability great enough to justify such an investment? Answers to each of these questions should become more fully developed as each additional aspect of the venture, which will be discussed in the chapters to follow, is worked out.

Pro Forma Breakeven Worksheet - First Year
January 1, 1990 to December 31, 1990
Sales = 100% projected

Net sales	Fixed expenses	Variable expenses	Total expenses	Profit or loss	Profit margin
$13,750	$20,928	$3,000	$23,928	($10,178)	−74%
$34,375	$41,833	$7,500	$49,333	($14,958)	−44%
$61,875	$62,714	$13,500	$76,214	($14,339)	−23%
$96,250	$83,572	$21,000	$104,572	($8,322)	−9%
$137,500	$104,406	$30,000	$134,406	$3,094	2%
$192,500	$125,216	$42,000	$167,216	$25,284	13%
$261,250	$157,801	$57,000	$214,801	$46,449	18%
$343,750	$190,350	$75,000	$265,350	$78,400	23%
$440,000	$222,863	$96,000	$318,863	$121,137	28%
$550,000	$255,339	$120,000	$375,339	$174,661	32%
$673,750	$287,777	$147,000	$434,777	$238,973	35%
$811,250	$320,177	$177,000	$497,177	$314,073	39%

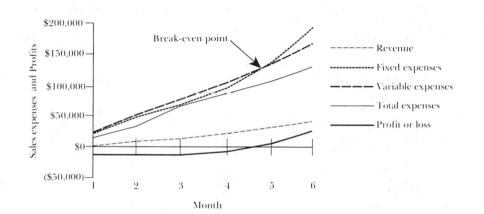

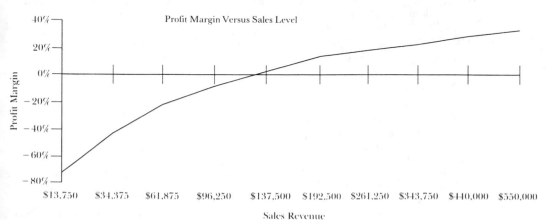

FIGURE 2-1 Mobile Clinik, Inc.

PLANNING QUESTIONS

The following questions are intended to stimulate thought about what should be considered in moving ahead with a venture. Which questions best apply can vary among entrepreneurs and ventures, as can the order in which they should be considered, the priority that should be placed on them, and which should be answered in a written plan.

Feasibility Analysis

- What will be the main customer application(s) of the venture's product or service?
- What will the venture's product or service actually do better (or worse) for the customer than competitors'?
- In what alternative basic terms can those applications be defined?
- What other alternative means can be expected to exist for accomplishing those same or similar functions for customers?
- What are the top priority items from a brainstorm list of possible problems and possible tangential opportunities for the new product or service?
- What government regulations or rulings can be foreseen that might appreciably influence the venture's fortunes?
- Can any "product life cycles," "rates of obsolescence," or "rates of new product introduction" be foreseen in the venture's market(s)?

Design Refinement

- What industry will the venture be in?
- Who are the individuals who will lead the venture's product or service development, what past accomplishments have shown that they can do it, and how will their loyalty to the venture be assured?
- What is the timetable for development through testing and introduction to the market?
- How far has development of the venture's product or service progressed to date?
- What physical models and tests of it have been made, and with what results?
- What contracts, if any, have been made with outside developers to help with technological upgrading, what do those contracts cover, and what are the contractors' qualifications?
- Are precautions arranged to cope with shortfalls in performance and any possible hazards of new features in the venture's product or service?

Market Fitting

- How, in terms of what it will do for customers, can the market for the company's product or service be defined and be segmented?
- How fast will each segment grow?
- At what point might its size make it attractive to larger competitors than the venture could contend with?
- What market share can the venture hope to capture in each segment, and how does that fraction compare to those of its two or three largest prospective competitors?
- What specific numbers might be used to characterize the segment sizes?
- How will the cost, quality, performance, and service of what the venture offers compare to what competitors offer?
- Have comparisons been analyzed on a grid?
- What data have been obtained that will allow objective analysis of these expectations?

- What will a customer have to change, if anything, in his or her present way of operating to take advantage of what the venture will offer?
- Have any asked to buy it?
- What prospective customers have been interviewed? Have they tried what the venture will offer?
- Is there a letter of intent or a purchase order to support salability expectations?
- If so, could it be attached as an appendix in a business plan aimed at garnering support for the venture?

Pricing

- By what procedure will prices be established?
- How hard will it be for competitors to match them and what would be the likely effects of their doing so?

POSSIBLE MILESTONES FOR A PLANNING TIME LINE

The most suitable milestones for a time line for a particular venture must be a function of the individual case. Those that follow are intended to help stimulate thought.

- Patent notebook begun
- Sketches worked out
- Theoretical feasibility computations performed
- Prototype prepared
- Prototype tested
- Market survey designed
- Market survey completed and analyzed
- Redirection designed

FUTURE
BUSINESS SYSTEMS

285 Washington Street
Winchester, Massachusetts 01890

COMPUTER STORE SURVEY
January, 1980

Dear Computer Store Owner/Manager:

Future Business Systems is an independent marketing research firm, which specializes in studying the computer industry. We are currently engaged in a nationwide survey to determine the current and anticipated future conditions of the desktop/personal/small business computer store marketplace.

We would greatly appreciate your help in our endeavor, and wondered if you could spare 5 to 10 minutes to answer our questionnaire. All results of this survey will be kept strictly confidential, and will be combined and used for statistical purposes only. A pre-stamped envelope is enclosed for your response. As a thank you for participating in this survey, all respondents will be mailed a summary of the findings. In addition, all names will be placed in a drawing for a Polaroid SX-70 Alpha I camera which is worth approximately $200.

Thank you in advance for your time.

Sincerely,

William L. Sellers
Manager Market Research

DEMOGRAPHICS

Number of stores in your organization? _____

How long has your store been in business? _____ Years _____ Months

What type of location do you have (large shopping mall, small mall, industrial park, etc)? _____

Which manufacturers' systems you offer are selling the best?

Manufacturers:
1st _____ 2nd _____
3rd _____ 4th _____

Anticipated best sellers 3 years from now-(Please also include any new or anticipated manufacturers' systems you feel may make your top 4 in this time period).

Manufacturers:
1st _____ 2nd _____
3rd _____ 4th _____

What other manufacturers' systems (not mentioned in the above) do you carry? _____ _____ _____ _____ _____ _____

SALES PERSONNEL

What do you look for in potential candidates? _____

How are they trained?

( ) Formal Training Programs which last __ weeks?
( ) Informal on-the-floor training program?

Approximate % of total sales each product area represents:

_____ % _____ % _____ % _____ % _____ % = 100%

Computers   Peripherals   Software   Books   Turnkey Sys.
                                                            (added value)

SALES BY MARKET SECTOR

Approximate % of total sales each market sector represents:

	Small Business	Home Hobbyist	Education	Scientific	Others	Total
CURRENTLY-	____%	____%	____%	____%	___%	= 100%
(Est. 1983)-	____%	____%	____%	____%	___%	= 100%

WHOLESALERS/DISTRIBUTORS

Do you foresee the need for distributorships which could offer major manufacturers' systems to retail stores because of benefits such as: small quantities without long range orders (which manufacturers sometimes demand), Open Terms, immediate availability, etc.?

(   ) Yes   (   ) No
If yes, which benefits would be im-   _____   If no, why not? _____
portant to you?   _____   _____
                                         _____   _____
                                         _____   _____

What percent of your equipment do you buy from the following sources? *(Each vertical column should equal 100%)*

	Systems-NOW	Systems-1983	Peripherals-NOW	Peripherals-1983
Manufacturers	_____%	_____%	_____%	_____%
Distributors	_____%	_____%	_____%	_____%
Patent Co.	_____%	_____%	_____%	_____%
Other:_____ Please Name	_____%	_____%	_____%	_____%
Totals	100%	100%	100%	100%

STARTUP

Please list the major factors you feel mfrs. look for when granting rights to sell their products. *(If none, say so)*:   _____   _____   _____

Your estimate as to the amount of capital needed to comfortably open a computer store.	$50,000 to 75,000 ( )	$76,000 to 100,000 ( )	$101,000 to 150,000 ( )	$151,000 to 175,000 ( )	Greater than $175,000 ( )

COMPETITION

Who do you view as your major competitors *now* and in *1983*? *(Please rank 1, 2, etc.—if not a factor put in 0).*	NOW		1983
	_____	Large computer chains (over 5 stores)	_____
	_____	Small independent stores (1 to 5 stores)	_____
	_____	Direct Sales by Mfr's sales force (IBM, DEC, etc.)	_____
	_____	Manufacturer owned stores (DEC, etc.)	_____
	_____	Sales thru office supplies sales forces. (Ex: Moore Business Forms sells for T.I.)	_____
	_____	Other:_____ Please Name	_____

SOURCES OF SOFTWARE

		Manufacturers	Independent Software Houses	User Developed	Other Sources	Total
Percent of total each source of software represents:	CURRENTLY-	_____ %	_____ %	_____ %	____ %	= 100%
	(Est. 1983)-	_____ %	_____ %	_____ %	____ %	= 100%

Who are your major *independent* software distributors?   COMPANY NAMES _____ _____ _____

How did these software distributors initially contact you? *(Please rank method most used 1, the next most 2, etc.—If not used, put in a 0).*

a) In-person ( ) sales call

b) Telephone sales call followed by ( ) in-person sales call

c) Telephone sales call ( ) only

d) Saw an ad and ( ) called them— (if so)—where you saw ad: Name of publication _____

e) ( ) Other: _____
    Please Name

If you were looking for additional software for your store to carry—how would you proceed—where would you look?   _____
_____

MAINTENANCE/REPAIRS

Where are your maintenance repairs handled? _____ % In House _____ % Send Back to Mfr.

Systems experiencing the most downtime to date—name of mfr: _____ 1st _____ 2nd _____ 3rd

Please circle if the above named manufacturers' equipment represents a serious recurring problem.   X   X   X

ADVERTISING

Advertising expenditures/month $ _____

MAIL ORDER BUSINESS

	NOW	1983	
Mail order as a % of total system sales	_____ %	_____ %	No Mail Order
Mail order as a % of total peripheral sales	_____ %	_____ %	OR Business ( )
Mail order as a % of total software sales	_____ %	_____ %	

BUYING MOTIVES

What major factors do you find attract customers to the retail personal computer marketplace in general?   _____
_____

What major factors do you find attract customers to your store in particular? (i.e. What are your strengths?)   _____
_____

PROBLEMS FACED

What do you find are the major problems facing computer stores in general, and yours in particular? *(Please rank 1, 2, 3, etc., in order of importance—if not a problem, put in 0)*

___ Unhappy with store location
___ Margins too low on the equip.
___ Getting good employees
___ Keeping good employees
___ Keeping abreast of technology
___ Training required with each new product or salesperson

___ Cashflow, lack of strong financial backing
___ Servicing equipment
___ Inventory control— (balance between cost and immediate delivery needs)
___ Other: _____
    Please mention

APPLICATION USAGE

What applications do you find users are looking for the most? *(Please rank only those of impor-tance — 1, 2, 3, etc.)*

(Please rank each column sep-arately — i.e. — rank Small Business applications and then rank Home/Hobbyist applications).

Small Business

_____ Word Processing
_____ General Accounting
_____ Accounts Receivables
_____ Accounts Payable
_____ Mailing Lists
_____ Billing
_____ Inventory
_____ Other:_____
                    Please Name
_____ Other:_____
                    Please Name

Home Hobbyist

_____ Games
_____ Personal Accounting
_____ Child Education
_____ Other:_____
                 Please Name
_____ Other:_____
                 Please Name

FUTURE

1) What year would be your guess as to when computer stores will peak or reach a saturation level? _____

2) What will allow smaller stores (1–5 Units) to survive the competition from large chains? (Will it be Turnkeying (Added Value) Systems — for certain market niches, price cutting, etc.?)
_____
_____

3) If you had capital to invest in the computer store marketplace, what would you invest in? (New stores, more inventory, a software company, a Turnkey system house, etc.)
_____
_____

4) Will you be seeking investment money in the near future, for some expansion aspect of your business?   ( ) Yes   ( ) No
            If "Yes" for what purpose? _____

5) Which manufacturers do you feel *are* (or *will be*) the growing or *new* important participants in this personal/small business computing marketplace?

GROWING: _____ _____ _____ _____ _____

NEW: _____ _____ _____ _____ _____

6) Do you foresee any technological developments which may have a profound effect on personal/small business computers within the next 5 years?
_____
_____

SALES REVENUES

	Under $100,000	$101,000 to $250,000	$251,000 to $500,000	$501,000 to $750,000	$751,000 to $1,000,000	Over $1 Million
Which annual sales revenue classification would your store fall into? (If not in business for a year yet, please estimate a yearly figure based on current performance.)	( )	( )	( )	( )	( )	( )
Three years from now, which classification do you feel you will have (realistically) achieved?	( )	( )	( )	( )	( )	( )

–THANK YOU FOR YOUR ASSISTANCE–

Chapter 3

DEFENSIVE MEASURES IN DESIGN

INTRODUCTION

Two additional design refinement topics are the subject of this chapter. They differ, but overlap in that both concern precautions that should be taken to protect the product and/or service ideas and the business itself. The first aims at protection from liability lawsuits, and the second at protection from imitation of the venture's innovations by competitors. The two intersect in the areas of patents, trademarks, and copyrights. Attention to these areas can help avoid illegal infringement on the protected rights of *other* companies and can also help the new venture protect its own legally owned ideas from being copied by others.

A common feature in both approaches is that they should begin early in the design process. Some specific actions to consider include the following:

- At the beginning of the design process, thought should be given to ways the product or service can be *misused* as well as used. Precautions should be incorporated in the design as well as warning labels and instructions. Liability insurance should be considered as a backup protection.
- If there is any possibility that any aspects of the new venture may be patentable, the inventor should begin keeping records in a bound notebook, dating and signing each page and periodically having it witnessed and signed by someone else.
- Possible infringement on the patents of other companies should also be considered. If conflict seems likely, legal advice should be sought and thought should be given to ways of "designing around" any conflicting claims.
- If it can be foreseen that a particular name and/or trademark may become important in the venture's future, then plans should be made early for discovering any possible

conflicts with those used by other companies and for securing rights to those the venture will use.

- If materials are being written that the entrepreneur may one day want to sell, then a date, the entrepreneur's name, and a circled "c" (©) indicating copyright should be written on the first page.
- If any of these precautions appear important to the venture's future, then the entrepreneur should (1) attempt to become better informed about topics in this chapter and (2) become acquainted with a law firm expert in intellectual property law.

This chapter looks first at protection from legal liability lawsuits through several approaches, including design methods, wording of warranties, buying insurance, and shaping the legal form of the venture. This is followed by a discussion of measures to protect the venture from imitation of its design ideas, including secrecy, legal devices, and strategies for continuing improvement.

CURBING LIABILITY

The possibility that someone may be injured as a result of operating the business or that a customer may be injured as a result of using the product or service it produces and may then sue the company for damages gives rise to the concept of *product liability*. But the concept reaches beyond immediate customers. Product liability problems can arise from product-related injuries that happen to anyone, whether a customer or not, whether the product is for industrial or consumer use, and at any time during the life of the product, even if the company that originally made it has changed hands. Liability can also arise from services that the company might offer (for example, malpractice lawsuits against physicians and hospitals).

The number of liability lawsuits has been increasing rapidly. At the same time, the courts have been shifting away from the notions of "buyer beware" and of placing blame on whoever is most capable of paying, regardless of where the fault lies. Because the maker of the product usually possesses more assets than the person who has been injured, the maker often gets sued and may have to pay for damages.

The legal doctrine on which such suits are most often based reads as follows:

1. One who sells any product in a defective condition unreasonably dangerous to the user or consumer or to his [or her] property is subject to liability for physical harm thereby caused to the ultimate user or consumer or to his [or her] property, if
   a. The seller is engaged in the business of selling such a product, and
   b. It is expected to and does reach the user or consumer without substantial change in the condition in which it is sold.
2. This rule applies although:
   a. The seller has exercised all possible care in the preparation and sale of the product, and
   b. The user or consumer has not bought the product from or entered into any contractual relation with the seller.

The first of these two paragraphs may not sound too threatening to a prospective manufacturer. But in practice, judgments have been applied to it by the courts in disturbing ways, as illustrated by the following examples:

■ *A helmet manufacturer was ordered to pay $5.3 million to a high school player who was paralyzed when a tackle forced his helmet against his neck. It was never proven in court that the youth was even wearing the firm's helmet at the time of the injury.*

■ *A papermaking machine manufacturer was hit with an $800,000 verdict for an injury that occurred on a fourteen-year-old machine that had been altered by the worker's employers [notwithstanding 1.b. in preceding list].*

■ *A gun manufacturer was required to pay $3 million in damages to a person who suffered a minor ankle injury when the gun he was unloading between his knees misfired.*[1]

One ironic advantage of a new venture in this da.igerous area is its own financial vulnerability. There is little point in suing a new company for $3 million, or even $800,000, because the company is not likely to have that much money. An injured party can sue for less, however, and for that reason there are three lines of defense that an entrepreneur should consider before putting a new product on the market. The first is defensive design of both the product and its manufacture. The second is incorporation of the business to shield the owner's personal assets from any potential liability suit against the company. The third is product liability insurance.

Some specialized education about product liabilities, both in general and in the particular industry, may be helpful. A horde of federal agencies may be involved. Depending on the industry, they may include the Consumer Product Safety Commission (CPSC), the Occupational Safety and Health Administration (OSHA), the Federal Drug Administration (FDA), the Environmental Protection Agency (EPA), the Interstate Commerce Commission (ICC), and the Federal Trade Commission (FTC).[2] By contacting them directly, the entrepreneur may learn about their areas of authority and how to minimize the risk of liability. These agencies set specific design requirements for some products. On bicycles, for instance, the CSPC specifies that control cable ends must be capped so people cannot stick their fingers with frayed ends.

Trade associations, such as the Society of Automotive Engineers (SAE) and the American Society for Testing and Materials (ASTM) can also be helpful in identifying areas of danger and advising how best to avoid them. If there are standards and codes in the industry, the associations will be able to point them out, and the entrepreneur should consider following them in the product design.

---

[1]"Litigation Medication," *Industry Week* (June 6, 1977), p. 54.
[2]Raymond D. Watts and Neal L. Thomas, "Product Safety and the Rulemakers," *In Business* (September–October 1983), p. 45.

There may also be certain testing agencies or laboratories, such as Underwriters' Laboratories, Inc., and the National Safety Council, which can help both in checking out the design and in certifying the product. In this educational process, the entrepreneur may also learn about negligence, statutes of limitations, implied versus express warranty, privity, strict liability in tort, and other topics that the law uses in discussing product liability. Taking defensive action, however, does not necessarily require an esoteric vocabulary.

Defensive Design

Defensive design begins with the inclusion of safety specifications for the new product throughout all stages of its life, including (1) production, (2) quality control, (3) testing, (4) distribution, (5) usage, (6) possible modification, and (7) ultimate disposal.

Different concerns apply for different products. A new stereo design may have potential electrical or even noise hazards, but it is unlikely to produce dangerous waste. A new wood-burning stove would not have any electrical concerns, but it might have all sorts of thermal and gaseous dangers, as well as possible problems of injury from cuts on sharp edges. Industry standards apply on products such as electrical appliances and gas heaters. Federal, state, or local standards apply to others, such as autos or smokestack emissions. These standards need to be identified for the particular product and worked into the design. Both private standards, such as those of the American National Standards Institute (ANSI), and governmental ones, such as those in the *Code of Federal Regulations*, should be considered. A guide to regulated products has been developed by Schaden and Heldman.[3] A catalog of regulations is offered by Hilyard et al.[4] It is important to note, however, that meeting these standards may not by itself be sufficient, as illustrated by the following:

■ *Riegel Textile Corporation had to pay $800,000 in damages plus another $1 million in punitive damages because a pair of pajamas it manufactured caught fire, seriously burning a young girl when she leaned across an electric stove to turn off a kitchen buzzer. The company had not treated the light, inexpensive, and highly flammable fabric with flame retardant. Riegel was able to prove that it had complied with federal standards; however, this testimony was not persuasive after it was shown that Riegel knew that the federal standards were inadequate.*

Whether or not established standards exist, it is necessary to apply what would generally be regarded as safe and prudent design principles. In the next case, it was judged that the company had not done so, even though the company thought it had:

[3]Richard F. Schaden and Victoria C. Heldman, *Product Design Liability* (New York: Practicing Law Institute, 1982).

[4]J. Hilyard, V. Roberts, and J. McElhaney, *Product Standards Index* (Durham, NC: Product Safety News, 1977).

■ *A three-year-old child knocked over a vaporizer. The lid, which had been designed to be loose-fitting so it could not stick and allow a dangerous buildup of steam pressure came off. Steam escaped and gave the child third degree burns. In court the plaintiff argued that the cap could have been perforated with small holes to vent excessive pressure and then threaded so it would not fall off when tipped, thus preventing the burn danger.*[5]

This example also illustrates the need to foresee possible error on the part of the user. Even misuse and abuse need to be anticipated in the design, lest some user become injured. In the next example, misuse, not of the product, but of the package, resulted in a lawsuit and judgment against the manufacturer.

■ *A door manufacturer packed a stack of doors for boat shipment by piling them 42 inches high and wrapping them with a sheet of cardboard and binding them together with steel straps. Because the doors had a large opening at one end for later insertion of glass, there was a void under the cardboard at that point. At the docks, a longshoreman walked across the stack carrying a 100-pound sack of flour, fell through the cardboard, and hurt himself. In the lawsuit that followed, the court found that his injuries were the responsibility of the door manufacturer, who consequently had to pay damages.*[6]

Care and thoughtfulness throughout the design and testing process can help minimize, though not completely eliminate, the possibility of lawsuits like this. Some important commonsense questions to consider, suggested in an article by Watts and Thomas,[7] include (1) whether the design process was adequate, (2) whether current state-of-the-art standards were observed, (3) whether the human element and alternative ways of protecting for it were considered, (4) whether suitable quality control was applied, (5) whether instructions and warning labels were adequate, (6) what express and implied warranties were given, and (7) whether marketing was misleading.

Beyond common sense, however, some formal techniques of engineering can help. These are discussed in the following sections.

Formal Engineering Analysis.   Engineering design, as was seen in the preceding chapter, includes many steps, each of which can be done well or badly. Configuring the device or process, selecting materials and components, choosing and getting help from suppliers, setting safety factors, anticipating possible problems, and devising ways to maximize performance, economy, and safety are all important elements of the process.

Mathematical methods, computer simulations, and empirical handbook formulae and data can be used to cross-check safety features such as strength and behavior of materials under load, melting and flash temperatures, electrical load limits, potentially destructive vibration frequencies, length of life under cyclical

[5]*McCormick v. Hankscraft*, 154 N.W. 2nd 488, Minn., 1967.
[6]*Simpson Timber Co. v. Parks*, 369 F. 2d 324 (1967).
[7]Raymond D. Watts and Neal L. Thomas, "How Liable Is Your Product?," *In Business* (November–December 1982), p. 53.

load and flexing, and so forth. A trained professional engineer experienced with devices operating under similar conditions can be engaged to apply such techniques. In some situations, such as calculating the amount of fuel to put into a rocket, or the trajectory the rocket will take, such formal methods are absolutely essential and can accomplish things that common sense and intuition never could. But they are only as good as the assumptions on which they are based. Grumman Corporation buses began to show structure damage in 1980, not because of a lack of formal engineering analysis, but because the analysis was predicated upon road conditions less severe than those that actually existed in major cities.

Testing. Jury rigs, breadboard models, and prototypes, as well as preproduction and production models, can all be used for extended tests under varieties of circumstances simulating actual operating conditions. These trials can be performed by the entrepreneur, by prospective customers (with the clear understanding that it is an experimental program only), and/or by independent testing laboratories. The disadvantage of testing as compared to more abstract methods of analysis is that it usually costs much more and takes longer. However, it is also a surer method of determining what will happen.

Some results, such as the sound from a new engine muffler, cannot be predicted by any other method than by trial. It is impossible to predict which new products will fail. Even with testing, in addition to extensive formal analysis during design, Lockheed's Electra aircraft continued to crash and kill people. Finally, a particular mode of destructive vibration resulting from dynamic interaction between the engine and the wing was identified and corrected. Although not an absolute guarantee of safety, testing, preferably under the widest possible variety of conditions, can vastly improve odds of success. Four types of tests that should be considered are (1) actual usage tests, (2) accelerated aging tests, (3) extreme conditions tests, and (4) standardized tests that have been established in some industries.

Anticipating Problems. Looking for all the ways an item can possibly fail and each way it could be a hazard is a somewhat different way of approaching the design. A variety of methods for doing so have been developed.

Failure mode analysis. Failure mode analysis, used particularly in spacecraft and electronic circuit design, begins with searching for possible ways things can go wrong then goes on to consider the probability of each mode of failure, the magnitude of negative effect or injury resulting from each failure mode, and calculation of a hazard index by combining these estimates into an overall picture of all the ways things can go wrong. The analysis can, if conditions call for it, be applied to each component, each type of application, and each stage of the product's development and life through disposal.

Fault tree analysis. If the failure mode analysis is broken down further into all the possible causes of each mode of failure, the causes of the causes, and so forth, a kind of decision tree, called a *fault tree*, can be diagramed. Basically, it is a systematic way of trying to explore all the possible implications of a failure of any given part of the system. Such analysis was used frequently in the development of the space program, where each missile launch was so enormously expensive that great investment in prior analysis to protect against failure was justified, and also in nuclear reactor design, where failure of a component could trigger a cascade of calamities leading to serious disaster. The manufacturing counterpart of this analysis is called a *zero defect* program—the aim is not to have just a reasonably small percentage of unacceptable parts, but to have none at all. In the auto industry, hydraulic valve lifters must be treated in this manner, because there are two or more of them for every cylinder of a car engine and to replace any of them requires major disassembly of the engine. The percentage of faulty lifters would be multiplied by the number of valves per engine to project the odds of failure due to lifter malfunction, which in turn produces huge rework costs.

Worst case analysis.   A combination of the most unfavorable extremes that can possibly occur in manufacturing tolerances or operating conditions constitutes the assumptions underlying a worst case analysis. What if the loads are worse than anticipated? What if the materials are of lower quality than expected? What if maintenance is not performed on schedule? What if production employees are careless? And what if all those effects combine at once? This sort of exploration can reveal a worst case for consideration. Coping with possible worst cases involves the use of safety factors to make parts several times as strong as they need to be, system redundancy, providing a backup system in case of failure (such as a spare tire), "fail safe" features (lack of pressure on the accelerator causes a car throttle to return to idle), and safety arrangements for emergencies (auto seat belts and air bags).

Hazard analysis.   Beyond the other types of failure analysis, systematic thought should be given to all the possible hazards the new product or service may create, regardless of whether the hazard arises from failure. Human factors experts may be able to help in assessing this task.

Design reviews.   A common practice in careful engineering is review by committee (not to be confused with design by committee!). Its purpose is to tear the design apart and find all its weaknesses so that it can be rebuilt stronger than before. This can be done in one or more meetings, together with presentations and homework assignments, by a committee composed of complementary specialists, each reviewing different facets of the design and considering all stages in the product's life. A start-up or small company that lacks a breadth of specialists may be able to draw from among business acquaintances, knowledgeable friends, and possibly hired experts.

Written Communication

Preparing effective written materials is also an important part of the design task. Notebooks on important design decisions should be kept (not the type that embarrassed Ford on its Pinto gas tank design, in which notes of company personnel indicated that they were aware a fire hazard in the event of a rear-end collision existed in the design of the car). This is not only for possible use in defense against liability suits, but also for possible use in obtaining patents to protect the design (as will be discussed later in this chapter). Drawings and materials lists should be unambiguous so that suppliers or shop workers will not err in production. Quality control procedures should be developed, formalized, and communicated so that breakdowns do not occur as operations move beyond the pilot or custom stage.

Instructions and Warnings. Instructions for installation, use, and maintenance must be developed and tested to be sure they can be understood and followed. The following instruction, for example, was considered inadequate because it did not more fully describe what could happen if someone plugged a 110 volt vacuum into a 220 volt outlet.

■ *Be sure to plug vacuum into the proper electrical outlet as indicated on the name plate. If the vacuum is plugged into an improper current serious damage to both machine and operator may occur.*

A worker who plugged the device into 220 volts and was injured by the resulting explosion won in court on grounds that "serious damage" did not adequately explain the danger.[8] "As a design engineer," Trombetta observed, "the small businessman is left in the vast area of discretion between 'absolutely safe' and the point at which enough has been done to make the product 'safe within reason'."[9]

Product Warranties. In addition to instructions, three types of important communications with customers that must be considered from a product liability standpoint are advertisement claims, warranty statements, and warning labels. The first two are connected. Advertising claims for the product are automatically part of an *express warranty*, which is defined by the Uniform Commercial Code to include "any affirmation of fact or promise made by the seller to the buyer that relates to the goods and influenced the sales." If a buyer can show that the seller, even unintentionally, caused him or her to believe that an express warranty was made, then it can be ruled that there was such a warranty. This would not apply to common overstatements such as "the best money can buy," which are regarded as statements of opinion, not fact. Any factual description, however, may be regarded as an express warranty. Examples include "100% wool," "won't shrink," or "meets SAE standards."

Breach of warranty is a legal basis on which the buyer can claim financial loss or damages from injury. By spelling out the warranty in a written or otherwise reproducible form, a producer is providing the buyer with convenient evidence that can be used as proof in a possible legal battle. Therefore, great care should be used in making claims for the product in catalogs, advertisements, brochures, samples, written descriptions, guarantees, and the like. The main safeguard is to avoid overstatement of virtues.

[8]*Post v. American Cleaning Equipment Corp.*, 437 S.W. 2d 516 (1968).

[9]William L. Trombetta, "Products Liability from the Small Manufacturing Industrial Distributor's Perspective," *Journal of Small Business Management*, 15 (No. 4) (October 1977), 32.

Even without such definite evidence, the buyer may be able to make a case on the basis of *implied warranty*. Simply offering the product for sale can be regarded as an implied warranty that it is safe and meets reasonable standards of quality. Someone who buys a typewriter, for example, is entitled to expect that it will hold margins and that the manufacturer warrants that it will. An exception to this general rule may be made if the seller does not regularly sell goods of that particular type or does not represent himself or herself as being expert about them. This might create more leeway for a new company than for one better established in the line of business.

Any recommendation by a salesperson that the product can be used for a certain purpose or in a particular manner tends to extend further the implied warranty. For instance, a recommendation that the seller's ball bearings be used on a particular machine may make the seller liable not only for the bearings if they fail, but for other repair costs on the machine as well. Therefore, the seller should be careful about such statements. Having the buyer agree to take the goods "as is" can further strengthen the seller's position. Having the buyer examine the product for possible flaws before buying protects the seller from claims arising from problems that should have been apparent to the buyer from such examination. Written disclaimers of warranty can also help in restricting sellers' responsibilities for dollar losses claimed by buyers if they are formulated in proper legal language, but they cannot protect the seller against legal claims of injury.

The Magnuson-Moss Warranty Act of 1975, which is only one of several warranty regulations,[10] sets forth some rules for warranty statements on products costing over $10. A company need not furnish a written warranty, but if it does, the warranty must (1) indicate whether the warranty is full (meaning no charges will be made for labor or repairs) or limited, (2) tell how to make a claim and the individual to contact, and (3) provide for refund if the product is repeatedly faulty.

If a product contains any possible but nonobvious dangers, there should be warning labels that clearly bring these potential problems to the attention of the user. These labels and instructions need to be designed with care so that (1) people will easily understand them, (2) they make clear what the nature of the danger is, (3) they are presented in such a way that they are certain to be noticed, and (4) they will last long enough to warn anyone as long as the danger exists. The authors of one helpful reference on product liability offer the following illustration:

■ *An apartment owner brought suit against the manufacturer and retailer of hair rollers that had been used by one of his tenants. The instruction urged the purchaser to use plenty of water when heating the rollers and not to let it boil away. The warning stated that "rollers may be inflammable only if left over the flame in a pan without water. Otherwise, they are perfectly safe." The tenant fell asleep after putting the rollers on the stove in a pan of water to heat. The water boiled away, a fire ensued, and extensive*

---

[10]Robert M. Springer, Jr., "Small Business Looks at the New Warranty Rules," *Journal of Small Business Management*, 15 (No. 4) (October 1977), p. 20.

damage was done to the building. The court held that the manufacturer should have anticipated that a user might fall asleep, and thus the caution on the roller box was inadequate.[11]

Development of warning labels must be given careful thought and probably expert treatment. Moreover, the company can still be liable if the warning does not reach the user:

■ *The user manual of a dump truck hydraulic lift did warn that the lift should be blocked before working under the truck. A mechanic, working on a truck axle, failed to block the lift and was injured by its collapsing. The court held the lift company liable for injury to the mechanic, noting that although there was warning in the manual, the mechanic had not been shown to have read it.*[12]

Subsequent Follow-Through. Beyond the first steps of getting a product ready, there are many other subsequent ones that should be taken to make sure something does not go wrong. These include (1) finishing the production specifications to assure that procedures are unambiguous and will not introduce problems, (2) developing inspection, functional testing, and quality control procedures, (3) developing maintenance procedures and possibly manuals, (4) pilot testing mass production methods, and (5) setting up procedures for gathering data from salespeople so that later problems and possible ideas for improvements will be picked up promptly when sales begin.

It should be borne in mind that if anyone is injured by something the company produces or does, there will probably be a lawsuit, and all records will be subject to examination. How good the records are and what they show about how the product or process was developed and refined will likely be a major influence on the outcome.

Liability Insurance

A start-up's scarce resources can work to both its advantage and its disadvantage when it comes to liability lawsuits. On the plus side, scarce resources present a less attractive target for lawsuits. If there are several possible defendants in a prospective lawsuit, claimants will generally focus on the one with the most assets. If none has sufficient assets, the suit may not be pursued at all, simply because the prospective payoff is not worth the time and expense of suing.

The disadvantage is that the start-up may not be able to afford the legal costs of defending itself, as well as the cost in terms of the founder's time. Tucker's auto company died, arguably, not because of product or market failure but because Preston Tucker's time and money were all consumed by having to contend with

---

[11]James F. Thorpe and William H. Middendorf, *What Every Engineer Should Know about Product Liability* (New York: Marcel Dekker, 1979), p. 60.

[12]Marisa L. Manley, "Controlling Product Liability," *Inc.* (February 1987), p. 103.

government litigation.[13] The issue was not product liability, but it produced the same effect that liability litigation might have.

Taking out insurance is another line of defense for the business. There are many forms of insurance to consider: fire, theft, business interruption, and so forth. Liability insurance is one category and includes such things as professional liability, personal injury, general liability, and product liability. Recalling the failure of a flight-planning software start-up that could not raise capital because no insurance company would cover it on product liability, an insurance executive commented that "In all that early planning about manpower, markets, sites and money you ought to be thinking about insurance coverage."[14]

Product liability insurance can be purchased through a general insurance broker as an "excess and specialty" line. There is typically no standard form or rate book for this insurance. Each policy must be tailored to the company taking it out based on the prospective risk of the particular product or service. The policy will provide that if the company is sued for injury caused by its product, the insurance company will cover the claim up to the amount specified in the policy. Taking out liability insurance can have the undesirable effect of increasing the size of the financial claim target that the new company represents, because now the value of the policy may be added to the company's own assets. But it also brings in the insurance company to help in fighting the claim. The entrepreneur must decide whether to pay the premium for this added protection or chance a lawsuit against the new company. Either way, the entrepreneur should make sure that his or her own personal assets are not mingled with those of the company, thereby making them vulnerable to lawsuit claims as well.

Avoiding Idea Infringement

Misappropriation of ideas can also get a new company into trouble. The new enterprise cannot use trade secrets or ideas that are protected by copyright, patent, or trademark unless it has permission from the owner of those ideas to do so. To be able to steer clear of such a pitfall, the entrepreneur needs to know about these forms of legal protection, how they work, how to find out whether a given idea enjoys such protection, and if it is not so protected, how the entrepreneur can preserve his or her right to use it.

Ideas are a form of property; therefore, it can be important to know who owns them and where the borders are. Obtaining rights to intellectual property through filing for patents, trademarks, and copyrights will be discussed shortly. But even if the venture does not pursue such rights of its own, it should be cautious about the possibility of infringing on such rights of others. A jury found that the Ford Motor Company did not know it was infringing on a patent owned by Robert W. Kearns when it introduced an intermittent windshield wiper it had developed

[13]Charles T. Pearson, *The Indomitable Tin Goose* (New York: Pocket Books, 1960), p. 88.
[14]Jim Jubrak, "Your Premium or Your Company," *Venture* (February 1986), p. 44.

independently. But it still owed him $5.2 million for continuing to make it after he filed a lawsuit. In cases of willful infringement, the penalties can be even worse, up to triple the damages of inadvertent infringement.

A new venture should consider hiring a patent attorney to perform a search of others' patents, because the search can both help the company steer clear of infringement and help prove that if any infringement does occur it was not willful. Unfortunately, it is not possible to search patents that may be pending. They are secret until the patents are issued. So the venture can still be "blind-sided," as was a company called Monoclonal Antibodies.

■ *"You can be merrily going along and kablooey, there's a patent issued," says Thomas Glaze, chief executive officer and chairman. "We had no intention of infringing a patent. We had products on the market in 1982, and the Hybritech patent was issued in 1983. Hybritech had said that they'd filed for something, but we didn't know what the patent claims were or if the patent would be issued."[15]*

Moreover, it is not just the company that makes the infringing product that may be liable. Patent law holds that anyone involved in making, selling, or using a patented article may be subject to an infringement suit. This is advantageous from the viewpoint of the company holding the patent because it is thereby permitted to go after the violator with the "deepest pockets." How a venture can protect *its* ideas from misappropriation will be further developed shortly.

Organizational Insulation

To some degree, it may be possible for an entrepreneur to become personally insulated from liabilities the venture incurs. Incorporation, for instance, is a way to make a business into an entity separate from the owner and can facilitate such matters as dividing ownership into shares, allowing people to pass their shares on to others, allowing the business to continue after the initial owners leave, and allowing separate taxation of the business with different rates than may apply to any of the owners.

Most important from the standpoint of liability, however, is that by separating the business from the owner through incorporation, the liabilities of the business can be separated from those of the owner. Under a proprietorship, where the owner simply operates the business as an individual, or a simple partnership, where two or more people operate it as individuals, the debts and liabilities of the business are debts and liabilities of the individuals as well. A corporation can be liable, but if it does not have enough money to pay, then creditors cannot go after the assets of its owners, as they can with proprietorships and ordinary partnerships.

To maintain this insulation, it is important to handle corporate formalities in a systematic and legal way. The owners must set up separate bank accounts for corporate versus personal use and take care not to mingle funds between the two.

---

[15]Doug Garr, "It Pays to Patent," *Venture* (October 1988), p. 39.

Meetings must be held according to the state requirements for corporations, with appropriate stockholders and officers present. Minutes of the meetings must be recorded, signed, and witnessed, and reports and fees must be filed in accordance with the laws of the state in which the firm is incorporated. Capitalization must also be maintained according to whatever requirements apply, and the business must be represented as a corporation, not a proprietorship or partnership, by including the word *Corporation* or *Inc.* in its name. Otherwise, the separation of corporate liabilities may be disallowed (technically referred to as *piercing the corporate veil*) by a court, and the advantages of incorporation may be lost.

Some limitations and disadvantages of incorporation should also be considered. Often, it does not provide complete protection from liabilities for owners. The Internal Revenue Service, for instance, can pierce the corporation to recover certain types of tax obligations. Some entrepreneurs have even been found personally liable for patent infringement, notwithstanding incorporation, as in the following case:

■ *In 1982 a district court ruled that Joe C. Eller, principal owner of Crystal Chemicals Co., Houston, was liable for Crystal's infringement on a Rohm & Haas Co. patent. The patent covered the use of propanil to kill grass in rice fields. The court ruled that Eller was personally liable for more than $5 million in damages.*

The decision was later reversed on grounds that the Rohm & Haas patent was fraudulently obtained. But for several years Eller lived under a cloud. "It just upset everything I was trying to do," he said. "Go try and borrow from your friendly banker with a $5 million judgment hanging over you. He'll say you're a good ole boy, and he'll offer to buy you lunch, but he won't lend you money."[16]

Banks and other creditors frequently require that owners personally guarantee loans made to the corporation, so that they have recourse to owners' assets in the event of default. Thus, the corporation's shielding effect again can be nullified. By forming the corporation, moreover, the owners invite investigation by many federal, state, and local agencies to make sure that proper business licenses have been obtained and that zoning and other ordinances are being complied with. There will be questions to answer from inspectors and auditors, forms to fill out, periodic filings to perform and fees to pay, as well as directors and officers to elect, formal meetings to be held and duly recorded, and taxes to be paid. Public disclosure of the incorporation as required by law will alert credit agencies and mailing list firms to take note of the new business, possibly to its disadvantage. Suppliers, noting that the business is being legally separated from the other assets of its owners, may put the firm on COD billing, whereas otherwise they might have extended credit to it through its owners.

Legal fees may or may not be incurred, both in setting up the corporation and later in dissolving or modifying it. The legal process is fairly simple. Some station-

[16]Garr, "It Pays to Patent," p. 39.

ery stores carry "boilerplate" forms—articles of incorporation and bylaws that attorneys use for the legal paperwork. Anyone can fill these out, mail them in to the state with the appropriate application fees, and set the corporation up without using an attorney. But there are technical decisions to be made regarding tax status and definition of the line of business. If there are a number of stockholders, then the terms for managing the business, buying each other out, and so forth may require informed decision making and phrasing. That is where the assistance of a lawyer experienced in such tasks can be worth paying for, and a legal fee upwards of several hundred dollars can be justified. Later, there may have to be amendments to the incorporation papers, and again an attorney may be needed. The more future needs that are anticipated in the first place, the fewer such modifications should be needed and the easier it should be to make them.

An alternative to incorporation as a means of insulating personal from business liabilities can be the formation of a *limited partnership*. *Limited* means that some specific statement in the partnership agreement puts a limit on the amount of financial liability any limited partner will assume for liabilities of the business. An advantage of this form of organization is that the state formalities that apply to corporations do not apply to it, and the paperwork involved is therefore more private and simpler.

However, it is a less standard form than a corporation and therefore more susceptible to the kinds of flaws that often crop up in custom designs. Moreover, in any limited partnership, there must be at least one "general partner" who *does* assume full liability for any of the company's debts. This general partner can be either an individual, in which case that individual is personally liable, or a corporation, which thereby shields all the partners, but puts the company back in the corporate form again. Thus, the corporate form is still the most common way of separating company from individual liabilities.

Other important aspects of incorporation as a device for joining partners in a venture will be considered further in Chapter 4.

FORESTALLING IMITATION

While the many facets of design described in the last chapter and this one are being worked on, precautions should also be taken to make sure designs do not infringe illegally on those of other companies and to lay the groundwork for protecting the venture's own ideas from imitation by competitors.

Three broad categories of actions to protect ideas are (1) to keep key aspects of the product or process secret, (2) to file for legal protection on certain features (which can then no longer be secret), and (3) to take strategic action aimed at staying out in front competitively. The first two apply more to some ventures than others. Sometimes they are extremely effective in combating competitors, other times they are worthless. The third can apply to all ventures but is not usually easy to do. Combining approaches may also be possible.

Secrecy

The most straightforward way to protect business ideas is to keep them secret. Secrecy did not help England win the jet engine race with Germany, but it did help in the development of radar. Both countries became aware of these technical possibilities at nearly the same time. The differences in outcomes were produced by how the technologies were managed in development and application.

A company may or may not be able to keep details of a new product or service secret during development and use. Coca-Cola's product is well known but the recipe remains a secret. Software companies develop products under wraps, but then they must "beta test" them at customer sites, so information about their features inevitably escapes before market introduction. However, the code in them usually remains secret. Thus, the role of secrecy necessarily varies among enterprises.

During development of a new product or service, notes and records should be kept, both to document its progress and to establish the company's ownership of the ideas. These records can be treated as confidential information and kept mostly out of sight. Other people whose assistance may be needed can also be asked to keep the information they have confidential. The selection of those people to whom the ideas are shown should be handled judiciously. If necessary, employees can be asked to sign an agreement promising not to reveal secrets, as follows:

> I will regard and preserve as confidential all trade secrets pertaining to the Company's business that have been or may be obtained by me by reason of employment. I will not, without written authority from the Company to do so, use for my own benefit or purposes, nor disclose to others, either during my employment or thereafter, except as required in the line of my employment with the Company, any trade secret or confidential information connected with the business or developments of the Company; and I will not take or retain or copy any of the Company's specifications, drawings, blueprints, reproductions, or other documents or things.

Such an agreement need not be written and signed, however. The law requires that employees preserve trade secrets of their employers anyway, provided it is made clear that they are secrets and that the company takes precautions to keep them that way. The exact definition of what constitutes a trade secret is spelled out in the Restatement of Torts, which reads in part as follows:

> A trade secret may consist of any formula, pattern, device or compilation of information which (issued in) one's business, and which gives him an opportunity to obtain an advantage over competitors who do not know or use it. It may be a formula for a chemical compound, a process of manufacturing, treating or preserving materials, a pattern for a machine or other device, or list of customers. . . . Generally it relates to the production of goods, as, for example, a machine or formula for the production of an article. It may, however, relate to the sale of goods or to other operations in the business such as a code for determining discounts, rebates or other concessions in a

price list or catalogue, or a list of specialized customers, or a method of bookkeeping or other office management.[17]

Merely having and maintaining something that the company regards as a trade secret does not necessarily prevent anyone else from using the same information. Another company is perfectly free to use the same information if it develops it independently. What another company cannot do is steal the secret or obtain it by hiring away an employee who then reveals it. If the information happens to be available in the public domain, then it cannot be construed as secret.

Other precautions the new enterprise can take to preserve trade secrets include (1) selecting partners and employees with prior reputations of high integrity; (2) briefing them regarding policies intended to preserve trade secrets; (3) putting those policies into writing; (4) using signed statements such as the one previously provided; (5) requiring the signing of agreements in which employees or partners agree not to compete with the company within a certain area and for a certain length of time after they leave it; (6) marking documents as confidential, storing them in secure locations, and attaching to them log sheets to be signed by each reader; (7) issuing periodic reminders in the company about the importance of preserving secrets; (8) debriefing anyone who leaves the company about secrecy responsibilities (and having the person sign a debriefing statement); (9) contacting the employee's subsequent employer about secrecy policies; (10) seeking a court injunction promptly if the company thinks a stolen secret is being used; and (11) suing for damages if the injunction does not give protection.

Legal action is generally a last resort. The other precautions serve to make it less necessary, or if it is necessary, they serve to strengthen the company's case. The company has to be able to show that there really was a secret, that precautions were taken to protect it, that the secret was not easy to discover through other means, such as "reverse engineering" (analyzing the end product to ascertain the underlying engineering specifications by which it is made), and that its loss really does damage the company. Note the following example:

■ *Two engineers had signed agreements with their employer, Sperry-Rand, not to divulge confidential information. They left the company and joined another, Electronic Concepts, Inc., taking with them a drawing with important manufacturing tolerances for a radar antenna they had designed and other documents important to the antenna. Then Electronic Concepts underbid Sperry-Rand for a government contract to make the antenna, and Sperry-Rand sued for theft of trade secrets. Both compensatory and punitive damages totaling $400,000 were awarded.*

Like other areas of law, trade secrets are bordered with gray areas, where decisions about what they are and what can be done about them under what conditions are subject to technical legal interpretation. An area of balance exists, for instance, between the right of an employer to have a secret protected and the

[174] *Restatement of Torts,* Sec. 757b.

right of an employee who knows the secret to be able to seek employment and practice his or her profession elsewhere. It is generally advisable to hire a lawyer to deal with the gray areas.

Legal Shields from Imitation

The government of the United States as well as those of many foreign nations offer other forms of legal protection besides the right to maintain secrets. These include patent, trademark, and copyright protection mechanisms.

Patents.   Patenting protects an idea very differently than secrecy does. Its purpose is to advance the progress of ideas by giving people incentives to come up with new ones and at the same time requiring that the ideas become public knowledge. In return for disclosing the idea, the inventor is given a monopoly on its use for a specified period of time—how long depends on the type of patent, which in turn depends on the nature of the idea being protected. A patent must be applied for within twelve months of offering the product for sale in the United States. In foreign countries, application must be made before offering the product for sale.

Utility patents.   The most common type of patent is a *utility patent*, which protects function rather than form. It gives the inventor exclusive rights for seventeen years and may cover a product, process, plant, mechanism, chemical composition, and the like. A full description of what is and is not covered is given in a set of rules and guidelines available from the U.S. Patent Office. This kind of patent does not apply to aesthetics, only to operation.

Design patents—protecting aesthetics.   A *design patent*, quite different from a utility patent, applies to the aesthetic shape or configuration of a utilitarian object. It could, for instance, apply to the street lamp designs that could not be utility patented. Examples of some items covered by design patents appear in Exhibit 3-1, reprinted from the *Patent Gazette*. It is important to note that the design patent covers only external appearance, not construction or operation. The patent of the Alarm Signal Transmitter in the upper left corner of the page, for instance, says nothing about the insides of the device or what it does.

The process of obtaining a patent should begin with a regularly updated, signed, and witnessed notebook describing the development of the idea. This process must document that the concept will work, referred to as "reduction to practice." An operational jury rig, breadboard, or prototype is typically used to accomplish this.

Next comes hiring a local lawyer, who in turn engages a Washington, DC, lawyer to research the patent records and see if the idea is really new. If it seems to be, the process continues with the drafting of an application (for which there are rules but no printed forms) complete with drawings, verbal description of the idea, and, most important, a list of "claims" about particular features that the inventor wishes to have protected. As an illustration, a copy of a patent application by Mark Twain (Samuel Clemens) appears in Exhibit 3-2. Normally, an exchange of corre-

EXHIBIT 3-1   Design Patent Descriptions

253,281
ALARM SIGNAL TRANSMITTER
Kiil Kim, 3450 Wilshire Blvd., Los Angeles, Calif. 90010
Filed Nov. 14, 1977, Ser. No. 851,550
Term of patent 14 years
Int. Cl. D10—*05;* D13—*03*
U.S. Cl. D10—121

253,284
VEHICLE PANEL GUARD
Richard E. Lauer, 6128 Ridgeway, Edina, Minn. 55436
Filed Nov. 30, 1977, Ser. No. 856,199
Term of patent 14 years
Int. Cl. D12—*16*
U.S. Cl. D12—190

253,282
BUTTERFLY CHRISTMAS ORNAMENT
Janet V. Lynch, Cactus Alley, Sp. #20, 2610 Salem, Lubbock,
Tex. 79410
Filed May 26, 1977, Ser. No. 800,964
Term of patent 14 years
Int. Cl. D11—*05*
U.S. Cl. D11—127

253,285
HOUSING FOR DASHTOP MOUNTED VEHICULAR
INSTRUMENTATION
Greg A. Wagner, P.O. Box 2270, Grass Valley, Calif. 95945
Filed Mar. 8, 1978, Ser. No. 884,723
Term of patent 14 years
Int. Cl. D12—*16*
U.S. Cl. D12—192

253,283
EARTHWORM FIGURINE
Jerome P. Mills, Scottsdale, Ariz., assignor to Susan Doolan,
Scottsdale, Ariz.
Filed Oct. 21, 1976, Ser. No. 734,652
Term of patent 14 years
Int. Cl. D11—*02*
U.S. Cl. D11—158

253,286
VEHICLE WHEEL
Kurt W. Lohmeyer, Fullerton, Calif., assignor to Tru-Spoke,
Inc., Anaheim, Calif.
Filed Oct. 11, 1977, Ser. No. 840,543
Term of patent 14 years
Int. Cl. D12—*16*
U.S. Cl. D12--205

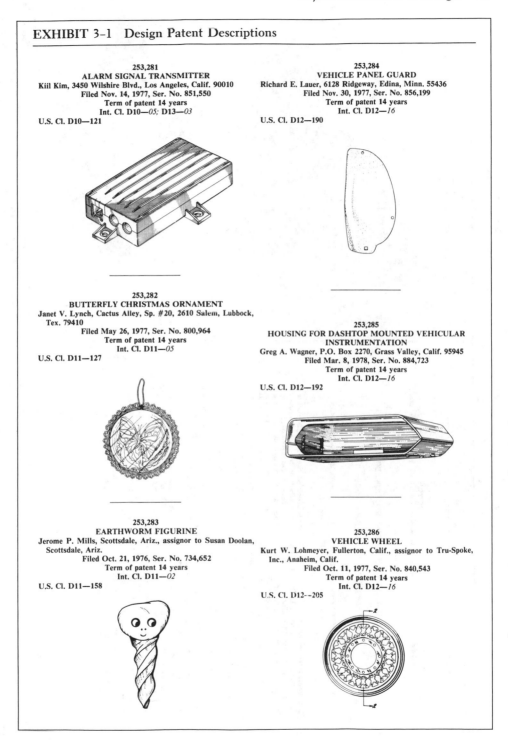

EXHIBIT 3–2   Clemens Patent Specification

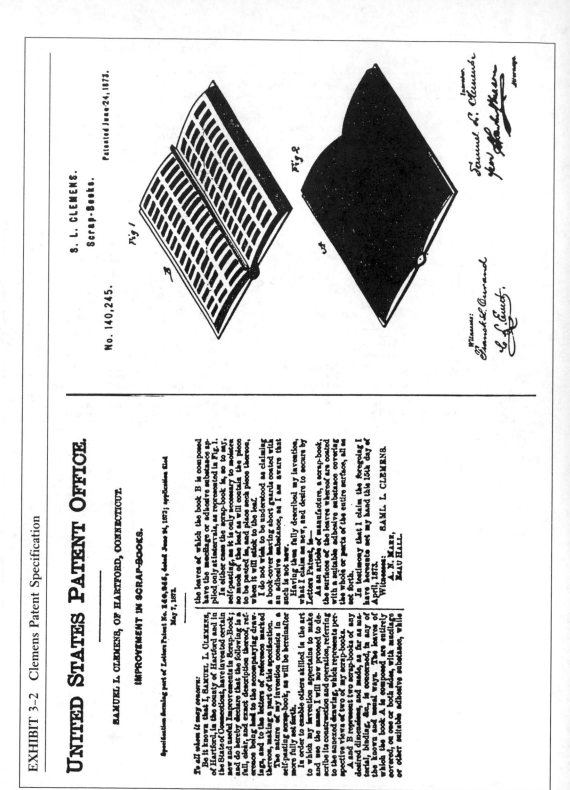

S. L. CLEMENS.
Scrap-Books.

No. 140,245.

Patented June 24, 1873.

Fig. 1

Fig. 2

B

Witnesses:
Inventor
Saml. L. Clemens

UNITED STATES PATENT OFFICE.

SAMUEL L. CLEMENS, OF HARTFORD, CONNECTICUT.

IMPROVEMENT IN SCRAP-BOOKS.

Specification forming part of Letters Patent No. 140,245, dated June 24, 1873; application filed May 7, 1873.

To all whom it may concern:

Be it known that I, SAMUEL L. CLEMENS, of Hartford, in the county of Hartford and in the State of Connecticut, have invented certain new and useful Improvements in Scrap-Book; and do hereby declare that the following is a full, clear, and exact description thereof, reference being had to the accompanying drawings, and to the letters of reference marked thereon, making a part of this specification.

The nature of my invention consists in a self-pasting scrap-book, as will be hereinafter more fully set forth.

In order to enable others skilled in the art to which my invention appertains to make and use the same, I will now proceed to describe its construction and operation, referring to the annexed drawing, which represents perspective views of two of my scrap-books.

A and B represent two scrap-books of any desired dimension, and made, as far as material, binding, &c., is concerned, in any of the known and usual ways. The leaves of which the book A is composed are entirely covered, on one or both sides, with mucilage or other suitable adhesive substance, while

the leaves of which the book B is composed have the mucilage or adhesive substance applied only at intervals, as represented in Fig. 1.

In either case the scrap-book is, so to say, self-pasting, as it is only necessary to moisten so much of the leaf as will contain the piece to be pasted in, and place such piece thereon, when it will stick to the leaf.

I do not wish to be understood as claiming a book-cover having short guards coated with an adhesive substance, as I am aware that such is not new.

Having thus fully described my invention, what I claim as new, and desire to secure by Letters Patent, is—

As an article of manufacture, a scrap-book, the surfaces of the leaves whereof are coated with a suitable adhesive substance covering the whole or parts of the entire surface, all as set forth.

In testimony that I claim the foregoing I have hereunto set my hand this 10th day of April, 1873.

SAML. L. CLEMENS.

Witnesses:
A. N. MARX,
BEAU HALL.

spondence follows; the Patent Office offers reasons why certain claims or perhaps the whole patent application is not approved, and the inventor's lawyer argues back to get the approval. If all goes well, the inventor may get a patent after spending perhaps $5,000 to $15,000 over two to three years.

Two easy ways to see what sorts of things are patented are to look for patent numbers on products and send away for copies of them at $.50 each from the Patent Office in Washington, DC, or to look at the *Patent Gazette*, which comes out weekly with abbreviated summaries of around a thousand newly issued patents. It too is available from the Patent Office and can be found in some local public libraries. Examples of utility patent summaries from a *Patent Gazette* are illustrated in Exhibit 33. Claims appear only in the full patents, not in these summaries. It is sometimes surprising to find that the claims issued on a particular product may be extremely limited and do not really prevent anyone from copying the product. In a chapter entitled "Patents Are a Force," George Ballas recalled:

■ *I have patents on several things: one is a lather warmer. This lather warmer involves a can of shaving lather and a process whereby the lather passes through hot water and warm, wet lather comes through a valve at the end of the long stem. My patent attorneys said they could get a patent on this. I said, "Wonderful!" When the attorneys sent the patent papers to be signed I read the claims. I had already spent hundreds of dollars in legal fees and I was looking at spending thousands in the future. I read the claim to see what he was actually patenting. The only thing that we were trying to patent was a crook at the bottom of a long stem. So I called a meeting and I asked my attorney, "Am I reading this thing right?" and told him what I thought I was reading. He said, "Yeah, that's what it says." I said, "What if someone made a straight stem at the bottom of the valve?" He said, "Well, you wouldn't be protected." I said, "You tell me what the hell these patents are going to be worth." He said, "I don't know, that's up to you to decide."[18]*

While waiting to see whether a patent will be issued, the inventor has no protection other than whatever speed or secrecy he or she chooses to apply to the idea. The government will not divulge the idea until it issues a patent, but competitors are free to copy the entire idea up to that time. After issuance of the patent, they may attempt to "design around it," as in the case just described, or they can infringe on it.

If they do infringe, the patent holder has the option to sue them. That is the only hope of stopping infringement, and it does not necessarily work. Some patents that are taken to court are ruled invalid. To make matters still worse, the lawsuit to enforce a patent typically costs several times as much as the patent, into the tens of thousands of dollars, and even winning the case may not pay the costs of bringing it.

Sometimes it is possible to make a near duplicate of the patented product legally. By noting the patent number, obtaining a copy, and examining the patent,

[18]George C. Ballas and David Hollas, *The Making of an Entrepreneur* (Englewood Cliffs, NJ: Prentice Hall, 1980), p. 135.

EXHIBIT 3-3   Utility Patent Descriptions

the lower end of said elongated portion having a rearwardly extending heel portion, and means cooperable with said stiffener heel portion for connecting said stiffener and, through said stiffener, the remainder of said neck to said body.

4,172,406
AUDIO-VISUAL HEADPHONES
Rosa E. Martinez, 1034 Shadwell, San Antonio, Tex. 78228
Filed Oct. 16, 1978, Ser. No. 951,489
Int. Cl.² *A63J 17/00*

U.S. Cl. 84—464 R   1 Claim

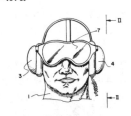

1. Audio-visual headphones for providing a user with sound from a sound input source and simultaneously providing the user with visible light in a pattern varying in accordance with variations in the sound, said headphones comprising
   a pair of headphones having a right speaker for the right ear of the user and a left speaker for the left ear of the user, said speakers being electrically connected to each other and to a sound input source whereby said speakers reproduce sound from said sound input source;
   a pair of goggles for covering the eyes of the user, said goggles being coupled to said headphones and having a plurality of lamps therein visible to said user;
   a source of electrical energy;
   a microphone electrically connected in circuit with the source of electrical energy and said lamps whereby sound reproduced by said speakers is picked up by the microphone, converted into electrical energy which varies in intensity with variations in the sound, and varies the energization of said lamps to provide a light pattern which varies in accordance with variations in the sound.

4,172,407
SUBMUNITION DISPENSER SYSTEM
Richard S. Wentink, La Jolla, Calif., assignor to General Dynamics Corporation, San Diego, Calif.
Filed Aug. 25, 1978, Ser. No. 937,682
Int. Cl.² *F41F 5/02*

U.S. Cl. 89—1.5 E   8 Claims

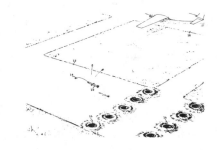

1. Submunition delivery system for attacking extended area targets which comprises:
   an elongated housing;

a plurality of sets of parallel tubes within said housing;
   the centerline of each of said tubes lying in a plane which is at an angle of at least about 60° to the longitudinal axis of said elongated housing;
   at least some of some sets of tubes oriented at different angles to the vertical than other sets of tubes;
   each of said tubes adapted to contain a submunition and a means of ejecting said submunition from said tube;
   first timing means actuating ejection means to cause said submunitions to be ejected in a selected sequence; and
   second timing means carried by said submunitions to actuate a flight drag means at a selected time.

4,172,408
LIQUID PROPELLANT GUN, BREECH PRESSURE AXIAL INJECTION
Steve Ayler, China Lake; John Holtrop, and Bruce Bartels, both of Ridgecrest, all of Calif., assignors to The United States of America as represented by the Secretary of the Navy, Washington, D.C.
Filed Aug. 29, 1977, Ser. No. 828,562
Int. Cl.² *F41F 1/04*

U.S. Cl. 89—7   7 Claims

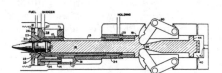

7. A liquid propellant gun having a chamber adapted to receive a projectile and liquid propellant in the form of fuel and oxidizer comprising:
   a substantially cylindrical hollow breech area having a central axis for loading a projectile into said chamber;
   fluid injector means contained within said breech area and having a central axis co-extensive with the axis of said breech area for injecting liquid propellant into said chamber;
   a bolt contained within said chamber for advancing a projectile forward from its initial placement in said chamber through said breech area;
   means for moving said bolt forward in said chamber located in the rear portion of said chamber;
   valve means contained within said breech area and also having a central axis co-extensive with the axis of said breech area for regulating the flow of fuel and oxidizer into said chamber in a predetermined manner, said valve means, fluid injector means and bolt cooperating such that when said bolt advances a projectile forward said fluid injector means pumps liquid propellant between said projectile and said bolt through said valve means; and
   sealing means within said chamber for preventing back pressure through said valve means or around said bolt.

4,172,409
FIRE CONTROL SYSTEM FOR VEHICLE-MOUNTED WEAPON
Helmut Looss, Hamburg, and Bernd Eschenburg, Uetersen, both of Fed. Rep. of Germany, assignors to Licentia Patent-Verwaltungs-G.m.b.H., Frankfurt, Fed. Rep. of Germany
Filed Jun. 8, 1977, Ser. No. 804,794
Claims priority, application Fed. Rep. of Germany, Jun. 8, 1976, 2625667
Int. Cl.² *F41G 5/14*

U.S. Cl. 89—41 E   5 Claims

1. In a fire control system for a weapon which is mounted on a rotatable platform installed on a vehicle and including a stabilized sighting mechanism and a stabilized weapon, a range

it may become apparent that a particular patent covers only features that are of little or no importance. Examination of the claims may reveal that they do not protect those features of the product that are really vital to its operation, or they may trigger ideas for other ways of accomplishing the same functions.

Many patents, probably most of them, are worth no more than whatever their sentimental or ego-fulfilling value happens to be. It is often said that at best a patent is nothing more than a license to sue infringers. Many people cannot afford to bring such suits, and the suits do not necessarily prevail. Hence, some companies, even in high technology areas, have policies of not bothering to patent anything. They just keep moving ahead with newer and better designs as fast as they can, to stay ahead of imitators.

But some patents have proven immensely worthwhile. For instance, Edwin Land's patents protected the Polaroid camera from all competitors for many years, gave him a monopoly on instant pictures, and made him a fortune. Eastman Kodak developed an "instant self-developing" film and camera, which it claimed did not infringe upon the patents held by Polaroid for such products. Polaroid disagreed, and filed suit to prevent Kodak from selling their products and to collect damages. After several years and millions spent on litigation, the court decided in favor of Polaroid. Kodak had to pay multimillion-dollar damages and to recall the film. Because customers were left with Kodak cameras that could operate only with that film, the company recalled the cameras as well. Thus, sometimes a patent truly does exclude competition.

Having a patent, or even simply filing for one in order to be able to write "patent pending" on the product, can discourage some potential competitors from even trying to imitate the product, even though they might in fact legally be able to imitate or at least design around the coverage if they tried. A patent application may sometimes win on psychology alone.

Another psychological payoff from patents is their effect upon prospective investors. One of the first questions investors will ask is whether the new company has a patent on its product or process. If it does, the new company typically will appear much more attractive, although the more seriously interested and sophisticated investors will likely want to look harder at just what the claims of those patents are, and how broad and strong they are. Some sales channels, such as Sears, are much more willing to handle a new company's product if it is protected by patents. If the inventor does not choose to start a new company to exploit the patented idea, then there is still the option of seeking to license it to someone else.

One definite advantage of having a patent is that it will protect the inventor's right to use the idea it covers without allowing someone else to patent it and block that use. A final advantage of seeking to obtain a patent is that the search required by that process will expose the inventor to other existing patents that may yield other useful improvement ideas.

Preparation for patenting.   As noted earlier, the preparation for patenting should begin as early as possible with the keeping of a design notebook to record development of the invention. The importance such a book can have is illustrated by the following historical example:

■ *Daniel Drawbach invented the telephone. Disputing the patent application filed by Alexander Graham Bell in 1875, Drawbach was able to produce hundreds of witnesses to testify that he, Drawbach, had talked over a telephone much earlier. However, Drawbach was not able to produce any notes verifying those earlier dates, and as a result the Supreme Court ruled four votes to three against him and in favor of Bell.*

Had Drawbach written out descriptions of his invention and had witnesses dated and signed those descriptions, the outcome might have been quite different. But it is not enough merely to document the starting point of development. If two inventors start at the same time, and both have initial witnesses, but one keeps track of progress with additional witnessed pages at subsequent dates and the other does not, then the former, who "demonstrates diligence in developing the idea," will win a patent dispute. Suggestions for keeping a design notebook appear in Exhibit 3–4.

There is good reason to keep the idea as secret as possible during this early notebook-keeping stage. Once the idea has been exposed through publication, through sale, or even through open testing, a twelve-month clock begins to tick toward the deadline for filing the patent application. The law starts the clock at time of use, and what constitutes "use" is subject to interpretation.

There is also good reason to move ahead promptly with patent application as soon as it appears that one should be made. Waiting leaves more chance that some other person may file for a similar patent and cause a dispute about who was first, something called "interference," at which time the notebook records will have to be used to settle the question. Interference has occurred historically on perhaps 1 or 2 percent of all patent applications. Hence, it is a matter of judgment for the entrepreneur whether the risks of waiting are justified by further checkout and development of the idea or not.

Foreign patents are also something to consider during the early secret phase. In some ways these can be even more effective than U.S. patents. In Japan, for instance, patent infringement is a crime, making patents much stronger. But many foreign countries grant the patent to the person who first applies rather than the one who first discovered the idea. In some foreign countries, the mere fact that a patent was filed elsewhere first renders the idea public. Almost no foreign countries allow a one-year grace period to apply after public exposure of the idea. Therefore, it may be important not to delay the foreign filings beyond the U.S. filing, or even to file them first. In the following example, the entrepreneur lost considerable royalty potential by neglecting to patent abroad:

■ *Papken Der Torossian, president of Silicon Valley Group, a manufacturer of semiconductor wafer manufacturing equipment, signed a distribution agreement for Japan in 1980 with Canon Sales Corporation. Canon asked for extensive information about the equipment to satisfy customers' requirements for modifications. Then in 1983 Canon terminated the agreement and Der Torossian found it was selling its own version of the product. Silicon Valley Group had never thought to patent its technology in Japan and so had no recourse.*[19]

[19]Marie-Jeanne Juilland, "Asian Money—and More," *Venture* (November 1988), p. 34.

EXHIBIT 3-4 Checklist for Keeping a Design Notebook

---

1. Obtain a bound notebook from a stationery store, preferable one with serially numbered pages.
2. Obtain a rubber stamp that includes blanks for "invented by," "date," and "read and understood by" (leave space for two people to sign) and imprint the stamp on every page of the book.
3. Use ink, not pencil, to describe each development of the idea on a page of the book, using works and sketches. Don't leave the ideas on loose pieces of paper. Photographs can be attached to the pages, but an entry should be written noting when they are attached.
4. Date and sign each entry. Explain any large gaps of time between entries to indicate insofar as possible that "due diligence" was consistently applied to bring the idea to practice.
5. Do not change dates or erase entries. Draw lines through any material to be deleted and through any large blank spaces on the pages.
6. Include any sketches, data, graphs, and other information that helps describe the idea and its development. If there are other things, such as large printouts or models that cannot be incorporated into the book, make entries noting their existence.
7. Periodically, such as every week or so, have the entries witnessed by one or two other people who had nothing to do with development of the idea but who are sufficiently knowledgeable about technical subjects to understand it. The more important the development, the more witnesses it is desirable to have.
8. Store the notebook in a safe place.

Clearly there is no point in moving ahead with a patenting effort if the idea falls outside the boundaries of what is patentable. In general terms, the patent law defines what can be covered by utility patents to include such things as:

- A product (e.g., lamp, wrench, circuit)
- Composition (e.g., plastic, dye, DNA life form)
- Machine (e.g., computer, stapler, jack)
- Method (e.g., fuel refining, drip production, cloth treating)

Things that are *not* patentable include the following:

- An idea that is not something physical
- A method of doing business (though a production process might be)
- An inoperable device, such as a perpetual motion machine
- An "obvious" improvement, such as substituting a more durable material (to someone skilled in a relevant art)
- A "new" assembly of old parts
- Something useless

Areas where interpretation is required and debate is possible arise from some words in this list, such as "new," "useful," and "obvious." The patenting of computer software programs is one such unsettled area. They can, in some forms (not read-only-memories), be copyrighted, but some decisions have gone against patenting them. It might seem that they should be patentable because they produce the same effects that mechanical cam, latches, levers, and gears sometimes produce, but it has not been clearly decided.

Help from lawyers.   Hiring a lawyer is the most common way to begin the patent application process. There are no government forms or a government list of procedures for making the application. However, an individual can apply personally without a lawyer, and this process has been described in books by Lynn,[20] Park,[21] and Pressman.[22] Either approach will produce one big advantage: Once a patent has been applied for, the inventor can write "patent pending" on the product. This may deter possible imitators, although there is no law against copying a not-yet-patented product. If a patent is issued, then the holder can imprint the notice of it on the product, and this does provide a legal base for suing infringers and sometimes customers of infringers as well. For the suing process, which may cost $20,000 to $50,000, hiring a lawyer is almost a necessity.

Patent lawyers, listed separately in the *Yellow Pages,* are the only lawyers who handle patent law, and they do not handle anything else. Seeing one immediately is the cheapest move in terms of time and the most expensive in terms of money, as one young entrepreneur who had an idea for a new type of travel trailer found out.

■   *A friend gave me the name of this lawyer, so I went to see him to ask if I could get a patent on my trailer. He asked me a bunch of questions and told me a lot of things about patent law. I mostly just listened to him lecture, although occasionally he would say something that would prompt me to ask him a question, which he would then answer. After about an hour and a half of this conversation he told me that, by the way, he was charging me at the rate of $100 an hour and had been since we started. It turned out that it was not worthwhile to go after a patent. Anyway, I couldn't afford to get it, let alone sue anybody to protect it.*

Even using a lawyer does not entirely spare inventors from the full task of working up the patent application. They still have to provide all the information about their ideas that the lawyer needs to write the application. The following entrepreneur was attempting to form a company around several new products. On the first one, he pursued a patent but was disappointed with his experience.

■   *Carl Nicolai was a "job shop" electronics technician and circuit designer, and Bill Wright was a professor of operations research and management science at the U.S. Naval Postgraduate School when they met socially in the mid-1970s. They found a common interest in communications theory, began discussing some potential new approaches to multiplexing (a way of putting several messages through one channel simultaneously) and how those approaches might be embodied in electronic circuit parts, and began to experiment. The results seemed to confirm their ideas, and they began to think about how to pursue them further. That, they decided, would take more money.*

---

[20]Gary S. Lynn, *From Concept to Market* (New York: Wiley, 1989).
[21]Robert Park, *The Inventor's Handbook* (White Hall, VA: Betterway Publications, 1986).
[22]David Pressman, *Patent It Yourself* (Berkeley, CA: Nolo Press, 1985).

They approached some California venture capitalists for financing to pursue the research but were turned down. What they needed, they concluded, was a working prototype of an actual product plus some patent coverage to show it was really new and had some degree of protection. "The protection is generally an illusion," they commented, "but it somehow seems to reassure investors. To have real protection the patent must be very basic and must be something other people can't design around. In addition, you have to have lots of money for taking people to court who violate it. Otherwise, there is nothing you can do about it. So you really aren't protected."

This was only the first of several surprises. They went to one of the largest firms on the West Coast and were startled to learn that as old and large as it was, the firm had never before processed a patent for an individual inventor. "They had only worked for the big corporations," Carl Nicolai said. "These companies bring in their hired inventors whom they pay $1 for the right to the patent, since the patent has to be issued in the name of the individual, not a company, and the law firm is then paid by the company for the patent application.

"Next, we did a search, and that cost us $800. There was no way to tell how good it was. We just had to take their word for it that the correspondent in Washington, DC, who did the search for them had been thorough. The results seemed encouraging, so we decided to go ahead with the patent application.

"We had imagined that the job of a competent patent attorney was to transfer our ideas onto paper in the appropriate form to get a patent. But that is not the way it worked. We tried to explain them to the attorney, and even switched to a different attorney. But what happened was that they wound up explaining patent law to us so that we would figure out what should be written on the patent application. It cost us another $4,000 in legal fees just to do that. It is amazing how much a patent lawyer will charge you for all the work you have to do."

Yet another entrepreneur who felt his patenting process had cost him too much money, even though it had provided him with the competitive edge needed to keep his profitable small manufacturing company in existence, said he thought he had learned how to handle the process better. He found a patent lawyer by asking his regular lawyer for a referral:

■ *Next time I would do it differently—I would not just turn the lawyer loose and let him charge me. Ask for an estimate in advance. Set a limit on the fee. Don't go after all the foreign patents. Minimize the nit-picking back and forth. Watch out for phone calls that cost $50.*

A different point of view was held by Roger Percy after he spent a great deal of money to develop and patent his TV commercial feedback evaluation system. He felt the expense was well justified and based future plans on following it up fully.

■ *Early in planning his company, he sought advice from several top executives in major corporations. "When I went to see them the first instinct of everyone was protection. Do you have something patentable? Have you seen a patent lawyer yet? One of them gave me a name and said to go see this patent lawyer. If that man would talk to me, he said, I would be halfway done.*

"So I flew down to Los Angeles to see that patent lawyer. He specialized in electronics. My impression is that all the best patent lawyers specialize in particular fields of

technology. He was also expensive; we spent $20,000 on patent work the first year alone. He was exacting, and he was one of the most difficult people I've ever dealt with in my life.

"I almost changed firms a dozen times. Finally, after almost a year of paying him and not seeing anything official back from the patent office, I flew down to see him again. I said 'Look we're not General Electric. We don't have all the money in the world, and I need to know. Are we going to get anything?' He said, 'Mr. Percy, I have to admit, I don't care about you or your company. I have my reputation to protect.'

"As it turned out, we filed 72 claims and after about eight months they gave us one of them, which was like nothing at all. Then this lawyer started working the appeals process, pointing out that this claim hung on certain others, and if this claim was approved, why not that one, and so forth. That steadily worked up the number of claims until he got us 68 of the 72 we originally filed for.

"Now we feel the product is very well covered, although we keep on developing it as fast as we can and tie down every additional patent a competitor otherwise might get. If anyone tries to infringe, we will go all the way to sue and protect our claims. We're convinced they are that important."

Defending patents.   After a patent is received, the question becomes what to do if someone infringes on it. Polaroid spent vast millions to sue Eastman Kodak on its instant camera and won, yielding a multimillion-dollar award and a market monopoly for Polaroid, while inflicting corresponding losses on its competitor. No matter which company won, however, both would have survived the suit. Windsurfer, a start-up company, was not as fortunate.

■ *The idea for combining a surfboard with a sail dawned on Jim Drake and Hoyle Schweitzer during a conversation in 1965. For a couple of years they experimented with ways of doing it and then in March of 1968 they filed for a patent. It was issued twenty-two months later as number 3,487,800. Applications in several foreign countries, unfortunately not including France, were similarly productive, and the two proceeded to develop a company, Windsurfing International, Inc., to exploit the idea.*

By 1981, however, there were 35 different companies selling sail boards in the United States and Windsurfer had named twenty of them as infringers of its patent. Meanwhile, the company had learned, after six years in business, that another inventor, S. Newman Darby, had made and used a sail board, which he never tried to patent, in 1963 which had been written up in Popular Science, *in 1965. Competitors rushed in and Windsurfer sued, claiming differences from Darby's design. One of the companies sued found another precedent design in a 1935 sailing magazine. By 1982, however, after claims had been denied by the Patent Office and appealed, and Windsurfer had refiled for clarified claims, it was asserting victory. However, other companies were still making and selling boards, and claiming it would lose the lawsuits it had filed against them.*[23]

An independent entrepreneur is more likely to face a "live or die" decision in considering whether to sue, and in any event will not be in a position to finance a multimillion-dollar legal effort. In a 1982 survey of 400 high technology small firms, Obermeyer found only one that had spent over $100,000 on patent litigation. Most

[23]Robert A. Mamis, "Hoyle Schweitzer's Decade of Discontent," *Inc.* (February 1982), p. 54.

actions by smaller firms cost less than $10,000 and took on average about two years to settle. Large firms, however, spent more and took longer to work things out. The study also found that large companies, particularly in chemical industries, tended to place more importance on patents and to make more use of the ones they had.[24]

Copyrights. A second means of protecting aesthetic features is through *copyrighting,* which gives the holder the exclusive right to reproduce and distribute a literary or artistic work for an initial term of life of the author plus fifty years. Copyright is normally associated with printed matter such as books, articles, and other writings. A company could use it on advertising copy or instructions for a product to keep others from using the same text. It could not protect the ideas embodied in what was said, but it would protect the exact wording or form of the expression. Application of copyright is automatic, simply by writing the copyright notice and author's name and date on the text. If need be, it can be filed at any time at the Library of Congress to provide the basis for an infringement suit. But this can be postponed until the need for a suit arises, because the application is automatic when the document (or speech, music, movie, computer program, or package design) is written.

Copyright can also be applied to works of art, such as paintings and sculpture, and therefore could apply to designs made by a company. The same product, an artistic lamp base for example, could possibly be protected by both trademark (for a surface logo) and copyright (for the overall shape). In applying to the Library of Congress for a copyright, only a picture of the work would be submitted, not the lamp base itself. The copyright examiner would decide whether copyright could be applied to the item. It has been decided, for example, that some lamp designs, such as those of highway lights, were primarily functional, not aesthetic, and therefore could not be covered by copyright. An advantage of copyrights is that they are good for fifty years beyond the life of the creator.

Trademarks. To protect the company logo, application can be made to the U.S. Patent Office and/or the secretary of state in any state(s) for a *trademark* registration. A trademark can be either a design (such as McDonald's arches) or a name (such as Pepsi-Cola) that identifies the source of the product or service. Common words or names do not qualify. The mark must not be similar to that used by another company for the same type of product in the same geographical area, but it may be possible to use the same name for different products. For example, Cadillac is used as both a car name and a dog food name. A *servicemark* is the equivalent of a trademark but applies to services (e.g., CENTURY 21) whereas trademarks apply only to products. A *certification mark* such as the Good Housekeeping seal of approval indicates that the product has met certain standards. This may help differentiate it from competitors, but it does not prevent copying.

[24]Judith H. Obermayer, "Protection Strategies for the Technical Entrepreneur" in Karl H. Vesper, *Frontiers of Entrepreneurship Research, 1982* (Wellesley, MA: Babson Center for Entrepreneurial Studies, 1982), p. 267.

Obtaining trademarks.   Trademark rights are acquired simply through use. Registration is not required but can greatly enhance the odds of avoiding infringement and combating infringement by others. Filing for a trademark is not the same as filing a corporate or assumed business name. To register the name as a national trademark, the company must first use it on the product in interstate commerce and then must file it with the Patent Office. The process is first to make sure the mark is not already registered, then to start using it, and finally to register it. Names that are in use can be found in the *Trade Names Dictionary, Thomas Register,* and the *Yellow Pages.* The U.S. Patent Office and the secretary of state of the area in which the company plans to do business can also be used as resources. More complete searches are offered for about $800 by search firms such as Thompson and Thompson in North Quincy, Massachusetts, Trademark Service Corp. in New York City, and Compu Mark, in Washington, DC.

Filing can be done personally, following instructions available from the Patent Office. Unlike patent application, for which there is no official form, trademark application can be made on a government form, which is illustrated in Exhibit 3–5, but it is usually better to engage a competent attorney. Bruce Milne recalled:

■   *Our first lawyer when we started said not to apply for a trademark right away, it was too expensive and could be done later. A year and a half later three other companies had filed on the same name and we had to spend a lot more money fighting them than we ever would have had to spend for registration. That's why we changed lawyers.*

Issuance of the registration usually takes about a year and is good for twenty years, after which it can be renewed for additional twenty-year periods. Proof of continued use must be filed between the fifth and sixth years or the registration lapses. Before issuance, the letters "TM" can be used to indicate ownership. After issuance, the company can use "R" or "Registered Trademark" in all advertising and can collect damages for infringements.

Defending Trademarks.   An example of a trademark dispute arose between two steak houses. One steakhouse chain was called Bonanza—the name of a TV Western series. An entrepreneur named Dan Lasater recalled what happened when he opened another steak house called Ponderosa, which happened to be the name of a ranch run by the heroes of the same TV series:

■   *We had run an ad in the paper—you know, local fellows going to start a steak house. When the Bonanza people saw that, they hot-footed down and trademarked the Ponderosa name, which we had forgotten to do. We were pretty upset, but I got to wondering how smart they really were. I wondered if they had trademarked the Bonanza name. And they hadn't. So I went down and trademarked Bonanza, and we swapped off with them.*[25]

[25]Lawrence A. Armour, *The Young Millionaires* (Chicago: Playboy Press, 1973), p. 80.

EXHIBIT 3-5   Trademark Application Form

TRADEMARK APPLICATION, PRINCIPAL REGISTER, WITH DECLARATION (Individual)	MARK (identify the mark)
	CLASS NO. (if known)

TO THE COMMISSIONER OF PATENTS AND TRADEMARKS:

NAME OF APPLICANT, AND BUSINESS TRADE NAME, IF ANY

BUSINESS ADDRESS

RESIDENCE ADDRESS

CITIZENSHIP OF APPLICANT

The above identified applicant has adopted and is using the trademark shown in the accompanying drawing for the following

goods: _____

_____

and requests that said mark be registered in the United States Patent and Trademark Office on the Principal Register established by the Act of July 5, 1946.

The trademark was first used on the goods on _____ ; was first used on the goods in
                                                              (date)

_____ commerce on _____ ; and is now in use in such
       (type of commerce)   (date)

commerce.

The mark is used by applying it to _____

_____

and five specimens showing the mark as actually used are presented herewith.

_____
(name of applicant)

being hereby warned that willful false statements and the like so made are punishable by fine or imprisonment, or both, under Section 1001 of Title 18 of the United States Code and that such willful false statements may jeopardize the validity of the application or any registration resulting therefrom, declares that he/she believes himself/herself to be the owner of the trademark sought to be registered; to the best of his/her knowledge and belief no other person, firm, corporation, or association has the right to use said mark in commerce, either in the identical form or in such near resemblance thereto as may be likely, when applied to the goods of such other person, to cause confusion, or to cause mistake, or to deceive; the facts set forth in this application are true; and all statements made of his/her own knowledge are true and all statements made on information and belief are believed to be true.

_____
(signature of applicant)

_____
(date)

The cost and complexity of obtaining design patents, trademarks, and copyrights are much less than those for obtaining utility patents.

Gray Areas.   Trademarks, copyrights, and design patents all apply to appearances of things, and it can be difficult to discern the boundaries between them. A fancy belt buckle, for instance, might have a squiggle design of some sort on the front that represents the company logo and could therefore be trademarked. If it could be construed as artistic, the squiggle, or perhaps even more of the buckle configuration, might also be copyrighted. And because of its functional purpose and distinctive appearance, the buckle could also be protected by a design patent. It would, moreover, be permissible to apply for all three types of protection, and all three might be granted. Each would require, however, that there be something distinctive about the appearance of the buckle. It is not possible to cover something that is regarded by the examiner as ordinary or identical to what has already been in existence. A trademark can even be nullified if it becomes so common as to be regarded as a generic name for a product. Some former trademark names that were lost to the public domain in that manner include aspirin, escalator, thermos, cellophane, shredded wheat, and formica. The name Weed Eater was threatened with this fate until it was saved by the introduction of the term *string trimmer,* which could be regarded as the generic name for the product.

The types of protection can be differentiated as follows: Trademarks are concerned mainly with logos; copyrights with "original works of authorship," mainly written works or art works; and design patents with outward appearances of utilitarian objects. Several types of protection may therefore apply to a single product, as illustrated by the belt buckle example or the illustration in Exhibit 3–6 of a ski pole with aesthetic and utilitarian as well as commercial features. The government puts out literature describing each type of protection, without distinguishing between them. A visitor can look at prior trademarks and design patents at the Patent Office, and at issued copyrights at the Library of Congress. However, there is no published information about the contents of applications that are turned down. Each of the three federal offices responds to questions about differences by describing only what it does and saying that questions about the others should be directed to them. The customary response is: "Send a description of the item to us and we will tell you whether our office will cover it."

Other Uses of Legal Protections.   The value of patents, and to some extent trademarks and copyrights as well, goes beyond simply protecting the company from imitators. A patent may help in trying to raise equity.

■ *Sanford Roth, who sought start-up capital for a bone healing monitor company in 1987 commented, "When we started looking for money we didn't have a patent. Investors weren't interested. As soon as we filed for a patent, interest definitely increased. All of a sudden people who hadn't been interested originally showed up to talk to me again."*[26]

---

[26]Doug Garr, "It Pays to Patent," *Venture* (October 1988), p. 39.

EXHIBIT 3-6   Illustrations of Idea Protection*

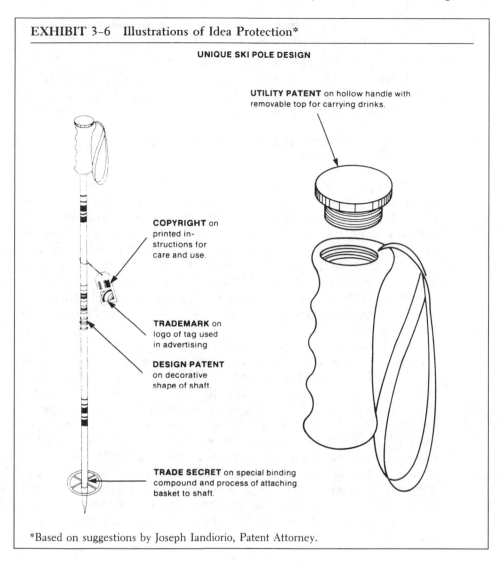

UNIQUE SKI POLE DESIGN

UTILITY PATENT on hollow handle with removable top for carrying drinks.

COPYRIGHT on printed instructions for care and use.

TRADEMARK on logo of tag used in advertising

DESIGN PATENT on decorative shape of shaft.

TRADE SECRET on special binding compound and process of attaching basket to shaft.

*Based on suggestions by Joseph Iandiorio, Patent Attorney.

A patent may also be useful as a trading device in exchange to obtain rights to use others' technologies. Finally, as will be noted later in connection with liabilities, the possession of a patent, trademark, or copyright can be a useful protection against lawsuits by others who claim *their* ideas are being unfairly copied.

Other Protection Strategies

Sometimes patenting is not possible, either because the odds of obtaining a strong and sufficiently long-lived patent are weak or because the inventor cannot afford the cost of obtaining or defending one. At other times patenting may seem inadvisable because it requires making the technology public and an entrepreneur might do better to use secrecy for protection from imitators, as does Coca-Cola, rather than patenting. Beyond that are still other strategic options.

Speed. At the very first, a start-up will have some advantage of newness setting it apart from competitors. Beyond that, even if its concept is not protected by patent or copyright, the new company may be able to keep going faster than the competition can keep up, like Kipling's shipping tycoon, who recalled:

■ *They copied all they could follow, but they couldn't copy my mind. And I left 'em sweating and stealing a year and a half behind.*[27]

For many, the best combination of safety and economy comes from moving fast, putting the new concept on the market before competitors can do anything about it, and then staying ahead by producing enough to meet demand, cutting prices to maintain a leading market share, and continuing efforts in research, development, and engineering so the competition cannot catch up. This approach is often used in toy and novelty industries where fads shift quickly and where more formal means of protection would take too long to acquire or would be inadequate in coverage. It is also sometimes used in high technology industries where the pace of innovation is fast and ideas are likely to become obsolete quickly, whether protected by law or not.

Emphasis on speed as a means of protection may also be justified by the fact that the same new idea often crops up in more than one place at nearly the same time; therefore, despite any secrecy precautions, there may be others who have thought of the same idea and gone to work on it. The jet aircraft engine, for instance, was conceived in both England and Germany at almost the same time by university students who knew absolutely nothing of each others' existence or efforts. It was not until Frank Whittle, the English inventor, saw aerial photographs of scorch marks in the grass of German airfields made by the jet engines that were already propelling German planes that he realized the Germans had, like himself, been building such engines. Regrettably for England, Whittle had not been given the same degree of support and freedom than Von Ohain had received in Germany, and German jets became operational first, with dramatic consequences for Allied bombers.

Continuing Improvement. Presumably, the longer the enterprise keeps working at improving its product or service, the cheaper, better, and more reliable that product or service will become. Ways will be found to eliminate some parts, simplify others, substitute cheaper materials, and enhance performance at the same time. Against this must be weighed the danger that competitors may enter while the company is doing its refinement, plus the problem of financing further development while no sales are coming in. Under these pressures, many companies move ahead with production and then live with the customer problems that follow.

---

[27]Rudyard Kipling, "The Mary Gloster," *Rudyard Kipling's Verse* (Garden City, NY: Doubleday, 1952), p. 128.

A technique called *value analysis* or *value engineering* is one method of extending the improvement process with the aim of cutting cost without cutting quality.[28] It starts by reexploring very basic questions about the underlying purpose of a product or service and goes on to examine how else it might be done better through such questions as

1. What is the basic purpose of the company's product or service? What is it fundamentally supposed to accomplish for the customer? Is there another better way to provide that? (Does the customer really want a better lawnmower, or would two-inch grass be the objective?) (Customers buy benefits.)
2. What is the value of each part or component of the product or service in providing that purpose for the customer? What other options might there be to replace each of these components in a more effective way? (Would rivets be better than screws, or casting in one piece better than riveting separate pieces?)
3. What is the cost of each alternative, and how does it compare to the one being used? Would it be worthwhile to let costs increase to provide more value, or can present value be provided at lowered costs?

Ideally, this analysis would proceed from raw materials through end use, looking for better ways of giving the customer more at lower cost. In practice, time is usually short, and it may be more feasible simply to keep questions of this sort in mind and apply them when opportunities allow. The main danger to be avoided is forgetting them and thereby giving competitors an opportunity to get ahead.

Even while testing and debugging of its first product or service is going on, it may be vital for the venture to be working on additional fresh ideas to maintain a lead on competitors. This was what Farallon Industries, a manufacturer of underwater recreational gear, found it had to do, as recalled by Norman H. Moore, a member of its founding team:

■ *Every forecast of time, money, performance and market was wrong. Only one of the original products was ever sold. And the company isn't completely out of the woods yet. . . .*

The above paper was delivered in February, 1973. It took another year to get all the bugs out of the digital depth gauge, but it is now in production. The company has continued to add new products — moldable mouthpiece snorkels and digital thermometers — and soon we will begin shipment of the Farallon "Decomputer," a cigarette-pack-sized wrist-mounted device that simulates the action of body tissues and accurately indicates to the diver his decompression status.

The company didn't climb into the black until January, 1974, three years and ten months after incorporation; but by June, 1974, sales and profits have risen so fast that possibly all operating losses of the first three years and nine months will be earned back by the five-year mark: March 31, 1975.[29]

At the same time that it was struggling to break even, the company was building in other strengths for the longer term, including not only new products,

---

[28]John W. Greve and Frank W. Wilson, *Value Engineering in Manufacturing* (Englewood Cliffs, NJ: Prentice Hall, 1967).

[29]Norman H. Moore, "Farallon Industries: A Case History." P. 43 in Donald M. Dible, *Winning the Money Game* (Santa Clara, CA: Entrepreneur Press, 1975).

but also a network of 500 dealers and production capability. "All the engineering and tooling didn't come cheap," Moore said, "but we try to design and fabricate everything we make so that no one else will be tempted to try to do it better or cheaper."[30]

Momentum.   With time and good performance, the venture should acquire progressively more advantages that are difficult or even impossible to imitate. Market knowledge, employee skills, reciprocal trading relationships, personal rapport with customers, reputation for good performance, and other ways of differentiating the company's product or service are examples. Whether the ideas are protected by patents or not, such other competitive protections are obviously worth considering. If patents are part of the picture, so much the better. It may well be worthwhile to keep developing new facets to those patents as well, as part of building the company beyond start-up.

Imitation of ideas and product or service liability are only two of many areas in which a new company needs to consider defensive measures. Any area of a business, including finance, sales, operations, accounting, and personnel, can have facets where protection can be important. Engaging appropriate advisers, complying with hiring and compensation laws, getting other needed forms of insurance, putting important clauses into contracts, securing shop facilities adequately, providing proper notification to customers, putting up safety signs and protective equipment for employees, guarding against shoplifting, and many other steps may be important in certain circumstances. The need for such measures will be considered further in subsequent chapters.

PLANNING QUESTIONS

The following questions are intended to stimulate thought about what should be considered in moving ahead with a venture. Which questions best apply can vary among entrepreneurs and ventures, as can the order in which they should be considered, the priority that should be placed on them, and which of them should be answered in a written plan.

Curbing Liability
- What cross-checks have been or will be made to avoid creating hazards with the venture?
- Has as long a list as reasonably possible of things that could break or cause injury been generated and provided?
- Have formal theoretical analyses been made to determine modes of failure and safety factors?
- Has testing of possible failure modes been performed?

[30]Ibid., p. 41.

- Have safety devices and warning labels been applied where advisable?
- How will the effectiveness of any operating and maintenance instructions be tested?
- Has the cost of liability insurance been investigated?
- What precautions have been taken to forestall possibilities of infringement by the venture against others' patents, lawsuit by a former employer of someone in the venture, or lawsuit arising from liability claims against the venture?

Forestalling Imitation

- What does it take to produce credibility with customers for a product or service the venture will produce, and how will the venture's offering accomplish that?
- To what extent will use of what the venture offers be dependent upon things provided by other firms, and what is the assurance those dependencies will be adequately provided for?
- What does a grid of product/service features versus competitive sources for what the venture will offer show about vulnerability of the venture to competition in the near term and the longer term?
- Will the venture be utilizing any trade secrets, and if so have precautions such as use of physical concealment and confidentiality agreements been taken to keep them secure?
- What can be patented, trademarked, or copyrighted for the venture?
- For any ideas that might be patentable, have dated and witnessed records been accumulated?
- Have names of some patent lawyers and information about their specialties that might apply to the venture been obtained?
- What specific claims may the venture be able to patent, and how powerfully protective will they be? Has the cost of obtaining them been checked?
- How will the venture continue to extend them further in the future?
- What other competitive protections will the venture have relative to each known or predictable competitor?
- What could possibly make the venture's product or service obsolete?
- What level of R&D spending has been arranged to keep a product or service such as the venture will produce at the forefront of competitive performance?
- What will future upgrading developments require in the way of money, facilities, and expertise, and how does the venture expect to obtain them?
- Where may its technology be in three to five years, and what can the venture best do to hold or extend its position amid such change?

POSSIBLE MILESTONES FOR A PLANNING TIME LINE

The most suitable milestones for a time line for a particular venture must be a function of the individual case. These that follow are intended to help stimulate thought about them.

- Patent applied for
- Trade name or mark applied for
- Copyright applied for
- Secrecy agreement for employees designed

Chapter 4

TEAMING

INTRODUCTION

Entrepreneurship requires collaboration, but not necessarily the sharing of ownership. Customers, suppliers, employees, and advisers must all be part of the process. Some types of help are free. Other types cost cash. Part ownership of the venture is sometimes offered in lieu of cash and is sometimes used to recruit help that can be obtained in no other way. When ownership is shared, there are decisions to be made about how much each partner will own, at what cost, and with what conditions. Success has been achieved by both solo and team-owned ventures. Some who have been successful with teams say they could not have done so otherwise. Sole owners often say that complete ownership and autonomy should be retained if at all possible. Which is "right" depends on entrepreneur, venture, and circumstance.

This chapter begins with what the entrepreneur can do alone and goes on to note different ways of obtaining help. Then consideration is given to sharing ownership and how it can best be done.

SOLO TAKEOFF

The most common reasons for going solo are to retain share value and control of the enterprise. If the founder has the expertise and financial capacity to start the venture alone, then going without partners is usually simplest. They can always be added later if the venture shows promise; the more progress it has made, the stronger the founder's bargaining position will be for bringing partners in.

Going without Partners

One entrepreneur who tried it both ways and preferred operating solo was Jonathan Holman:

■ *He had operated an executive recruiting firm with two partners. His partners were several years older and wanted to take cash out of the company, while Holman wanted to let his stake build up in the company. They preferred to have the company and its profitability grow by hiring lower-paid people for some of the search tasks. He liked to perform more of the tasks personally, rather than specialize in delegating and managing. Consequently, he left and started his own one-man firm.*

A major competitive advantage with prospective clients, he said, was to inform them that he personally would perform the whole job and to suggest that they ask any competitor whether its chief executive would be handling their business personally or would be delegating any important parts of the job to lower-level, less-experienced staff personnel. This, he said, was yielding a 90 percent win rate for him on bids. The rest of his business, all he could handle, was coming on referrals. "I have yet," he commented, "to meet a successful solo practitioner who has any enthusiasm at all for going back to a corporation, no matter what the size."[1]

The advantage of not having to answer to anyone has been echoed by others. John Haley ended up with 100 percent of his company, Southeastern Telecom, which in 1983 had over 8 percent profits on sales of $6 million, because he could not find anyone willing to invest when he was starting the company. He commented, "I make the decisions—I'm not waiting for someone in another city to tell me what to do." Another entrepreneur, Richard Thalheimer, 100 percent owner of The Sharper Image, which he started in his apartment in 1971 and built to sales of $85 million in 1985 commented in a similar vein, "I'm a confident individual who doesn't like to be told what to do. I haven't met anybody yet who I'd work for."[2]

Most ventures that have been successfully created by lone entrepreneurs are simple types of enterprises, such as small retail stores and services, mail order firms, real estate, and various kinds of "wheeling and dealing." But they also include some manufacturing companies and enterprises that grow large. Testimony can be seen from "one-man shows," such as McDonnell Aircraft, that ultimately go public or merge with other firms. Care should be taken in noting these examples, however, to ascertain whether the dominant owners of these companies actually started them alone or whether they started with partners and later bought them out, as did Henry Ford.

Substantial wealth can be saved by sole ownership. If the company grows to be worth $1 million, then a 40 percent partner would own $400,000 at the expense of the entrepreneur who shared ownership. Many entrepreneurs have used stock

[1]Jonathan S. Holman, "Why I Went Solo," *Inc.* (May 1987), p. 156.
[2]"When It Pays to Go It Alone," *Inc.* (June 1984), p. 154.

to pay for help in early stages when cash was scarce, only to decide later that the payment was too high. For instance, by paying an attorney 5 percent in stock for forming a corporation, as has often been done, an entrepreneur may be paying thousands for a service that normally costs only a few hundred dollars. The words of one entrepreneur who concluded from sad experience not to take in any partners again were recalled by Collins and Moore as follows:

■ *Why should I take somebody in who is a millstone, who eats off you because he owns part of you, and you cannot buy him off because the value of his investment has increased due to your very own efforts?*[3]

An even better reason for operating solo can be to retain total control of the company. Although it may at times be demoralizing to have a silent partner who shares the rewards without sharing the work, it can be worse to have a silent partner who, out of concern for his or her investment, becomes a pest with questions about how the company is doing, and why it is not taking this or that action to do better. These questions can take time and attention away from getting the job done and at the same time lower the incentive needed to do it well. Going one step further, a working rather than silent partner can be an asset when he or she truly carries part of the load and complements others but can be a substantial drag when he or she works at cross-purposes, either out of disagreement over policies or because of a personality missmatch.

Such problems can be avoided by sole ownership but may saddle the owner with an enormous number of tasks. If the company has enough money, it can hire others to help. But if not, then the owner must work alone or with the help of family, as Danco has described:

■ *The battles of the early years are fought in the foxholes of the basement, the garage and the trunk of the car. While the founder operates a drill press in the garage or keeps stock in the basement, and hopes the zoning commission doesn't shut him down, Mom learns to keep books on the kitchen table. . . . When the children are old enough to lick stamps and address envelopes, they are "employed." In order to survive, the "work" and the "profits" must be kept within the family. So the children and the relatives all come in at odd hours to help and to pick up a little extra money on the side. In some cases family members swap sweat and muscle for a needed job. Since the owner can't pay them much, he substitutes fancy titles for money, and plays upon their family loyalty to keep them involved. This early participation in the business provides them with tenure in later years when key management positions are up for grabs.*[4]

This level of dedication can work either way in the family — knitting it closer together or driving it apart. And it may not be sufficient to build the business.

---

[3]Orvis Collins and David G. Moore, *The Organization Makers* (New York: Meredith Corporation, 1970), p. 149.

[4]Leon Danco, *Beyond Survival* (Cleveland, OH: Center for Family Business, 1975), p. 28.

■ *In one northwest trailer manufacturing company run by a family, the father died of a heart attack under the pressure of the business. The mother carried on with her two sons, working long hours, seven days a week. Each of the three gave the effort of two, skimping and making do, eventually buying materials at retail on personal charge cards at the hardware store after cash ran dry and suppliers began requiring payment on delivery. Somehow they kept the trailers coming out the door for several months, but more slowly each month, until finally the Small Business Administration cracked down on its loan, padlocked the plant, and brought in an auctioneer who disposed of the meager remaining assets.*

But it is also possible for a business to survive and eventually prosper despite weaknesses in solo management, as Danco describes:

■ *Because his pride and his fear and his lack of trust made it impossible for him to ask for help from those who might have guided his efforts, the founder of a business learned mostly from trial and error. He was a protozoic pragmatist, re-inventing the wheel each time he made a business decision. It didn't matter if his answer was right or wrong for the long run. What mattered was whether it worked then. He made so many decisions so fast, and he made so many mistakes that enough were bound to turn out right in the end, so he prospered. Those things which did turn out right were called "management decisions." Suddenly he was the boss.*[5]

Generally, the farther along an entrepreneur is able to carry a venture solo, the stronger his or her bargaining position becomes because greater value has been created in the venture. The idea creates some value. Getting a prototype in operation creates more. A patent and a first customer add still more value, and so forth. The greater the value, the less ownership and control the founder should have to share to attract a partner. The price required for this enhanced position, of course, is that the founder will have had to commit more time and other resources on the hope that the idea will pan out. Not sharing the ownership also means not sharing the risk.

Legal Formats

There are two legal formats for a solo venture. It is automatically a proprietorship if no action is taken to make it something else. If registration is needed, to get licenses or to do business, for example, the company can be given a name that will appear on paperwork beneath the owner's own name followed by DBA (meaning "Doing Business As") and the company's name. Essentially, the business and the owner are one entity.

The other option is incorporation. As discussed in the last chapter in connection with insulation from liability, the corporation is an entity separate from its owner. It has some advantages in terms of different tax options, protection of the owner from liability, continuity beyond the owner's death, and possibly greater convenience in later decisions about sharing ownership. It also requires more

[5]Danco, *Beyond Survival*, p. 31.

paperwork. The owner can prepare and file for incorporation personally by obtaining forms from a commercial stationery store or references on forming corporations.[6] Alternatively, an attorney can be hired, either to save time or to anticipate possible complexities if the addition of other partners is contemplated, as will be discussed shortly. Table 4–1 summarizes the contrasting advantages and disadvantages of alternative legal forms.

Low-Cost Help Sources

Notwithstanding talented and resourceful entrepreneurs, plus availability of encyclopedias as well as textbooks on how to develop businesses,[7] a new venture usually needs help from outsiders to get started and to operate. Help sources can be divided into those who require direct payment for their services and those who do not. The latter low-cost sources can be grouped into six categories:

Customers.   Customers are often willing to help because they will benefit directly if the start-up succeeds.

Suppliers.   Also standing to benefit are suppliers for whom the start-up may become a good customer. They can help with selection of materials and services during the process of refining the business concept. They may also be able to provide information about potential customers and likely competitors for the start-up.

Bankers.   A supplier that is likely to become particularly important to the start-up is the bank that will benefit from its deposits and also possibly "rent" it money. Hence, bankers have an interest in helping start-ups. They have an occupational bias toward conservatism but can help as sounding boards for business plans and as providers of contacts and information. An entrepreneur should not hesitate to ask and to shop around for the banker who offers the most help. Selecting and dealing with bankers will be further discussed in the next chapter on raising capital.

Government.   The federal government's official policy is to assist entrepreneurship. Part of the mission of the Small Business Administration (SBA) is to help start-ups as well as established small firms. It offers lectures by successful entrepreneurs, literature written by experts from private industry, and the services of both retired and active executives who donate their time to help entrepreneurs. Other agencies of government must favor start-ups and small firms in contracts. Making contact with the SBA as well as state and local agencies can quickly generate a list of low-cost assistance sources, such as volunteer executives under its ACE (Active

---

[6]Ted Nicholas, *How to Form Your Corporation Without a Lawyer for Under $50* (Wilmington, DE: Enterprise Publishing, 1971).

[7]Ron Christy and Billy M. Jones, *The Complete Information Bank for Entrepreneurs* (New York: Amacom, 1988); and David E. Gumpert and Jeffry A. Timmons, *The Encyclopedia of Small Business Resources* (New York: Harper & Row, 1984).

TABLE 4-1 Comparison of Legal Entities

	PROPRIETORSHIP/ PROPRIETOR	PARTNERSHIP/ PARTNER	LIMITED PARTNERSHIP/ LIMITED PARTNER	CORPORATION/ STOCKHOLDER
Possible Concerns				
Insulation of owner from liabilities of company	None	None	As specified by partner agreement	Yes
Double taxation	No	No	No	S-Corp. No C-Corp. Yes
Setup cost	Lowest	Varies	Highest	Varies
Periodic paperwork	Less	Less	Less	More
If an owner dies	Company stops	Company stops	Depends on agreement	Company continues
Reallocating shares	Depends on next form	Hardest	Depends on agreement	Easiest
Able to go public	No	No	Hard	Yes
Ability to change form	Easiest	Second easiest	Second hardest	Hardest

109

Core of Executives) and SCORE (Service Corps of Retired Executives) and SBI (Small Business Institute) programs. Further consideration of government relationships, particularly concerning governmental red tape and other hurdles, is found in Chapter 9.

Other Institutions.   Two other types of organizations worth contacting for low-cost help are trade associations and universities. There are trade associations, described in the *Encyclopedia of Associations,* for virtually all lines of business, and they usually have useful information that is shared among their members about how to operate effectively. The cost of joining can be inexpensive relative to the value of information and contacts that it may buy. Universities often provide information through their business libraries and free help through student research projects done for course credit.

Other Contacts.   The story of nearly every successful start-up includes parts played by personal contacts of different types. Other entrepreneurs can often be particularly helpful, and many are glad to help. Venture capitalists who are approached with a carefully prepared business plan will sometimes give helpful feedback, even if they do not provide investment capital—although under the weight of the many plans they screen, there is not much time for them to give counsel to those they reject.

The importance of networks found by Birley's study was noted earlier in Chapter 2. The catch in making use of assistance sources and networks, even if there is no charge, is the time cost to the entrepreneur. Cultivating a network can absorb great amounts of time, particularly if the entrepreneur does not know which contacts will be most helpful. For some types of help, it may be more economical simply to wait for the need to arise and then pay for the assistance needed.

Judith Daniels, who in the fall of 1976 quit her job as managing editor of the *Village Voice* to start *Savvy Magazine,* recalled what she learned from navigating a network of contacts in search of capital:

■ *You must follow up every lead, every contact, because you never know who will introduce you to someone who will introduce you to someone who knows somebody who will turn out to be the right person. I never made any cold calls, but that's not necessarily my advice to you, because I know it has worked for others. In my case, I contacted names only when I was referred by others.*

It is important to realize what networks are not . . . consciousness raising groups, social clubs, career counseling seminars, encounter group therapy or sales calls. . . . A network cannot make up for lack of talent . . . [it] is not a crutch . . . [it is] not a substitute for working hard.[10]

---

[8]*Encyclopedia of Associations* (Gale Research Corporation, Book Tower, Detroit, MI 48226).

[9]Sue Birley, "The Role of Networks in the Entrepreneurial Process." P. 335 in John A. Hornaday, Edward B. Shils, Jeffrey A. Timmons, and Karl H. Vesper, *Frontiers of Entrepreneurship Research, 1985* (Wellesley, MA: Babson Center for Entrepreneurial Studies, 1985).

[10]Judith Daniels, "A Cliff-Hanging Saga," *HBS Bulletin* (November–December 1980), p. 100.

In attempting to answer questions and solve problems, it is often natural to consider who might be able to help and to call that person. What may be even more helpful is to start by generating a *list* of people who might help, including as many names as possible, and then to seek more names from each person contacted, so the list is not shortened by crossing off contacts made, but instead grows longer with each contact.

EXTERNAL TEAM

People who help advise management on a continuing part-time basis can be regarded as its outside team. They include several types of professionals plus other advisers who receive compensation in either money or stock.

Professionals

In addition to bankers, who as previously noted usually do not charge directly for their services, there are several other types of professionals who do. They will be discussed more fully in later chapters, but briefly they include the following:

Lawyers. One of the first paid professional advisers to be engaged will be an attorney. The role of the patent attorney was discussed in the preceding chapter. A second important legal area also treated in the last chapter is product liability, which requires a different specialist. Still other types of attorneys are valuable for dealing with the creation and maintenance of the company's legal form, as noted in Chapter 2 and this chapter. Other legal areas discussed in subsequent chapters include

- Loan agreements, Chapter 5
- Investment agreements and securities requirements, Chapter 6
- Contracts with sales channels, Chapter 7
- Contracts with landlords, suppliers, and labor as well as permits and governmental requirements, Chapter 8
- Taxes and other forms of liability, Chapter 9

There is some tendency for these legal needs to arise in sequence. According to a study by Brown, Colborne, and McMullan, issues of intellectual property and business format are the most common, but the former tend to taper off in earlier stages of the venture. Issues of taxation and contracts tend to arise later, though never to as great an extent as the first two.[11] How to choose and use attorneys will be discussed further in Chapter 9.

[11]Catherine A. Brown, Carmen Colborne, and W. Ed McMullan, "Legal Issues in Venture Development." P. 359 in Neil C. Churchill, John A. Hornaday, Bruce A. Kirchhoff, O. J. Krasner, and Karl H. Vesper, *Frontiers of Entrepreneurship Research, 1987* (Wellesley, MA: Babson Center for Entrepreneurial Studies, 1987).

Accountants.   Accountants, like attorneys, can become specialists in such areas as setting up accounting systems, keeping financial records up to date, auditing, tax preparation, and more general management consulting (see Chapter 9). They, like bankers and lawyers, can be particularly helpful in networking to find other needed contacts.

Advertising Agencies.   Not all start-ups need the help of advertising agencies, but, in some cases, they are vital (see Chapter 7). If the company needs to advertise, even on as small a scale as distributing brochures or putting an advertisement containing graphics in the *Yellow Pages*, the help of professionals may be the only way of avoiding clumsy and inefficient performance.

Insurance Brokers.   Only one form of insurance, product liability insurance, has been discussed so far. Later in this chapter, brief consideration will be given to some other forms — directors' liability insurance and insurance to cover key personnel and buy-sell agreements. Other forms, as well as procedures to select and obtain them, will be considered in Chapter 9.

Consultants.   Consultants can provide advice on a wide range of topics. Some consultants have specialized knowledge of topics ranging from vibration analysis to statistical quality control, plant layout, package design, market research, pension plan design, data processing, investment counseling, environmental regulations, plant safety, labor relations, computerization, and countless others. Others are more generalized, providing help in areas such as management consulting, although most of those listed under that topic in the *Yellow Pages* specialize in recruiting and job search. Many consultants specialize in anything that pays, and it is easy to spend money for valueless advice.

As noted earlier, some types of consultants, government volunteers and students, for example, cost no money, only time. One way to minimize risk on using consultants is to tap this source. Another is to select any paid professionals with great care to be sure that they have experience and references from satisfied prior clients on exactly the type of work they are needed to do. They can be found both through networking and through contacting well-known major consulting firms and accounting firms with consulting divisions.

Giving the consultant a written proposal, delineating what is to be done and by when, choosing one who is clearly in the right specialty by virtue of similar experience, and checking with other clients can raise the odds of receiving what is needed. As with accountants, bankers, lawyers, and other professionals, it is important to know which individual(s) in the firm will do the work and to minimize the risk of paying "tuition" for a junior person's education.

Sounding Boards

In contrast to consultants, who are usually hired on a short-term hourly basis for solving isolated specific problems, there are longer-term advisers who, although they are not part of the internal team of employees, develop an advisory relationship that continues over time with the business.

Directors.   There can be any combination of three reasons for having a board of directors: (1) to satisfy the law if the company is incorporated, (2) to provide oversight for outside investors, and (3) to advise the chief executive.

Directors should be considered at two levels: formal and informal. If the company is incorporated, then it is required that the company have a board of directors. The minimum number of directors is set by the state in which the company is incorporated. If the company has more than one investor, then probably the major investors will have preferences as to the people they would like to have represent them on the board. Stockholders vote to elect directors according to how many shares they have, and the directors in turn elect the officers who run the company. Hence, the corporation will be formally forced to comply with the wishes of the investors in choosing directors, and the president will have to answer to them.

At a less formal level, the founder(s) must decide what kinds of people with what qualifications they want to have on the board. Books have been written on this subject, plus numerous articles, and no attempt to summarize them will be made here. In general, however, the entrepreneur should be aware that by selecting directors wisely, he or she may be able to obtain considerable assistance and support for the company. It is often desirable to have on the board the president of a company that is just a stage or two beyond the new company, not so far that this president will have lost touch with the reality of a start-up, but far enough that he or she can share the learning gained by successfully surviving and growing.

There can be problems associated with having the company's banker, lawyer, or accountant on the board. They and the employees of the company are already available to advise the company. It is often preferable to recruit people who are detached from the company and in a better position to be unbiased in advising the president. Finally, it is easier to vote a director onto the board than to expel one without hard feelings. Many companies prefer to make the appointments on an annual basis.

A 1984 *Venture* poll of 277 companies found that the likelihood of a company's having outside directors went up with company size. One-third of companies with sales less than $2 million had no outside directors. For the other companies, the main contribution of outside directors, according to respondents, was objectivity. Major shareholders and business associates were considered most valuable as directors, while bankers and consultants rated in the middle. Lawyers and academics came in last. The most common meeting pattern was "as needed."[12]

Advisers.   A problem with recruiting outside directors can be the specter of liability lawsuits against them. Directors' liability insurance can be purchased but is costly and may not be affordable.

One way to get the counsel that directors might give without subjecting them to such liability is to form a "board of advisers" without authority or formal

[12]Cathy Hedgecock, "Who Sits on Your Board?," *Venture* (April 1984), p. 32.

connection with the company. If there is a corporation, there still must be a board of directors, but that board can be comprised of people such as family members who are not so concerned about such liability. The advisory board can include any of them plus others whose continuing counsel the entrepreneur would like to have but who are uneasy about potential liability.

Advisers, like directors, may be able to help not only in counseling the CEO, but also in lending credibility to the company for raising money and making sales. Advice from people experienced in such roles, according to *Venture*, includes using them for more than "window dressing," however. It also suggests they should be chosen only with a clear purpose and after the direction of the company is clear; they should not include friends; they should be paid on the order of $1,000 to $10,000 per year each; and that amount should be scaled to a specific commitment on their part.[13]

Any mix of advisers, professionals, directors, and other help sources is possible. What combination will work best must be decided for each venture. Egge and Simer reported that 91 percent of a sample of entrepreneurs agreed that a founder should seek out and listen to an expert who has gone through a start-up.[14] From interviews with 110 entrepreneurs, Hutt and Van Hook found that accountants were the most frequently used external advisers, followed by attorneys, then friends and relatives. Interestingly, the authors found that entrepreneurs with weaker ties to advisers got more information from them. Whether it was better information, however, was not reported.[15]

Assessment of Additional Needs

One entrepreneur who in hindsight said he used too little help was George Morrow, a pioneer in microcomputers. His company, Morrow Designs, filed for Chapter XI bankruptcy in mid-1986, even though it had produced a successful product, the Pivot II, of which 15,000 units were ordered by the Internal Revenue Service, but from a licensee, Zenith Data Systems, rather than Morrow Designs. He commented:

■ *I was too much of a one-man band, the head of engineering and the chairman. If you're wearing two hats you can get in the way of products. All of us in the early microcomputer industry were scared to death of giving up equity. We had an attitude of antiestablishment.*[16]

---

[13]Margaret Kirk, "Building an Advisory Board," *Venture* (October 1984), p. 42.

[14]Karl A. Egge and Frank J. Simer, "An Analysis of the Advice Given by Recent Entrepreneurs to Prospective Entrepreneurs." P. 119 in Bruce A. Kirchhoff, Wayne A. Long, W. Ed McMullan, Karl H. Vesper, and William E. Wetzel, Jr., *Frontiers of Entrepreneurship Research, 1988* (Wellesley, MA: Babson Center for Entrepreneurial Studies, 1988).

[15]Roger W. Hutt and Barry L. Van Hook, "The Use of Outside Advisors in Venture Start-Ups." P. 216 in ibid.

[16]Marie-Jeanne Juilland, "Bootstrapping Backfires," *Venture* (June 1986), p. 96.

For some entrepreneurs, lack of *time* is the key factor that makes working with outside sources of assistance difficult. The alternative is to create additional time by recruiting partners to share the load. A way to decide whether to add partners can be to list the main functional areas of the business: technology development, marketing, production, finance, accounting, human relations, and leadership, as well as any appropriate subdivisions of each. Then consider for each subarea how another person with different capabilities and experience might be able to help, and so on to consider whether it would be most effective to engage such a person as an outside helper, hire that person as an employee, or recruit him or her as a partner.

A highly successful entrepreneur who saw the value in complementary talent when his company's performance slipped was Kemmons Wilson, founder of Holiday Inns, who observed:

■ *I have never claimed to be any kind of administrative man at all. It kills me. I hate detail work.*[17]

Another way to look at teaming is to consider what sort of team might make the most formidable competitor for the new venture. Again, which members of such a team might it be worthwhile to recruit and on what basis?

SHARING OWNERSHIP

Aside from the case of 100 percent personal financing and ownership from the start, there can be any number of variations with other working partners and/or investors at various stages, a subject that will also be discussed in Chapters 5 and 6 in connection with financing. There may also be stages where partners are squeezed out for one reason or another, as will be discussed shortly.

Team Takeoff

A strongly favored view among professionals who deal with start-ups, particularly venture capitalists, is that teams are better bets than individual founders and that teams with a balance of talents are even more preferable. Relatively little empirical data have been gathered on this subject, but the information that is available seems to support these views. For instance, Teach, Tarpley, and Schwartz found from a study of 237 software start-ups that most were started by more than one founder and that founding teams that were larger and included members with engineering and business education backgrounds tended to be more successful. The most powerful indicator of success was the

---

[17]"Holiday Inns: Trying the Comeback Trail," *Business Week* (July 5, 1976), p. 64.

inclusion of members with more software experience, preferably including some in middle, though curiously not top, management positions.[18]

A quick reflection on the number and variety of different functional areas of a business immediately reveals how unlikely it is that a given entrepreneur will be highly competent in a large number of them. Product or service design subdivides into technical and aesthetic factors; finance allows innumerable avenues of choice; accounting requires precision as well as understanding of its purposes; tax rules are constantly changing; selling calls for talent in understanding customers as well as initiative and great amounts of time. All these diverse activities must be attended to in the new company in addition to the central function of producing and delivering what the company has to sell and recruiting, training, and managing the people who do it.

An illustration of how teaming can give a venture a considerable advantage over its competitors appears in the remarks of Tom Melohn, who learned the value of specialized help in a big corporation and then applied it to a venture:

■ *It was a happy surprise for me to find that there was very little systematic problem solving or creative marketing in our manufacturing segment when I bought my company 10 years ago. We were competing with "classic" entrepreneurs — self-made, visceral, intuitive, with a hands-on technical background, light in marketing experience and with a ferocious need for personal control.*

In that competitive environment, the corporate management skills I brought with me helped us to increase sales tenfold, boost pretax profit by 2,100 percent, and raise our ROI [return on investment] to the same level as those of companies in the top 10 percent of the Fortune *500 — all within 10 years.*

But the single most important thing I brought with me from my corporate experience was the wisdom to know that I couldn't do it all alone. I recognized that other people in the company could care just as much as I, and that our success depended on my ability to delegate to them. I did, and we grew. The entrepreneur who can't let go can't compete with me.[19]

The help needed, depending upon the developmental stage of the venture, may be technical expertise in how to design, produce, or sell what the company is going to offer. Or it may be for obtaining capital, facilities, or sales outlets. Sometimes the need is to round out management so that all business aspects — accounting, marketing, finance, operations, and engineering — will be covered. It may be for another set of hands to work on creating the business. Or it may simply be to get psychological support. Generally, it is some combination of these needs that impels the entrepreneur to team up. Many entrepreneurs who team up are glad they did or feel that it was an inescapable necessity. Some are sorry and wish they had not teamed the way they did. Still others did not and wish they had,

[18]Richard D. Teach, Fred A. Tarpley, Jr., and Robert G. Schwartz, "Software Venture Teams." P. 546 in Robert Ronstadt, John A. Hornaday, Rein Peterson, and Karl H. Vesper, *Frontiers of Entrepreneurship Research, 1986* (Wellesley, MA: Babson Center for Entrepreneurial Studies, 1986).

[19]Tom Richman, "The New American Start-up," *Inc.* (September 1988), p. 64.

usually because they can see in hindsight that teaming could have saved a business that failed to survive.

From the entrepreneur's perspective, reasons for sharing equity include (1) raising money or providing compensation in lieu of it, (2) recruitment and motivation of key people, (3) a sense of fairness, and (4) a need for companionship. Reasons against it are (1) loss of wealth, (2) reduction of control and decision-making freedom, (3) becoming "stuck" with other owners, (4) reduction of privacy, (5) reduction of future ability to raise money, and (6) having to answer to others.

In an intensive study of 105 start-ups, Gartner asked entrepreneurs how they obtained necessary start-up skills. Forty-three percent said they already possessed them, and 32 percent said they learned as they went. The remainder recruited them, 11 percent from partners, 8 percent from employees, and 6 percent from consultants. The percentages varied, however, with areas of expertise and type of venture. Partners were most often recruited for adding production talent in ventures whose founders were technical experts. Partners were least often recruited for general management capability. Most of the founding entrepreneurs reserved that activity for themselves.[20]

A study by McMullan, Long, and Tapp found that the two most common reasons for sharing ownership were to raise money and to attract needed expertise or employees. Some other reasons that, in the founders' hindsight, seemed less well justified were to acquire influence or credentials and to affiliate with a complementary organization.[21] Taking on partners to raise capital (see Chapter 6) is illustrated by the experience of the following entrepreneur, as reported by Collins and Moore:

■ *I began to see I could make out. I quit and began working it night and day—not just nights. But leaving my job like that meant I didn't have a paycheck coming in, and it was going to be weeks before I could make a delivery. This Al, he had three thousand and I tried to talk him out of it on a loan basis—a personal loan—but he wouldn't and so I took him in as a partner. He was hard-working, but he couldn't read a blueprint; he was so dumb.*[22]

Regrettably, capital appears to have been the only positive thing this entrepreneur gained from his partner. Collins and Moore go on to say that trouble between the partners followed, as it does many times for reasons that will be described later.

Judicious teaming can help in making the venture attractive to outside investors. Bruno and Tyebjee concluded from their study of high-technology start-ups that had sought venture capital that "The entrepreneur should form a manage-

---

[20]William B. Gartner, "Problems in Business Startup: Relationships among Entrepreneurial Skills and Problem Identification for Different Types of New Ventures." P. 496 in John A. Hornaday, Fred Tarpley, Jr., Jeffry A. Timmons, and Karl H. Vesper, *Frontiers of Entrepreneurship Research, 1984* (Wellesley, MA: Babson Center for Entrepreneurial Studies, 1984).

[21]W. Ed McMullan, Richard Long, and Jay Tapp, "Entrepreneurial Share Transaction Strategies." P. 39 in ibid.

[22]Collins and Moore, *The Organization Makers*, p. 146.

ment team which is well rounded in technical and management skills before initiating a search for capital. The entrepreneur should think in terms of a venture team in search for financing rather than a single individual with a business plan."[23] One reason for preferring teams is to get a balance of capability among production, sales, engineering, and control. Another is that the entrepreneur who can lead a team is more likely to be good to deal with and to be capable of building a bigger business. Collins and Moore quoted an entrepreneur who appears to have appreciated this fact:

■ *There had to be four of us. First, we needed an engineer. I knew something about production, but with what I knew we would never get beyond the alley shop stage. We needed someone who could set up an operation, and I thought right away of Tom. Tom is a graduate engineer, and I started figuring how to get him. Then we needed somebody who could get out and find jobs for us. Ned was the man because he was already in selling and knew quite a few people. Then, we needed somebody who could handle the financial side—taxes and all that. Actually, we never found that person. I put that on myself by default, and actually in the process I've become a pretty good accountant.*[24]

This entrepreneur envisaged and recruited a fairly full array of needed talents at or near the inception of the enterprise. Most build a team more minimally and as needed. The team members, moreover, are usually not so much sought out as encountered by coincidence—which may be enhanced by building contacts and cultivating awareness of what complementary talents may be needed.

The next example illustrates how another team need—competence in engineering design—can come about and how it can be met:

■ *In late 1959, a civil engineer employed by a large aerospace company to work on runway instrumentation began talking with one of his neighbors, a mechanical engineer, about how to design a hydraulic system to control a road scraper and keep the scraping blade at constant height as the scraper moved along. The civil engineer had worked in surveying with the highway department ten years earlier. Finding it cumbersome to adjust the position of survey stakes by pounding them into the ground, pulling, and moving them around, he had invented an adjustable stake that he patented. At the suggestion of another engineer, he incorporated a string attachment into the stake that would provide a continuous reference line for survey work.*

He contracted with a manufacturer to produce stakes, quit his highway department job, and went on the road to sell them. After a year of traveling and unsuccessful talking with skeptical highway engineers, he gave up and in late 1951 took another job, this time on a dam construction project. Five years later, the dam completed, he wandered from job to job, never content, always looking for something better, but not working on the stake. Ultimately, in late 1958, he signed on with the aerospace company. There, on the runway work, it occurred to him that perhaps an attachment might be designed for a road grader that would cause it to guide on the string of his patented stake. If it were successful, he

[23]Albert V. Bruno and Tyzoon T. Tyebjee, "The Entrepreneur's Search for Capital," *Journal of Business Venturing* 1 (no. 1) (Winter 1985), p. 63.

[24]Collins and Moore, *The Organization Makers*, p. 151.

might finally have a way to sell stakes and get into business for himself. The trouble was that he did not know how to design the hydraulic control system. Maybe his neighbor, a mechanical engineer, could help.

The mechanical engineer had joined the aerospace company following graduation from college, but a year later, he became dissatisfied with working in the large organization. After returning to college and earning another engineering degree in graduate school, he and some friends formed a concrete products company, at which he served as plant engineer. When the civil engineer described his hydraulic controls problem, it looked to the mechanical engineer not only like one he could solve, but also the chance to start another company.

The two men each put up $6,000, agreed to become partners by shaking hands (no written documents), and began development work during evenings and weekends of late 1959 in the civil engineer's garage. From a nearby university the two obtained further technical and testing help. The president of a paving company, whom the civil engineer had met several years earlier on another job, gave them use of road grading machines for testing prototypes of the new control unit. He also arranged their introduction to the manufacturer of the machines, who became the first customer for the new product. Patent application was made in both men's names, and both quit their jobs to work full-time on their control device. Even with application of full-time effort, completion of product development took three years. Through the paving company, the partners met a lawyer, who set up their corporation in exchange for 10 percent of the stock. Sales began to pick up and gradually the company moved toward the black, though neither quickly nor without difficulty. By now the product consisted of laser-aimed control equipment, having nothing to do with adjustable surveying stakes.

There are any number of conceivable ways this product or this company could have come about. Although no such product was on the market when the two men began designing theirs, a large company also began developing one independently before the two men had finished, apparently with neither competitor knowing about the other. The big company's first design was, in the opinion of the two entrepreneurs, decidedly inferior, much to their relief. Consequently, their new company was able to survive against this competition. But had the two men not developed their product, the big company still would have.

Either of the two men could also have developed the product. The civil engineer first raised the possibility, with the objective of selling stakes, but he did not have the technical knowledge to get them made. Nor could he afford to hire the technical talent. He might have borrowed money from friends to hire the technical talent, but that would not directly have done much, if anything, to help generate demand for surveying stakes, his objective at the time. He needed the mechanical engineer as a partner to help with the technical work.

The mechanical engineer could also have developed the product on his own. But he too did not really have enough capital. He also lacked the kind of understanding of the application of the control device that the civil engineer had.

Interestingly enough, both men had prior entrepreneurial experience, and in both cases it was less than satisfactory. The civil engineer had failed to sell enough stakes to sustain a business. The mechanical engineer had helped start a concrete products company, but after twelve years, it finally failed. This new joint effort survived, although in 1970 the mechanical engineer left the company, filing a lawsuit to obtain cash for his share of the ownership. The company continued and prospered, illustrating that the entrepreneurial team needed for creating a company may be different from the managerial team needed to lead it in the long run.

Venture teaming was not over for the mechanical engineer when he left this venture, the second of his start-up experiences, however:

■ *In 1963, while the two engineers were still struggling to get their new control device ready for market, an electronic technician working for the same large aerospace company also became discontented working as "just a number" in the huge organization. It occurred to him that perhaps he could build upon the love he felt for boats and his knowledge of electronic hardware to set up a repair service for marine electronic equipment, particularly boat radios and depth sounders. With $1,000 in savings, he opened a small shop, starting as a repairman and then expanding into installation and sales, taking in a partner along the way to increase his company's capacity to grow. By 1970, when the mechanical engineer was quitting the control device business, the marine electronics enterprise was prospering with fourteen full-time employees, a solid set of market contacts and a good reputation.*

Among other things, it had become the second largest dealer for a particular line of electronic depth sounders. They were high in quality, but the company that made them had found greater profit potential in a different product line and began to neglect the sounder market. Deliveries became slow and service poor. The technician sensed market opportunity for a competitive product. But he felt incapable of designing a new sounder by himself. Then a rush order came for a sounder that was not in stock. The technician called the manufacturer for help and was outraged to be told that it could not be shipped because the manufacturer was having a picnic for its employees that day.

Inspired to seek a new source of supply, the technician learned that one of his neighbors, the mechanical engineer who had left the controls company, was currently consulting on design jobs and might be able to help. The mechanical engineer became interested, talked to a few boat dealers to assess the market and the nature of what was needed. But he too had a problem, in that his knowledge of electronics was limited. He had been in touch with a colleague who was an electronics engineer at the controls company, however, and this man decided to leave the controls company and join in the formation of a new company as a partner.

With that, two new companies were formed. The mechanical and electronic engineers formed a company to manufacture a new depth sounder, and the electronics technician formed a new company to sell it, cashing in his share of the former repair and sales partnership to provide seed capital for the new enterprise. Each of these two companies then went on to develop its own new directions. The mechanical and electronic engineers pursued custom product design and manufacturing, eventually developing their own product lines. The electronics technician expanded his sales company beyond the depth sounders to include other lines, including proprietary lines of his own, which were basically copies of existing products manufactured for him in Asia.

Thus the breakup of one partnership, after it had successfully created a new company, opened the way for the formation of two more companies. It can be difficult to pick out "the" entrepreneur in these formations because they are truly joint efforts. It may be possible to attribute discovery of the venture idea more to one partner than the other, or the contribution of physical resources, personal contacts, and other needed key ingredients. Sometimes, one partner contributes more time than the other to a venture, especially in the earliest stages, but often the full energies of both are required, as was true in this last chain of start-ups.

Two important questions that quickly arise in the development of partner-ships are how to find the "right" partners and what to include in the partnership contract, particularly concerning the division of ownership. If an active partner is needed, as in the previous example, the first of these questions is likely to be answered by work experience. People's accomplishments on prior jobs should be the first consideration. Beyond that are questions of personal compatibility, which can be trickier. Finding out what each partner is likely to add to the picture and what each partner expects out of the venture has to be negotiated individually for each partnership.

Legal Formats

There are two legal formats to be considered: the corporation and the partnership. A partnership, like a proprietorship, identifies the business with its owners, so that liabilities of the partnership become those of the owners personally as well. If a partner withdraws or dies, the partnership terminates. For tax pur-poses, income of the business is considered income of its owners. Its terms and conditions need not be written down to be in effect, or they can be spelled out in detail. In other words, a partnership can go into effect automatically, in which case all partners will be considered equal owners by law, and one partner can commit the others to obligations whether they know it or not. Hence, it needs to be regarded with caution.

Alternatively, the company can be set up as a separate entity in a corporate form. This requires formal paperwork but offers the advantages, as noted earlier, of limiting owners' liability, of continuing whether individual owners do or do not, and of certain tax options. Paradoxically, attorneys generally recommend the corporate form to their clients but use the partnership form for their own law firms.

Often entrepreneurs operate as a proprietorship if there is only one owner and the business is small. If partners are involved and/or the company starts to grow substantially, most elect to form a corporation. Partners usually have little idea about what is in the articles of incorporation or the bylaws once the company gets going, unless trouble turns up in the form of an Internal Revenue Service audit or a dispute among shareholders. Those are the times when handling pro-cedures according to the book becomes important. The figure or formula setting forth the value to be placed upon shares, for example, can be important if one of the partners wants to withdraw.

Finding Potential Partners

In assessing a venture's initial requirements, it may be possible to foresee some need for additional partners at various times in the future and to develop a time schedule for developing the team. Perhaps there will be more need for technical people at first, then marketing and production experts later on. Like any forecast, the expectation may be wrong. It will be well both to anticipate such needs and to maintain flexibility to respond to unforeseen needs. Partners can discuss situations that might occur and require additional partners to set aside shares of ownership specifically for future unknown recruitment.

Only the end result of the searching process for partners is obvious — the way the new partner became connected to the venture can be traced. There may have been a host of other connections that were attempted without success along the way. The entrepreneur mentioned earlier who recalled that "We needed someone who could set up an operation" apparently had already acquired an appropriate contact earlier and needed only to scan his memory quickly to identify that person, recalling "I thought right away of Tom."

A wide search had to be performed by the electronic technician who could not find a good source of depth sounders. All the elements of his searching, including the scanning of his own memory, are not known. But he did discuss the need with his partner, who in turn scanned his own memory and recommended a neighbor. That was still not the end, because the mechanical engineer had to search among his own contacts, where he found the needed link to the electrical engineer.

All these instances illustrate the vital role of collecting and building personal contacts, even though it may not be clear that any given contact will be needed later. When the need does arise, the list can be scanned and action can be taken to draw together a workable alliance. Even if the "right" contact is not already at hand when the need comes, accelerated contact development activity can be undertaken. Although it will cost valuable time, it should be able to turn up the people needed. James I. Stockwell, a founder of Adage, Inc., described how this can be done:

■   *Suppose you are looking for a marketing man, a financial specialist, and a foreman. Here are some examples of the type of talent search you might initiate.*

1.   *You and your co-founder are both engineers for a large corporation. Together you have invented a new computer memory device, and now you need a marketing specialist to complete your team.*
   a.   *Pick a successful man in one of the smaller companies that will be a competitor. Arrange a meeting, and discuss your plans with him. Ask him if he would be interested in joining you. If he isn't, does he know someone who might be? If he is frustrated in his present job, he may be ready for a change. If he has enjoyed building up his present company and wants to remain, he may want to give a similar opportunity to one of his subordinates or to a friend in a competitor's plant.*
   b.   *Talk to a salesman who is familiar with your product, someone you might want to hire when you can afford a full-time salesman. Ask him about his boss's marketing experience and interests. If his boss seems to be the type of person you are looking for, ask the salesman to set up a meeting for you.*
   c.   *Visit a supplier for your major source of raw material. He should know marketing men in your field and may be willing to recommend potential associates if he considers you a future customer.*
2.   *You have invented a biodegradable detergent and, together with a marketing man, are ready to form a new company. Neither of you has a business or financial background.*
   a.   *Visit a bank where you are known. Talk to a loan officer about your plan, and ask him if he can suggest a financial specialist for your company. If he has no suggestions*

of his own, ask for the name of a loan officer in a larger bank who might provide
leads. (If a bank executive recommends someone whom you eventually hire, you may
be on your way to establishing a line of credit.)

b. Contact a member of an accounting firm that prepares audits for a competitor of
yours or a company in a similar field. Independent auditing firms are identified in
corporate annual reports, which are on file in most business college libraries. Tell your
story to the person you have chosen, and ask for leads. There may be a manager or
junior manager in his firm who is eager to get into industry.

c. Ask your physician for leads. Since he is probably in a high income bracket, he may
know investment bankers or other financiers and may have heard of a financial man
looking for a change.

3. You are starting a new company that will make printed circuit boards. You already have
financial and marketing experts on your team, but you need a foreman to oversee plating
operations.

a. Visit a plant where similar devices are manufactured, in the role of a potential
customer. Ask for a tour of the facilities. Take careful note of the best-run facilities.
Find out the foreman's name, and call him later on to see if he can give you a contact.

b. Make a "sales call" on a large manufacturer with facilities of his own who may use a
small company for specialty runs. Tour the plants, and look for well-organized
facilities. Then make your own contacts.[25]

All these actions involve getting out and talking to people about the need.
The list of possible people to ask and conceivable ways they might be able to help
can easily be extended by further thought. Beyond that are the more formal
approaches of advertising and engaging professional searchers. These methods can
turn up any number of additional candidates. Clearly, there will be time constraints for obtaining the help, and this raises two points. It is advantageous to have
developed contacts in advance of the need, so that quick mental scanning, rather
than further visits and conversations, may lead more directly to the needed person.
Second, the searching should be done judiciously, working from leads most likely
to pay off and selecting with care. In addition to saving time, this shrewdness
should help avoid the cost and pain of getting into an unsatisfactory partnership
arrangement—unfortunately, there seem to be many of those in the annals of
entrepreneurship.

Selecting

According to conventional wisdom, becoming partners with friends is not a
good idea. But according to a *Venture* poll, only 6 percent of respondents, mostly
among the older ones, ruled it out. Almost half indicated some reluctance to deal
with friends, but a third thought friendship was irrelevant, and 14 percent said they
preferred to deal with friends. "When you go into business with a friend, you have
to deal with everything on two levels, which sometimes produces negative results,"
one respondent said.[26]

[25]James I. Stockwell, "How to Find and Attract Your Key Employees." P. 41 in William D. Putt, *How to
Start Your Own Business* (Cambridge, MA: MIT Press, 1974).
[26]Nancy Madlin, "Do Business and Friendship Mix," *Venture* (March 1985), p. 27.

Depending on the reason for having a particular partner, there will be several important criteria for selection. One concerns values and personal compatibility with the founder and other members who may be on the team. Second is technical competence appropriate to the candidate's anticipated role. Third is the time and energy that the person can contribute to the venture. Put another way, will the person pull his or her weight? Finally, there is the matter of ownership division. Will there be enough for all, and can agreement be reached on how to "cut the pie"?

It is most important to avoid clashes in values between the partners. These range from relatively minor ("he was too careless about money") to major ("she was a crook"). Sometimes the undesired qualities may be readily apparent ("I didn't like his smoking"). Other times they may only be revealed by the pressure of crises in the venture.

There may be little choice but to accept a conflict in values going into a partnership. Collins and Moore claim, in fact, that conflict is inevitable because the typical entrepreneur's need for autonomy is bound to impel him or her sooner or later to squeeze partners out to escape "the dominating, unreliable figures which have plagued him all his life."[27] In the following example, the entrepreneur foresaw problems from the outset but went ahead anyway, as he describes here, to get needed capital from a partner.

■ *He wanted a deal that he could take his money and get out any time he wanted to. Right then I smelled a rat. That tipped me off to the kind of guy he was. My lawyer advised me, "Don't make that kind of a deal under any circumstance. It's not a real partnership." All right, but what could I do? I needed the money that week, or the whole deal fell through. I signed the partnership papers. He thought he had me over a barrel.*[28]

The squeeze-out to come was also based upon the company's need for capital. Unbeknown to the partner who invested, the entrepreneur in this case stretched out accounts payable to suppliers to an extreme degree, something he was able to accomplish because those suppliers were hard up for sales. The partner, upon learning this, was very upset and stormed out. Now he was set for the kill, as the entrepreneur continued:

■ *I called him and told him there was no way out. I told him there was just enough money to buy him out, and I'd buy. I'd gotten him into the mess and if it was the last thing I did, I'd get him out. The damn fool. If we were going under he couldn't get out. We couldn't take his money out with all the debts we had. That would have been fraud. The firm bought him out for exactly what he put in. Not a cent more. Hell, we'd been making deliveries and the checks were coming in. We were in good shape, although we didn't have much cash. He didn't stop to think or investigate. He was a coward.*[29]

[27]Collins and Moore, *The Organization Makers*, p. 91.
[28]Ibid., p. 163.
[29]Ibid., p. 166.

How the squeezed-out partner felt about this outcome was not reported. He took a chance with his investment, entered under a cautiously written agreement, did not put much effort into the venture, apparently experienced a period of fear, and eventually came out with his money intact but no profit. He took a gamble and did not happen to win. But at least he came out even and with the benefit of an adventure and some education. So it may not have been too negative an experience, but the next time he would likely choose his partner with more attention to personal values.

A second important criterion for selecting a teammate is competence for the role he or she is to play in the enterprise. The following case illustrates how problems can arise along this dimension:

■ *An entrepreneur had worked in rebuilding and repairing a certain type of machine. From this experience, he had conceived of a new design that would perform better. He made and demonstrated a prototype that worked well, and now he wanted to go into business to produce and sell it. Because his expertise was technical, he decided it would be desirable to bring in someone with strong business experience to help raise the half million dollars needed from investors to get the company going. After a brief search, he succeeded in recruiting a man who had previously been president of a company with annual sales of $50 million.*

The new executive went to work and soon, as the entrepreneur recalled it, had the company in serious trouble. Lacking specialists to assure that details were properly cared for as they had been in his former large company, the new man handled things himself and blundered. Among other things, he negotiated terms with investors that in effect would turn the company entirely over to them. To head this off, the entrepreneur utilized the controlling interest that he still held to discharge the new president and kill the deal. The company now was strapped for cash. The entrepreneur took the extreme action of canceling all outstanding sales orders and scaling activities back once again to rebuilding and repair work. Later, after a period of retrenching, he again embarked on a capital raising effort, succeeded, and went into manufacturing.

Many other entrepreneurs can report unhappy results from bringing in executives whose prior experience in big businesses or governmental agencies did not qualify them to develop embryonic companies, although there have obviously been success stories of executives turned entrepreneurs (though very rarely from government employment).

Lack of balance between founders in the degree of commitment to the enterprise is a third area where problems frequently arise during start-ups, and later on as well. It is far easier to contemplate and discuss prospects and actions required for launching a venture than to buckle down and put in the long and often frustrating hours of work needed. The following entrepreneur found it was easy to sign people up on the prospect of jointly creating a new enterprise, but somehow they all disappeared when pressed by other commitments:

■ *An architecture graduate student had spent several years as an officer in the U.S. Army where he had given thought to a novel design for a camping trailer that would be compact when towed but would fold out several times larger for use when set up. When he left the army, where he had managed several large projects, and returned to school, the trailer idea stayed with him. To get his degree, he was required to develop a major project, and he decided to fulfill this requirement by building a working model of his trailer, which he would use to solicit sales for additional units and thereby create a trailer manufacturing business.*

This project was for only one course. Because he was taking several other courses, it was clear that he could not do the whole job alone. He began recruiting other students with the prospect that they might participate in the business. Some other architecture students, a law student, and several from business administration joined him. Soon he had nearly a dozen, a small number compared to groups he had run in the army. The trailer began to take shape as they eagerly pitched in. But their enthusiasm waned a bit after the first excitement of "joining." Then as the school term wore on, their other studies began to load up. When their midterms arrived, most dropped everything to study. The entrepreneur soon found that working time of the typical member had shrunk to where he was spending almost as much of his own time directing each of them as they were spending on the trailer work. By term end, with final examinations approaching, he was working almost single-handedly with the aid of one man whom he hired with money borrowed from the bank to get the trailer ready for display at a recreational vehicle show. As it turned out the trailer was finished and displayed, but sales failed to materialize.

Failure of team members to "come through and deliver" happens not only in hours of work, but often also in terms of contributing resources to the enterprise. Withdrawal of one member puts an even heavier load on the others and can thereby cause the whole team to collapse. This is why venture capitalists like to see all founders in a venture put up their own money as evidence of commitment before looking for capital from others.

A fourth potential partnership problem seen in this venture was having too many members on the team initially. This cost the entrepreneur an inordinate amount of coordination time, much more than he received back in effort from the participants. Had his enterprise succeeded, it would have cost in salaries and ownership as well. This would have diluted the rewards and consequently the participants' incentive. That dilution alone can be enough to wreck a partnership, as the following example from Collins and Moore illustrates:

> ■ *Although things were getting better, they were also getting worse. We were coming up against a stone wall. Ed and Bill were getting increasingly restless. They had sunk their savings in this thing, and they were getting less out of it than if they were on wages somewhere else.*[30]

To avoid outcomes like these, entering into partnership calls for caution and moderation. Self-assessment is often stressed in writings on entrepreneurship as important for determining *whether* a person should undertake venturing, and it may indeed have value for this purpose. But an even more important reason for doing self-assessment can be to define clearly whether partners are needed, just what they are needed for, and at what stage in the development of the enterprise. Then the prospective partners themselves need to be carefully evaluated as well. In

---

[30]Collins and Moore, *The Organization Makers*, p. 192.

general, it is often better to go as far as possible without them first, then add only those whose special ability happens to fit what is needed and who can be counted upon to deliver. A good way to test this quality can be to invite informal participation of the prospective partner first as a test. An example of this approach is recalled by Putt from his own experience as a team member:

■ *Harry Forster's approach to selecting partners for the Holograph Corporation was typical, I believe. When the potential of "holographic" signs became apparent, he invited six friends and associates to help him develop a company around his idea. The group included men with strong technical, marketing and financial abilities. I had been a friend of Harry's since our undergraduate days and was one of the people he approached. We were all invited to participate in the startup process on weekends and, later, for longer periods. Harry asked us to help in writing proposals, developing the product, raising money, making sales, and defining the business. He found that some assignments were done well; others, not so well. The problem was that several people were inconsistent. When they had free time, they were happy to work on the project. But family, job, and recreational activities always took precedence. This is a good way to tell if a prospective partner is willing to make sacrifices for the new enterprise. But it would be a mistake to reject anyone too early. It takes a certain length of time for a person to become so committed to a venture that he is willing to change his life-style.*

Further along in the development of the business, Harry needed small amounts of money to pay rent, hire a secretary, send out mailings, and so forth. He periodically asked us to help — not with large sums, but as much as $100 or $200 at a time. He also asked us to take some time off from our jobs to visit potential investors and customers.

After several months, Harry decided to formalize the company's structure. We all worked together on the terms of incorporation and the division and price of company stock. Harry had the final say on all decisions. We determined that any partner who decided to withdraw from the company must sell his stock back to the company at its original price. Harry then offered ownership to several people. All of us were interested, but some balked at the investment of $700 to $1,000 for stock before more conclusive product tests were made. When the negotiations came to an end, Harry and I were the only ones left. Harry then proposed terms that I found reasonable. The split was approximately 65 percent for him and 35 percent for me.

It might well be asked why I did not request 49, 50, or 51 percent, since there were only two of us remaining as founders of the company. Several considerations influenced my thinking about the appropriate percentage. The first was that, as the creator of the idea around which the company was being built, Harry was contributing more to the formation of the company than I was. Second, I was not concerned about management control at that stage of the company's history, since I felt that on important issues I would be able to exert a certain amount of reason to affect such decisions. Third, I believed that if a voting confrontation developed, I could form a coalition with the investors of outside funding, which was going to be required. Finally, although Harry originally offered me 40 to 45 percent of the company, I turned it down because I thought doing so would solidify our working relationship. I also felt that 35 percent was sufficient to allow me to earn a great sum of money if we achieved our goals.[31]

Here the entrepreneur started off with a fairly large number of people on the team, but only informally. When it came time to formalize relationships, only two

---

[31]Putt, *How to Start Your Own Business*, p. 24.

partners were left, so the company began essentially with a small but proven relationship between its founders.

Dividing Ownership

As soon as two or more people agree to work together as partners, questions arise. An early one is the matter of ownership. The law automatically assumes an even split, unless formal arrangements are set up differently. Baty urges his readers to be especially frugal with ownership and says "do not take on a partner if you can hire a person for the same role . . . do not allow your normal sense of democracy to cause you to part with more stock than is needed to give your partner the motivation to use his full energies."[32] In his study of equity distribution in start-ups, McMullan found that stock sharing often led to later problems.[33]

The resolution of responsibilities can be especially important in setting up a partnership. Amid the flurry of start-up activities, such division can be glossed over, but doing so can come to haunt the firm later, as Eliot Hoffman and two other founders of Just Desserts, Inc., recalled:

■   *"We all baked and washed dishes. Then I generated sales by taking whole cheese cakes to restaurants. Soon we developed a waiting list of 40 restaurants. We couldn't keep up." However, before long conflicts arose and, as another founder, Barbara Radcliff, recalled "it was a nightmare." For instance, Hoffman took on growing problems in leasing and financing, but then other partners found him unavailable when needed in production. But, he said, "giving up the kitchen was like tearing my heart out." Another partner, Fay Sills, responded "Just let me know where your [authority] stops and mine starts." Eventually a consultant was hired to help sort out the organization.[34]*

Bruno and Tyebjee reported in a 1985 survey of 145 high technology firms that there were typically two to four founders who shared ownership equally. They observed:

■   *While this distribution arrangement can later create animosity and lead to difficulties due to disproportionate contribution in time and skill by founding members, rarely are such difficulties anticipated by the founders. . . . The division of ownership must reflect past, present, and future contributions to the success of the enterprise. In addition, the probability of the premature departure of a founder to the detriment of the start-up must be minimized. Probably, the most satisfactory approach is to use a vesting provision that accrues common stock ownership over time, thus inhibiting premature departures.[35]*

---

[32]Gordon B. Baty, *Entrepreneurship for the Eighties* (Reston, VA: Prentice Hall, 1981), p. 42.

[33]W. Ed McMullan, "In the Interest of Equity." P. 397 in Karl H. Vesper, *Frontiers of Entrepreneurship Research, 1982* (Wellesley, MA: Babson Center for Entrepreneurial Studies, 1982).

[34]Nina Easton, "The Art of Partnership Survival," *In Business* (May–June 1984), p. 34.

[35]Bruno and Tyebjee, "The Entrepreneur's Search For Capital," p. 63.

The split of ownership determines who has control and can be handled in a number of ways. Ray Stata tried two of them, which he recalled as follows:

■ *In my first company, all three of the partners were equal, and the president was picked by flipping a coin. We made the naive assumption that this office would rotate annually, a very convenient way to avoid the question of leadership. Communication between two partners is difficult, but agreement can usually be reached through a process of give-and-take. Among three people communication is impossible. You seldom can reach a unanimous agreement. Someone almost always ends up on the losing side of a two-to-one vote. The result is an environment frought with insecurity. . . .*

In my second company, partnership conflicts became less intense because there were only two of us. Nevertheless, the basic problem was not resolved. Our first experience should have taught us something, but once again we ignored the need to choose one boss. This time, we divided the company in half, each partner having total authority in his own fiefdom. . . . As the company grew, this separation caused severe problems.[36]

Deciding how ownership should be split in a working partnership can become complicated, even to the extent that it defeats the advantages of joining forces. A first step can be to divide everything equally. From there, readjustments could be considered in cases where each partner contributes something different. Reasoning about readjustments can be based on the following:

- If one partner is contributing most of the money, that partner should have a larger share, or should be entitled to repayment of the money, guaranteed by the other partners, with interest.
- If one partner is contributing the core concept and will be the leader in running the business, that partner should have control and a larger share of ownership.
- If one partner will be both more indispensable and harder to replace, that partner should receive a larger share of ownership.

If one partner brings the venture idea and certain technical expertise, while the other contributes more financial savings and business contacts, how should the balance of control and/or ownership be struck? The answer may depend on other factors, such as which partner needs a job more in the new venture, or which will have the most time to give to it. How hard it would be to replace either person may be another crucial element.

What each partner most cares about may be an additional consideration. If, for instance, one is more concerned with financial security to support a family, then perhaps that partner might prefer to contribute through a loan to the enterprise, rather than to take equity. If one partner can go with little or no salary, while the other has financial responsibilities and needs a steady salary, then the sharing of ownership in the venture might be shifted accordingly. Ideally, partners with smaller shares would take the view that a small piece of something is better than a bigger piece of nothing, and what's most important is to make the business a

[36]Raymond S. Stata, "Opening Strategies," in Putt, *How to Start Your Own Business*, p. 17.

success. If they feel the division is unfair, however, it may be hard for them to see it that way.

A starting point, as suggested above, could be an agreement that if each partner contributed the same amount to the venture idea, the capitalization, and the job of building the venture while taking the same salary out, then ownership shares should be equal. The discussion can then go on to explore why anything other than equal might be more appropriate. If agreement on how a departure from equality cannot be arrived at, then any partner who feels shorted can decide whether to drop out or simply to accept the perceived short-change in order to get on with the venture, figuring that if the venture is successful enough, the short-change will not matter.

For investors who take a more detached and less personal perspective, and are involved more for the return on capital, there are more systematic approaches to determine how ownership should be divided, such as analysis of return on equity. These can add helpful insights in the division of seed stage ownership as well as later stage investments. They are discussed in Chapter 6. In the next example, however, the investor believed equality of ownership would be most effective in motivating and retaining the talent needed, so he used his resources to make that possible.

■   *An entrepreneur who was already wealthy from other ventures wanted to purchase shop facilities to make travel trailers, but he felt he needed two key partners, one expert in production and the other experienced in sales. Although he could finance the whole company himself, he believed the odds of success would be higher if the other key people had a vested interest in the business through major personal financial commitment. After a search he located two men whose prior experience and accomplishments seemed appropriate and who seemed willing to consider trading their present jobs for employment in a company where they could be co-owners.*

The three discussed how much money each could contribute to the company. One of the two recruits could come up with enough to cover his third of estimated needs for fixed assets, working capital, and start-up expenses, as could the wealthy founder. But the other man could not. So the wealthy founder offered to loan the company enough on a personal basis to cover that man's share until he could make it up out of salary. The wealthy founder further said that if the initial capitalization proved insufficient to get the company running profitably, he would personally loan enough additional cash to the business to see it through. That way, he pointed out, ownership of the other two partners would not be diluted by the additional capital he provided, while he would be able to recover his money without being taxed on it. He would be taxed on interest received, but the business would be able to take a tax reduction on the interest as an expense.

A systematic scheme for entrepreneurial team design has been suggested by Timmons.[37] Based upon experience with numerous venture teams, he observed that an "extended mating dance" can help appreciably in forming an effective

[37]Jeffry A. Timmons, *New Venture Creation*, 3rd ed. (Homewood, IL: Dow Jones Irwin, 1990), Chapter 7.

team, but that agreements reached early will likely become obsolete eventually, regardless of how carefully they are developed.

Forestalling Problems

All sorts of unforeseen and even improbable problems can arise in a partnership, even with a satisfactory beginning, as the following example illustrates:

■ *In early 1971, an eastern Washington man entered into a partnership agreement with an Oregon man for joint ownership of a laundromat that was part of a real estate enterprise the Oregon man was trying to develop in a small resort town on the Pacific Coast. It seemed to the Washington man to be an excellent opportunity. The Oregon man came well recommended and held a Ph.D. in psychology from a prominent California university. The laundromat was the only one in the town of 700 people where construction was soon to begin on 400 condominium apartments. The Oregon man had committed all his capital to buy the enterprise and now wanted to upgrade its fourteen-year-old equipment.*

A well-reputed attorney was engaged to draw up a partnership agreement in which the Washington man invested $5,000 to pay for eight new Maytag washers and a large Hitachi dryer, paid $400 worth of delinquent utility bills, and paid $1,500 to the Oregon man. In return, the Washington man retained ownership of the new machines for three years until fully depreciated, as a tax hedge, and received a half interest in the business. The agreement, carefully drawn, also provided that the Oregon man would collect and deposit the receipts in a joint account with the deposit slips sent to the Washington man and included conditions regarding resale and dissolution. Profits were to be divided equally. Both partners worked together to renovate the plumbing and install the new machines.

Opened in March 1971, the enterprise initially showed a loss because of the cold season and consequent lack of seaside tourist traffic, plus the expenses of start-up, travel, accelerated depreciation, and attorney's fees. By summer, however, receipts grew to $450 per week, and by September sales since opening reached $8,000, with a profit of $1,500.

In late summer, the Oregon man began upgrading the building, installing second-floor sleeping rooms, a dance floor, pool tables, and a soft drink area for teenagers. He arranged financing for a share of the interest in the enterprise, and to minimize labor costs, he helped work on the building. Then the problems began.

The Oregon man fell off a scaffold and required hospitalization, leaving care of the laundromat to an acquaintance. Receipts reported on deposit slips to the Washington partner dropped 75 percent. By the time the Oregon partner was released from the hospital, there were medical bills to pay on top of the creditors from the building work. He took a second job to pay off the bills, but then he was arrested on drug charges. He posted bail through a bondsman and arranged to trade his share of the laundromat for a relative's car. After selling off all the loose furniture and taking the rent checks and available cash, he then jumped bail and vanished.

The relative now had the laundromat keys and collected the money, but the building began to run down quickly and business dwindled. By early 1972, the utilities had been turned off and there was no hot water. Transients and vagrants began using the building, and the city council complained it was an eyesore and fire hazard.

The Washington partner sued for full title to the Oregon man's share of the laundromat, claiming the partnership agreement had been violated by the attempted transfer to the relative. He won that plus a judgment of some $400 from the relative. Not all of it could be collected, however, because the relative did not have that much. In addition, the Washington man found that the Oregon man had never owned the laundromat outright *and still owed $700 on it. Negotiation with the note holder obtained a settlement for $400.*

Now there were offers from several others in the coastal town to team up. They offered to run the laundromat in return for half the profits. But the Washington man had now become leery of distant partners, fearing skimming, shirking, and the like. Instead he put the business up for sale and rapidly succeeded in parting with his investment, coming away with a capital gain and a heightened awareness of the risks of partnership.

The Washington man learned several lessons from this experience. First, he should have done more checking on his prospective partner's background and prior behavior. Second, he had done well in choosing an attorney who had protected him with the written agreement so that when the Oregon man traded his share of the laundromat to another, he violated the agreement and gave up legal ownership to the Washington man. He further saw that he could have tended his interest better by sticking to a venture nearer his home. Still, he did come out with a small profit, and he was ready to enter more joint ventures.

Lessons about how to make a partnership work were learned by the engineering and architectural firm of Daniel, Mann, Johnson, and Mendenhall of Los Angeles in the 1950s. At that time, the company had over 300 employees and was doing business around the world, but problems of cooperation among partners with different personalities forced them to stop and reconsider how they worked together. These problems occurred substantially downstream from start-up but nevertheless could have helpful implications for how to develop a partnership. In brief, the problems they encountered were as follows:

1. Lack of consensus on votes
2. Suspicion and quarrels between partners
3. Imbalance between partners in workload
4. Partners' "pulling rank" and upsetting the work of subordinates
5. Confusion over partners' duties
6. Partners' operating outside the company strategy
7. Lack of coordination in such things as hiring
8. Confusion about what was going on ("Don't ask me")

A wide variety of remedies for these problems were explored, including hiring consultants, subjecting partners to psychological tests, putting a consultant in charge with an incentive contract (which worked until they made him a partner), rotating roles among partners, attempting to take on so much work that it would smother the problems and give them all more information than they needed, dividing into autonomous divisions, and hiring a team of professional managers. They found the following remedies to be helpful:

1. All partners draw equal salaries, with half of the profits reinvested.
2. Partners lead separate social lives.
3. Every job has at least one partner on it.
4. Each partner sees through at least one job per year.
5. All partners pass on all major designs.
6. All partner decisions must arrive at unanimous consensus.

7. One partner is a general manager clearly in charge.
8. All partners have dual roles: owners on policy matters, otherwise employees.
9. Annual meetings are held at which
    a. Each partner's performance is reviewed.
    b. Long-range plans are hammered out.
    c. General managers report on happiness, output, and suitability of each partner's job.
10. Monthly update meetings are held.
11. Any partner can call a complaint meeting.
12. A code of ethics operates in which each partner
    a. Takes responsibility for bringing in pro-rata share of business.
    b. Agrees not to make disparaging remarks about other partners.
    c. Agrees not to take arbitrary positions.

These policies were arrived at through a period of trial and error, and over time they have no doubt been further modified as conditions changed. Similarly, a new firm should expect that its relationships among team members will evolve and change. A start can be made by recognizing this fact and recognizing the value that conscious attention and thought can have. The process can begin, as Forster suggests, during a "moonlight" phase prior to startup when team members get together informally to design and plan the company, so that the formal relationships to follow will be soundly based.

Three rules for getting along with partners came from the experience of Stephen Thomas, who with two others formed a partnership in early 1979 that broke up two-and-a-half years later. These rules were

1. *Share equally.* In contributions of effort and money and in withdrawals of benefits such as time off and pay, there are continual pressures for inequality. These should be frankly discussed and resolved equitably.
2. *Write it down.* Although it seems tedious, recording expectations and understandings on paper can help prevent disappointments and disputes. This view is also stressed in a book by John Howell on how to prepare partnership agreements.[38]
3. *Be candid.* Untruths, even white lies such as to cover up subordinates' mistakes or other temporary bad news, undermine the company with false information that causes bad decisions.

As he looked back, Thomas said success followed when these rules were observed and failure followed when they were not.[39] The moral of these experiences appears to be that although many arrangements are possible, and may even work at times, it is generally necessary to have a clearly designated leader with authority for success in the long run. As experience in the partnership grows and problems arise, there may be repeated occasions when revision of operating rules is necessary. Consideration of such possibilities in advance may also provide a better basis for initial arrangements.

---

[38]John Howell, *Prepare Your Own Partnership Agreements* (Englewood Cliffs, NJ: Prentice Hall, 1980).
[39]Stephen G. Thomas, "Why Partnerships Break Up," *Inc.* (July 1981), p. 67.

Breakups

Regardless of how high the hopes for partner compatibility are, there should be a formal written contract with provision for parting of the ways if unresolvable disputes arise. The partnership agreement or corporate bylaws may provide that an owner must sell back shares to the company at a stipulated price upon leaving. Such a "buy-sell agreement" may also provide, through a "shoot-out clause," that a partner wishing to buy another partner out must be willing and must offer to sell at the same price he or she wants to buy. Then the other partner must agree either to sell at the offered terms or to buy at those same terms. How this can work appears in the following case from Collins and Moore.

> ▮ *He wanted either to buy my half or sell his half to me. He thought he had me in a bind because I had no money personally. I'd even mortgaged my house to put up my original investment. It was insulting. He was offering me just about what I'd put in in the first place. There was nothing to show for my year's work. I told him "All right, please put it in writing." That made it a firm offer which he was stuck with if I could meet it.*
>
> *Then I went to this young friend of mine, he was rich—that is, his father was rich. He talked to his father, and told me, "Okay, we're in." What actually happened was this. We went to the bank and he made me a personal loan which went into my personal account. I then got a certified check and went to this guy's office. "Here's your money. I'm meeting your offer." His face fell a mile. He had no idea I had that kind of money in cash. He tried to renege and withdraw his offer, but we had anticipated that. I laid another check for five thousand on his desk and said, "This is for getting out without making trouble. Of course, I can always take this to court and cost us both plenty." He accepted.*[40]

A "shoot-out clause" may or may not fully solve the problem of breakup. When founders of CMI Corp. sold out to an insurance company, then bought back some shares and sold others to employees, a "dual-option" or shoot-out provision was included in the deal. Subsequently, the founders offered to buy on the shoot-out provision. The insurance company responded by finding another buyer, then buying out the founders and reselling to the buyer. Next, the founders started another company that competed with the buyer, and lawsuits followed alleging theft of trade secrets by CMI's founders.[41]

In conjunction with buy-sell agreements, it is a common practice to have the corporation buy "key partner life insurance" that provides money for the company to buy out the shares of any partner who dies. An advantage of this insurance is that the premiums are tax-deductible expenses for the company.

An important contingency to consider is the possible death of a partner and what will happen to that person's interest in the company. Buy-sell agreements cover such possibilities, by providing either for *redemption* by the company of that person's shares, possibly paid for by a life insurance policy carried by the company on the person, or through *cross-purchase* of the person's shares by the surviving partner(s), possibly paid for by insurance carried by the surviving partner(s). Which is preferable depends largely on tax considerations.

---

[40]Collins and Moore, *The Organization Makers*, p. 166.
[41]Robert Preston, "It's Show Time Again for Encore," *Venture* (July 1988) p. 21.

Webster suggested as an archetypical entrepreneur one whose objective was to use partners as investors during the high-risk early part of start-up and then force them out by a "rapacious act" as soon as the risk drops and profit growth impends.[42] McMullan, Long, and Tapp found evidence that reacquisition of stock by founders does occur. In the view of those who acquire it, the main reasons are either "to reflect changing role expectations" or "to provide cash to the seller," and such acquisitions are most frequently made at what the buyers consider fair market value. Sellers' views, however, were not reported.[43]

PLANNING QUESTIONS

The following questions are intended to stimulate thought about what should be considered in moving ahead with a venture. Which questions best apply can vary among entrepreneurs and ventures, as can the order in which they should be considered, the priority that should be placed on them, and which of them should be answered in a written plan.

Solo Takeoff

- What are all the major tasks to be performed for start-up in each functional area of the venture: product development, testing, sales, finance, shop setup, production, quality control, servicing, accounting, and so on?
- Which tasks can the founder perform most effectively and which ones can others do better?
- How will the tasks be sequenced in time, and how long will each take to complete?
- List the potential sources of free help for this particular venture and what each might add.
- What are the pros and cons of going solo versus sharing ownership for this particular venture and founder(s)?
- If the venture does begin solo, what would be the pros and cons of incorporating?

External Team

- Who will be the company's legal, banking, accounting, and other professional advisers?
- In what ways, if any, are they different from those of competitors?
- Who will the directors be and what special capabilities, relative to competitors, will they bring to the venture?

Sharing Ownership

- What partners, if any, will most strengthen the venture and for what purposes?
- What experience and accomplishments (track record) will they bring that apply specifically to the needs of the venture?
- Who will the CEO and the key manager for each area of the venture be? (Include brief resumes in the appendix to the business plan.)

---

[42]Frederick A. Webster, "A Model for New Venture Initiation: A Discourse on Rapacity and the Independent Entrepreneur," *Academy of Management Review* (January 1976), p. 26.

[43]W. Ed McMullan, Richard Long, and Jay Tapp, "Entrepreneurial Share Transaction Strategies." P. 41 in Hornaday et al., *Frontiers of Entrepreneurship Research 1984.*

- What prior experience and accomplishments indicate their capacities to perform the managerial functions they will be assigned?
- How will these managers compare to competitors'? Are any key members of the venture team embroiled in problems outside the venture that could impair their performance inside it?
- Have checks been made with past references of key people to be sure backgrounds are as supposed?
- How will they be organized? (Include a chart in the appendix to the business plan.)
- What will the schedule of salaries and other compensation be, and how will it compare to competitors?
- What enticements will the venture use to retain key people and attract others needed in the future?
- How will shares (and possibly options) of the company be divided and among whom? What is the rationale?
- What additional shares will be set aside for future investors or employees?
- What can be done to cope with the possible loss of "irreplaceable" people in the venture?
- What means will be used to upgrade managerial skills if the venture grows?
- Has anyone left the venture in anger so far, and if so why and what threat, if any, might they represent?
- Have ground rules, both informal and formal, been worked out for getting along and possibly for breaking up?
- If the venture takes on partners, what would be the pros and cons of organizing as a partnership versus as a corporation?

POSSIBLE MILESTONES FOR A PLANNING TIME LINE

The most suitable milestones for a time line for a particular venture must be a function of the individual case. These that follow are intended to help stimulate thought about them.

- Completion of inventory of needed capabilities versus time
- Needed professionals identified
- Founder capabilities assessed
- Necessary team members identified
- Background checks completed
- First team member recruited
- Directors, if any, recruited
- Entire starting team recruited
- Company's legal form set up

Chapter 5

INSIDE EQUITY CAPITAL

INTRODUCTION

Marshaling capital is a crucial step in most ventures. It can be viewed as permission to apply society's resources, which is virtually always necessary for any substantial enterprise. The exception is an entrepreneur who needs only his or her own personal energy and time, and nothing else. An independent sales agent may be able to start that way, although even then he or she will need business cards and stationery and possibly an office, phone, and travel resources. Most start-ups require more than that.

There is much folklore on this popular and intriguing subject:

"It takes money to make money."
"There's always money available for a truly good idea."
"The best idea in the world is worthless if nobody buys it."
"The best time to find capital is when you don't need it."
"Failing companies often believe more money would save them, but in fact it would not."

Start-ups typically begin by using founders' personal savings for initial business necessities and income while the venture gets started. After that, borrowing may be possible, and as the business develops, its own earnings may help. If those sources, which include the first nine listed in Table 5–1, are sufficient, the founders may be able to retain all ownership, as this chapter will

TABLE 5-1 Sources of Capital

Inside Equity Sources

1. Savings
2. Working partners
3. Employees

Debt (Sometimes Outside Equity) Sources

4. Friends and relatives
5. Customers
6. Suppliers
7. Banks
8. Leasing
9. Community development corporations
10. Asset-based lenders

Outside Equity Sources (see Chapter 6)

11. Private placement
    Angels and silent partners
    Corporate investors and joint ventures
    Foreign
12. Venture capital
13. Public offering

discuss. If not, then equity must be shared with outsiders to obtain additional capital (see Chapter 6).

Retaining Equity

How much ownership to sacrifice in order to obtain capitalization during start-up is a common dilemma among founding entrepreneurs. Recognizing the conflict, Raymond Stata, the founder of two successful high technology companies concluded that retaining as much equity as possible for as long as possible was usually best:

■ *In the earliest stages of start-up, the value of your company's stock will be negligible. But value increases rapidly with even the most meager accomplishment. If you quit your present job, spend $300 to incorporate, rent a building, and hang out a shingle, you are creating value. You are also making it clear to potential associates that you are in charge. If you can finance the development of your product with your own money, you are making a healthy start. If you can book even one purchase order, you are on your way to convincing investors that you have a viable operation. Go as far as you can before looking for outside backing. And then fight to hold on to a major share of ownership, even if it means less working capital.*[1]

---

[1]William D. Putt, *How to Start Your Own Business* (Cambridge, MA: MIT Press, 1974), p. 13.

Some well-known companies that started with borrowed money include Avon (1886, $500), Goodyear (1898, $13,500), and Singer (1850, $40). Most start-ups are seeded primarily or exclusively with founders' savings. Hewlett and Packard, for example, began their company in 1939 with combined personal savings of $438.[2]

The National Federation of Independent Businesses reported that among its members, most of whom are small firm entrepreneurs, 48 percent used personal savings and 29 percent used bank loans for start-up, as shown in Table 5–2. Other important sources were the savings of friends, relatives, and partners and then, as the company got going, and trade credit from suppliers. For an extremely small fraction of ventures, support from professional venture capitalists and even public offerings were used for initial funding.

The financing of the following start-ups did not involve sharing equity outside the business:

■ *Tracy Barnes and two fellow balloon enthusiasts pooled their savings to make prototypes for display at the world championships, then required 50 percent payment in advance on orders to finance production.*

■ *John Rector borrowed $2,000 from family, $1,000 from friends, $8,000 from a bank and persuaded a supplier to give him 120 days credit to open a bar.*

■ *Beverly Red borrowed $8,000 from family to start manufacturing toys.*

■ *Bill Grady raised $5,000 from his savings and the cash value of his life insurance, which he extended with a $5,000 bank loan to start a blower manufacturing company.[3]*

■ *Rudi Wiedemann started LaserSense, an electronics company, initially with personal savings augmented with $100,000 from sale of rights to use his technology in a specific application for a single six-month period.[4]*

TABLE 5–2 Use of Different Financing Sources[5]

Savings		48%
Banks, other institutional lenders		29
Friends		13
Individual investors		4
Venture capital firms	less than	1
Government	less than	1
Other		5
TOTAL		100%

[2]Royal Little, "Shoestring Financing of Great Enterprises," *Journal of Business Venturing*, 2 (no. 1), 1.

[3]The four examples listed here are from "Seeds of the Future," *Venture* (October 1979), p. 53.

[4]"Alternatives to Venture Funding," Santa Clara, Silicon Valley Entrepreneurs Club, *The Achiever*, 2 (no. 4) (November-December 1988), 5.

[5]"Where Entrepreneurs Get Start-Up Cash," *The Wall Street Journal*, November 24, 1980, p. 33.

These examples also illustrate how financing sources work in combinations and vary from one venture to another.

Financing Stages

Those whose profession is the financing of ventures often view the ventures in terms of such stages as the following:

Seed Money is a relatively small amount of cash, typically up to a couple hundred thousand dollars, to enable an entrepreneur to prove out a concept with such things as prototype development and market research.

Startup Capital is money provided to set up production and develop initial sales of the venture's product or service. It may be several hundred thousand dollars or more, depending upon what is appropriate to carry the venture through the first year or so.

First Stage Financing is a term sometimes synonymous with startup capital and other times used to distinguish the cash provided by outsiders to extend the startup capital, which may have been more provided by founders themselves. It is associated with commencement of full scale operations and market development which may extend beyond startup.

Second Stage Financing is usually used to finance expansion through provision of more working capital for receivables, inventory, advertising and other production and sales efforts. For a venture seeking this capital, which may be a year or so into startup, achievement of a net profit is typically becoming an important issue. However, some ventures, particularly in services, are expected to become profitable earlier while others, such as those requiring major product development efforts may take several years to reach a breakeven point.

Mezzanine Financing is typically for major expansion well into profitability.

Bridge Financing is provided sometimes when a company sees still further major expansion ahead for which it will go public to raise the funds. The bridge money carries it during the period that the public offering is worked out and sold. This is usually a fairly short period, on the order of a few weeks; and the bridge money, while it may be large in amount, is not needed for long. Those who put the money up, because they see it as both a bother to pull the money together and a fairly high risk if the public issue does not sell, are able to ask for a fairly stiff payment in interest and possibly options. When viewed in relation to the time the money is out, these payments typically constitute a tremendously high rate of return for the financiers and correspondingly high cost of capital to the venture. To avoid this cost the venture may be wise to anticipate the time gap to public offering and begin the process earlier rather than waiting until the capital from public offering is desperately needed.

Although these stages can be conceived of as fairly orderly and sequential, there is no necessary match for any particular venture, each of which may have its own special departures from any norm.

Classifications

Which sources should be used for a given venture may depend on many things—personality, economic times, contacts, location, and other idiosyncratic factors. Some determinants include the following:

Entrepreneur—Experience, wealth level, qualifications.

Venture—Capital intensity, profitability, types of customers, liquidity, repayment schedule.

Industry maturity—A more mature industry usually requires more massive start-up capital.

Amount needed—Later stages usually need larger amounts, raising the probability of more widespread ownership.

Applications—Product development, legal services, working capital (receivables versus inventory), fixed assets (custom versus general purpose, real estate), advertising, and so on.

Preference for debt versus equity—The two are different, with debt requiring repayment and usually carrying interest and with equity conveying ownership not requiring either repayment or interest. But often the distinction is blurred by use of debt, possibly at no interest but allowing the option of repayment or conversion into equity. Other variations include preferred stock requiring redemption or allowing conversion to common stock, use of options, warrants, and so forth.

Time and circumstances of need—Varies from case to case.

Financing options discovered—Financing opportunities vary greatly with the times, the source, and the entrepreneur who wants it; it is common for an entrepreneur to have approached many sources to find the one that is appropriate.

Considering these factors can help avoid the pitfall of wasting time in pursuit of capital sources that are not appropriate to the venture. Other pitfalls can be avoided by having a lawyer look over the terms of any deal, especially if it is not in standard form and/or from an experienced and highly reputable source.

CASH REQUIREMENTS

Varying capitalization needs from one venture to another can be seen in the following examples, as well as others to be described later:

- Proctor & Gamble, 1837, began with capital of $7,192.
- Eastman Kodak, 1880, invested capital of $3,000.
- Gillette Razor, 1901, invested capital of $5,000.
- Ford Motor, 1903, invested capital of $28,000.
- Textron, 1923, began with no equity and a $10,000 bank loan.[6]

Financial needs also vary with the industry, as can be seen from the results of a 1986 *Venture* poll that drew 843 responses (Table 5–3).[7] Most service industry firms started with smaller amounts, whereas over 80 percent of high technology and manufacturing firms required more than $50,000 to start and almost none were started with less than $10,000.

[6]Royal Little, *How to Lose $100,000,000 and Other Valuable Advice*; also Joseph Mancuso, "Shoestring Financing," *The Entrepreneurial Manager's Newsletter*, 2 (no. 5) (1981), 6.

[7]"Financing Your Business," *Venture* (October 1986), p. 24.

TABLE 5–3   Start-Up Capital Needs by Industry

INDUSTRY	<$10,000	$10,000	>$50,000	TOTAL
High tech and manufacturing	2%	16%	82%	100%
Finance/Other	18	29	53	100
Retail/Wholesale	20	48	32	100
Service	39	34	27	100

Needs may also vary within an industry, not only because of the specific function and strategy of a given start-up, but also because of the stage of development of the industry. Firms that start with more capital often tend to be more successful, but not always. For instance, among ventures set up to supply fresh-squeezed orange juice, Duchesnau and Gartner found that during the early stages in the development of the industry, lower initial capitalization tended to correlate with higher long-run company success, while later in the development of the industry, companies that started with higher capitalization tended to be more successful. The reason was that equipment improved as the industry matured, and those firms that invested in it earlier found themselves saddled with obsolete equipment later on. Those that entered later with little capital could not afford the improved equipment.[8]

Minimizing Needs

One approach to making financial ends meet is to reduce the amount needed by cash conservation. Each line of the income statement and of the balance sheet can contain alternatives. By going through the statements line by line, it is fairly easy to think of many ways to conserve cash. Consider the following:

From the Income Statement

- *Rent*—If location is not important to customers, bargain for low-cost space and renovate minimally.
- *Salaries*—Founders can go with little or no pay (they can keep other jobs or get help from a spouse); hire as few employees as possible; use temporaries, consultants, part-timers; do not hire people to do what managers can do themselves, even if it is menial work.
- *Product components*—Adapt off-the-shelf items wherever possible, rather than tooling up for new ones.
- *R&D*—Suppliers may contribute greatly without charge.

From the Balance Sheet

- *Tools and equipment*—Buy from used equipment dealers and auctions; buy on time or lease.

---

[8]Donald A. Duchesnau and William B. Gartner, "A Profile of New Venture Success and Failure in an Emerging Industry." P. 372 in Bruce A. Kirchhoff, Wayne A. Long, W. Ed McMullan, Karl H. Vesper, and William E. Wetzel, Jr., *Frontiers of Entrepreneurship Research*, 1988 (Wellesley, MA: Babson Center for Entrepreneurial Studies, 1988).

- *Accounts receivable* — Scck prepayments; plead for prompt payment; offer discounts for prompt or early payment.
- *Inventory* — Order smaller batches; take care not to overstock; reach for "just-in-time" where possible, by having suppliers deliver to the venture precisely when needed and not before. No inventory piles up at the venture, which reduces capital needed for inventory and also reduces the need for space to store it. Against these advantages must be balanced the need to have variety and flexible quantities available for customers or for production. There may also be adverse effects on purchase quantity discounts.
- *Accounts payable* — Plead for credit, but do not delay withholding payments, employees' pay, or paying key suppliers unless they agree to it.

Trade-offs will often be required between minimizing cash needs and maximizing other desirable performance variables such as profitability, quality, speed, and demand on the entrepreneur's time.

For example, leasing, rather than buying, equipment reduces the need for paying cash out immediately. Moreover, the lease payments are tax deductible; hence, they reduce the cash that must be paid to the government in the short run. However, the equipment costs more to buy on a lease, and in the long run, leasing reduces profits more than buying would. Reducing cash needs is often advantageous in the short run, but profits are important in the longer term — both must be kept in mind.

Trade-offs also occur in connection with time. Rather than hiring a lawyer right away to do a patent search or set up a corporation, an entrepreneur could do some of the legal work personally. That would reduce legal expenses and corresponding cash outflows. But it will also take the entrepreneur's time away from other activities, and the entrepreneur will be slower than a lawyer at performing the legal work and progress of the venture will be correspondingly slowed.

Make or Buy

A decision that has major implications for the cash needs of the venture as well as other strategic elements is the extent to which it makes versus buys what it sells. Working in-house usually gives the founders tighter control, less need to travel, faster responses to communications, and less need to share profits. But farming out can require less capital investment for both equipment and inventory, easier changing of capacity, lower fixed costs, and a richer depth of experience in specialized functions performed by outside experts.

The notion of setting up a plant can be alluring. It provides solidity to the company. It can be built and equipment can be bought largely on borrowed money. Manufacturing margins tend to be higher than those in retailing and service. Physical structures may impress employees, bankers, associates, friends, and, in some lines of work, customers. But they require and hence immobilize large amounts of capital, and they diminish flexibility, because they usually cannot be modified easily or sold readily if the company shifts strategy — something small companies often do that gives them a substantial advantage over larger companies. Arthur P. Alexander, the president of one successful chemical company, recalls:

■ *"In 1962 my partner and I started our company with a total initial capitalization of $25. At the beginning we had no plant or equipment and no technical expertise in our particular field, the formulation of industrial chemicals."*

Alexander recalls that the choice of product was dictated by ease of entry considering the many aspects of capital investment, technology, competition, plant and equipment requirements, product development, sales effort, time to make first sale, simplicity of use, location of market, and so forth. Industrial adhesives seemed best to satisfy these criteria. They next contacted potential customers to test the idea of making those, asking whether there was room for another formulator, what products were needed, what were they now using, how much would they buy from the new company, and how much would they be willing to pay. They found that competitors were selling through sales representatives and concluded that by offering industrial adhesives in a small, clearly defined geographic area through direct salesmen, they should be able to enter the market.

By contacting suppliers they learned what formulas were used for the products, what technology was needed for each product line, and what industry should be easiest to penetrate. They also learned how to accomplish production without a plant, as Alexander recalled.

"Remember, we had no plant and equipment or money to invest in manufacturing. The raw material supplier told us that the type of equipment used to formulate our products was also used in several other noncompetitive industries. Thus we located a company that had the necessary equipment and available equipment time (nights and weekends) and was willing to subcontract the manufacture of our product line."

A disadvantage of this approach, using another company to make the product, is that there will likely be cost disadvantages to the entrepreneur, who consequently can have difficulty keeping up with competitors on price. Alexander commented on this aspect as follows:

■ *In our initial product line, we decided to price as high as the highest competitor's price. We justified this position by being able to offer something to the customer which he was not getting at the time from the existing suppliers—service. In a word, we were being more responsive to the customer's needs. This pricing technique was so successful over the years that it became yet another facet of our corporate image—high prices. This was probably the single most important factor in shaping the format and image of our company. In effect, we said "We will operate under the philosophy of low volume–high margin." This is not a bad philosophy for a small company starting out.*

In addition to capital needs, deciding what the new venture should make and what it should buy from others involves considering the following questions:

1. What elements of value make up the product or service to be offered? If it is a product, some possible elements include design, testing, purchasing, production, packaging, delivering, stocking, displaying, advertising, selling, financing, upgrading, customizing, installing, and servicing. Any particular product or service may break down into different categories and subcategories.

2. Which of these elements might the venture become best at performing itself, rather than having others perform them? How long will it take to become competitively proficient at elements the venture contemplates performing versus farming out? When will any farmed-out elements have to be paid for? How will required production amounts, flexibility to change output, and costs of various run lengths compare between farming out and in-house production? How will speed of delivery compare? How difficult and costly will contracting, communication, and quality checking be?

3. Based upon answers to the preceding two questions, what will be the likely forecasts of investment, profitability, and risk involved in performing each of the functions or having others do them? Which will build the best base for discovering further opportunities in the future? Which tasks would the founders most enjoy performing versus having others do? Which potential subcontractors "feel" right after meeting them, seeing their facilities, and checking their references?

A central question will be just how the venture adds value. That, after all, is the main factor that justifies its existence. How two contrasting enterprises added value without plant and equipment is illustrated by the following examples:

■ *Mike Lieberman, operating in a Riverton, Wyoming, storefront, buys microcomputer parts from U.S. and foreign suppliers and adds value by selecting, purchasing, and assembling them into machines which he sells directly with personal service to local governments in his state and those nearby.*

■ *Florence Sender, operating in a Newton, Massachusetts, storefront, adds value by formulating cheese snack food, designing the packaging and advertising, ordering the production and delivery by a supplier, Beatrice Foods, and doing the billing, collecting and bookkeeping in her business. Beatrice adds value to her product by manufacturing to her formula, packaging, controlling quality and shipping.*[9]

Except for very personal services, virtually any value-adding operation can be kept in-house or farmed out at will. Impact on cash flow can be a major consideration in make or buy decisions.

Pitfalls

Financial hitches can arise at any point in the development of a venture, regardless of whether it is growing or not, profitable or not.

■ *Roger Melen of Cromemco, a "high end" microcomputer manufacturer, observed that "cash flow can kill faster than profits can cure. Running out of cash is the greatest threat to a small company." Accordingly, he and his partner, Harry Garland, took measures to conserve it, including renting rather than buying plant space, advertising through "free" publication of articles written by themselves, keeping their jobs as Stanford professors during start-up so they would not have to draw out cash personally, and maximizing tax deductions [see Chapter 9]. They managed to build their venture from $50,000 in 1975, the company's first year, to $50 million in 1981, with no outside equity capital beyond the $5,000 savings originally used for start-up.*[10]

Some companies must have more capital to start and/or grow. Inadequate financing at the outset may mean the venture does not start at all. A shortage later on can mean that the entrepreneur spends excessive time worrying about needs,

[9]Tom Richman, "The Hottest Entrepreneur in America," *Inc.* (February 1987), p. 50. (Emphasis added.)

[10]Robert A. Mamis, "Cromemco's Never Taken a Dime from Anyone," *Inc.* (November 1981), p. 117; also, Robert Levering, Michael Katz, and Milton Moskowitz, *The Computer Entrepreneurs* (New York: New American Library, 1984), p. 36.

cutting corners to conserve cash, looking for possible sources of more cash, or negotiating to obtain it. How increasing cash needs can quickly develop was illustrated in the experience of George Ballas with his Weed Eater, as he recalled:

■ *When I first started I may have had five thousand dollars in inventory (parts, spools, line, and so on). This was all the inventory I needed to take care of what I was selling. One year later, I had to have $150,000 in inventory in order to meet my expected demand for parts, line, and so forth. I had to buy this material for my warehouse. I had to have it there in order to be able to take care of my customers.*

Where does the money come from to buy this $150,000 in inventory materials? This inventory is not only for sales that you have already made; it is also needed for projected sales. These sales may or may not materialize, but you have to be ready to deliver if and when sales come. You don't want to miss sales because you don't have the product available. So the problem is, where do you get the $150,000 for your inventory before you have sold the inventory? It's a financing problem and you're spending most of your time on financing the growth.[11]

A venture with growing sales, even though it may be profitable, can be entirely wiped out if it is not adequately capitalized. If creditors sense a cash squeeze, they may clamp down on supply, so they will not have as much at risk. Debtors may begin to think that the venture is going under and if it is becoming weaker, the venture will not be able to pressure them to pay. Some may decide to hold off payment, which will help bring about collapse, as happened to the following producer of a new aircraft radio:

■ *At a time when the small plane radio market was dominated by two manufacturers, King and Narco, a floundering upstart Seattle company, Radair, which had recently been taken over by a small team of entrepreneurs, introduced a new radio design. Three features set it apart: incorporation of the first digital readout to appear in such a product, a lower price with higher margins for distributors, and a service policy under which immediate replacement of a defective unit was offered so users would not be without a radio while repairs were made. These features produced virtually instant market success, and sales of the company shot from nil to over $1.5 million within a year.*

As cash became needed for inventory and receivables, the entrepreneurs repeatedly turned to their banker. When he balked, they found a new banker who was interested in flying. "We'd need more credit. He'd get nervous. We'd take him flying. He'd get all enthused about the company. And we'd get the new loan," one of the entrepreneurs recalled. Bank debt grew and growth continued.

Until credit reached $350,000. At that point the banker could not approve further extension without approval of his bank's distant parent in southern California. "He balked," the lead entrepreneur recalled. "So we took him for a ride, gave him our pitch and turned him around as usual. But then he sent the paperwork to L.A. for approval, and that was the end. They turned down our loan request, we couldn't pay our bills, our creditors threw us into receivership and we were out of business, even though we were making profits and growing like mad." Assets of the venture were subsequently acquired by another company and moved to San Diego, where Radair continued. But the entrepreneurs were out.

[11]George C. Ballas and David Hollas, *The Making of an Entrepreneur* (Englewood Cliffs, NJ: Prentice Hall, 1980), p. 88.

Waiting until the last minute to look for capital can be disastrous. It takes time, often a matter of weeks, for an institution to make a loan. Other sources, such as individual lenders or investors, can take even longer if they have to be sought out, acquainted with the entrepreneur and the business, negotiated with, and sometimes left at that point to find others who are more ready to act. Moreover, when the money is needed, there are usually other crucially important matters for the entrepreneur to work on without having to drop everything else and look for cash. Calculation of needs in advance can help.

Guidelines

To the extent that an entrepreneur's personal resources may be limited relative to the needs of the venture, it is important not only to take measures for conserving cash, but also to do a cash flow forecast as a precaution against running out of money. The forecast may reveal whether cash needs of the business will require infusions from other sources, such as banks, partners, and other investors. When such needs are determined, the cash flow forecast coupled with explanations of how it was arrived at should help persuade those other sources to provide the money.

How much money it takes to start a business is not determined by whether the founders will work full- or part-time, whether it is a product or service business, or even how big it will be. Rather the amount needed is determined by a set of individual payments made to the company by customers at specific times and cash disbursements by the company to pay bills at other specific times. The cash needs depend on what it buys and how quickly it must pay its suppliers. Sometimes it is possible to suggest "typical" amounts for starting some types of businesses, such as those listed in Table 5–4. But any actual single business may vary widely from these amounts. The best way to estimate capital needed for start-up is to make a line-by-line cash flow forecast.

Forecasting

"There's no excuse for running out of money," according to Stan Rich, a veteran venture capitalist.[12] The good thing about capital needs is that they usually can be planned for in advance. By making a cash flow forecast, an entrepreneur can estimate how much outside cash will be needed for different possible scenarios of business growth. There are four approaches to forecasting financing needs:

1. Use "ballpark numbers" or rules of thumb for capital needed for start-up, such as the figures in Table 5–4.
2. Scale values proportionately from the financial statements of other companies, particularly other start-ups.
3. Generate *pro forma* income statements and balance sheets, using percentages of sales for expenses and estimated delay periods for receivables, inventory, and payables.
4. Generate a cash flow forecast by projecting sales, collections from those sales, and cash expenditures by date needed to support those sales.

[12]Edmund L. Andrews, "Running out of Money," *Venture* (January 1988), p. 32.

TABLE 5-4   Start-Up Capital Needs by Various Businesses[13]

START-UP CAPITAL (in thousands of dollars)	VENTURE
25	Software for tracking computer program revisions
95	Bank foreclosure property magazine
125	Wind-deflecting seat covers for convertibles
140	Vacuum packed meals for baby sitters to serve
200	Underwater voice projecting scuba mask
225	Simplified, beginner's scuba gear
300	Nutrient sealing vial for flower stems
350	Federal regulations on floppy disks
400	System for packaging in inflated mylar bags
410	Data intercom for office computer equipment
420	Massaging machine manufacturer
450	Prerecorded dial-in *Yellow Pages* advertisements
500	Cancer diagnostic service
750	Elasticized Velcro-fastened cloth diapers
1,500	Franchised golf course system using bigger balls
2,100	Manufacturing cigarette-dispensing machines

Examples of such financial forecasts from a computer disk drive start-up, Priam, can be seen Appendix B. One way to generate such statements is to imitate those of a "look-alike" enterprise, adjusting it as needed for differences in the businesses. A look at the statements of operating businesses and/or financial statement ratios published by Dun and Bradstreet and by Robert Morris Associates can yield other helpful ideas about how statements for the start-up should differ from those of the look-alike.

Each of these approaches has its merits and limitations. Easiest to use are the ballpark numbers, but they are probably only helpful in forming general ideas about which types of ventures will likely cost more than other types. Their applicability to any particular venture is unlikely, except perhaps in a hazy way.

Scaling financial statements proportionately from those of a prior similar venture is also fairly easy. Entered on a spread sheet program, the numbers can easily be multiplied by a single percentage to scale them up or down according to how sales of the new venture are expected to compare to those of the prior one. The difficult part may be to find a similar venture whose statements are available for such a purpose. This approach may seem unlikely to work, because no two ventures are truly alike. But it was used to raise venture capital by a start-up that turned out to be very successful, Stratus Computer, Inc.

Generating original *pro forma* statements is more complicated, but it allows

[13]"100 Ideas for New Businesses," *Venture* (December 1987), p. 35.

closer tailoring to what will actually happen in the new venture. The easiest way to make them is first to estimate sales, perhaps by month for the first year, quarters for two years, and annually for two more years to make a five-year forecast. Then, receivables can be estimated as a percentage of sales by guessing how long it will take to collect them, and inventory as a percentage of sales by guessing gross margin and estimating how many months of inventory should be kept on hand. Expenses can be estimated by breaking them into fixed versus variable costs and scaling the latter as a percentage of sales. Payables can be estimated by guessing how quickly expenses will have to be paid. Fixed assets may require more direct item-by-item estimation and depreciation on some simple schedule, such as straight line over ten years. For cash balance, a ratio of sales or expenses similar to that of other companies and "eyeballed" for reasonableness may do. Investment needed should then be revealed as a gap on the liabilities side of the balance sheet.

To check for reasonableness of the *pro forma* statements, it may help to compare them against three other things—ballpark numbers and scaled numbers obtained as previously suggested; ratios from published reports of such services as Robert Morris Associates, Dun and Bradstreet, and possibly relevant trade associations; and a carefully developed cash flow forecast. Squaring projected statements with the latter will provide the tightest check.

The cash flow forecast is most essential for actually operating the venture. A company can go without sales, profits, or even a positive net worth at least for a while. But it cannot go without cash if there is a payroll to meet or a tax bill to pay. The company must have enough cash at the right time to meet its expenses.

The cash inflows come from collecting on sales. They depend on what will be sold, when it will be delivered, when the bill will be sent and, most important, when it will be collected. This must be determined month by month.

The next considerations concern what the company itself will have to pay for and when to produce those sales. If product development work must be done, what is the schedule, what will it cost, and when will the bills have to be paid? Similar questions will arise for buying equipment, setting up shop, getting out advertisements, and starting production. If an inventory will have to be built up and maintained to support the sales, a corresponding schedule of purchases and payments to cover them must be laid out. All these payments will constitute a schedule of cash outflows that will start before inflows begin. If the company begins to show signs of success, the inflows will increase until a cash balance begins to build up.

The cash flow forecast looks much like an income statement, with receipts shown above the expenditures and the difference between the two below that. The bottom line shows the cumulative total the company will have to raise from other sources to be solvent. In the illustration presented in Table 5–5, the company will be out 5 (dollars, thousands, or whatever) the first month, rising to 16 by the third month, after which the situation improves as receipts exceed expenditures.

A somewhat more detailed worksheet, which can readily be adapted to a particular business and set up on a microcomputer spreadsheet to allow both forecasting and comparison of actual versus forecast expenditures, appears in

TABLE 5-5 Cash Flow Forecast Example

	JAN	FEB	MAR	APR	MAY	JUN
Units						
Orders		1	2	4	6	8
Shipments			1	2	4	6
Cash in						
Billings			10	20	40	60
Receipts				10	20	40
Cash out						
Salaries	1	1	1	1	1	1
Advertising	1	1	1	1	1	1
Rent	1	1	1	1	1	1
Equipment	2					
Labor		1	1	2	2	2
Materials		1	2	2	2	2
Taxes				1	2	4
TOTAL	5	5	6	8	9	11
NET IN	−5	−5	−6	2	11	29
CUM IN	−5	−10	−16	−14	−3	26

Exhibit 5-1. It is usually preferable to show more detail for the short term and less long term as the uncertainty becomes greater. Making forecasts monthly the first year, quarterly for the next two years, and annually for the two after that is typically advisable.

Reconciling the cash flow forecast with projected income statements and balance sheets is more complex. Problems are introduced by the fact that receipts usually lag behind sales, disbursements sometimes lead and sometimes lag behind expenses, and expenditures on labor and materials do not correspond directly to changes in inventory. Rather, they swell and contract depending on the timing of shipments and may be seasonal or erratic. Reconciliations can be made by making simplifying assumptions (e.g., receivables are collected after sixty days and payables are paid after three) and using a spreadsheet, by using more sophisticated software that allows more complex assumptions, or by working the whole process out in detail as if the company were operating. The last of these allows the most tailoring to reality, but the first is quickest and easiest. Welsh and White provide helpful illustrations of how these elements work together.[14]

In deciding which approach to use, another consideration must be how valid the estimates of individual items of projected sales and expenses will be. If they are

[14]John A. Welsh and Jerry F. White, *The Entrepreneur's Master Planning Guide* (Englewood Cliffs, NJ: Prentice Hall, 1983), p. 257.

EXHIBIT 5-1 Monthly Cash Flow Forecast

YEAR MONTH	Pre-Start-up Position		1		2		3		4		5	
	Estimate	Actual	Estimate	Actual	Estimate	Actual	Estimate	Actual	Estimate	Actual	Estimate	Actual
1. CASH ON HAND (Beginning of month)												
2. CASH RECEIPTS (a) Cash Sales												
(b) Collections from Credit Accounts												
(c) Loan or Other Cash injection (Specify)												
3. TOTAL CASH RECEIPTS (2a + 2b + 2c = 3)												
4. TOTAL CASH AVAILABLE (Before cash out) (1 + 3)												
5. CASH PAID OUT (a) Purchases (Merchandise)												
(b) Gross Wages (Excludes withdrawals)												
(c) Payroll Expenses (Taxes, etc.)												
(d) Outside Services												
(e) Supplies (Office and operating)												
(f) Repairs and Maintenance												
(g) Advertising												
(h) Car, Delivery, and Travel												
(i) Accounting and Legal												
(j) Rent												
(k) Telephone												
(l) Utilities												
(m) Insurance												
(n) Taxes (Real Estate, etc.)												
(o) Interest												
(p) Other Expenses (Specify each)												
(q) Miscellaneous (Unspecified)												
(r) Subtotal												
(s) Loan Principal Payment												
(t) Capital Purchases (Specify)												
(u) Other Start-up Costs												
(v) Reserve and/or Escrow (Specify)												
(w) Owner's Withdrawal												
6. TOTAL CASH PAID OUT (Total 5a thru 5w)												
7. CASH POSITION (End of month) (4 minus 6)												
ESSENTIAL OPERATING DATA (Non-cash flow information) A. Sales Volume (Dollars)												
B. Accounts Receivable (End of month)												
C. Bad Debt (End of month)												
D. Inventory on Hand (End of month)												
E. Accounts Payable (End of month)												
F. Depreciation												

fairly solid, then a more detailed forecast may be worthwhile. But if they are highly uncertain, then it will probably be best to look for worst-case possibilities by making a larger number of simpler forecasts using a variety of assumptions. In either event, it will be desirable to have best, worst, and most likely cases worked out.

INTERNAL SEED CAPITAL SOURCES

Personal Money

Founders, employees, and friends or relatives of the founders may be the ones who invest in the venture or lend it money.

Founders' Money.   George Ballas, inventor of the Weed Eater, described his seed capital approach as follows:

■   *I've started all types and in most cases I never had any money. . . . Whenever I had an idea, I just started doing it. After I'd developed the first stage, I would ask friends to invest in it. I'd form a corporation, sell stock and/or borrow money from someone I knew, or someone I'd just met, or from a relative. If I had a good idea that I had faith in, and I could explain it to somebody else, it was always easy to get money as I needed it. Sometimes it was five hundred dollars and sometimes it was five thousand dollars. I think the most I've ever borrowed from an individual was fifty thousand dollars. This was for the Weed Eater after it was going pretty good.*[15]

Personal savings become the price of starting a company. If the entrepreneur is already wealthy, perhaps from prior ventures (e.g., William Lear) or from inheritance (e.g., Howard Hughes), he or she may be able to launch the start-up with available personal capital. But most founders squeeze out their savings, life insurance cash value, securities, home mortgage, and other investments to produce a stake. (To raise start-up cash for Apple Steve Jobs at one point sold his Volkswagen and Steve Wozniak sold his pocket calculator.) Obviously, one way to expand a meager ante is to multiply the number of founders, one of several arguments for starting with a team.

By investing and risking their personal assets for the new company, founders gain several advantages. They can become sensitized to disciplines of economy and the importance of not spending carelessly, as they might be more likely to do with other people's money, particularly if it is available in abundance.

Second, in their dealings with suppliers, bankers, employees, and later possibly venture capitalists, those founders who have contributed substantial proportions of personal assets to the company can offer this fact as persuasive evidence of their commitment and dedication to the success of the enterprise. The firm is less likely to fail if owners cannot personally afford such failure. Conversely, if an

---

[15]Ballas and Hollas, *The Making of an Entrepreneur*, p. 98.

owner has not contributed a substantial share of his or her assets, others who are asked to take risks on the firm may wonder, "If you aren't chancing much on it, why should I?" Lenders do not always require countersigning by an entrepreneur, so he or she may not have to commit his or her total assets to the company, only a substantial portion.

Third, the longer the founders are able to operate on their own capital, the further the company should progress in sales and profits and the more favorable the terms it should be able to obtain when it must eventually draw on outside capital. A company that has not yet made sales will have a difficult, if not impossible, time raising outside capital. One that has made sales but not yet broken even will have it easier but will still have difficulty, especially if it cannot clearly prove how greater profitability is likely to come. After breakeven, financing becomes much easier—now the outside capitalist can start to feel some assurance that the company is bound to win and the only question is the extent of the success. By holding off on their own resources still longer, founders may be able to build a history of earnings, which becomes still more convincing.

Working Partners. *Stakeholders* are those who have selfish reasons to want the venture to succeed. Consequently, it may be in their best interests to help with its financing. They include formal lenders, such as banks, and also investors, such as working partners.

Much as an individual entrepreneur might prefer to retain 100 percent ownership and control, it may not be possible and may not be best for the venture. In some lines of business, such as high technology manufacturing, partners are more the rule than the exception. From a survey of 145 such firms, Bruno and Tyebjee found that only one-third had a single owner-manager, whereas 38 percent had two founder-owners, 12 percent had three, and 16 percent had four or more.[16] Teaming with partners may give the venture much more strength and a broader base to build on, as well as the cash it may need beyond what a single owner can muster. Sharing ownership with working partners can be a way of keeping control within the company, although as will be discussed later, it may be necessary to share it further with outside investors as well.

Employees. Employees can become a source of capital if they buy stock or lend the venture money. The fact that they are insiders, however, does not mean that soliciting money from them will be legally construed as a private offering.

■ *Alfred Knief figured he could beat high interest charges at the bank and offer his employees higher interest than they could get elsewhere by having his supply company borrow money from them at a rate between the two rates. He wrote a letter to his twenty-three employees proposing the deal, and within a week seventeen accepted. Federal law allowed solicitation of up to thirty-five people without registration, but the law in Wisconsin, where he had his company, allowed only fifteen. The state went after him but*

[16]Albert V. Bruno and Tyzoon T. Tyebjee, "The Entrepreneur's Search for Capital," *Journal of Business Venturing*, 1 (no. 1) (Winter 1985), p. 63.

backed down when the press applauded his initiative. Instead of fines of $5,000 and five years in jail, he was given an exemption permitting him to solicit up to $400,000 from up to thirty-five individuals.[17]

More will be said in the next chapter about public offerings and how to avoid the drastic penalties that can result from the violation of securities laws.

Relatives and Friends.   When founders do not have any savings at the outset or begin to need outside financing because they have used up their savings, the next source of funding may be the savings of family and friends. Apple was started using the home of Steve Jobs's parents and to some extent their labor as well.[18] Whether to sacrifice some ownership to obtain such help or to borrow with an obligation to repay depends upon the nature of the venture and the desires and expectations of both parties.

There are countless "horror stories" ending with lost friends and hostile relatives when setbacks afflict ventures, leading some to believe that relatives and friends should never be involved. Others say it is all right to do so provided the basis of involvement is sufficiently businesslike, with "full disclosure" of risks and formal contracts. Such an agreement can include provisions for interest, repayment, equity rights, reporting requirements, buy-sell arrangements, and insurance to cover the repayment and/or replacement of key individuals should they die or be injured. The agreement can be drafted by the individuals concerned, but it should then be reviewed by a lawyer who has appreciable experience with just such contracts. With "friendly" lenders or investors, sometimes less formal contracts work as well.

■ *Three people working for a travel tour wholesaler became frustrated with their inability to advance further in the firm and also with the fact that they were putting in full workdays making the company go while the two owners were appearing for one or two hours each day and taking home much more money than the three. After trying unsuccessfully to work out terms for buying out the owners, the three, one of whom specialized in operations, the second in sales, and the third in finance and control, decided to start their own company.*

Based upon pro forma financial projections, they estimated $230,000 would be needed to get the new firm going. This money would be used mainly for travel to negotiate tour arrangements with hotels, for printing and mailing brochures to travel agents who would sell the tours, for visits to travel trade shows and individual agents to sell them on selling tours, and finally for salaries of the three plus secretarial staff to handle correspondence and incoming phone calls.

The three had a good track record in the industry, which was currently expanding. Consequently, two sources offered them capital. One was a wealthy venture capital group that wanted 60 percent ownership for full capitalization. The second was a travel agent with a chain of offices who offered the same capital for only 50 percent of the ownership. In addition, he offered some valuable tour connections. Quitting their jobs, the three took his deal and started organizing tour packages for the new company.

[17]"An Innovative Borrower Gets the Law to Bend," *Inc.* (October 1982), p. 21.
[18]Lee Butcher, *Accidental Millionaire* (New York: Paragon House, 1989).

A few weeks later some major shifts in airline schedules upon which their financier's own firm depended heavily caused his business suddenly to collapse. The three founders found themselves stranded in mid–start-up with an empty bank account.

Frantically, they sought assistance from other acquaintances as well as the capital sources they had tried before. But those whom they had turned down before now rejected their deal. Then a personal acquaintance of one member of the team offered to help. He extended a loan on the basis of a simple note bearing no interest with repayment to occur only as soon as they were able to accomplish it. With that they were able to complete their start-up, and as promptly as cash flow allowed, they returned their benefactor's money.

Surprising as it may be from a business standpoint, this kind of philanthropy is not highly unusual in entrepreneurial sagas. There seem to be many entrepreneurs who themselves were once saved by such acts and who take pleasure in passing the good deed along to other struggling entrepreneurs. "Somebody helped me once," the reasoning goes, "so this time I figured it was my turn."

Other Stakeholders

Aside from owners, the interests of two other types of stakeholders may be strong enough for them to help with financing—those who want to buy something from the business and those who want to sell something to it.

Suppliers and Trade Credit. Although they will not usually extend credit until a start-up's ability to pay its bills is apparent, suppliers are a universal source of credit among established businesses and can be an important source of help for a company attempting to grow on internal capital. There is usually a lag between placing an order and having it shipped; between shipment and arrival; arrival and acceptance after inspection; and checkwriting and processing as requested on the invoice. A normal lag time is between thirty and sixty days, with the supplier wishing payment in ten days and the customer wanting ninety or more.

Where the balance is struck is usually a trade-off against other things, such as the importance of the customer to the supplier, the kind of service the customer wants, how badly the supplier needs sales or the customer needs prompt shipment, and, finally, the reliability of the customer for payment. This reliability is gauged in terms of the customer's financial strength and track record of payment. On these last two counts, new companies are typically weak; consequently, it can be hard to get trade credit when starting a new business, although not necessarily impossible.

Suppliers can be helpful in several ways. They (1) allow goods to be bought on consignment, where the purchaser pays only after they are sold; (2) allow extended payment terms, such as 120 days instead of only 10 days or C.O.D.; and (3) allow the return of unsold goods. However, the entrepreneur must also consider the prices a supplier is charging, the dependence of the venture upon the supplier that can result from such help, and the reliability of a supplier who may be unwisely overgenerous.

Generally, a middleman-type of business gets trade credit for inventory easier than a manufacturing company because the inventory for a middleman will be finished goods. One option for the supplier of a middleman is to provide the supplies on consignment, retaining title to the inventory until it is sold. The new company taking on the inventory then operates as an agent for the supplier. After some sales have been made, the new company will have proven its ability to do business and should also have somewhat greater financial strength from profits on the sale. Then the trade credit may be forthcoming.

Obtaining trade credit for a manufacturing company is complicated by the fact that the company modifies what it buys and may thereby make it unsalable. If the founder can demonstrate that the venture is beginning with substantial equity capital relative to its debt, or if the owner is known and well regarded by suppliers, possibly from a prior business success, or if the owner is personally able to guarantee payment, then suppliers may grant credit. Otherwise, they will probably not, at least until the start-up is well underway and making a profit. Even then they will likely watch the account closely, and if the new company starts to draw out its payments, they may clamp down and put it on C.O.D.

A variation on financing to obtain supplies is the use of confirming houses. A *confirming house* will arrange for supplies by guaranteeing to pay the supplier for the venture, then collecting from the venture itself. This approach is used particularly in purchasing from overseas suppliers.

A final way to get trade credit is to buy supplies on personal credit cards. Debbie Galant, writing for *Venture*, cites the following example:

■ *Take Robert Townsend, a black actor who wanted to make a film satirizing Hollywood's portrayal of blacks as pimps and junkies. After running through $60,000 saved from acting in* A Soldier's Story *and other jobs, Townsend ran out of cash in February, 1986. Then he noticed those credit card solicitations he had been receiving—and throwing away—since his acting career had begun to take off. Townsend accumulated 25 credit cards and finished the film by charging $40,000 worth of film stock, camera rentals, costumes, lumber and other items. "I found out there's nothing you can't charge," he recalls.[19]*

Galant goes on to claim that "using credit cards in the start-up stages of a new business is extremely common—especially for entrepreneurs not yet considered creditworthy by more conservative lenders." Unfortunately, credit card bills require repayment in the near term and carry high interest charges. The total amount that can be borrowed, moreover, is limited to begin with or will rapidly become so if the bills begin to mount. Moreover, credit cards are used for buying at retail, and retail prices are much higher than competitors are likely to be paying for materials. Consequently, using credit cards for start-up capital represents a rather desperate measure.

In sum, except for middlemen types of enterprises, the entrepreneur had better not plan to rely on trade credit for financing initially. Once the venture gets going successfully, however, it will become a helpful way of financing growth.

[19]Debbie Galant, "Don't Start Up Without It," *Venture* (July 1988), p. 87.

Customers. There are a number of ways that customers who want to buy from the start-up can help with its financing, aside from simply buying its product. Paying promptly for what is bought, rather than dragging out payments and taking advantage of the new company's weakness, is of great help. Advance deposits, prepayments, and progress payments or standard retainer payments are other ways a customer can help the supplier financially. To obtain such help, the start-up may, of course, have to yield on other things, such as providing price discounts or special service.

■ *In 1977 Robert Harar borrowed $700 from his father, bought a mailing list and with brochures and phone calls recruited companies to exhibit at a trade show he planned to organize on office systems. Recalling that he managed to rent 100 booths at $400 each, he commented that "It boggled my mind that you could come up with a brochure, mail it to someone, then call him up and convince him to send you money for something that's not going to happen for another year." By 1987 the show had become annual with 1,300 booths and Harar had added seven other shows to create a $5 million business.[20]*

Advance payment for gift certificates and subscriptions is a way of obtaining financing from retail customers. An illustrative example was a magazine start-up described by *In Business:*

■ *The firm gave away 100,000 free subscriptions, then obtained advertisers by guaranteeing a circulation of 100,000. The money paid by the advertisers to reach this audience served as the basis for the magazine to begin. A few years ago, the magazine dropped the 100,000 free subscribers since it no longer needed them because it then had enough paying subscribers.[21]*

Yet another way to raise customer money early is to sell some form of memberships. Some types of enterprises, such as discos, can be started, at least in some states, as private clubs. *Venture* described the start-up of one disco by an entrepreneur who required membership fees of $200 initially plus $72 annually. Before opening, he had signed up 511 members.[22]

For a manufacturing start-up, raising money through the sale of dealerships is another possibility. When Henry Ford's company became strapped for cash due to pressure from creditors, he required dealers to advance money and was able to pull through. Sometimes, a customer will prepay on orders to help out a new supplier, possibly to cultivate it as a competitor with other suppliers and thereby improve supply costs or supplier service. In the next example, the customer did so to an extent it later found was too great:

■ *He had worked for a couple of years as salesman for certain types of advanced technology office machines and then became a consultant on them. In the course of this work, he*

---

[20]Jay Pridmore, "Another Niche, Another Show," *Venture* (January 1987), p. 38.
[21]Robert N. Allen, "Customers: A Money Source," *In Business* (September–October 1980), p. 19.
[22]William G. Shepard, Jr., "Disco Fever," *Venture* (June 1979), p. 43.

conceived of a new type of advance in these machines that he thought should be of interest to a certain type of industrial customer. He approached a company in that industry and described the machine he had in mind. The company became highly interested and encouraged the entrepreneur to help it obtain a number of those machines for its own use.

Next, the consultant, whose company at this point consisted of only a corporate registration, a mail drop, answering service, and business cards, approached a company with the engineering capability to develop the new machine and the manufacturing capability to produce it. He asked for a quotation of price and delivery to develop and ship ten units. The price he received was $30,000 each.

Now he returned to his prospective customer and proposed that he do a study of its operations to assess how much the new machine could save the company. When the customer company asked how much he would charge for the study, he replied, "Nothing, I'll do it for free." The customer company agreed.

When the study was done, the consultant showed the customer company figures supporting the conclusion that if the company installed ten machines for $125,000 each, they would realize savings sufficient to pay for them in three years. Not only that, the consultant argued, but on further expanding the use of the machines throughout the company, even greater savings would be realized. In addition, he said, this new technology would make the company a leader in its industry.

All he needed to begin, he offered, was a drawing account of $350,000—enough to pay for the machines plus some operating capital. If the customer would advance the money, he would put it into an escrow account pledged against satisfactory delivery, installation, and performance of the machines. He would further give the customer company 10 percent of the stock in his own company and pledge the rest as a guarantee of performance.

The customer company signed a contract of agreement and advanced the cash. The engineering company signed a contract guaranteeing delivery of the machines as specified. The consultant was happily on his way to a profit of nearly one million dollars—a sale of $1,250,000 that would cost him about $350,000 to deliver on.

But then the customer pushed for changes in the machine's specifications, and the producer began slipping the delivery schedule, producing a gradual collapse of the deal. The entrepreneur sued the customer, charging that the customer had caused problems by meddling during development of the project and changing the specifications. After winning a small settlement in this suit and getting all his stock back from the customer company, he next sued the supplier for failing to deliver and won another settlement. The product was superseded by further advances in technology and never made it to market.

An unusual aspect of this deal was that it included a supplier who was willing to engineer as well as produce the new product to the entrepreneur's specifications on a fixed price and delivery schedule. It also included a customer who was willing to buy the first shipment at a price that would leave the entrepreneur with a healthy profit. The upshot was that the customer was financing virtually the entire start-up of the company. It was not quite a no-equity-outside-at-all deal, because the customer was getting 10 percent of the stock. But the fraction was very small, and in the end the founder got it all back.

Financial advances by customers in cases where the product or service is a known quantity, rather than speculative as in the previous example, are much more common, although some of those too are unusual. One entrepreneur, for example, obtained an advance from a division of a large chemical company to provide a certain chemical, which he then bought, unbeknownst to that division, from another division of the same company. Others have advertised products by mail order, requiring money in advance. After receiving the money, they would make or obtain the product and ship it, later paying suppliers, so that in effect the customers were financing the whole operation. Still more common is the use of an order from a large customer as evidence to persuade a bank to loan the new company money.

The fact that some entrepreneurs have been able to use customers as a source of equity does not mean it can be done for any venture. In fact, it tends to be a fairly rare occurrence made possible only in exceptional circumstances. Being alert to that possibility, however, may provide the would-be entrepreneur with one more trick to use if the right circumstances arise.

Federal SBIR Funds. The federal government sometimes provides start-up capital as a customer. In particular, each of eleven federal agencies with large research and development budgets is obliged to set part of those budgets aside for grants to small firms. These grants, called "Small Business Innovation Research" (SBIR) grants, are provided on the basis of competitive proposals. Awards are made in stages; the first is typically $50,000, to support development and demonstration of new technological ideas. If the first stage is completed successfully by the grant recipient, he or she becomes eligible for the second stage, with a maximum of $250,000 to $500,000 depending on the agency and other factors. The point of contact to learn about the availability of such grants is whatever federal agency might most likely be interested in the technology. The Department of Energy, NASA, the National Science Foundation, and the Department of Defense are some examples. An advantage of such funds is that they require neither giving up equity nor repayment. The disadvantages are that they require a fairly long-shot gamble of effort on proposal preparation; they are restricted to technologically innovative ideas; and they are limited in amount. Literature on SBIR programs is available without charge from the Small Business Administration.

State and Local Support. Localities interested in economic development have set up many ways to help entrepreneurs. These include state development funds, such as the Ben Franklin Partnership in Pennsylvania, which provides expansion capital to ongoing small firms but also helps start-ups, typically on some sort of matching basis.[23] Other sources are private, state and university incubators. The incubators typically do not put up capital, but some offer low-cost rentals for start-ups, and many offer low-cost assistance. Local development funds are described in a Small Business Administration booklet, *Capital Formation in the*

[23]Marie-Jeanne Juilland, "Alternatives to a Rich Uncle," *Inc.* (May 1988), p. 62.

States. Incubators can be found through local economic development offices and chambers of commerce.

BANK BORROWING

Start-ups rarely begin with bank loans. They begin with the personal savings of the founders and their acquaintances, and bank loans come later. But exceptions occur. Personal loans are made to founders and commercial loans to start-ups.

Personal loans may be obtained through mortgaging a house or borrowing against such assets as stocks and bonds. Borrowing from insurance companies against the cash value of life insurance policies is another source of personal loans. Personal loans are easier to obtain before a future entrepreneur quits his or her prior job, however, because the banker will consider salary from an established employer more reliable than income from a start-up as a source of loan repayment. Taking out a personal loan early and repaying it on schedule can also be a way of becoming acquainted with a banker and building confidence to apply for a commercial loan for the venture itself.

Commercial borrowing takes the following forms:

Short Term

- Line of credit
- Inventory loan
- Accounts receivable financing

Longer Term

- Equipment loan
- Commercial mortgage
- Guaranteed term loan

At first, a start-up will not have any accounts receivable, so that type of financing is ruled out. It may be wiser not to invest initially in real estate or expensive equipment. Bank borrowing options for a start-up thus become very limited at best.

Raising money by bank borrowing is serious business. Bank borrowing, unlike founders' savings, must be paid back. Using personal savings for a start-up will mean giving up the interest that might have been earned but will not require paying out interest. Using bank-borrowed cash will require paying interest—at about twice the savings interest rate. Just to pay that interest, the start-up will have to earn a fairly high return on the money—around twice what depositors can earn. In addition, the start-up will have to earn still more to be able to make the required repayments of the principal as well.

From a bank's point of view, the most important consideration is the degree of certainty that a loan will be paid back on the agreed schedule of interest and timing. The bank has a responsibility to remain able to pay back the people who deposited their money with it. Also, the bank is limited on what it can charge in loan interest and the only protection it can seek is to be prudent in lending.

By law, a bank may lend out only part of the money it receives in deposits. Some money must be held in reserve and some must be kept on hand as cash, so that only about three-fourths can be loaned. From the limited interest it receives on this fraction, it must pay all its expenses, cover any bad loans it makes, and earn income for its shareholders. A bank cannot afford to have as much as 1 percent of its loans defaulted on or it will go out of business. Banks fire loan officers who make loans that default, and bankers consequently take care to make loan decisions that will assure repayment.

Hedges for assuring repayment, which can help in obtaining bank loans, include both collateral and guarantees. Collateral can come from whatever equity has been invested in tangible assets of the start-up, such as real estate, equipment, or inventory that can easily be sold. Occasionally, a bank will loan against the strength of orders the start-up has landed, if it is clear the company will be able to perform on those orders and that the customers are big companies or the government and have the financial strength that assures they can pay.

Guarantees

Guarantees, or promises from others besides the start-up itself to repay the loan, typically come from two general sources, individuals and the U.S. government.

Individual Guarantees. Two potential sources of individual guarantees are the entrepreneur and others outside the company who may for one reason or another accept such risk. By cosigning or countersigning a loan, one person can make credit available to another without actually putting up any money. The catch, of course, is that if the person or company that takes out the loan does not repay it, then the cosigner must. Thus, the cosigner carries the risk but does not have to put up money except in case of default. In the following case, the entrepreneur offered to pay for this risk with a gift of stock to be repurchased by the company:

■ *He had set up shop to manufacture furniture and other wooden items but had not as yet broken even. His initial financing had come from personal savings plus a mortgage on his house plus a bank loan against accounts receivable. After some searching he had run across a product he felt had much higher profit potential than what he had initially started to produce. Office space was encountering high and increasing demand locally, and the company making office partitions seemed to have more demand than it could handle. "It really surprised me," he said. "I visited a company making these things and they told me all about how to make them, since they could not handle all the orders they were getting."*

Meanwhile, some customers of the entrepreneur had become very slow in paying what they owed him and this had begun to stretch out his bank loan against the receivables. As a way to solidify the loan and finance entry into the partitions business, his banker had suggested that the entrepreneur get someone capable of covering his note to cosign it. In return for the guarantee, the entrepreneur offered to give 30 percent of the company's stock under terms that would require that the company repurchase it after two years for the full face amount of the cosigned loan.

Although used here for financing somewhat downstream from start-up, this approach could be applied to a start-up as well. The variety of incentives that could be used for obtaining personal cosigning or guarantees, and the variety of parties from whom they might be obtained, are virtually limitless.

There are numerous and important technicalities that can be incorporated into the guarantee. How long will the guarantee run? Must the one who signs the guarantee put up any collateral? Will the venture be restricted from other borrowing or in any other way during the guarantee period? Should the borrower also personally guarantee the loan? What would constitute default by the borrower, and what sequence of events would then follow? Could the guarantor go after the borrower, or only the venture for recovery in case of default? Can the guarantor sell his or her rights to anyone else? What financial reports by the venture, if any, is the guarantor entitled to? To what extent, if any, can the guarantor meddle in management of the company or be prevented by the entrepreneur from doing so?

It is important to remember, however, that if the bank ever clamps down on the loan, the guarantee will pull the entrepreneur's personal assets down with it. An example was that of Bill Rodgers, a world champion marathon runner, who used $40,000 of personal savings to open a running-equipment store in 1977, then a year later with some partners he added another $60,000 to start producing his own running gear. To get bank loans for working capital, Rodgers and his principal partner, Rob Yahn, cosigned notes with the Bank of Boston. Ten years later, *Inc.* reported:

■   *After shutting down the ailing business, the bank subsequently opened even deeper wounds for Rodgers and company president, Rob Yahn. To guarantee the company's loans, both had pledged personal assets as collateral, including second mortgages on their houses. Now, the two were being held accountable for an estimated $700,000 shortfall, and Rodger's 17-room house in Dover, Mass., was under imminent threat of foreclosure.*[24]

Rodgers lost the business and his house. In addition, he had to perform free commercials for the bank that took the business and house away.

Government Guarantees.   The Federal Small Business Administration frequently guarantees bank loans, as it did in the Rodgers case. However, to the extent that the government must cover anything the bank cannot get from the borrower, it too will hold the borrower personally responsible. So in effect the entrepreneur must personally guarantee the loan also. To obtain an SBA guarantee for a start-up loan, the entrepreneur must have invested one dollar of personal cash in the business for every two dollars to be borrowed.

---

[24]Joseph P. Kahn, "Heartbreak Hill," *Inc.* (April 1988), p. 68. Also, Hank Gilman, "Rodgers and Company Runs on a Fast Track," *Inc.* (May 1981), p. 142, and "Letters to the Editor," *Inc.* (July 1988), p. 8.

The procedure for seeking such a guarantee is to approach a bank with a written proposal, as will be further discussed later, for a direct loan. If it is declined, then the banker should be asked to make the loan under the SBA Loan Guaranty plan. If the bank agrees, it will then deal with the SBA directly. However, the guarantee will cover only 90 percent of the principal on loans up to $150,000 or 85 percent on loans up to $750,000. Thus, if the loan becomes uncollectable, the bank must cover at least 10 to 15 percent of it. The amount of interest the bank can charge, moreover, is limited to between 2 to 3 percent over the prime rate.

Finding a Banker

That bankers, not banks, make loans is a cliché of the banking business. Certainly, banks establish guidelines, rules, and standard procedures for evaluating, deciding upon, and handling loans, particularly small ones for routine transactions. But when an entrepreneur wants to borrow for starting a company, the loan he or she is proposing is no longer routine. The process then either produces an immediate rejection or else becomes much more involved.

■ *Charles Pierce had obtained a $6,000 customer contract in late 1975 and hired four employees to help him carry it out. But now he lacked the cash needed for payroll in four days. Deciding to apply for a bank loan to cover it, he entered the Attleboro Trust lobby and asked, "Who loans the money here?"*

Thereupon, he met a loan officer, Dana Bishop, and learned why a loan would be hard to get. His enterprise, which would rent crews of nuclear technicians to utilities, was not only new and unproven, but a service business with no collateral to pledge against a note. The nuclear industry itself had risks, and a payroll loan in particular could leave the bank responsible for withholding taxes if Pierce's venture failed.

"I guess I'd always assumed bankers were experts on any business," Pierce later recalled. "That isn't true. If you want them to deal with your needs intelligently, you've got to spend time going over every last nut and bolt. If there's anything you forget to explain, they're sure not going to pick it up out of thin air."

There wasn't much risk as Pierce saw it, only as the banker did. The market he aimed at was growing, he had extensive personal experience as a nuclear technician and Navy contacts to find others with similar skills, and he had helped his own prior employers do so.

Pierce set about educating the banker, Dana Bishop, about exactly how the business worked and why these advantages were important. Bishop recalled Pierce's supplications. "He was one of the most sincere, persuasive people I've ever met. But I also began to see he had something definite to offer. He knew the industry, he knew his customers and he knew what he wanted to do. In fact, he'd already started on a contract with Northeast Utilities for a four-month radiation survey, and had four guys on the job."

Bishop agreed to propose to the bank's president that a loan of $1,500 be approved, less than a third of the $5,000 Pierce requested, with a requirement that Pierce personally guarantee it. He got the loan, hit sales of $400,000 his first year, $1.4 million the second and $8 million the fifth. Many of his competitors who were less able to manage cash needs failed.

Recalling how crucial bank credit was to this rise, Pierce said: "Out of every dollar's worth of business, 80 cents goes right out in weekly payroll to our crews in the field. That doesn't leave much margin for overhead, but the tough part is that we deal with big utilities—and they'll easily take three months to process an invoice before we see any cash. It became routine for us to charter planes to fly out to pick up a check that was still warm from the computer. And then we'd have to get the check back to our bank in time to cover the next payroll, or it would've been all over for us." Because his balances swung widely with payrolls, collections and loans, he and Bishop met frequently to watch them, and consequently "there weren't a lot of surprises for either of us," he recalled.

Eventually, Pierce moved on to another bank, partly because he knew Bishop was leaving the bank, and partly because the bank's president reacted adversely to the growing size of Pierce's needs. What clinched his decision to leave, though, Pierce said, was a meeting with the bank's president. "He came to my office — and you've got to remember I'd been at the bank for three years and was one of its biggest customers — and said, 'Can you refresh my memory on what it is exactly that you do?' At that point, I definitely knew my days there were numbered."[25]

Setting up a checking account at a bank will be one of the first steps in starting a company. That action will provide the opportunity to meet one or more bankers. The early seed capital stage may be too soon to apply for a loan, but it is not too soon to start learning what it takes to get one.

The choice of both bank and loan officer can be crucial in the development of a venture. Successful borrowing relationships often depend upon having a loan officer who is close to the business, truly understands it, and takes a personal interest in it. Sad stories in borrowing relationships are usually associated with the opposite. Such stories often begin when the entrepreneur finds out that the loan officer has been changed by higher management of the bank. The venture now has to deal with a new person who does not understand it, is frightened by that lack of understanding, and either denies expansion of a loan needed by the venture to cope with growth or, worse yet, cracks down on an existing loan to ward off possible blame for anything that might go wrong.

One way for the entrepreneur to cope with such possible negative consequences is to choose the bank with care. Consider the following questions in making this choice:

1. How highly placed is the loan officer with whom the company will deal? (An ambitious young officer at a low level in a big bank may be more likely to move away from the venture to larger clients.)
2. How much lending authority does the person have, and how many levels of required approval lie above that person?
3. How willing is that person to learn details of the venture and take an interest in it?
4. How close is the bank to its loan limit? (The closer it is, the less likely it may be to take an interest in a new venture.)
5. How much experience has the bank and the loan officer had with start-ups and/or with companies in a similar line of business to the start-up? How well did those relationships work out?
6. How many directors of the bank have worked with start-ups themselves?
7. How does the bank compare with others on such things as frequency of loan committee meetings (more often is probably better), both short- and long-term inter-

[25]Jeffrey Tarter, "What Do Bankers Know about a Service Business?," *Inc.* (October 1980), p. 87–90.

est rates, willingness to make different types and lengths of loans, and requirements for compensating balances?

8. How does it compare on services such as payroll processing, credit references, help with other business contacts, and any other functions that may be important to the start-up?

The best time for the start-up to become acquainted with prospective banks is before it needs any money from them. It may take as much as six months or longer before a loan is needed. Getting the company started, developing financing plans, submitting a loan proposal, and waiting for it to be checked out all take time. If the founder can get some of these tasks underway well before the money is actually needed, he or she will be under less pressure to obtain financing and better able to concentrate on customers and making the company go when the financing is actually needed.

It may be advantageous to choose a small bank when the company is first starting out. That way there will be less bureaucracy between the entrepreneur and the bank CEO. Later, when the start-up grows and needs more funding, it may be better to move to a bigger bank with greater lending power, more services, and wider contacts.

Some banks are more aggressive, active, and experienced with small and start-up firms than others, and within those banks some officers are better qualified than others. The way to find the right bank, banker, and other sources of financing as well is to start with personal contacts and ask questions. These contacts can be professional acquaintances, such as someone in the bank where the entrepreneur has his or her personal account, as well as accountants or attorneys with whom he or she is acquainted. Other entrepreneurs and prospective suppliers or customers can be asked for recommendations. It will probably be advantageous to talk with more than one prospective banker.

Having identified a prospective banker, phone for an appointment in advance. Even on a get-acquainted visit before the time when a loan will be requested, it will be helpful to take along a written profile of the anticipated venture. There is no harm in suggesting that although the entrepreneur currently banks at another location, he or she will likely open one or more other accounts at another bank or banks in the future as the venture develops. Banks prefer not to have competition but, like other businesses, must contend with it anyway.

Ask what the lending officer's specialties in banking have been and to what extent he or she likes dealing with start-ups and has had experience with them. Also ask in what ways the bank might be able to help the venture aside from serving as depository and lender (e.g., credit check), as well as what procedures and advice the banker can suggest in preparation for requesting a loan in the future. None of these actions will obligate the entrepreneur to return to that particular bank or banker.

Additionally, the entrepreneur may find it wise to develop back-up contacts at more than one bank, in case a change of loan officer or bank policies occurs. One way to do this is to keep the business account at one bank and a personal account at a second bank that serves as a back-up.

Loan Application

Actions that will help an entrepreneur "look good" to a banker are (1) writing a loan request that includes a high-quality business plan (see Chapter 10), (2) demonstrating personal commitment to the venture by being prepared to invest personal resources to the maximum and to devote as much time as the venture will need, and (3) asking acquaintances to provide introductions personally and to serve as references if asked.

Before presenting a loan request, the entrepreneur, possibly with the aid of an adviser, should consider how a banker might answer five questions: (1) What are the strong points in favor of this loan request; (2) what are the weaker or negative aspects of the proposal; (3) what information should be disregarded as unimportant, dubious, irrelevant, or unclear; (4) what other information might be desired for further clarification; and (5) what terms and conditions could be incorporated in a loan agreement both to help the start-up and to protect the bank? Some specific questions a banker will want answers to in considering whether to make a loan to a venture include the following:[26]

The Money

1. How much is needed by when?
2. What will it be used for?
3. What will be the source of repayment?
4. When will it be repaid?

The Entrepreneur(s)

1. What assets do they have?
2. What is their prior credit record?
3. What is their prior business experience?
4. What professional help do they have?
5. How fully committed to the business are they?
6. What buy-sell agreements and life insurance have they?

The Venture

1. What assets does it have?
2. What is its forecasted earning power?
3. What are its competitive strengths and weaknesses?
4. What is its plan of action?
5. What other money does it owe?
6. What might make it a safer borrower?

The Collateral

1. What is available to pledge against a loan?
2. How much bigger than the loan is it?
3. Who owns it, the business or the entrepreneur?

[26]For an illustration, the reader is referred to Don Alexander, *How to Borrow Money from a Bank* (New York: Beaufort Books, 1984).

4. How can its security be assured?
5. How hard will it be to sell?

Making the formal loan proposal should begin with a phone call to request an appointment long enough to make a clear presentation. How much time will be needed can be estimated by rehearsing in advance to a colleague who role-plays the banker, which should also help in polishing the presentation. The entrepreneur should take along the business plan and any supporting documents, such as brochures, sketches of the proposed company, and personal financial records. Central to the presentation should be a detailed cash budget and the ability to explain how the numbers on it were derived. Most crucial to a bank is to know how and when any money to be borrowed will be repaid.

Questions the banker asks should be answered fully but without promising anything that cannot be delivered. It is also appropriate to ask the banker questions on any unclear points. It will probably take the banker time to digest the information, ask and receive further clarification, and make a decision on the loan. The banker may signal this need by saying he or she "will have to take this proposal to the bank's loan committee." Approaching another bank will be appropriate if either the response is negative or processing starts to take too long.

Giving up too easily in a search for capital can be a mistake. Many entrepreneurs found what they needed only after being rejected and moving on to try other sources. Each source should be asked for referrals to other possible sources as well as what the reasons for rejection were and for any suggestions as to what might be done about them. Some "reading between the lines" and tactful questioning may be necessary to determine all the "real" reasons for rejection. One entrepreneur, Robert Tracht, who finally landed a bank loan for his import-export start-up in soft goods, recalled his search:

■   *We called thirty-five banks, and they all gave us the same answer. Everyone said you have to have been in business for at least two years and have $100,000 in working capital. It was like they were all reading from the same cue card.*[27]

Eventually, they found a banker with extensive experience in soft goods, Sam Simons, who made the loan. Simons recalled making the decision:

■   *They seemed to understand soft goods, and really wanted to get ahead. They knew the risks, but they were very careful. But I really can't say I made my decision from the numbers. In this business, it boils down to instinct. You have to have the smell.*[28]

Looking long term also helps. Small loans of under $100,000 such as a start-up might need frequently carry more risk and may be discouraging unless the company demonstrates that it will grow into a greater financing customer in the future.

[27]Joel Kotkin, "The New Small Business Bankers," *Inc.* (May 1984), p. 112.
[28]Ibid.

Loan Terms, Covenants, and Restrictions

A lender, whether a bank, insurance company, other institution, or individual, may choose to impose any number of restrictions on the venture to protect the venture's ability to repay the loan. These can include the following:

- The agreement contains interest and repayment schedules.
- A provision that receipts from certain anticipated sales will be applied directly to loan repayment is included.
- The venture must take out insurance assigned to the lender on the entrepreneur's life sufficient to pay off the loan.
- Other insurance, such as liability insurance and business protection insurance, must be taken out by the venture.
- Certain assets to be purchased by the venture must be pledged against the loan.
- The entrepreneur must personally guarantee the note and may not take out personal loans or guarantee notes for others.
- Certain expenses in the venture's business plan, such as executive salaries, must be capped or even reduced.
- Any other borrowing by the venture must be subordinated.
- The venture must provide quarterly (or even monthly) financial statements and audited annual statements.

In addition, the lender may suggest certain other actions by the entrepreneur that, although not formally required in the loan agreement, are advisable for obtaining the loan itself or anticipated extensions beyond the first loan. Such other actions might include retention of particular types of attorneys, accountants, or consultants; participation in business training programs; or other actions that seem likely to build more managerial strength in the venture.

There can be any number of ways of collateralizing loans. For instance, warehouse receipt financing is a way to borrow against finished goods inventory. The lender, such as a bank, actually keeps the goods in a warehouse and pays for them, allowing the venture to draw down the materials as needed and under close controls. Payment for the goods then carries not only a charge for interest but also a fee for the cost of storing and managing the inventory as well as collecting for it. Therefore, it can be expensive. Good bankers are ingenious at suggesting situations in which various arrangements such as these can help.

Development of a good bank relationship is a continuing process that is helped by staying in close touch with the banker, providing reliable information about developments in the venture as early as possible to avoid surprising the banker, and scrupulously living up to commitments made to the bank. At the same time, there should be no hesitation about asking the bank for help in obtaining information or for referral to other contacts useful to the business.

FINANCING GROWTH – RETAINING EQUITY

Whether a start-up succeeds or does poorly, it will need additional capital. Equity must often be shared to raise it. But sometimes it is possible to grow without sharing equity through some combination of low capital intensity, high margin, and debt. Examples include a software company growing to $20 million in sales, a ski apparel company growing to $35 million, and a solar products company growing to $73 million, all without outside equity sharing.[29]

Clearly, part of the task is to manage existing equity well by controlling cash. It is usually possible to foresee needs for more cash by making cash flow forecasts frequently, and it is also possible to minimize needs for raising more by carefully watching how it is spent. Although Vector Graphic eventually was eclipsed in the microcomputer market by the IBM PC, there were many things it did well. One of them seems to have been managing cash. Lore Harp, who with her friend, Carol Ely, founded the company, described her cash control activities as follows:

■ *"I'm a hawk. I sign all the checks. I still authorize all invoices for payments. Once every couple of weeks I get a big stack. It takes me about fifteen minutes. Just yesterday, I discovered a $1,000 mistake in one invoice. In the context of umpteen million dollars that may seem very small, but it could happen many times. I make people more aware of the importance of these mistakes being eliminated.*

"In receivables I look over the credit limits and see what can be shipped out. I sign off every shipment over $1,000." Keeping her eye on the twenty most expensive items in inventory, she tried to avoid having any of them in stock over six weeks. "We turn our inventory seven or more times a year, which is good," she said.[30]

Other Debt Possibilities

Several other sources of debt to finance expansion without sacrificing equity ownership to outsiders can be noted. Most apply only after the venture is up and running.

1. *Finance companies*, or *asset based lenders*, require collateral, but they are much more flexible about what they will accept as collateral than banks. They also charge much higher interest rates than do banks.[31]
2. *Factors* are companies that buy accounts receivables and take over their collection. This yields cash from sales billings quickly, but it can be an extremely expensive way of getting it.[32]
3. *Community development corporations* can help raise loans, particularly for real estate under some "SBA Debenture 503/504" programs wherein banks take a first mortgage and the SBA takes a second mortgage.[33]
4. *Buying on time* as a way of getting a dealer to finance the purchase of equipment is a common practice.
5. *Leasing* rather than buying equipment can be viewed either as a way of reducing cash needs or as a way of borrowing. The latter may be more realistic, because leases include extra costs similar to interest, they tie up collateral, and they impose fixed payment obligations. *Sale and leaseback* of assets, if the venture has them, is a variation on leasing.

---

[29]Jeffrey L. Seglin, "Growing by Their Bootstraps," *Venture* (July 1985), p. 48.

[30]Susan Benner, "Next Stop Wall Street," *Inc.* (March 1981), p. 37.

[31]Robert A. Mamis, "Lender of Last Resort," *Inc.* (May 1987), p. 149.

[32]Robert A. Mamis, "Factors to Consider," *Inc.* (October 1986), p. 131; also Susan E. Currier, "Selling Receivables for Quick Cash," *Inc.* (July 1983), p. 63.

[33]Eileen Davis, "The Long Arm of the SBA," *Venture* (October 1988), p. 74.

6. *Industrial revenue bond* sales by various state and local governments can sometimes be used, particularly for purchase of real estate, though not usually by start-ups.[34]

Splitouts

A final way to retain ownership of a venture and still raise money for it can be to sell off some part, such as R&D royalties, real estate, or distribution rights, on some basis, possibly by setting up a limited partnership to handle it[35] or by selling rights directly from the venture, as was done in the following case:

■ *A man who had spent all his capital developing and producing for sale a "voice stress analyzer" needed more cash to market it. His plan was to advertise in airline magazines. To those who would pay for the advertisements he offered a full refund from the first revenues received, plus a royalty on sales until investors had received their money back with a substantial return. He got the money.*

To look for possible splitouts, the venture can be divided into parts, which can be envisaged as separate businesses—the more the better. It can be divided into different markets, different business functions, and/or different categories of assets. Each of these can be a candidate for a different form of financing with different types of potential tax incentives and other features to appeal to different types of lenders or investors. Most alternatives will probably not be practical—the subdivisions will be too small. But some may, perhaps by recombining pieces.

■ *Five ex-Xerox employees wanted to set up a Ricoh copy machine dealership. Cash was needed to set up a sales organization and obtain machines for lease and rental. The men were prepared to invest $150,000 from personal assets but considered this insufficient to contend with well-financed major companies in the market. A small investment banking firm devised an approach that financed each part of the business differently. Under a holding company, personal equity was used for creating the sales organization. A separate subsidiary was set up for the leasing activity. When a lease was signed the bank would advance cash to buy a machine. Another subsidiary in the form of a limited partnership was established to buy machines for the rental side of the business and $300,000 worth of shares were sold by the investment banking firm to outsiders.[36]*

Franchising

A special case of selling off selected rights is the familiar phenomenon of franchising. The buyer gets the rights to use the venture's name and formula within a designated region, and in turn the venture is able to expand through use of the franchisee's investment in setting up shop as well as franchise and royalty fees. Sometimes franchisees expand by "subfranchising" to smaller units within a region.[37]

[34]"1986 Plant Directory," *Venture* (October 1986), p. 86; also, "Directory of Incentives for Business Investment" (Washington, DC: Urban Institute Press, 1986).

[35]Edmund L. Andrews, "I'll Take a Limited Partnership with a Twist, Please," *Venture* (May 1988), p. 70.

[36]Bruce G. Posner, "A Rare Case of Bourgeois Values," *Inc.* (June 1983), p. 71.

[37]Ralph Raffio, "Double-Decker Franchising," *Inc.* (November 1986), p. 60.

PLANNING QUESTIONS

The following questions are intended to stimulate thought about what should be considered in moving ahead with a venture. Which questions best apply can vary among entrepreneurs and ventures, as can the order in which they should be considered, the priority that should be placed on them, and which of them should be answered in a written plan.

Cash Requirements

- What has been done to economize capital in the venture?
- What else could be done to economize further if it were absolutely necessary to do so?
- What trade-offs for economizing capital will the venture face in the future, and how will they be struck?
- How will future cash needs of the venture be staged over time? (Include *pro forma* financial statements and cash flow forecast, monthly for first year, quarterly for next two, and annually for next two in business plan appendix. Also include a list of assumptions, including executive salaries, underlined and footnoted to the numbers in the forecasts.)
- What seasonal patterns are projected for inventory, receivables, labor, and servicing demands?
- What effects would variations in assumptions of the forecast have on cash flow needs (sensitivity analysis), and how could they be coped with?

Internal Capital Sources

- Which financing source has given what promise to help cope with cash flow needs?
- What personal resources have the founders committed to the venture? What fraction have they held back?
- What are the targets for distribution of ownership and why?
- Are back-up plans available in case expected cash sources go back on what seem to be their promises? Are the promises written and signed and if not, why not?
- What will the venture do if customers are slow in paying and/or suppliers demand higher prices or faster payment?
- How do operating costs at various production levels compare to each other and to start-up costs?
- To what extent can they be reduced if need be and how fast?
- Has the salability of receivables been discussed with a bank or factor, and if so, what valuation basis was projected?
- What amounts of credit, if any, have the venture's bank and suppliers expressed willingness to extend so far?
- What restrictions, if any, have they imposed?
- What credit will the venture apply for from them and when?
- What additional resources can they and will they commit in the future and under what conditions?
- If individual sales are to be large, will there be advance deposits or progress payments?

Financing Growth Internally

- Has the possibility of customer advance payments, loans, or loan guarantees been explored?
- Are there any present or prospective problems with regard to personal guarantees on loans to the company?
- How salable will its inventory, if any, be?

- What threats to personal or venture solvency, such as loan guarantees, leases, or mortgages, are in force?
- What ones, if any, are contemplated for the future?
- What will the main applications of loans be and how will they be repaid?
- What will be the creditworthiness of any of the venture's customers who will pay other than by cash or credit card?
- Could any product lines, territories, fixed assets, or other pieces of the company be sold off for growth cash?
- Could cash for growth be raised by selling dealerships or franchises of some sort?

POSSIBLE MILESTONES FOR A PLANNING TIME LINE

The most suitable milestones for a time line for a particular venture must be a function of the individual case. These that follow are intended to help stimulate thought about them.

- Sales and costs estimated
- Cash budget completed
- Initial capital lined up
- Banking connection arranged
- Contingency financial plans developed
- First supplier credit obtained
- First bank loan obtained

Chapter 6

OUTSIDE EQUITY CAPITAL

INTRODUCTION

Although there are strong reasons for retaining ownership entirely inside a venture, they are sometimes outweighed by others for sharing ownership with outsiders. The principal reason is to raise larger amounts of capital. Some ventures can be started and can even grow significantly with a small amount of initial capital and retained earnings and debt, but most cannot. It is not always possible or practical to split off assets for separate financing. Therefore, to meet capital needs, the founders must share equity with outsiders, particularly the founders of high–growth-oriented firms, such as those in high technology industries.

A study by Freear and Wetzel illustrates this point. In a sample of 284 out of 1,073 new technology based ventures founded in New England between 1975 and 1986, 177 (62.3 percent) had, by 1987, raised outside equity financing.[1] From another study, Bruno and Tyebjee observed that

> Although outside investment results in the founders' share of the pie decreasing this is often offset by a substantial increase in the size of the pie. Ventures with outside capital achieved average sales of $4 million, sales growth of 157 percent, and growth in

[1] John Freear and William E. Wetzel, Jr., "Equity Financing for New Technology-Based Firms." P. 347 in Bruce A. Kirchhoff, Wayne A. Long, W. Ed McMullan, Karl H. Vesper, and William E. Wetzler, Jr., *Frontiers of Entrepreneurship Research, 1988* (Wellesley, MA: Babson Center for Entrepreneurial Studies, 1988).

TABLE 6-1 Comparison of Capital-Raising Methods

CONSIDERATIONS	DEBT	COMMON STOCK	PREFERRED STOCK
Must Pay Back	Yes	No	No
Must Pay Periodically	Interest	No	Depends on terms
Control through Voting	No	Yes	No
Restrictive terms	Maybe	No	No

number of employees of 77 percent, compared to $8 million, 48 percent and 35 percent, respectively, in the case of companies which did not receive outside capital.[2]

There is room for considerable virtuosity in making financial deals to obtain capital because of the variety of items that can be shared for money and the choices of amounts and terms that can be worked out for each. An entrepreneur can use any of the following to raise money:

1. Common stock—voting or nonvoting
2. Preferred stock
3. Bonds or notes—subordinated or not
4. Royalties
5. Consulting commitments or paid positions
6. Warrants, options, or rights for any of these items
7. Combinations of any of these items

This chapter describes three main ways of sharing ownership to raise outside capital: (1) private placements, (2) formal venture capital, and (3) public offerings. Finding the source that will work best or at all may require considerable searching. As mentioned earlier in connection with finding a bank that will make a loan, the entrepreneur should not give up easily. Each rejection may yield ideas for ways to improve the venture and the funding proposal as well as other leads to try for the capital. A long list of possible sources can therefore be a worthwhile searching aid. A summary of the three main ways of raising capital—debt, common stock, and preferred stock—appears in Table 6-1.

When Seed Plus Debt Is Not Enough

Much as an entrepreneur or founding team might like to retain 100 percent ownership, it is sometimes not the best idea for the venture or not even possible, as the following sequences show:

[2]Albert V. Bruno and Tyzoon T. Tyebjee, "The Entrepreneur's Search for Capital," *Journal of Business Venturing*, 1 (no. 1) (Winter 1985), 63.

- The founders have a good idea and skills for start-up but no savings or at least not enough savings and borrowing capability to get started.
- The founders have enough savings coupled with borrowings to get started but not enough for adequate product development, testing, advertising, or production volume to reduce costs enough to withstand competition.
- The founders have enough to get started, but a successful start may lead to such growth in demand that more outside capital than can be borrowed will be needed to keep growing. To go looking for capital at that point may so distract the founders from managing well that the company will lose momentum.

Table 6–2 shows some industries that have particularly high start-up capital needs.[3]

Faced with such needs, many founders have no choice but to seek capital through sharing ownership. Amdahl Corporation, for example, required $50 million to start, so Gene Amdahl had to sell ownership to a syndicate of large corporate investors. The money-raising process took five years.[4]

The alternative, running out of liquidity, can create problems, as illustrated by the experience of Joseph J. Turek, developer of a Massachusetts intrusion detector company whose sales began to grow. This should have been cause for celebration but was not because of the increased need for cash that was not available, as *Venture* reported:

■ *Turek is hardly rejoicing. Money is so tight that he can't afford to fund new R&D, market his products or build up inventories. Instead of getting components on a weekly or monthly basis, he must reorder almost daily in a desperate attempt to shorten the gap between accounts payable and accounts receivable. The consequence: an administrative nightmare where delayed shipments can throw his production process out of whack. And that's not the only problem. Early last year, when his bank suddenly reduced his line of credit 77 percent to $150,000, Turek had to ditch plans to promote and expand his products. He found himself unable to support four newly hired technicians and a sales*

TABLE 6–2 High Start-up Capital Industries

INDUSTRY	START-UP CAPITAL NEED (in millions)
Satellite communications	$ 100–200
Specialty airline	75–100
Surface transportation	50–100
Specialty chemical processing	50–100
Lease financing	40–50
Biotechnology	25–50
Data communications network	25–50
Semiconductors	25–40
Oil exploration	25–30

[3]Pavan Sangal, "Ten Expensive Startup Fields," *Venture* (September 1981), p. 67.
[4]Susan Benner, "Starting Over," *Inc.* (January 1981), p. 33.

manager, and to continue advertising in trade magazines. Turek still worries about production. Assembly by hand adds 10 percent to his expenses, yet he can't afford the $500,000 he needs to automate the assembly line. To make matters worse, competition is looming. "I've heard about products being developed in West Germany that would cost $1 to $2 less per unit," Turek laments. "If they come in we won't be able to compete. We'll keep our customers, but we'll never grow."[5]

Stages and Outside Equity

A perspective on the variety of financing avenues that may apply at the various stages of development is provided by the Freear and Wetzel study mentioned earlier. They studied 445 equity capital deals (rounds) accounting for $671 million raised by 284 young technology-based firms.[6] A percentage breakdown of the total $671 million among five sources as it applied to three stages — seed, start-up, and later — appears in Table 6–3. Several observations can be made:

- About one-fourth (25.4 percent) of the total outside equity was raised by these young firms during seed and start-up stages.
- Seed-stage ventures drew less than one-fifth as much outside equity as start-up–stage ventures (3.9 percent versus 21.5 percent). This is near the low end of the range found by Timmons and Bygrave for highly innovative technology seed-stage ventures financed by venture capital firms, which ran from 3.5 to 10.3 percent depending on time period.[7]
- Private investors and venture capital firms accounted for about the same amounts of seed-stage outside equity, and together for nearly all of it.
- Venture capital's share of outside capital was over twice that of private investors' share at the start-up stage and over eight times as much at still later stages.
- Public offering's share was zero at seed stage and grew with successive stages.

Private investors did over four times as many seed-stage deals and one-and-one-half times as many start-up–stage deals as did venture capital firms. They also did typically smaller deals than venture capitalists. For the former, median deal size

TABLE 6–3   Breakdown of $671 Million Raised by Young Technology-based Firms

STAGE	AMOUNT (in millions)	%
Seed	$ 26	3.9
Start-up	144	21.5
Later	501	74.6
TOTAL	671	100.0

[5]Edmund L. Andrews, "Running out of Money," *Venture* (January 1986), p. 32.

[6]Freear and Wetzel, "Equity Financing," p. 347.

[7]Jeffry A. Timmons and William D. Bygrave, "Venture Capital's Role in Financing Innovation for Economic Growth," *Journal of Business Venturing*, 1 (no. 2) (Spring 1986), 169.

was in the $100,000 to $200,000 range for all rounds, whereas for the latter it was around $400,000 at start-up and from $1 million to $3 million at later rounds.[8] An implicit rule of thumb might be to choose a funding source according to the amount needed—private investors if it is under $1 million, venture capital firms for $1 to $3 million, and public offering if it is above $3 million. Even so, all sorts of exceptions apply.

A logical progression for financing starts with personal savings and borrowing, moves to private placements and then to venture capital, and finally ends with a public offering where founders and capitalists alike are able to cash in on the venture. So-called "bridge financing," wherein a few individuals put up short-term cash at high rates of return is sometimes used to tide a venture over between stages when the financing of a succeeding stage does not come together quite as fast as it is needed. But such a sequence is rare. Most ventures do not get beyond founders' savings plus debt, and successively fewer ventures use each additional stage. The value in learning about them, however, is that although they happen rarely, they remain possibilities.

PRIVATE PLACEMENTS

Some well-known companies formed with private financing have included Du Pont (1802, 18 shareholders, $36,000) and the Ford Motor Company (1903, 11 shareholders, $28,000).[9]

Silent Partners

Financial backers who take a close personal interest as well as equity but not an active role in running the business are sometimes known as *silent partners*. They may be friends and relatives or others interested in making money simply by investing, as in the following example:

■ *A prosperous retired surgeon complained to his investment adviser about problems he had in handling physical objects because one of his hands had been amputated due to an infection. The adviser thought about the problem and devised improvements for an artificial arm to help his client.*

After trying the new attachment, the surgeon was so pleased and impressed that not only did he begin giving lectures about it to professional groups but he also proposed to the adviser that he set up a company which they would jointly own to produce and sell it. The adviser, in addition to having come up with the product idea, would do the work of setting up the business, while he, the surgeon, would provide the capital.

Terms for the partnership, which were formulated by the adviser and accepted by the surgeon, would divide ownership fifty-fifty. In return for this investment, the surgeon

---

[8]Freear and Wetzel, "Equity Financing," p. 347.

[9]Royal Little, "Shoestring Financing of Great Enterprises," *Journal of Business Venturing*, 2 (no. 1) (Winter 1987), 1.

would receive preferred stock. The adviser would take no money out of the business personally until the surgeon's preferred stock had been fully redeemed by the company.

On that basis the company was started. The surgeon took no active role in the business whatever. Within a couple of years, the surgeon had been repaid. The adviser then bought out his common stock as well.

A more complicated arrangement could have attempted to specify the terms of buyback on the surgeon's common as well as preferred stock. It could also have specified preferred stock dividends for the surgeon in lieu of interest on the money. In fact, however, the two men agreed to keep the arrangement simple and work out whatever terms would be mutually agreeable at each successive stage. That way, neither had reason to claim he was being short-changed by unforeseeable developments.

Partners who intend to be silent sometimes turn out not to be. If well chosen, they can provide expertise, contacts, and more cash as the company grows.[10] George Ballas, inventor of the Weed Eater, commented on the importance of choosing investors with care:

■ *In a start-up situation, the investor must have confidence in you. If he doesn't, if he's the type that checks with accountants, attorneys and bankers, I'd say forget him. He will probably continue to question, investigate and cite the law to you regarding your actions and his rights after he has invested. In general, he will cause a lot of unnecessary problems that will impede the progress of the venture by creating added expenses and taking a lot of time from many key people. In the end he will either threaten legal action or file suit against you.*[11]

Finding silent partners can be likened to finding someone with whom to have a party, start a game, or even marry. It happens through personal and professional acquaintances, such as advisers, associates, and even employers. Sometimes there is no harm in telling other people about a desire to start a business and to obtain help, possibly through finding a partner. Each person told may tell others, so lines of communication to potential partners can multiply geometrically. Undertaking the process gradually should help control its direction and speed, so the person seeking a partner is not besieged by supplicants too numerous or unsuitable. The following example appeared in *Venture:*

■ *Allen Michels began Convergent Technologies, Inc., with $16.22 in 1979. "About enough," he says, "to run it for three hours." William D. Rollnick had been one of Michels's best customers when Michels ran the microcomputer systems division at Intel Corp. "He was also my friend," notes Rollnick. "I could tell he was a friend, because we could fight and still like one another."*

Rollnick had also just sold one of his computer rental companies. "I bought cheap and sold it for more than I paid," says Rollnick, "Just like my daddy always told me."

[10]Robert A. Mamis, "New Money," *Inc.* (April 1984), p. 93.
[11]George C. Ballas and David Hollas, *The Making of an Entrepreneur* (Englewood Cliffs, NJ: Prentice Hall, 1980), p. 104.

"I asked him if he'd like to spend it," says Michels. "To my astonishment he said yes."
In 40 minutes they cut the deal for a $2 million investment from Rollnick and two of his
friends; Michels gave up 64 percent of Convergent.[12]

Having such a wealthy and available friend is more than most would-be
entrepreneurs can hope for. But it does not hurt to look.

Informal Investors

Informal investors are similar to silent partners but are less personally connected to the entrepreneurs. Wetzel defined them as having a net worth over $1
million, annual income over $100,000, substantial business and financial experi-
ence, the ability to evaluate investments, no affiliation with the founders or their
ventures, and the willingness to take high risks over extended time to earn high
profits. He estimated that in 1987, such investors accounted for $50 billion, or over
twice the amount managed by professional venture capital firms at that time. The
average deal, he estimated, involved three such investors and around $250,000.[13] It
takes on the average about six months to arrange financing with individual investors with whom the entrepreneur is dealing for the first time, at least for high
technology start-ups, according to Bruno and Tyebjee.[14]

Finding Investors. Although they sometimes know each other and collaborate on deals together, many informal investors prefer not to be known as such.
Rather than having large numbers of entrepreneurs coming to them looking for
money, they prefer to seek out, possibly with the aid of a few select personal
advisers, the kinds of ventures in which they want to invest. They most often get
leads from trusted associates, such as lawyers, bankers, stockbrokers, accountants,
insurance and investment advisers, suppliers, customers, business brokers, and
fellow entrepreneurs. Hence, these are sources that the entrepreneur may be able
to work from the other end.

The entrepreneur can, for instance, ask at a stock brokerage whether any
salesperson there might have a client who occasionally likes to invest in private
companies, as opposed to listed stocks. Requesting personal referrals from people
who can vouch from experience for the entrepreneur's integrity and competence is
particularly effective as a way of setting the venture apart from many others
seeking capital. Even asking for referrals by prospects who say the venture is not
for them can help.

Some contacts, such as investment brokers and real estate brokers, regard
themselves as professional intermediaries entitled to be paid for such service—
perhaps as much as 7 to 10 percent on deals under $1 million. Lipper points out

---

[12]William Bryant Logan, "Finding Your Angel," *Venture* (March 1986), p. 38.
[13]William E. Wetzel, Jr., "The Informal Venture Capital Market: Aspects of Scale and Market Efficiency," *Journal of Business Venturing*, 2 (no. 4) (Fall 1987), 299.
[14]Bruno and Tyebjee, "The Entrepreneur's Search for Capital," p. 63.

that such a finder becomes the entrepreneur's agent, not that of the investor, and should be paid by the entrepreneur according to a clear understanding. A percentage of the deal, he suggests, could start with 5 percent on the first million then drop a percent each million to a minimum of 1 percent, plus such expenses as the agreement details. There should be a written agreement that specifies these points as well as a time limit and just which services the finder will be paid for.[15]

Country clubs and other social networks can also serve as a less expensive route than professional intermediaries. Some examples described by Posner are illustrative:

■ *Jim Poure was active in his country club, where he convinced a fellow board member to invest $100,000 in a limited partnership which would own a plant needed by his venture. Based upon that he was able to borrow another $500,000 from his bank.*

■ *Henry Stickney contacted two old Air Force buddies to help him find limited partners among doctor acquaintances of theirs to own a building which his venture then leased.*[16]

It can be noted that both these cases involve splitoff deals where the partnership will own real estate. Moreover, both also involve raising resources for businesses that are ongoing. The problems may be different for start-ups, but the concept of seeking limited partners through social acquaintances and through business contacts can still apply.

Inquiries must be done with some care so as not to be construed as a public offering, as will be further discussed later. It is important not to offer shares in the company either to "unsophisticated" investors or to more than around twenty in total without first obtaining permission from the state agency governing the sale of securities and the federal Securities and Exchange Commission. If unsure at all about legality, an entrepreneur should contact these agencies and/or a lawyer specializing in securities law.

As a more formal mechanism for matching informal investors with potential deals to aid this process, Professor William Wetzel established a "Venture Capital Network" at the University of New Hampshire, which maintains a confidential database of such investors and their interests. Entrepreneurs can enter information on their ventures to allow computerized selective matchmaking. He reported that during the first twelve months of its operation, the network arranged introductions for over 200 entrepreneurs and 300 investors. Both can be listed in the computer confidentially to allow matching to be selective without risk of public exposure. The number of actual deals was not tracked, but at least seven were

---

[15]Arthur Lipper III, *Venture's Financing and Investing in Private Companies* (Chicago: Probus Publishing, 1988), p. 172.
[16]Bruce G. Posner, "A Limited Success," *Inc.* (February 1988), p. 114.

noted in the first twelve months.[17] Other such networks have sprung up in other states.[18] In some areas, there are also venture capital clubs that may be helpful.[19] The MIT alumni office can provide leads to meetings of the MIT Start-up Forum, where entrepreneurs in search of capital meet with potentially interested investors.

It is important to note that actions taken with regard to seed capital can have major implications for the future prospects of obtaining growth capital. A venture with many seed investors is typically less attractive for later investors. At the same time, seed capital investors may resist application for later growth capital if it threatens to undermine their control or dilute their ownership. Informal investors tend to be both less tolerant of setbacks in venture performance and less likely to increase investment if difficulties in the venture create the need for it. However, some, such as entrepreneurs who have been through start-up themselves, can contribute much helpful guidance in addition to investing.[20]

An aspect of this process that can sometimes be tricky is the signing of a secrecy or nondisclosure agreement. The entrepreneur may want a prospective partner or investor to do so in case the deal does not go through. But the investors or partners may not want to sign because doing so may make them vulnerable to a lawsuit even though they may not do anything wrong. It could be that the person signing might already know the information or might be working on something similar, and the nondisclosure agreement might restrict that person without real cause. Or it could be that some other party might reveal the secret and somehow the person who signed the nondisclosure agreement is accused of violating the agreement. Typically, professional investors refuse to sign such agreements. One rationale is that if the entrepreneurs do not trust them, they should not come to them in the first place.

Getting the wrong private investors can also cause problems. "Some angels are just making a cocktail party investment," according to one entrepreneur. "They're too passive or too nervous, and you can't count on them when more money is needed or a crisis comes. Too often the angel is playing golf in Barbados when you really need him."[21] Other complaints include investors who meddle too much and others who fail to deliver on promises of support[22] and still others who resist efforts to raise further capital from outside, out of concern for dilution. Consequently, it can be prudent for the entrepreneur to check the references and reputations of prospective investors just as they may want to check those of the entrepreneur. Careful structuring of the deal can also help.

[17]William E. Wetzel, "The Informal Venture Capital Market: Aspects of Scale and Market Efficiency." P. 275 in Lipper, *Venture's Financing and Investing in Private Companies.*

[18]Logan, "Finding Your Angel," p. 42.

[19]"Letters," *Venture* (November 1986), p. 12.

[20]Mamis, "New Money," p. 93.

[21]Logan, "Finding Your Angel," p. 38.

[22]Pamela J. King, "Showdown at U-Cart," *Venture* (July 1980), p. 72; also, Michelle Bekey and Edward J. Doherty, "When Investors Pull the Plug," *Venture* (April 1980), p. 68.

Deal Terms.   The variables that can be shaped to make a venture financing deal work include control, ownership, pricing, security, restrictions, amount, staging or timing of infusions, and types of financial instruments — common or preferred stock, bonds, warrants, options, convertibility, and other covenants.

Many informal investors, for instance, write control provisions into their investment agreements, expect to be kept abreast of developments, want to be on boards of directors of ventures they are involved with, and sometimes take over management entirely when they think either that they must or that they can run things better than the founders. Agreed-upon reporting requirements can relieve investors of the need for asking questions and shield the entrepreneur from meddling inquiries later. Including an arbitration clause in the investment contract can be helpful for both parties.

How much control and ownership a founder must give up to get financing is a question that comes quickly to the minds of would-be entrepreneurs. In two words, the answer is "it depends." How much the founders are investing, how much money the venture can be expected to make with different levels of probability, how much of the investment will be lost with different levels of shortfall in performance, how soon the investor will be able to cash in, and how much help the entrepreneurs will need besides the money all affect the answer, as do the current cost of money in the market, how well the expertise and type of business of the investors fit the particular venture, how much capital the investor has to apply, and who else might have to be brought in now or later and at what cost.

Arthur Lipper's book on investing in private companies suggests several different methods of formulating a deal and also for drafting the terms.[23] He prefers not to invest money for stock, or in fact to invest any money at all. Rather, he offers to guarantee a bank loan in return for a "Revenue Participation Certificate" that prescribes that a royalty percentage (between 1 and 5 percent) on total sales of the venture be paid to the backer in return for providing a guarantee, backed up by a letter of credit, for a loan from a bank or other institution. The guarantee would be for one or two years and the royalty would last much longer ("in perpetuity," he suggests, though noting that negotiation might arrive at a different duration).

The following questions should be answered in setting up such a deal:

1. How much is the royalty, how long does it last, and can it be sold or assigned?
2. What is guaranteed, all of the loan or only part, and for how long?
3. In case of default (defined how?), who goes after the borrower first, the bank or the guarantor?
4. What collateral must the guarantor put up?
5. Under what conditions, if any, can either party get out of the deal?
6. What reporting requirements, if any, does the borrower have, and to whom?
7. What promises or predictions of performance should the entrepreneur make in writing, and what should happen if they do not come true?

[23]Lipper, *Venture's Financing and Investing in Private Companies*, p. 338.

8. Should the entrepreneur be required to have anyone else such as family or friends also sign on the loan?

In a case where some sort of security, rather than a royalty, is used for a loan guarantee, Lipper recommends, from the investor's point of view, debt that is convertible into equity based on a formula that lets the entrepreneur keep more of the company to the extent that the company meets its forecasts and less if it falls below them.

A basis for pricing the security should be a comparison with listed companies' securities. Noting that the venture will involve higher risk and its stock will have no initial market, he suggests that it should promise the investor a correspondingly greater multiple of return than a listed security. The multiple of earnings to price over a given investment period, he says, should be five times as great for seed capital in a venture as for a listed stock, three times as great for start-up capital, and two times as great for "second-stage" financing after the venture is up and running.[24]

If an entrepreneur is personally unable or unwilling to invest, but the prospects of the business are still attractive, Lipper suggests the following:

■ *My proposal in such a case is that investors receive 100 percent of the initial equity of the business (perhaps structuring to qualify for the benefits of S corporation status), and that entrepreneurs receive an option from the company to acquire within 5 to 10 years 50 percent of the then-to-be outstanding shares at 150 percent of the investor's cost with, of course, the money going to the company. The investor could permit a lower exercise price if the option was exercised earlier than agreed or could adjust the exercise price to the performance of the company. . . . If entrepreneurs suggest that this (or any other proposed deal) is too tough a deal, I usually ask if they have any friends or family members who would like to participate with me in this overly unfair deal favoring the investor.*[25]

Another basis for pricing an investment is to compare it with available returns an investor might expect to get through investing in comparable companies that are listed on the stock exchange. Venture capitalists use rules of thumb for pricing, as will be discussed later. They tend to focus on multiples of return on their investment that they hope to realize through selling out the investment after a few years. Thus, they might specify a desire to recover three to five times their money in three to five years.

The next example illustrates the use of preferred stock. John Cheever wanted to develop a chain of stores without giving up control. An investment company, 3i, which had been set up for investment in U.S. industry by three British banks proposed the following deal, as described by *Inc.:*

24Ibid., p. 148.
25Ibid., p. 128.

■ *The investment company proposed putting up $2 million in two types of nonvoting preferred stock. The first would function much like an eight-year fixed-rate loan: Cheever would receive $1.5 million and have to pay a dividend of 6 percent per year. In years six through ten the venture would pay off the $1.5 million in equal installments to redeem the shares. The second type of preferred would pay a 3 percent royalty on sales in return for the other $500,000 of investment. This participating preferred would not be redeemable, but if and when the venture were sold it would convert to around 30 percent of the common stock.*[26]

Yet another variation is to combine splitoff with rights to buy equity in the parent as well as the part split off, as illustrated by the next example:

■ *A man who had developed a new drug and needed money to market it set up a limited partnership to finance the marketing effort separately. Through private placement of $15,000 units, $2.5 million was raised. Costs of setting up and selling the financing were about 15 percent. In return, the partnership received a 10 percent royalty until the investment was repaid threefold. Additionally, investors received warrants to buy 6 percent of the parent company's shares for another $1 million, which would in turn further help capitalize the company by sharing equity.*[27]

Other Private Placement Sources

Corporate Investors.   Established corporations occasionally provide money for start-ups, sometimes to get "windows on technologies" through the ventures they invest in, sometimes to find potential acquisitions, and sometimes simply as profit-generating mechanisms. Some invest in the ideas of employees who are leaving to start new ventures and even work out licensing arrangements with them. That way the corporation retains at least some interest in new ideas it might otherwise fail to benefit from.[28] Foreign corporations, particularly in Asia, often consider acquisition of technology the major reason for investing in U.S. start-ups.[29]

Development Corporations.   Capital for either start-up or growth is available in some regions through community development corporations. Such a corporation is put into operation by citizens of a local area in need of economic development. If the region has high unemployment, the federal government's Community Services Administration will grant money to extend the development corporation's capital. The corporation can invest or lend the capital to anyone who will set up shop and create jobs in the area. Use of such capital for a start-up is illustrated by the following case:

■ *James Egnew and John Moore, co-workers in a tent manufacturing company wanted to start a new tentmaking company but needed $700,000 to finance it. Between their savings and those of some prospective sales representatives, they could raise only $130,000.*

---

[26]Bruce G. Posner, "Equity Without Tears," *Inc.* (August 1984), p. 116.
[27]Edmund L. Andrews, "I'll Take a Limited Partnership with a Twist, Please," *Venture* (May 1988), p. 70.
[28]Richard Barbieri, "When a Former Employer Backs Your Startup," *Venture* (November 1983), p. 64.
[29]Sabin Russell, "The Yen for Capital," *Venture* (November 1985), p. 134.

> "We were told," Egnew recalled, "that a community development corporation, Kentucky Highlands Investment Corporation, had money to invest in a venture like ours. But there was a hitch. Firms it invested in must move to and operate in a ten-county area in the economically underdeveloped mountains of Kentucky. A back-country location had been far from our plan, as had been accepting a socially motivated institution as a significant stockholder."
>
> The development corporation was willing to put up $100,000 for 25 percent of the common stock and to loan another $120,000 on six-year 14 percent subordinated debentures. Two local banks offered a $350,000 loan, and a local coal company offered free use of an unoccupied warehouse.
>
> When 36 initial job openings were offered 2,000 people applied. Sales of $790,000 the first year carried the startup, Outdoor Venture Corporation, past breakeven, and sales the second year were over $1.2 million. Additional loans from the development corporation enabled construction of a new and larger plant. By year seven sales exceeded $8.1 million.[30]

Public and private business development corporations are created from time to time in various parts of the country.[31] Because they apply resources locally, the way to look for them is through local agencies, such as economic development offices and chambers of commerce. Many states also have incubators that can provide leads to such financing.[32]

Foreign Investors. Deals with overseas financing sources can take many forms. Costs of making contacts, becoming sufficiently acquainted to establish confidence, and dealing with new technicalities that often require intermediaries who must be paid can make such deals expensive.[33] Consequently, they tend to apply mainly to larger deals, often later financing rounds for established companies that can afford the cost in both money and time. Exceptions can occur when dealing with single foreign individual investors on a personal basis or when a start-up has technology or marketing rights abroad to offer to a foreign partner as part of the package.[34] Points of contact include U.S. offices of foreign banks, securities firms, chambers of commerce, trading companies, and consulates, as well as U.S. banks with foreign-trade specialists.

FORMAL VENTURE CAPITAL

Professionals whose full-time occupation is managing pools of capital that finance start-ups and small growth-oriented companies have grown in number to an estimated 470 over the past forty years and now comprise what has become known

---

[30]"A New Business Takes Off from an Unlikely Launching Pad," *The Business Owner* (September-October 1978), p. 11.

[31]A. David Silver, "Flexible Lenders," *Venture* (June 1979), p. 18.

[32]Udayan Gupta, "More Incubators Used to Hatch Small Firms," *Wall Street Journal*, January 24, 1990, p. B1.

[33]Curtis Schroeder, "We Went Overseas for Easier, Cheaper Cash," *Inc.* (February 1980), p. 75.

[34]Marie-Jeanne Juilland, "Asian Money—And More," *Venture* (November 1986), p. 34.

as the "venture capital industry."[35] As of 1988 it represented an estimated $31.4 billion in funds, including independent private funds of $24.9 billion (80.0 percent), corporate funds of $3.9 billion (12.6 percent) and SBICs (small business investment companies), which were augmented with government lending to represent $2.3 billion (7.4 percent).[36]

The larger venture capital firms have tended to concentrate in California, New York, Massachusetts, and Texas. But many other states also include large as well as small venture capital firms, and the larger firms often do deals outside their localities. Many specialize by industry or level of technology. They often collaborate on larger financings. Operators of these firms constitute a common-interest group, many of whose members know each other fairly well, meet through associations and financing syndicates, and exchange information and advice.

Venture capital is a term whose romance has been enhanced by association with spectacular ventures such as Apple and Intel, by attention in the press, and through study by researchers, possibly because of the romance and because easy identification of such successful firms makes them an inviting population to study. But the fraction of ventures in which venture capital is invested is extremely small, only a couple of thousand out of millions of small firms and hundreds of thousands of start-ups. It is not available to most entrepreneurs.

Most venture capital firms do not invest in seed stages or small deals. They have found it more lucrative to concentrate on young companies already operating and ready to take off on rapidly rising growth trajectories and on leveraged buyouts. In the latter, heavy use of borrowing (leverage) against the assets of a company is used to generate cash for buying the company from its owners. If some nonborrowed cash is also needed, the venture capitalists may provide that in return for a substantial share of the equity. Thus for a relatively small amount of cash they can become major shareholders in a company that is already going and has progressed beyond the risks of start-up.

One venture capitalist who did set up a seed-capital fund for startups described his somewhat disappointing experience as follows:

■ *In early 1981 we reorganized our seed capital into a limited partnership small business investment company. This structure enabled us to work a three-stage financing plan: $100,000 to plan and launch the enterprise; $200,000 to develop products and begin manufacturing and marketing operations; and a later $250,000 or so to bring the venture to economic viability. Even with this kind of financing we found our venture projects very tightly constrained with little margin for error. We ran with too thin a startup management team and depended too much on outside contractors. We had difficulty recruiting skilled people even when we thought we could afford them because of the modest capital base.*

We've experienced delays, performance shortfalls, and technical problems in every venture we participated in thus far. They are often far under sales forecasts during the

---

[35]John C. Ruhnka and John E. Young, "A Venture Capital Model of the Development Process for New Ventures," *Journal of Business Venturing*, 2 (no. 2) (Spring 1987), 167.

[36]*Venture Capital Yearbook* (Wellesley, MA: Venture Economics, 1988), p. 7.

first year or two. People who haven't been through it cannot believe how hard it is to sell unique new products offered by an unknown new company.[37]

Some venture capital firms, such as the $5 million Zero Stage Capital fund of Boston, do specialize in seed-stage investments. Some have even gone so far as to pick a product area and assemble founders in order to finance a start-up.[38] By the mid-eighties, *Venture* reported that some major venture capital firms had established a growing number of "feeder funds" to help get ventures started and up to a point where the larger funds could take serious interest in them.[39] Timmons and Bygrave took further note of these as aids in venture development.[40] Perhaps the most spectacular example to date of a seed venture capital investment was that of Digital Equipment Corporation:

■ *Harlan Anderson and Ken Olsen, engineers at MIT's Lincoln Laboratory in the early fifties had been invited to join a new business venture. Disappointed when it failed to materialize, the two decided to develop one of their own. To learn about business they read management texts from the public library, and with what they learned undertook to plan for starting a computer company. For capital they approached the only venture capital firm in town, American Research and Development. The firm asked them to submit a formal written plan, and in response the two wrote out four pages. When they were asked for more details, they went back to the library and developed the plan further, including four year financial projections.*

Next they were told to prepare a formal presentation to the venture capital firm's board, and were advised to project profits of at least five percent and early breakeven but with no mention of computers, since some major companies such as General Electric and Honeywell seemed to be demonstrating currently that headway against IBM in that field was not possible.

AR&D's response was to offer $70,000 in equity plus a $30,000 loan in return for what turned out to be 77 percent of the start-up. Fifteen years later, in 1972, the venture capital firm sold its $70,000 stake in the company for $400 million.[41]

At the very first stages of a venture, it is the considerable expense and time it takes to work out a deal on an enterprise (little deals, it is said, take about as much time and trouble to work out as big ones) that causes many venture capitalists to avoid investment at the very start.

Whether to Seek Venture Capital

Some people claim that formal venture capitalists increase the odds of success in a venture through their guidance, arrangement of useful business connections, ability to provide more money when needed, and experience in

[37]William R. Chandler, "Prestartup Seed Capital." P. 38 in Stanley E. Pratt, ed., *Guide to Venture Capital Sources* (Wellesley Hills, MA: Capital Publishing Corp., 1981).

[38]G. Thomas Gibson, "How Early Is 'Early Stage'?," *Venture* (March 1984), p. 120.

[39]Lori Ioannou, "The Lure of Feeder Funds," *Venture* (January 1985), p. 28.

[40]Jeffry A. Timmons and William D. Bygrave, "Venture Capital's Role in Financing Innovation for Economic Growth," *Journal of Business Venturing*, 1 (no. 2) (Spring 1986), 169.

[41]Glenn Rifkin and George Harrar, *The Ultimate Entrepreneur* (Chicago: Contemporary Books, 1988), p. 14.

taking companies public. The reasoning goes that because some professional venture capitalists have records of successful investing, selection by them enhances a company's success. They may require a substantial share of equity, but it is better to have a small piece of a big pie than a big piece of a small pie or a pie that is likely not to survive at all, as the following example from *Venture* illustrates:

■   A *classic case of hanging on too long is that of Michael and Charity Cheiky, who founded Ohio Scientific in 1975. Their technically advanced, low-cost computers built company sales to $20 million. Recalls Charity Cheiky: "We were determined to do things our own way." But Ohio Scientific needed capital to maintain market share against competitors and the Cheikys finally sold to M/A Comm, which soon divested it. Although $1 million richer from the sale, the Cheikys were without a company.*[42]

Venture capitalists usually require membership on the company's board of directors, monthly financial statements with annual audits, and substantial life insurance policies on key executives of the venture. They mete money out as needed, requiring that entrepreneurs live up to business plans and keep coming back for support to advance further. They may also require a buy-sell clause in the investment agreement to leave open the option of taking over the venture entirely to save it from failure.

Arguments against using venture capitalists point out that such requirements burden the founders unduly while robbing them of a great amount of equity capital. Some studies claim that professional venture capitalists do not really add value, as indicated by the fact that their investments do not seem to fare any better than the overall average. A study by Cherin and Hergert reported that no evidence of superior performance by venture capital-backed firms was found and in fact the market performance of non-venture capital-backed firms was actually superior to their venture backed counterparts.[43]

However, MacMillan, David M. Kulow and Roubina Khoylian found that performance seemed too dependent on the nature and extent of the venture capitalists' involvement. In some cases involvement enhanced performance and in others it appeared to affect performance of the venture adversely.[44] Some attained portfolio performance far above average and others substantially below average. Within the portfolio of each, moreover, were some ventures that did well and others that fared poorly.[45] The individual entrepreneur is left with the question of which venture capitalists to do business with and the more important task of

[42]G. Thomas Gibson, "Holding Onto Equity," *Venture* (May 1983), p. 62.

[43]Antony Cherin and Michael Hergert, "Do Venture Capitalists Create Value?" P. 342 in Kirchhoff et al., *Frontiers of Entrepreneurship Research 1988* (Wellesley, MA: Babson Center for Entrepreneurship Studies, 1988).

[44]Ian C. MacMillan, David M. Kulow and Roubina Khoylian, "Venture Capitalists' Involvement in their Investments: Extent and Performance." P. 322 in ibid.

[45]William D. Bygrave, Norman A. Fast, Roubina Khoylian, Linda Vincent and William Yue, "Rates of Return of Venture Capital Investing: a Study of 131 Funds." P. 275 in ibid.

seeing to it that his or her venture is one of the winners within the capitalist's portfolio.

What Venture Capitalists Want. A necessary but not sufficient requirement for venture capitalists, according to a study by Rea, is that the venture exploit a market where there is opportunity for rapid growth. The product, he found, required a competitive edge but did not have to be a major improvement over others in the market. Also, a strong team was considered essential, although it did not have to be fully in place at start-up.[46]

Bruno and Tyebjee found that "the entrepreneur should have a significant amount of experience working in several other companies before trying to start a company of his own. Whether this experience is gained in small or large companies is not as important as whether the entrepreneur gained experience in a variety of business functions. Engineering, marketing, and R&D-related experience was most prevalent among the founders in our study. Manufacturing and sales experience was less prevalent." Also, "the entrepreneur should form a management team which is well rounded in technical and management skills before initiating a search for capital. The entrepreneur should think in terms of a venture team in search for financing rather than a single individual with a business plan."[47] MacMillan et al. conducted structured interviews with venture capitalists and found a variety of venture selection criteria, with a similar emphasis on the qualifications of the entrepreneurial team.[48] The cliché that "it is better to bet on a grade 'A' entrepreneur with a grade 'B' idea than a grade 'B' entrepreneur with a grade 'A' idea" has endured.

There has been a trend toward venture capitalists typically preferring to invest later, after the venture is at least partly going. *Inc.* reported that whereas in 1980, 48 percent of venture capitalists expressed interest in start-up investments, that number had fallen to only 25 percent by 1990.[49] The most likely combination has typically been for founders to furnish the initial capital and the venture capitalists to wait and come in later, as illustrated by the experience of Priam, a manufacturer of computer disk drives:

■ *In the late 70's Bill Schroeder, a Harvard MBA who worked for Memorex, a manufacturer of main frame computer disk drives, and Al Wilson, Memorex's engineering vice president, met Paul Wythes, a venture capitalist, when Memorex was working out financing with Wythes' firm, Sutter Hill Ventures. The three discussed possibilities for applying big computer disk drive technology to produce drives for microcomputers.*

---

[46]Robert H. Rea, "Factors Affecting Success and Failure of Seed Capital/Start-up Negotiations," *Journal of Business Venturing*, 4 (no. 2) (March 1989), 149.

[47]Bruno and Tyebjee, "The Entrepreneur's Search for Capital," p. 63.

[48]Ian C. MacMillan, Robin Siegel, and P.N. Subba Narasimha, "Criteria Used by Venture Capitalists to Evaluate New Venture Proposals." P. 126 in John A. Hornaday, Edward B. Shils, Jeffry A. Timmons, and Karl H. Vesper, *Frontiers of Entrepreneurship Research*, 1985 (Wellesley, MA: Babson Center for Entrepreneurial Studies, 1985).

[49]"Hotline," *Inc.* (July 1990), p. 27.

> *Schroeder and Wilson quit their jobs and each invested $20,000 to underwrite market prospecting and product development investigations. Sutter Hill offered free office space and help in organizing and financing the startup. It insisted on addition of an experienced marketing person to the team, and it sought participation of other venture capital firms, all to provide long-term balance and support.*
>
> *After evaluating Priam's proposed product against others displayed at the 1977 National Computer conference, Sutter Hill and a second venture capital firm, Bank-America Capital Corp., agreed to finance the venture. The founders put up $175,000 for 350,000 shares of common stock. The venture capital firms put up $169,000 for 325,000 common shares and an additional $1,261,000 for 325,000 shares of convertible preferred stock. The bank also supplied a $700,000 line of lease financing for setting up shop. First shipments of Priam's product began in mid-1979.[50] (Their business plan appears in Appendix B.)*

In this example, although the outside venture capital came in early, founders still provided the very first cash and also invested another substantial amount when formal venture capital came in. Thus the financing came from a combination of sources.

Venture capitalists want returns that justify the high risks ventures carry as well as the considerable time and expense it takes to deal with them. They have no interest in acquiring control, unless it is necessary to protect their stake, and they do not want to get involved in running anyone's venture, because they are not expert at that.

A benchmark for some venture capital firms, according to Lipper, is that a venture, to be attractive, must be clearly aimed toward profitable sales of $100 million per year within five to seven years and require a minimum investment of $250,000.[51] Robinson found that the predominant priority of venture capital firms is a return on investment of 20 to 40 percent,[52] while Golder reported a target return range of 25 to 50 percent, but he noted that it would depend upon stage of investment, with the high end applying at start-up and the lower end applying at third-stage financings. He also noted that these target returns were based on straight cash investment and would shift with risk and with such variations as use of leverage and seniority.[53] One seed-capital fund, Vanguard, reported a target of multiplying an initial $300,000 investment by ten by the time of first-stage financing and by fifty by the time of public offering.[54]

Rather than rate of return, venture capitalists tend to think in terms of multiples on their money, such as a three- to fivefold return in three to five years, which indicates the following range:

[50]John Thackray, "Putting Together Quality Deals," *Venture* (May 1979), p. 28.

[51]Lipper, *Venture's Financing and Investing in Private Companies*, p. 41.

[52]Richard B. Robinson, Jr., "Emerging Strategies in the Venture Capital Industry," *Journal of Business Venturing*, 2 (no. 1) (Winter 1987), 63.

[53]Stanley C. Golder, "Structuring and Pricing the Financing." P. 210 in Lipper, *Venture's Financing and Investing in Private Companies*.

[54]Gibson, "How Early Is 'Early Stage'?," p. 120.

Threefold return in five years	25 percent
Fivefold return in five years	41 percent
Threefold return in three years	44 percent
Fivefold return in three years	71 percent

The actual experience of a given venture capitalist is, of course, a portfolio mixture of winners, losers, and in-betweens, such as 5 percent big winners, 10 percent total losses, 25 percent moderate winners, and 60 percent "walking dead" investments where the capital remains tied up in firms that seem able neither to go public nor to sell out for a satisfactory price. It is to cover overhead and nonwinners that venture capitalists have to seek high returns.

Average performance has ranged widely among firms. Poindexter, for instance, reported a mean rate of return among 59 venture funds of only 13 percent, with a range of 35 percent down to minus 40 percent.[55] An extensive study of 131 institutional venture funds started between 1971 and 1984 and reported by Bygrave et al. in 1988 found that the internal rate of return depended both on the year it was computed and the year the fund was created. For all funds together, the high was around 32 percent in 1980, and the low in 1985 was less than 7 percent. Moreover, funds started earlier did better than those started later. After three years, funds started in 1978–1979 showed an annual return of 40 percent while those started in 1982 showed less than 10 percent after three years.[56] Thus, although the target return sought in a particular financing may seem exorbitant to a venture founder who is seeking money, the risk and consequent average return accruing to the capitalist, particularly after considering the expenses of dealing with the venture, may not be unreasonable at all.

What Venture Capitalists Contribute.   Robinson found in a 1987 study that the investment contributed by a venture capital firm ranged from $5,000 to $20 million, with an average just under a half million dollars. The holding period ranged from one to 12 years and lasted on average 6.3 years,[57] as opposed to 5.6 years found by MacMillan et al.[58] A somewhat higher average investment figure, $865,000, was found in another study of 100 venture capital firms by Maier and Walker.[59]

The venture capital deal usually involves more than money. In the next example, the entrepreneur believed he could have developed his venture with only

[55]J. B. Poindexter, *The Efficiency of Financial Markets: The Venture Capital Case,* Ph.D. dissertation, New York University, 1976.

[56]William Bygrave et al., "Rates of Return of Venture Capital Investing: A Study of 131 Funds." P. 275 in Kirchhoff et al., *Frontiers of Entrepreneurship Research,* 1988.

[57]Richard B. Robinson, Jr., "Emerging Strategies in the Venture Capital Industry," *Journal of Business Venturing,* 2 (no. 1) (Winter 1987), 67.

[58]Ian C. MacMillan, David M. Kulow, and Roubina Khoylian, "Venture Capitalists' Involvement in Their Investments." P. 303 in Kirchhoff et al., *Frontiers of Entrepreneurship Research,* 1988.

[59]John B. Maier II and David A. Walker, "The Role of Venture Capital in Financing Small Business," *Journal of Business Venturing,* 2 (no. 3) (Summer 1987), 212.

debt plus retained earnings, but he chose to share ownership with venture capital-ists anyway:

> ■ *In 1976 Steve Edelman received his bachelor's degree in electrical engineering from Cornell, worked for NCR in Ithaca for a few months, and then decided to start his own microcomputer company. He had seen NCR "wrap $10,000 worth of hardware around $5 chips and sell those machines for God-knows-what," he recalled. He began with a $4,000 stake in March 1977, buying blank printed circuit boards and components for $10 and reselling them for $35 to hobbyists. By year end from his one-room $30 "factory," he had sold $300,000 worth. The next year he developed new completed modules that he sold for $175–$300 to other producers who combined them with further parts and software for resale. Edelman's sales doubled to $600,000.*
>
> *By 1979 with the aid of no outside equity but a $220,000 SBA guaranteed loan, his company, Ithaca Intersystems, had grown to sales near $2 million. Because his invest-ment requirements were mainly just for inventory and receivables financing and his profit margin was high, Edelman believed he could go on expanding from reinvested profits plus debt alone. He chose, however, to share equity instead with a venture capital firm, Oak Capital. For $600,000 he gave preferred stock convertible into approximately one third of the company's common shares.*[60]

The reasons the twenty-six-year-old entrepreneur gave for sharing his ven-ture, aside from the obvious purpose of raising money, were threefold: first, to get help in building a management team; second, for help in recruiting a board of directors that would add credibility "with the IBMs of the world"; third, to start a relationship from which he could draw another $1.5 million he expected to need within two years to reach sales of $13 million.[61]

Other reasons could be added, such as the help venture capitalists can provide in responding to setbacks and eventually in either selling out or going public to cash in on the venture. It is to be remembered, however, that other types of investors may also be able to contribute beyond capital. For example, Systek chose investment by a major corporation, General Instrument, to that of some highly distinguished venture capital firms not because the financial terms were different (they were not), but because Systek's top managers believed General Instrument's expertise, reputation, and contacts were valuable elements venture capitalists could not add to the package.[62]

MacMillan et al. found that the degree to which venture capitalists interacted with ventures after investing varied considerably. The most frequent activities engaged in by the 62 respondents were serving as a sounding board, helping arrange further financing, interfacing with other investors, and monitoring both financial and operating performance. Least frequent were activities concerned with running the venture, such as selecting vendors and working on technical development.[63]

[60]J.D. Lovinger, "When It's Time for More Cash," *Venture* (February 1980), p. 30.
[61]Ibid.
[62]Bruce Posner, "Big Deal," *Inc.* (January 1984), p. 109.
[63]Ian MacMillan, David M. Kulow and Roubina Khoylian, "Venture Capitalists' Involvement in Their Investments: Extent and Performance." P. 303 in Kirchhoff et al., *Frontiers of Entrepreneurial Research,* 1988.

Venture capitalists who do invest at earlier stages tend to specialize more narrowly by both industry and geographical location, according to a study by Gupta and Sapienza.[64] They also spend over twice as much time working with the ventures after investing in the early stages, according to Gorman and Sahlman.[65] However, it has been estimated that over 75 percent of venture capital deals are done with ventures having several years' operating experience behind them.

Terms of Venture Capital Deals

A favorite way of investing by venture capitalists is through convertible debentures—bonds that may or may not carry interest and allow the capitalist to choose at some future date between repayment in cash or in a specified amount of common stock. The conversion rate may be contingent upon venture performance, with higher results meaning that less stock will be taken, because less will be needed to attain the venture capitalists' desired multiple of return. There may also be terms allowing the appointment of one or more directors by the capitalists and requiring maintenance of certain performance levels by the venture. If the venture falls too far short of the goals, the capitalists may require that they be able to take control to save their investment. Thus, involvement with a venture capital firm does encroach on an entrepreneur's degree of managerial independence.

Bruno and Tyebjee observed from their observation of firms seeking venture capital that

■ *The entrepreneur should recognize that outside capital comes at a significant cost in terms of equity relinquished. The amount relinquished will depend on the amount of money raised. In our study, ventures gave up an average of approximately 50 percent of equity to outside investors. Of course, additional rounds of financing entail increased dilution in the founders' equity. On the average, 31.5 percent equity is given up for the first round, an additional 19.7 percent equity is given up in the second round, and 10 percent more in the third.*[66]

One sample of 193 entrepreneurs revealed that they had given up on average 45.1 percent of their equity. In another sample of 179, 54.5 percent had given up less than 49 percent. The average was 35.8 percent and the median was 40.1 percent. Generally, the amount of capital raised from venture capitalists was related to the amount of equity relinquished. For deals in which less than 5 percent of the equity was relinquished, the average amount of capital raised was $22,000. For deals relinquishing between 5 and 50 percent, the average raised was $246,000, and for deals giving up over 50 percent, the average amount was $4.7 million.[67]

[64]Anil K. Gupta and Harry J. Sapienza, "The Pursuit of Diversity by Venture Capital Firms." P. 290 in ibid.

[65]Michael Gorman and William A. Sahlman, "What Do Venture Capitalists Do?" P. 414 in Robert Ronstadt, John A. Hornaday, Rein Peterson and Karl H. Vesper, *Frontiers of Entrepreneurship Research, 1986* (Wellesley, MA: Babson Center for Entrepreneurial Studies, 1988).

[66]Bruno and Tyebjee, "The Entrepreneur's Search for Capital," p. 63.

[67]Andrew McWethy, "A Sweeter Way to Give Up Equity," *Inc.* (October 1982), p. 159.

■ *One venture capital deal provided that if the venture achieved its goals the venture capitalists could claim 15 percent of its equity in return for advancing $750,000 on ten-year convertible debentures yielding the larger of 13 percent or 3 percent over prime. If, however, it achieved only 75 percent to 90 percent of target, they would get 20 percent, and at less than 75 percent they could claim 35 percent of the equity. Additional requirements of the venture were that it provide monthly financials, audited annual statements, maintain certain working capital and net worth levels and not take on additional debt, pay dividends, merge or go public without permission.[68]*

A customary practice is to spell out the conditions of the investment in what is called a *term sheet.*[69] An example of a term sheet given by Halloran, Benton, and Lovejoy for preferred stock venture capital investment covers such things as number of shares, price, liquidation preference, options for redemption, conversion price, automatic conversion events, antidilution protection, voting rights, closing conditions, registration rights expenses, waivers, and more. Their book, discussing and illustrating the intricacies of such investments, runs to 900 pages in length and is updated annually.[70] The terms and legalities of venture capital investing can be immensely complex, which puts a premium on having competent professional guidance for anyone who is not a specialist in it.

Finding Sources

Venture capital firms fund less than 2 percent of the deals they consider, according to a survey of 100 venture capital firms by Maier and Walker,[71] and 47 percent of venture capital firms fund less than 1 percent of them. Bruno and Tyebjee observed that

■ *The founder should anticipate that raising money will take longer than he would like and plan accordingly. In particular, the search for funds should not result from imminent cash crises but rather from a growth plan based upon a tenable strategic plan. In our study, the median amount of time spent in the search for funds was in the vicinity of four to five months, with 20 percent of the sample indicating that it took over eight months. This process can be further elongated if it represents the first attempt to raise outside capital. The founders should anticipate that the search for capital will require a substantial amount of their time. Moreover, the search will divert them from the day-to-day management of their venture. This latter development often has serious repercussions for day-to-day control of the enterprise.[72]*

They go on to note that

■ *If a venture is denied venture capital by a venture capital firm, it may still be possible to raise venture capital. Of 135 ventures which we knew to have been denied venture capital at least once, we found that over two-thirds were still in business. Of these,*

---

[68]Ibid.

[69]Paul Troop, "Coming to Terms with Investors," *Venture* (October 1988), p. 77.

[70]Michael J. Halloran, Lee F. Benton, and Jesse Robert Lovejoy, *Venture Capital and Public Offering Negotiation* (New York: Harcourt, 1990), p. 259.

[71]Maier and Walker, "The Role of Venture Capital in Financing Small Business," p. 212.

[72]Bruno and Tyebjee, "The Entrepreneur's Search for Capital," p. 63.

approximately 60 percent were able to raise outside capital elsewhere. However, it may be necessary for the entrepreneur to lower his sights regarding the amount of capital required and/or be willing to give up a higher share of equity.[73]

Moreover, those who failed to get the venture capital they sought but managed to raise funds elsewhere typically fell further short of their fundraising goals.

Finally, they found that on average it took entrepreneurs about six months to arrange financing with venture capitalists with whom they were dealing for the first time, the same as for obtaining individual investors. Subsequent rounds took less time in both cases. Those who sought but failed to raise venture capital spent on average 39 percent longer seeking funds.

Sometimes entrepreneurs are lucky enough to have venture capitalists come after them. One venture capitalist recalled that "I can think of companies in our portfolio that we heard about in a restaurant."[74] But waiting for such a contact is not likely to be enough in any particular case.

Personal contacts, unsolicited proposals directly to the capital firms, and venture capital conferences are three ways of seeking out a venture capital connection. Contacts such as bankers, other professionals, and other entrepreneurs may be able to provide leads. Names of venture capital firms can be obtained from them as well as from listings in magazines such as *Venture*;[75] from Venture Economics, 75 Second Avenue, Needham, Massachusetts 02194, which maintains a venture capital database; from the National Venture Capital Association, 2030 M Street NW, Washington, DC 20036; and from the Venture Capital Hotline in Carmel, California (1 800 237 2380), whose founder, Lance Strouss observed, "A personal contact makes all the difference in the world."[76] The Small Business Administration can give names of SBICs, but the odds are still long. One venture capital firm reported getting as many as 150 unsolicited calls per week, none of which it ever invested in.[77] However, venture capitalists operate in networks,[78] and it is always possible that a contact with one will lead to others that will work out. Venture capital conferences, sometimes sponsored by universities, clubs, associations, or chambers of commerce, can be another way to enter the network, although they tend to favor established ventures that are beyond start-up.[79]

Types of Formal Venture Capital Firms

Independent Venture Capital Firms. Typically, independent venture capital funds are organized as partnerships, with up to four general partners who do the managing plus up to twenty-five limited partners who put up 99 percent of the

---

[73]Ibid.

[74]"News and Trends," *Inc.* (November 1983), p. 50.

[75]James P. Roscow, "The Changing Venture Capital Marketplace," *Venture* (June 1987), p. 72.

[76]Nora Goldstein, "Venture Capital Savvy," *In Business* (January/February 1988), p. 49.

[77]"News and Trends," *Inc.* (November 1983), p. 50.

[78]Edward Doherty, "How Venture Capital Networks Work," *Venture* (July 1980), p. 44.

[79]Steve Johnson, "Where Technology Can Find Capital," *Venture* (March 1981), p. 14; also, Dave Lindorff, "Where Ideas and Money Mingle," *Venture* (October 1983), p. 58.

money. The general partners receive management fees of around 2.5 to 3 percent plus 20 percent of profits after return of invested capital. The limited partners receive the remaining 80 percent of profits. Most of the general partner money usually comes from pension funds (47 percent), followed by foreign investors (13 percent), corporations (12 percent), endowments and foundations (11 percent), insurance companies (9 percent), and individuals and families (8 percent).[80] Some independent firms are in corporate rather than partnership form, and some are publicly held and traded, mostly over the counter.[81] All these forms operate in much the same way, at least from the entrepreneur's point of view.

Small Business Investment Companies (SBICs). SBICs are investment companies licensed by the Small Business Administration to leverage their investments with federal money to provide debt and equity capital to American firms. In return, each SBIC agrees to restrict investments to firms smaller than $6 million in net worth and to limit the fraction of its total investment that goes to any one venture. A free list of these investment firms can be obtained from the Small Business Administration or from the National Association of Small Business Investment Companies, 618 Washington Building, Washington, DC 20005. Although sponsored by other firms, such as other venture capital firms and banks, as well as individuals,[82] the number of SBICs has been declining in recent years.[83]

Corporate Venture Capital Divisions. Large corporations, as noted earlier, sometimes help finance start-ups for a variety of reasons. Some, such as General Electric and Monsanto, operate venture capital divisions to perform this function. When they do, they usually become part of the broader network of venture capital firms and operate in the same ways, often participating in syndicated deals.[84]

Institutional Venture Capital. Other institutions with venture capital arms include banks, pension funds, insurance companies, endowments, foundations and universities.[85] These, too, operate much like the others, although with perhaps more emphasis on established rather than start-up ventures.

Venture capital firms and their divisions often specialize, but their specialties shift over time.[86] Thinking in advance not only about whether venture capital is appropriate but also about which venture capital firms may be best suited to the particular venture may help focus the search on more promising prospects. It is important, for instance, to deal with capitalists who will be prepared to provide more money when it is needed. Changing investors can be expensive, difficult, or

[80]*Venture Capital Yearbook*, p. 78.
[81]Loretta Huerta, "Venture Capital's Small Investors," *Venture* (February 1981), p. 18.
[82]Udayan Gupta, "SBICs," *Venture* (October 1983), p. 66.
[83]Sabin Russell, "1986 Was a Sad Time for SBIC's," *Venture* (January 1987), p. 103.
[84]Clint Willis, "The Other Risk-Takers," *Venture* (September 1981), p. 48.
[85]Lori Ioannou, "Venturesome and Loaded," *Venture* (February 1983), p. 38.
[86]James P. Roscow, "The Changing Venture Capital Marketplace," *Venture* (June 1987), p. 72.

even impossible. If the search turns up more than one likely firm, some questions to consider in choosing the best one include the following:

1. Which venture capital firms invest in industries similar to that of the new enterprise?
2. What reputation does each firm have with prior investees? How are its current investees doing?
3. How much available capital and ability to raise more does the fund have?
4. What will the firm's goals with respect to the venture be, and how well do they match those of the founders?
5. Which partner will deal with the venture, what qualifications and reputation does he or she have, how accessible will that person be, and what level of personal rapport do the founders have with him or her?
6. How attractive is the prospective deal?

The deal itself is only one factor and may not be the most important. Stanley Pratt, operator of the leading database on the venture capital industry commented that most entrepreneurs interviewed by his company said that "it is far more important whom you get your money from than are the specific terms of the deal."[87]

When entrepreneurs were turned down by venture capitalists, according to Bruno and Tyebjee, they usually attributed the rejection to different causes than the venture capitalists did. The former felt rejection was due to weakness in market potential, management competition, and product feasibility. Fewer than 20 percent ascribed rejection to their own managerial abilities, whereas over 30 percent of the venture capitalists gave that as the reason.[88] A well-known venture capitalist, Fred Adler, further commented that spendthrift symptoms such as expensive offices and high-priced dining by capital seekers inspire rejection.[89]

GOING PUBLIC

The advantages of going public with a venture are that it paves the way for entrepreneurs to cash in (even though there may be some legal restrictions on how fast they can do so) and they can, depending upon registration choices, go after any amount of financing from any number of people. Public selling of shares may eventually lead to owners becoming quite wealthy.[90]

But there are also good reasons why going public, particularly at start-up, is a relatively rare approach to financing and why considerable caution should be taken in doing so. Reasons include the following list.

[87]Stanley E. Pratt, "What Companies Are Saying about Venture Capital," *Inc.* (November 1984), p. 12.
[88]Bruno and Tyebjee, "The Entrepreneur's Search for Capital," p. 63.
[89]Burton W. Teague, "Venture Capital, Who Gets It and Why," *Inc.* (June 1980), p. 70.
[90]Kevin Farrell, "100 Who Made Millions in 1981," *Venture* (April 1982), p. 34.

1. There are legal restrictions, known as "Blue Sky Laws," on public offerings. It is crucial to check with the Securities and Exchange Commission and probably a lawyer before advertising or trying to sell shares beyond a small group of investors. Such terms as *full disclosure* and *insider trading* should be understood before going public. Alternative types of offerings such as "Regulation D," "Intrastate," and "Full Registration" (and its subcategories—S-2, S-18, etc.),[91] should also be understood. Until government approval is obtained, the offering and company should not be touted publicly.[92]

2. Going public can involve considerable legal, accounting, and other costs. Liability insurance against potential shareholder lawsuits can be very expensive but also worthwhile.[93] Audited statements are usually required, sometimes for several years or as long as the company has been in business. It is not usually possible to go public for less than $1 million. The typical costs of a major offering can be

   - Legal and filing fees: $50,000 to $350,000
   - Accounting: $25,000 to $200,000
   - Printing: $100,000 to $115,000 (for prospectuses)
   - Underwriter fee: 6 to 40 percent (to sell the issue)[94]

   Thus, a company needs prior seed capital just to be able to start paying the costs of raising money publicly. Terms of the offering, including what an underwriting firm would get, are customarily spelled out in a letter of intent.[95]

3. Once legal permission is obtained, the hard part, selling the issue, begins. The most effective way is to hire a professional underwriter. But it can also be hard to find a willing underwriter, particularly on a "firm underwriting" or guaranteed basis, as opposed to a "best efforts" (no guarantee of sale by the underwriter) basis. One underwriter may succeed in engaging buyers' fantasies of success where another fails. It is very rare for ventures to go public early in life because people who buy stock issues in ventures first want to see a record of profitable performance with clear indications of high growth. As one expert put it, "What people want to invest in is growth and the potential to be a big company."[96] Timing plays an important part. In rising markets, new issues, along with other stocks, sell best, but in other periods, new offerings, unlike other stocks, do not sell at all.[97]

4. After going public a first time, it can be complicated or impossible to tap venture capital sources for more money. It can also be hard to tap the public markets again unless the venture is growing very successfully.

5. Some or all of the entrepreneur's own shares of stock may be subject to restrictions when the venture goes public and for some time after that. The federal laws on securities trading aim to make sure that those who might buy the shares will have full information about the risks they are taking. Hence there are requirements for "full disclosure" of the company's financial status to those who might buy the issues. Also, there are prohibitions about "insiders," people who have special private knowledge of

---

[91]Loretta Kuklinsky Huerta, "The Ups and Downs of Going Public," *Inc.* (November 1980), p. 20.

[92]Ron Scherer, "A New Underwriter: The Quiet Rule," *Venture* (October 1980), p. 18.

[93]Ellen James, "How Not to Get Sued," *Venture* (April 1987), p. 52.

[94]John Verity, "The Underwriter's Fee," *Venture* (October 1981), p. 12; Neil L. Beregman, "Now Is Not the Time," *Inc.* (January 1982), p. 103; and David P. Sutton and Tom Post, "The Cost of Going Public," *Inc.* (April 1986), p. 30.

[95]"Negotiating a Letter of Intent," *Venture* (May 1984), p. 35. Examples can be found in Arthur Lipper, *Venture's Guide to Investing in Small Firms* (Hangwood, IL: Dow Jones-Irwin, 1984).

[96]Robert J. Koxma, "High Hopes for 1980," *Venture* (January 1980).

[97]Udayan Gupta, "Initial Public Offerings Set New Records," *Venture* (September 1983), p. 102.

the company's affairs from working inside of it, from taking advantage of that knowledge to the detriment of outside buyers who lack it.

6. After the company becomes publicly held, there will be more reporting requirements and more owners for the company to report to and interact with. Any of these investors who become "nervous" about the company's performance for any reason can become a severe annoyance and possibly a troublesome legal expense.

Even though it is unlikely that a start-up will go public early, it can still be wise to learn about what is required to go public. Some forms of public offering, for example, require a history of audited financial statements.

When Is It Done?

Public offerings, even more than capital infusions from formal venture capital firms, usually occur well downstream from start-up, but occasionally they are also used at an early stage. When Cetus Corporation went public for a record $120 million initial offering, the company was already nine years old. However, Muse Air used a $35 million public offering (of 2.2 million units at $17.50, consisting of a share of common plus half a warrant for five years to buy a common share at $16) to raise start-up capital. The former case is probably more typical, but the latter is a reminder that exceptions are possible.

In Freear and Wetzel's 1988 study, none of the outside seed capital and less than 20 percent of the outside start-up capital came from public offerings. However, in 1984 *Venture* cited a Securities Data Corporation report that 181 start-ups with no operating history went public for an aggregate of a half billion dollars simply on expectations.[100] *Inc.* reported that in 1985 a total of 147 companies with sales of $10,000 or less went public.[101] Why might these findings be inconsistent? Different timing, different definitions of start-up, and different populations sampled are probably all part of the explanation.

Of more value is an understanding of how and when public offerings can be used early. Illustrations cited by *Venture* include the following:

- Edgewater Films, $2.2 million at $1 per share to produce low-budget films.
- Chem-Tech Labs, $1.2 million at 25 cents per share to develop an over-the-counter drug.
- Lo-Jack, $1.5 million at $1 per share to develop a stolen car tracking system.
- Sports Information Database, Inc., $4 million at $5 per share to develop and market a computer database.[102]

All these companies went public before generating sales and at least part of the funding was to complete the development of proprietary products with high

---

[98]Pavan Sahgal, "The Mega-Offering Boom," *Venture* (August 1981), p. 14.

[99]Freear and Wetzel, "Equity Financing for New Technology-Based Firms," p. 347.

[100]Sid Kane, "Start-Ups Go Public," *Venture* (August 1984), p. 54.

[101]David P. Sutton and Tom Post, "The Cost of Going Public," *Inc.* (April 1986), p. 30.

[102]Alan Gersten, "An Entrepreneur's Penny Stock Startups," *Venture* (July 1980), p. 68.

profit potential. In each case, other seed capital had to be previously invested in order to create a business platform on which to seek capital publicly. In the case of Sports Information Database, Inc., for example, the founders first invested $150,000 to create such a platform. The next example illustrates in further detail how a public offering may be part of the financing sequence in a start-up:

■   *Dr. John Altschuler incorporated Applied Medical in February 1979 with an investment of $15,000 to develop and produce a device used in bone marrow transplants. By chance he was contacted by Gregory Pusey, a stockbroker who was making "cold calls" in search of companies for whom he might seek to float stock offerings as well as clients whom he might serve as a broker. Three months later, in May, Pusey helped Applied raise another $230,000 through a private placement with thirty investors Pusey knew from his brokerage work. He also invested $15,000 himself in return for 27 percent of the stock, a three-year contract to serve as president for $30,000 per year, and thereafter a 5 percent royalty on sales. Altschuler took a four-year contract at $45,000 per year and thereafter a 1 percent royalty on sales.*

In the fall of 1979 Pusey undertook to raise another $1.5 million at $1 per share in public offering through a Denver investment bank. The offering failed and he made another attempt through a different underwriting firm, which succeeded. Pusey's shares were now worth $400,000. Next, he split the stock ten for one. By July of 1980, although the company had still as yet not reported any profits, the stock was selling at 63 cents per share. Pusey and Altschuler were each holding shares now worth close to $3 million.[103]

Government Constraints

If proposals to put money into a venture are made to a large number of people, the activity is defined by the federal government as a public offering, which requires that legal permission to proceed must be obtained. There is no requirement for such permission if the offering is sold only to "sophisticated investors," which typically includes "persons who have access to information about the company and are able to fend for themselves (such as those directly managing the business)." However, the government warns, "You should be aware that if the security is offered for sale to even one person who does not meet the necessary conditions, the entire offering may be in violation of the Securities Act."[104] It also notes that "There has been much uncertainty as to the precise limits" of what constitutes a private, as opposed to public, offering. If the offering is public, then governmental permission to make it must be obtained. Penalties for failing to obtain permission when required are severe. Hence, it is important to check with governmental offices at both state and national level, because both are involved in the regulation of public offerings.

There are several alternative types of permission. They range from relatively restricted selling freedom that is fairly simple to obtain to much greater freedom that is much more costly and complicated to obtain. The main options are as follows:

---

[103]Ibid.

[104]*Q&A: Small Business and the SEC* (Washington, DC: U.S. Small Business Administration; June 1990), p. 14.

1. *Intrastate offerings.* If state authorities give permission to offer a securities issue, such as stock, bonds, or partnership shares, and if 80 percent of revenues, assets, and spending of the proceeds are limited to the state, the issue is automatically exempt from federal filing.[105] However, the permission to sell only applies within the state where it is obtained and to a company incorporated and headquartered there.

   States vary in the degree to which they constrain offerings.[106] In Wisconsin, for example, an entrepreneur who wrote to twenty-three employees offering 12 percent three-day demand notes to finance the purchase of a computer found out through being forced to sign a consent letter that the state rule limited solicitation to fifteen people, even though federal regulations, with which he had been familiar, allowed more liberal solicitation.[107]

2. *Regulation D Offerings.* Federal permission is granted to sell to any number of investors in any state, but only up to a certain amount of money—$500,000 with no audited statements. Different rules apply to larger amounts. Paperwork is simple enough that an entrepreneur can do it personally by visiting a Securities and Exchange Commission office, examining the filings of other offerings, and imitating them. However, state approval is also required and states differ on rules. Engaging a competent lawyer to help will cost money but will save time.

3. *Full Registration Offerings.* Federal permission can be obtained for selling any amount of the security to any number of people. A history of audited statements is required, and the paperwork to obtain permission is substantial. Engaging a lawyer is practically essential.

The heart of a public offering is the company's prospectus and the terms it extends to investors. Of central interest to government agencies regulating the process is that the prospectus render "full disclosure" of all the risks and dangers of the offering. Examples of prospectuses can easily be examined at the offices of stock brokers or of the Securities and Exchange Commission.

Normally, the process of obtaining approval proceeds through several cycles of application, followed by critical rejection, modification, and resubmission until the government agency is satisfied. As with venture capital terms, the array of details to be borne in mind can be hopelessly complex for someone who does not work with them constantly over years. Professional help for obtaining permissions and guiding the execution of the offering can be valuable.

It is worth noting that there can be "end runs" around governmental regulations for selling public securities. One is to buy the shell of a company that is already publicly held and start the venture inside that.[108] A second is to sell shares on a foreign stock exchange rather than in the United States, such as the Vancouver Stock Exchange[109] or the London Unlisted Securities market.[110] Then there will be foreign regulations to deal with, but they are sometimes less restrictive. A third is a novel scheme that has not been proven illegal, although whether it ever will be remains to be seen. That is to give away shares free, develop a list of

[105]Tom Wolpert, "Home-State Offerings," *Venture* (November 1982), p. 98.

[106]Michele Bekey, "Easing California's Blue Sky Laws," *Venture* (February 1981), p. 12.

[107]"An Innovative Borrower Gets the Law to Bend," *Inc.* (October 1982), p. 21.

[108]A. David Sliver, "The Shell Game," *Venture* (May 1981), p. 25.

[109]Edmund L. Andrews, "The Siren Song of Vancouver," *Venture* (July 1987), p. 35.

[110]Cathy Hedgecock, "Going Public Overseas," *Venture* (February 1984), p. 100.

shareholders thereby, and then sell these shareholders other rights, such as a newsletter or additional shares.

Selling a Public Issue

Hard as it may be to obtain government approval of the offering, that is not the hardest part. Rather it is to sell the issue after receiving approval. The main alternatives for selling a public offering are either through a brokerage firm or selling the issue directly. The most likely brokerage firm for a small public issue is a smaller local firm because there should not be a need to tap a wide geographical area.[111] Initially, the objective will simply be to get the issue sold to raise capital. Later, it will be desirable to have some sort of active market so that shares can be traded. This can be a difficult problem with small issues, because few shares and a small market remove the incentive from the broker to work on finding customers for trades. A large firm will not likely be interested at all, and even a small one may not want the trouble of making a market.

Issues can be sold through brokerage firms, as noted earlier, on a "firm underwriting" basis and a "best efforts" basis. With the former, the broker buys the shares and resells them, thereby guaranteeing their sale; with the latter, the broker merely handles sales on a commission basis with no guarantee that anyone will buy the shares. Unfortunately for the entrepreneur, a firm underwriting is not usually possible. A small brokerage firm may not have the money to buy the issue, and a big one will not find either the smallness of the issue or its riskiness attractive enough to do so, though it may have a venture capital arm that is willing to invest.[112]

The best efforts sale reduces risk for the broker, and possibly also the incentive to make sure the issue sells, and it correspondingly increases the risk for the entrepreneur that the issue will not sell. Many do not. The companies that handle best efforts sales, according to a *Venture* survey, tend to be small and not very reliable.[113] Seven out of twenty-five brokers who handled best efforts sales tracked by the magazine in 1985 were not answering their phones after one year. The issues themselves also did less well, at least in the first year, for investors. But if no more established broker will offer to buy the issue on a firm underwriting basis, there may be no choice except either best efforts or self-underwriting.

Self-underwriting, in which the founders must find their own contacts, either through personal contact or advertisements, is by far the cheapest. Indications from a *Venture* sampling of self-underwritings in 1984 were that the cost could be cut as much as 90 percent.[114] There are two catches in this procedure, however. First, the entrepreneur will not usually have the connections a broker does for finding people to buy the issue. Second, the broker may be able to get a better price for the offering. Moreover, in some cases the savings from self-underwriting

[111]Jerry Buckley, "Using Regional Underwriters," *Venture* (June 1981), p. 14.
[112]Dave Lindorff, "Investment Bankers Take the Venture Plunge," *Venture* (January 1981), p. 42.
[113]Marie D'Amico, "In the End, Are Best Efforts Your Best Buy?," *Venture* (July 1985), p. 20.
[114]David Sutton, "Going Public and Selling It Yourself," *Venture* (November 1984), p. 182.

have been nil because the self-underwriter ended up selling the shares through various different brokerage firms rather than directly to customers anyway.[115]

Thus, the sale of stock publicly as a means of raising money for a venture may offer no easy solution to the difficult problem of capitalization. But it can work, as illustrated by the experience of Robert A. Citron, founder of Spacelabs, Inc., a company that makes experimental modules for space shots. Having previously lost control of a venture to venture capitalists, he avoided them this time through personally selling a Regulation D issue, as described by *Venture*:

■ *"The hardest financing was the first," he recalled. He had to talk to seventy people to get the first six investors, beginning with a core from his earlier ventures, who in turn told their friends. Some investors surfaced as news of the company spread through the space industry. Later, the venture's accountants and lawyers referred potential investors.*

They were impressed in part, he said, by the fact that he had invested $200,000 of his own money and two years into the start-up. He priced 860,000 shares, 15 percent of the company, at 23 cents, and limited the number of investors by setting a $25,000 minimum. Three subsequent additional rounds completed the financing.[116]

COMBINATION DEALS

For many ventures, the path to financing includes a variety of sources. One entrepreneur, for example, said he financed the prototype on his savings, took on a consulting contract, and then joint ventured with another company to get into production. The following example illustrates a very different combination of sources:

■ *In 1990 James H. Olmstead, partner in a small Colorado construction company, and Kenneth Lucas, manager of a small publishing company, formed a company to make sawhorse kits for home remodelers. They raised $33,000 from friends and relatives and borrowed $150,000 from a local investment banking firm, which in turn helped them open a $425,000 line of credit at a Denver bank. Through another brokerage house they floated 6 million shares on the "penny stock market" at 50 cents per share. Acquiring $1.5 million worth of automated equipment they started shipping kits for as little as one third the price of competitors and started producing for sales of $4.5 million the first year, while developing other wood products such as rocking horses, tool boxes and work benches.[117]*

The combination can also include foreign investors and splitoffs, as illustrated by a final example:

■ *Vitalec Corp., San Jose semiconductor start-up, could not afford $100 million for a plant to manufacture chips. Alex Au, the founder, arranged to have manufacturing performed by one company in Japan and another in Korea in exchange for manufacturing licenses*

[115]Ronald Tanner, "Is a Self-Underwriting Worth It?," *Venture* (July 1981), p. 12.
[116]Debbie Galant, "A Four-Stage Launch for Spacelab," *Venture* (June 1987), p. 87.
[117]"Riding a Sawhorse to the Hardware Market," *Inc.* (November 1982), p. 17.

on his product. He also made an agreement with a Taiwanese government laboratory for facilities to perform development and testing work. Two other Japanese companies each bought $2 million worth of common stock to become involved with the company. To work out the deals, Au flew 17,000 miles in a two-week period to four Asian countries. He commented that although it cost him a lot of time the multiple alliances reduce risk of licensing all his products to one source and also yield a greater combination of strengths in manufacturing and marketing.[118]

Without straining the imagination, it can be seen that other sources, such as employees and venture capitalists, could be added to such a combination. Knowledge of more possible sources can lead to more practical options. Hence, it is in an entrepreneur's interest to become informed about many possible sources and to develop contacts who may be able to help in tapping them.

PLANNING QUESTIONS

The following questions are intended to stimulate thought about what should be considered in moving ahead with a venture. Which questions best apply can vary among entrepreneurs and ventures, as can the order in which they should be considered, the priority that should be placed on them, and which of them should be answered in a written plan.

Stages in Capitalization

- When, if ever, will the venture need further equity capital from outsiders?
- What milestones of accomplishment will signal appropriateness of future equity capital injections?
- Can "look alike" companies be identified whose capitalization stages are similar to projections?
- What sources for additional capital have been or will be approached under the present plan?

Private Placements

- What contacts with brokers and wealthy individuals might the company draw upon for private placement?
- How are the shares presently spread, and what changes in spread over time through exercise of any options plus sale to new investors are contemplated?
- Is there good reason to believe that additional investors will find it attractive to buy in?
- What should be their motivations, and how well do those fit with the company's goals and projections?
- What combinations of common, preferred, and debt securities might fit the circumstances?
- Are there potential individual tax implications that should be discussed with appropriate experts?
- What special tax advantages or disadvantages will the venture or its investors have?

---

[118]Juilland, "Asian Money—and More," p. 34.

- To what extent can they be expected to enhance the venture's credibility?
- Are the legal groundrules for private versus public placement clearly in mind? (If not, call the SEC and/or legal experts.)
- What other investment inducements might be offered to investors, such as employment or tie-in contract deals?

Venture Capital

- Is the venture's projected potential market and competitive edge likely to be great enough to interest formal venture capital?
- Has a list of nearby venture capital firms been obtained? (Getting an SBIC list from the SBA and asking around can be the way to start.)
- When will audited financial statements become available to potential outside funding sources?
- How attractive a return on equity will the venture be able to offer, and how does that compare to very low versus very high rates of return available elsewhere?
- How do other performance ratios of the forecasts, such as those indicating riskiness, compare to other firms in similar lines of business?
- What level of R.O.I. (return on investment) is projected for capital in the venture, and how does that compare to the rate sought by investors?

Going Public

- Have up-to-date publications of the Securities and Exchange Commission (SEC) about going public been obtained and looked over?
- Have nearby brokers who might handle such an offering been identified?
- Have prospectuses of similar offerings available at the SEC and/or brokers been obtained and examined?
- Have one or more law firms and accounting firms familiar with public offerings been identified and met with?
- What has been learned from discussion with other entrepreneurs about their experience in going public with roughly similar companies?
- What reason is there to expect that a securities issue by the venture, if permitted, could be sold?
- What would be the specific steps in doing so?

POSSIBLE MILESTONES FOR A PLANNING TIME LINE

The most suitable milestones for a time line for a particular venture must be a function of the individual case. These that follow are intended to help stimulate thought about them.

- Full venture plan developed
- Prospective investors identified
- Plan presented to prospective investors
- Investment agreements worked out
- Public offering or sell-out completed

Chapter 7

LINING UP SALES

INTRODUCTION

Founders usually make a venture's first sales. The sales will often come as part of the transition from former employment: customers brought forward, contacts utilized, even requests from clients of a former employer. Sales can also begin through running an advertisement or submitting a bid for a job. But it will be the founder's actions that make the sale happen. This initial selling action may take any of the following six alternative forms, which are further elaborated in Exhibit 7–1:

1. Accepting an order that has grown out of a relationship prior to the venture
2. Responding to requests for quotes, such as those run regularly by the federal government in the *Commerce Daily*.
3. Running an advertisement
4. Renting space in a storefront or at a trade show or fair and "hanging out a shingle"
5. Making a sales call on someone, either by phone or preferably in person
6. Paying someone else to sell for the venture

A venture may use any of these methods for its first sale, either alone or in combination. This chapter explores each of these possibilities.

Do not forget, however, that customers must ultimately make the sales happen. This was illustrated by the experience of the first highly successful microcomputer spread-sheet program:

206

EXHIBIT 7–1   Some Possible Actions to Seek Sales Orders

Respond

Accept a spontaneous order or request
Contact the government and bid on a contract

Advertise

Distribute flyers with how-to-order information
Run a newspaper or magazine advertisement
Rent TV time to pitch what the venture will sell
Prepare and mail a catalog
Rent a mailing list and send a sales letter
Publish an article about the venture's product or service
Arrange a publicity stunt highlighting the product or service
Give away free samples

Display

Rent a storefront and open for business
Outfit a van to serve as a mobile store
Rent a trade show or fair booth
Piggyback on someone else's booth
Demonstrate in space rented from a store
Hawk on a street corner

Sell Personally

Make sales calls by phone
Sell door-to-door
Set up a seminar and invite potential customers

Pay Others to Sell

Hire a salesperson
Engage an independent sales representative
Negotiate with a wholesaler to carry your product or service
Contact a company purchasing agent and ask for an order
Ask a store manager what it would take to get an order
Have a party and recruit others to sell on commission
Ask purchasing agents about private label possibilities

■ *Dan Bricklin, who originated VisiCalc in 1978, his first year as a Harvard MBA student, thought sales would most likely come through selling the program door-to-door among Massachusetts's high tech executives. His actual outlet turned out to be a publishing company, Personal Software, Inc., which was compiling a catalog of programs to sell. By May of 1979 Bricklin and Bob Frankston, an MIT friend who had joined him as co-developer, thought it was ready for display to computer dealers but, according to a 1982* Venture *article,[1] the dealers were "not impressed."*

[1]Stewart Alsop II, "Software Arts Wrote the First Best-Seller," *Venture* (January 1982), p. 71.

One month later, the two made a presentation on their program at the National Computer Conference in New York City. But only about 20 people listened to the talk. Only two were not family or friends, and those two walked out before it ended. Even though an industry pundit declared their program "the software tail that might wag the personal computer dog," their first reception by the public also was disappointing.

It took another year before word of the program's effectiveness began to spread. Then, according to Venture, *"people began showing up in computer stores to buy Apple computers just so they could use VisiCalc."*

Thus, customers, not selling, ultimately built the sales of VisiCalc, and for that matter Apple as well. Later, customers decided that another start-up's product, Lotus 123, was a better spreadsheet program, and VisiCalc was eclipsed.

Variety of First-Order Sources

The following examples indicate the range of sources from which the first sales orders in a new company can come:

1. A manufacturer of aircraft radios took a mock-up of the product, before a working model had been produced, to distributors. It would be the first general aviation radio to incorporate an electronic digital readout; existing brands had only mechanical digital readouts. He also offered a service policy with the new radio under which a pilot would receive an exchange immediately if the radio failed, so the aircraft would not be grounded for radio repair as happened under existing service policies of competitors, and he offered a larger discount than competitors. The typical reaction of distributors was, "Where do I sign?" Before his first unit was produced, orders were already rolling in.
2. A laid-off aircraft worker designed a fish smoker for himself. He also made some as presents for friends. These friends asked to buy some for their friends. He took some units to sporting goods stores, which immediately placed small orders. He filled these; customers bought them; and larger orders followed.
3. A graduate student earning his way through school by repairing TV sets devised a very powerful hi-fi amplifier (700 watts). Friends asked him to make units for them, and then other people began calling him. Soon dealers were asking and orders were coming in.
4. The designer of a new hobby product asked if he could demonstrate the product in a discount supermarket. He rapidly sold out his stock and started making more. The market offered to stock the product, and he went to other markets, building sales.
5. An inventor of a new type of bicycle lock approached the buyer for Sears, Roebuck. When Sears agreed to carry his product, he was in business.
6. Three aerospace engineers devised a new solid waste disposal concept. They began contacting government agencies until they found one that was interested. Their first sale came in the form of a government contract.
7. A hi-fi speaker maker began by running the following classified ad in the newspaper: "For sale: Engineering Prototype Hi-Fi Speakers," but without success. He opened a storefront, and still few customers appeared, nowhere near enough to achieve break-even. Then he ran larger newspaper advertisements, and customers began to come into his store and buy.
8. An employee found that his employer was having trouble obtaining screw machine products locally. The employee contacted a machine dealer, bought his own screw machine, and obtained orders from his former employer.

9. A college dropout bought photographic enlarging equipment for a hobby and taught himself how to use it. When a friend offered to buy the first print, the young man decided to ask drugstores if he could make high-quality prints for them. They gave him orders and he was in business. Later, at the suggestion of a friend, he tried advertising his service in a photo magazine. Within two years his sales were over a million dollars annually through mail order.

10. A man who was manufacturing plastic shrunken heads in his garage rented a booth at the county fair. Soon he was sold out, and shortly after that he had the opportunity to sell his garage operation to a larger company for a substantial profit.

11. A Seattle man started in the hi-fi business by purchasing components wholesale and selling them door-to-door. Then he arranged to have speaker cabinets made by a local carpenter. Advertisements for these brought not only more sales, but inquiries from distributors who also wanted to sell his speakers. He was soon selling through distributors instead of door-to-door as his manufacturing expanded and sales of his speakers spread to Canada.

This list includes only some of the possible ways of obtaining first orders. It by no means exhausts the possibilities. Many service enterprises get started simply through word-of-mouth that draws customers to the company. Others begin with advertisements in the *Yellow Pages*, newspapers, and flyers distributed either by hand or through the mail. Some products obtain first sales through magazine advertisements or direct mailings of flyers or catalogs. Still others are sold by television display or by the entrepreneur's personally calling on purchasing agents of other companies who then become the company's sales channels.

RESPONDING TO PROSPECTIVE CUSTOMERS

The amount of effort required to develop sales for a new company varies. Among the previous examples, the second (fish smoker), eighth (screw machine parts), and ninth (photographs) illustrate situations in which the entrepreneurs did not have to go after their first sales at all, because the customers were already at hand or came to them.

The following is a more detailed example of such a case:

■ *In 1970 Len Muller was approached by Heath-Techna, an aircraft subcontractor, for help on the design of some seats for Lockheed. He had worked briefly for Lockheed after graduating from the University of Michigan in mechanical engineering in 1959, then as a contract engineer, employed by a company that sent its engineers on a short-term basis to work for other companies that did not want to expand their full-time staffs. In 1965 he joined Boeing where he had worked on a variety of engineering jobs for five years, most recently the design of cargo doors, when the Heath-Techna invitation came. Along the way he had also been a part-time MBA student. Throughout his studies he reached for variety to broaden his capabilities, in case he might encounter an opportunity to develop an independent enterprise.*

The Heath-Techna invitation came at the suggestion of a friend at Heath-Techna who knew Len Muller's capabilities as a design engineer. The Lockheed seat project had run into difficulty in the hands of a Heath-Techna subsidiary. Its design was failing tests required by Lockheed, and time for the job was running short.

Muller spent Christmas vacation sketching alternative design concepts for the seats. Heath-Techna looked at them and invited him to continue working on the job. He negotiated a contract and in January 1971 invested $5,000 to set up shop in his apartment. Hiring one employee in January, he began to build a work force that reached a dozen by year end. Halfway through the year, he incorporated and engaged an accountant to handle the books.

He recalled the hectic pace: "It was a 16-hour job. I arrived at 7 for coordination meetings with Heath-Techna, then after a half hour left for my 8 A.M. job at Boeing. At night it was back to the office by 5 to catch my employees before they left at 5:30. Then in the evenings I worked on the project myself."

By October he had begun to acquire other work for his moonlight enterprise and decided to take a leave of absence from Boeing, to which he didn't return. Subsequently, he branched his company into writing technical manuals, then through acquisition, job machine work, and finally a proprietary product consisting of a remote control for fireplugs. He had done this diversification as a hedge against one part of the company's business hitting a downturn. By 1979, however, the company was growing so fast that he was searching for ways to pare parts of it off.

Although the first sale came to Len Muller without his directly pursuing it, he still had to do the work of preparing a proposal and working out the terms. Beyond that, he had to seek other work and keep other sales coming in to build the business rather than simply working his way out of it by completing the first job. And, of course, he had to have performed well previously in order to attract the first sale to begin with. Thus, selling could not be regarded as either unimportant or effortless. But the first break did come to him. From his prior experience in contract engineering and his varied education, he knew what to do with it.

The following company, like Muller's, began in contract engineering from a customer inquiry but followed a considerably different pattern:

■ *Milton Lewis and Ted Warner were engineering managers in the nuclear laboratory of Douglas Aircraft at Richland, Washington, in late 1973 where they had seen the need from time to time for temporary engineering employees on critical phases of technical projects. There were companies in business to provide such temporary help, but none were headquartered locally. Consequently, several of the local nuclear industry companies serving the Hanford Atomic Works would hire employees from each other on a moonlighting basis.*

Because requests for such temporary technical help seemed to be coming frequently, the two men proposed that their employer create a formal operation to respond, but the idea was rejected. Consequently, the two began to plan an independent company on their own. It seemed to them that they might seek to reach twenty employees by year end, and they decided $4,000 was the limit they would be willing to invest. Problems they had to solve were how much overhead cost to expect and how much to charge for engineering service.

They listed prospective employees among personal acquaintances, some of whom agreed to provide resumes and make themselves available for specific amounts of time. Later the list was expanded by advertising in other geographical areas to avoid competition for engineers with their prospective customers. Discussions with an accountant helped on the overhead and rate problems; they estimated overhead requirements to be about half those of their employer. With an attorney they worked out details of a corporation, deciding against Subchapter S (taxation on personal rather than corporate rates) on the advice of their accountant.

Still working their regular jobs, they placed their first employee on a contract with the local Westinghouse operation in March 1974. By July the number of employees on their payroll had grown to ten and Ted Warner quit his Douglas job to join the new company, Columbia Engineers, Inc., full time. Six months later in January 1975 employment had reached the target of twenty and Milton Lewis also quit Douglas to join full time.

In contrast to Len Muller, who was personally solicited by a prospective customer, Milton Lewis and Ted Warner found the customers coming to their employer, Douglas Aircraft. Only after that employer had turned down the business did they pick it up. Otherwise, the start-ups were fairly similar. Beyond start-up, Columbia Engineers also sought to diversify, beginning with the acquisition of a consumer electronics manufacturing company.

Bidding

Bidding opportunities are normally open to anyone qualified to perform the work. They crop up particularly on construction projects and government jobs, although certain lines of industrial work such as job shop machining and other subcontracting (e.g., in the auto industry) use this mode of buying as a standard practice. Which jobs to bid depends on what kind of work the entrepreneur is capable of doing. To locate bidding opportunities, the following types of lists are available:

1. The *Commerce Business Daily* lists bidding opportunities for federal jobs. Public libraries have copies. The Small Business Administration helps entrepreneurs find opportunities to sell to the government and can be a helpful information source. The SBA can also provide other literature and information about how to land government contracts.
2. Local governments, state universities, and other public nonfederal organizations (such as community hospitals, highway patrols, and junior colleges) typically have bidders lists that are open to inspection in their purchasing offices.
3. In construction, the major contracting companies, architects, and contractors' associations are sources of information about jobs up for bid.
4. Purchasing departments in companies handle bid buying, and personal contact with them is normally required to learn about available jobs.

There are often people with an "inside track" on bid work because they helped develop specifications in the request for proposals. At other times, proposals that are referred to as "unsolicited" are in fact solicited or negotiated outside of the formal channels. It can be helpful to become acquainted with the people who write the request to learn what sort of proposal they are interested in receiving on an "unsolicited" basis.

Even so, it may be necessary to keep "playing the numbers" in pursuit of a contract. Typically, several bids are received for every request for proposals and all but one fail. Most bids fail most of the time. Hence, a bidder must be prepared to "strike out" a number of times for each time he or she is successful, as illustrated by the following case.

■ *A Seattle man who grew up in the construction business, working with his grandfather on construction projects as a small boy, serving four years as a carpenter's apprentice after high school while picking up a degree in mechanical engineering and additional courses in business from the University of Washington, then finally moving up through a series of managerial positions over ten years with a major construction company, finally decided in 1973 that his future with that company no longer offered a sufficiently attractive horizon. Although he faced loss of substantial profit sharing and other fringe benefits, he began to consider quitting to start his own commercial construction business. He solicited advice from some of the many contacts he had developed in the business and received the virtually unanimous reply that this would be a very bad time to make such a move because commercial construction was down roughly 12 percent in the area and competition had become cutthroat. Nevertheless, he prepared* pro forma *financial forecasts for business he thought he could perform and took them to the bank to request a loan. The banker too pointed to the grim industry conditions and in no uncertain terms turned down the request.*

Despite the rejections, he kept searching for capital among private sources, and when three personal friends expressed enough confidence in him to offer backing, he told his employer of his plans and submitted his resignation. His employer asked him to stay on part-time to finish jobs he was supervising, and for a year he did so, meanwhile seeking leads on jobs being opened for bid. Industry conditions continued to worsen, however, and two of his backers withdrew, leaving only one and very limited capital. Still, he moved ahead with his plan, formed a corporation, opened an office and worked up his first bid, for a $600,000 restaurant job. He failed to win it. He continued working up more bids as he learned of prospective jobs. Seven more bidding attempts failed, then finally success came on a warehouse construction job. From there sales rose to $2 million the first year with a solid profit and kept rising thereafter.

Government Customers

Sources of information about government sales opportunities were previously noted. Although the government is the world's largest customer, purchases thousands of different items, and specifically favors small companies in procurement, it can still be a hard sell.[2] Some companies with more experience may know how to bid. Others may be selected even with a higher than the lowest bid because of their established track record of dependable performance. Still others may have helped prepare the bid specifications or may simply have personal contacts who will favor them.[3] One small company president, John C. Rennie of Pacer Systems, Inc., described the need for working contacts:

■ *The technical people are usually willing to say what is coming down the pike, where their future needs will lie, and where and when they will put a given piece of work out for bids. From their point of view, they want to speed up the process as much as possible. Once a request for bids comes out on the street, you are prohibited from talking to technical people until the award is made.[4]*

How a new company may be able to capitalize on related experience and contacts in bidding on government work is illustrated by the next case.

[2]Michelle Bekey, "Selling to Uncle Sam," *Venture* (February 1982), p. 23.
[3]Dexter C. Hutchins, "Entrepreneurs Ride the Defense Boom," *Venture* (August 1980), p. 74.
[4]Dexter C. Hutchins, "Landing Government Contracts," *Venture* (March 1980), p. 19.

■ *In late 1969 when the Boeing Company was cutting its basic research programs, three of its scientists in environmental research began a series of evening meetings to discuss possibilities of starting a new company in that field. They enrolled in night courses on small business and recruited the wife of one of the three with a background in accounting to help with a business plan. For three months discussions continued, considering different options for the type of business they might create, centering primarily around schemes for remote sensing of air pollution. They seriously considered manufacturing a transmissometer on which one of the scientists held a patent but calculated that option would require too much capital. Instead, they chose to start with services as a more conservative way to gain start-up experience.*

They engaged a lawyer friend of one of the three to draft and file incorporation papers, obtained a city business license and chose a name, all before soliciting any business. Then they began contacting acquaintances asking about possible contracts to bid on. One friend, a scientist at Stanford Research Institute, mentioned a project for which the institute was slated to become program manager and which would include sub-projects that might be appropriate for their new company. Writing to the federal Advance Research Projects Agency responsible for the overall program, they requested and received a copy of the Request for Proposals (RFP). Within a month they had submitted their proposal for a $20,000 contract. A month and a half after that they received an acceptance which put them in business.

Now with a contract in hand, which they attributed partly to their prior record of experience, partly to the proposal which drew upon that experience, and partly to personal acquaintance with decision makers and influencers involved, they rented an office. Based upon prospective progress payments scheduled in the contract, which was for design, construction, testing, and operation of an interferometer system for upper atmospheric research, they started buying equipment. One scientist quit his Boeing job and went full-time with the new company. The other two joined full-time after further contracts were lined up.

One of these other contracts came from an unsolicited proposal they submitted to the Department of Transportation for research on fog prediction at airports. To their surprise they learned that the department just two weeks earlier had put out a request for proposals for very similar work. Modifying their unsolicited proposal to fit this RFP, they landed another contract for $165,000.

Booklets are available from all levels of government with such titles as "Selling to the Government," "Selling to the City," "Doing Business with the State," and so forth that tell where to go, whom to see, what the rules and conditions are, how to learn about opportunities and submit bids, and what the governmental policies are. But they do not reveal how the human interactions that can be so important to success on such contracts work. For those the best teacher is experience and the second best is discussion with others in similar lines of work who have that experience and are willing to tell about it and offer advice.

ADVERTISING

Some start-ups generate sales almost entirely through advertising. MITS, which introduced the first microcomputer kit, ran a small advertisement for the product and to its astonishment was swamped with orders. Other start-ups never advertise and still prosper. Two well-known examples are Haagen-Dazs ice cream and Mrs. Fields' Cookies, neither of which spent any money on advertising. For them, the substitute was a timely product that people would reach for, plus free publicity (such as newspaper and magazine "human-interest" stories), which could be regarded as taking the place of advertising.

Seeking Free Publicity

The potential for free publicity may lie in the unusual nature of the venture, the personalities of the founders, or local human interest. New local restaurants are usually written up in newspapers, for instance. Free publicity can be obtained through publicity stunts, though sometimes they cost money, and it can be obtained through technical publications when scientific discovery or engineering innovation is involved. An example of free publicity through article publication was related by Dible:

■ *One businessman I know sent out new-product releases describing a $200 device to 12 trade journals serving his industry. He received more than 1,500 inquiries in response to articles carried in the two journals that printed his story. His total cost was less than $15.*[5]

The power of publicity, however, can work either way. Its negative influence was vividly illustrated by the case of United Sciences America:

■ *Robert M. Adler II, inventor of the automatic telephone dialer, had already made millions when he decided to form a company to produce and sell nutritional supplements through development of a "multilevel" (sometimes characterized as "pyramid") salesforce. Under such a scheme, people recruited as "distributors" buy the company's products at discount and resell them at 35 percent to 50 percent markup. They also recruit others to sell and receive 10 percent to 15 percent override royalties on sales of the recruits, who in turn recruit still others for similar overrides. On products that retail for five times manufacturing costs, some such companies become highly profitable.*
In 1985, Adler invested $2.5 million of his savings and recruited an advisory board of distinguished physicians, including Nobel Laureate Julius Axelrod, and famous athletes, including Joe Montana, to help develop the products and program. To recruit salespeople videotapes were made which touted the illustrious board and made impressive benefit claims for the products, including mention that they included ingredients that had been proven useful in preventing many incurable diseases. So effective were the tapes that within six months the company had recruited 100,000 "independent distributors." Sales after six months had risen to $10 million per month and were heading to surpass the start-up sales record of $110 million set earlier by Compaq Computer.
Then other physicians began reacting in alarm to the ways their distinguished colleagues were being used in the tapes and to health benefit claims the company was making. Those whose names were used in advertising began to protest and to deny claims made in their names. The Federal Drug Administration said the company was mislabelling its products with false health claims, and an NBC television show exposed the company nationwide for these and other problems, such as the American Heart Association's demand that its name be removed from company advertising. "Sales died totally," a

---

[5]Donald M. Dible, *The Pure Joy of Making More Money* (Santa Clara, CA: Entrepreneur Press, 1976), p. 160.

Manhattan distributor recalled. "People said 'forget it, I don't want to sell this thing.'" Three months later, in January 1986, the company filed for bankruptcy, with 130,000 distributors, no products, and a negative net worth of $1.3 million.[6]

Publicity usually influences the fortunes of a company in a positive direction, but in less spectacular ways. For E. Joseph Cossman, an elaborate publicity campaign produced orders for over 600,000 "spud guns" within ten days:

■ *The toy gun, which shot a potato pellet formed by jamming the end of its barrel into a potato, had previously failed to sell, which enabled Cossman to buy, for 10 percent of its original cost, the tooling used to make it. In anticipation of the National Toy Show, he then wrote potato associations across the country asking them to contribute potatoes to fill a room as a stunt for which they would receive recognition from the press as producers of "America's most important vegetable." He invited a local orphanage in New York, where the show would be held, to send twenty-five children for a "shootout" on the pile of potatoes, which in turn would be contributed to the orphanage.*

The campaign had many other features—a potato sack with potato and gun was sent to newspaper city desks, feature writers, and home economics editors, as well as television stations; publicity materials went to major news magazines; displays on potatoes and the gun were widely distributed; sheriff badges with "Spud Gun Patrol" were issued to all who visited the display; and hostesses dressed in potato sacks welcomed visitors.[7]

The result was wide press coverage and orders for far more guns than Cossman could produce, which obliged him to expand production—all for a toy that had previously been a complete market failure.

Buying Exposure

An implicit rule shown in Cossman's successful promotional experience is to involve multiple media sources, including the purchase of space in magazines and newspapers as well as on radio and television. Engaging top-quality professionals to take photographs and design packaging, displays, brochures, and advertisements may be more costly, but it can increase the effectiveness of advertising far out of proportion to the extra charge. Such help on the design of letterheads, business cards, signs, store layouts, and decor can similarly be well worth the price. Sometimes advertising agencies will do work in return for stock and/or give unusually low prices to start-up companies, anticipating that they are entering on the ground floor with an account that may grow much larger and more lucrative with time. It is also sometimes possible to get low-cost help from highly talented commercial artists who are just beginning their own enterprises.

The Written Word. Selling directly through written advertisements prevails in many industries and can be seen by noting the advertisements in newspapers and magazines that solicit orders by mail and phone. From its inception, the

[6]David M. Roth, "The Rise and Fall of USA, Inc.," *Venture* (May 1987), p. 66.

[7]E. Joseph Cossman, *How I Made $1,000,000 in Mail Order* (Englewood Cliffs, NJ: Prentice-Hall, 1963), p. 129.

microcomputer industry has included start-ups that obtained their first sales directly through advertising, and some companies, such as Dell Computer, have continued to operate that way. A couple of early examples included companies that were highly successful in gaining early sales, although they ultimately failed, primarily due to management problems, not selling difficulties.

■ *The first popular microcomputer, sold in kit form, was the Altair. It was developed by MITS, a company in Albuquerque which began as a mail order company selling radio controls for model airplanes. Thereafter, it tried selling pocket computer kits but was unsuccessful. Next, it tried Microcomputer kits, which were featured in a January 1975 cover story of* Popular Electronics. *That article galvanized the start-up of many other microcomputer companies, including Microsoft, and also apparently stimulated a market for the MITS product. When the company ran a small classified advertisement for it, the response was a deluge of orders.*

One of the kits shipped by MITS was examined by a California consulting firm, IMS, which was looking for a way to link together within car dealerships some limited purpose Wang computers used exclusively for computing car payments. A GM dealer had hired IMS to develop linkage hardware and software that could also be used for accounting. Wang had no solution for it at the time, so IMS after hearing about the MITS computer began looking for ways to adapt it. However, MITS would not agree to extend trade credit to tiny IMS, so IMS "reverse engineered" the product to build its own. As a way of generating short-term cash, it also ran a small classified advertisement in Popular Electronics *offering the machine by mail.*

IMS's founder described what happened next. "I mean, here are five people—two of whom are myself and my wife—in this little place in San Leandro. And we're just trying to survive, okay? The mailman came in with the mailsack. We got 3,500 responses to our ad—our little one inch ad. And he spilled it out on the counter, and we began opening these envelopes. And this would be on tablet paper, 'Here's my order for the IMSAI 80 kit.' And there's a check—$699."[8]

Before long other companies had followed suit, as another computer entrepreneur, George Morrow, recalled. "There were 50 to 60 microcomputer kits around and everyone wanted me to do memory products for this, that, or the other one. I got typecast with memory. I had ideas for other products, but I couldn't get the people I had been dealing with to do them. I became frustrated, and one day sitting at home discussing my problems with my wife, I said damn it, what's the difference between doing these products for somebody else or for ourselves? All it takes is an ad in a magazine."

For $500 he bought a half-page ad in Byte Magazine's *February 1976 issue for some product ideas he had. Around $5,000 worth of orders resulted, and he started shipping products he had made from the ideas. Sales were $50,000 between March and December of 1976, $600,000 in 1978, $1.5 million in 1979, and $22.5 million by 1984.*[9]

Yellow Pages advertisements, flyers, and posters are other printed media alternatives for soliciting orders directly. The mail can be used for sending advertisements, catalogs, and/or samples.

---

[8]Robert Levering, Michael Katz, and Milton Moskowitz, *The Computer Entrepreneurs* (New York: New American Library, 1984), p. 351.

[9]James Ridgeway, "Living the Computer Future," *In Business* (February 1984), p. 28.

■ *Robert Kaldenbach obtained the first 800 subscriptions for his* New England Farm Bulletin *by renting four mailing lists and sending samples to 10,000 people.*[10]

The next entrepreneur obtained the first subscriptions for a vastly larger enterprise, one ultimately worth hundreds of millions of dollars, by sending only a letter, no samples, using a list that was borrowed rather than rented.

■ *On November 1, 1942, while waiting to be drafted, John H. Johnson borrowed $500 on his mother's furniture to start his magazine,* Negro Digest. *On the same date in 1945, he started* Ebony, *and in 1951,* Jet. *[Johnson] started at Supreme Life Insurance as Office Boy and Gofer. His 1989 estimated net worth was $200 million. As a high school student in the mid-thirties, he organized a mimeographed magazine* (Afri-American Youth) *for the National Youth Administration.*

Upon graduating from high school, he was given a $200 scholarship, not enough to attend the University of Chicago. At a luncheon for outstanding students, he managed to meet the main speaker, Harry H. Pace, president of Supreme Liberty Life Insurance. Upon hearing of Johnson's financial plight, Pace offered him a part-time job to help out.

For the first three months, he was given nothing to do but sit at a desk outside the president's office. The company printed a monthly newspaper, The Guardian, *and eventually Johnson was made assistant editor and then editor. But the idea for starting his own magazine came after President Pace asked him to prepare for him personally a weekly briefing on what was happening in the black world, so Pace would be better able to discuss race relations with people he encountered. Why not, [Johnson] thought, a pocket-sized magazine "that would summarize newspaper and magazine articles about Negro life"? He looked for support among personal acquaintances and black leaders but was told the idea would not work. Other attempts at black commercial magazines had all failed.*

The only way he could see to create such a magazine would be to produce it himself. Pondering this idea, it struck him that one resource he had was knowledge of his employer's automatic addressing machine, which held names and addresses of its 20,000 policyholders. "Why not," he thought, "send a letter to every person on the list asking for a two-dollar prepaid subscription to a new black magazine? If I got a 30 percent response ($12,000) or even a 15 percent response ($6,000), I would have the money to publish the first issue of the magazine."

He asked for and received permission from Pace to use the machine and mailing list, drafted a letter designed to follow an injunction he culled from reading self-help books: "Ask not what you want, but what the customer or potential customer wants." "It aimed," he said, "to say to blacks that I intended to put out a magazine that would increase their respect and add to their knowledge and understanding." He sent it with stamps paid for by borrowing $500 against his mother's furniture. Three thousand replies brought in $6,000 and Johnson Publishing, which by 1989 had made Johnson worth some $200 million, was in business.[11]

There are two general types of mail selling: (1) direct mail, which involves mailing letters to people to solicit orders, as Johnson did, and (2) mail order, which

---

[10]Nancy Frazier, "Thriving at Home," *In Business* (March-April 1982), p. 37.

[11]John H. Johnson with Lerone Bennett, Jr., *Succeeding Against All Odds* (New York: Warner Books, 1989), p. 114.

makes use of any advertising media to solicit customers to place orders so they can receive merchandise through the mail. This requires buying space in someone else's catalog, magazine, or other medium, but on a per-person-reached basis, it is substantially cheaper than direct mail. Both approaches are described in many magazine articles and books on the subject.

Electronic Media.   Telephone, radio, television, and computers are all channels through which start-ups can generate sales. There are few examples of their doing so, however. A notable exception is the story of Home Shopping Network (HSN):

> ■   *Based on a precedent radio shopping program run by Lowell Paxon, he and Roy Speer in 1982 introduced a local TV buying show to 10,000 cable subscribers in a local area of Florida. Within three months it became profitable and the two expanded nationwide, using software they had developed specially for giving quick response on orders phoned in. By 1986 the firm was so successful that they went public, pulling in over $30 million on the offering, only to see it rise over tenfold in the aftermarket.*[12]

OPENING AN OUTLET

Setting up a point of contact where customers can walk up and buy the new venture's product or service is the most common approach used. As will be illustrated shortly, the display may be a formal storefront or something more temporary. A store can be in a rented building; a vehicle such as a mobile dispensing van; or simply a temporary space in someone else's store, a sidewalk fair, or a trade show that produces both immediate sales as well as links to selling agents, wholesale agents, and retailers for the product of a manufacturing venture.

Storefronts

Renting a place to display and sell the product or service of the company is probably the most familiar of all selling methods, one customers might use several times a day. With a storefront, the entrepreneur does not have to go looking for customers. They come to the company. Stores that open up in locations where other stores have closed are obvious examples of new ventures seeking to get sales started.

A problem with this kind of a start-up is that it may be too easy. Finding a storefront to rent, either through an agent or by driving around looking for a vacant window, is simple and so is signing a lease. Fixing the place up, painting, installing shelves or counters, putting up a sign—all these may take manual labor, time, and some money, but they are basically simple and straightforward tasks that do not require the will power, drive, and self-discipline that some other types of selling do. Getting inventory may take some capital and negotiation, but it can usually be

[12]Ellen James, "So What's a Billion to Speer?", *Venture* (May 1987), p. 40.

arranged, because the suppliers of that inventory are interested in getting the store started and generating sales for their own businesses. Such simplicity leads many to open stores as a way of entering business. All these entries intensify competition, drive margins down, and raise odds of failure.

It may be possible to hedge against such risks by starting small and growing. Tech Hi-Fi, for example, began as a sideline retailing activity in the dormitory room of an MIT student, Sandy Ruby, then expanded to a vacant janitor's closet, and finally, in 1967, to a formal storefront when they were evicted by school officials. Thus, the venture began on a low-risk basis that extended into the rental of a store only after sales were established.[13]

In other cases, a larger initial commitment may be required. If, for instance, major advertising or a large selection of inventory is part of the start-up strategy, a slow start may not be possible. When Debbi Fields wanted to start a cookie store, for instance, she needed to sign a lease and invest $25,000 borrowed from the bank for the installation of commercial cooking equipment, decoration of the shop, and working capital for an enterprise that almost did not make it.

■ *Debbi Fields had been told repeatedly by people with extensive business expertise and people without it that her idea of opening a store to sell chocolate chip cookies would not succeed. Market research studies had indicated that the public preferred crispy cookies, and hers were gooey. Bakeries sold cookies for nine cents each and hers would have to sell for twenty-five.*

But she could not let go of the idea. Now twenty years old, she had been baking them for friends since she was a child, and knew people liked them. Even "experts" munched on them while telling her they would not sell, and emptied the plate. So she rejected their advice and, with her husband's somewhat reluctant cooperation, took out a bank loan, rented a storefront in Palo Alto, bought equipment and supplies, and started baking.

For three weeks she baked and tested. Then the night before opening for business, she decided it would not work. She recalled crying and pacing the house, "It was obviously going to fail and I didn't know why I'd persisted so hard in trying to make it happen. Probably I'd done it because everyone said it couldn't be done. Now I was stuck with it."

The next morning at 9 A.M. she opened the store. People walked by, asked the price, and left without buying. "By noontime," she said, "my smile was beginning to fade. I had sold not one cookie."

"Well, I thought, if I can't sell them, I'm going to give them away." Leaving a friend to tend the counter she took a tray of cookies and walked around the arcade, but could not give them away. Going further in to the streets of Palo Alto, however, she began to encounter people who would sample the product. Some even asked where it could be bought, and she gave them the store's address. Eventually, they emptied the tray.

"I went back to the store and started baking," she continued. "An hour later, some of the people who'd tried a cookie on the street wandered into the arcade and presented themselves at the counter. They found me! And they bought cookies."

By the end of that day she counted fifty dollars in sales. The next it was seventy-five. She was on her way to creating a multimillion-dollar chain of over 500 stores in the U.S. and abroad.[14]

---

[13]Jeffrey Tarter, "Can He Keep His Customers Tuned In?," *Inc.* (November 1980), p. 73.
[14]Debbi Fields and Alan Furst, *One Smart Cookie* (New York: Simon & Schuster, 1987), p. 80.

What makes the difference between the stores that close and those that stay open? The wrong combination of products on display, not enough inventory, high prices, and lack of effective advertising may all be part of the problem.

The most reiterated cliché concerning retail success seems to be that "location, location, and location" is the key. Certainly there are examples in support of that claim. Donald Hauck, a former department store operator, attributed the failure of his new store to being located "40 ft too far north."[15] Others have offered rules for selecting location and indicated that the best location depends on the type of business,[16] as well as local population density and income level, density of foot traffic past the door, availability of convenient parking, driving distance or traffic flow rate. The types of other stores in the vicinity may be a factor. Fast food establishments, for instance, often do best near other similar businesses, whereas veterinary clinics fare better when there are no other similar businesses nearby.

In the following case, the entrepreneur found he had to change location to get a viable volume of sales:

■ *A Seattle man who had taken a job in a language institute in Peru was informed that the Peruvian government would not extend his work permit beyond twelve months. He had traveled in the back country where he had seen handicrafts that he thought should sell well in the United States. Because he would have to return there and find employment, he and his wife decided to try importing some of the goods. When their time was up in Peru, they returned to Seattle with $600 worth of goods, all they could afford.*

Supported in part by his wife, he set up a table at a downtown marketplace and attempted to sell the goods. Sales were very small, averaging only $30 per day for the first six months. Then one Sunday on a visit to Tacoma he noticed a historic building being renovated as a shopping center. He found the building very appealing, and after discussing the possibility with his wife decided to rent a small space in it to display his wares. Sales now suddenly averaged $165 the first month, well above breakeven, and continued to rise thereafter.

Another crucial dimension in retailing is the choice of what the company sells. In the next case, changing that was the key:

■ *In late 1969 two Seattle men decided to try starting a new movie theater. Neither had ever worked in such a business before, but both were intrigued by the idea. They found a suitable building, renovated it largely with the help of friends, bought their city business license, paid the amusement tax, contacted the newspapers for publicity and film distributors for films to show.*

In mid-1970 they opened to an audience that was disappointingly small and composed mainly of friends and relatives. They had been told by the film distributors and other advisors that a small theater such as this would never make it. Their banker had said he was certain it would fail.

As the weeks rolled on and the theater continued to operate in the red with small audiences, eating up the remainder of the two men's savings, they kept trying different

[15]Donald Hauck, "Location, Location, Location!," *Venture* (April 1987), p. 100.
[16]Gregory and Patricia Kishel, "Choosing a Business Location," *In Business* (January-February 1983), p. 28.

films, but to little avail. Finally, in August they tried a film called The Pride of Miss Jean Brodie *and threw their reserves into an advertising campaign to promote it as a great movie, although it had been regarded as having a bad title and had received almost no publicity when first released. Suddenly things changed. Their customary audience quickly doubled and then kept on growing. Customers went home and told their friends about the new people-oriented theater with free cheese and crackers in the lobby and a good show, and soon the partners were looking at the alternative of opening a second theater.*

Time can be yet another important dimension in developing store sales. For some, sales may be immediate, whereas for others, it may take a while for people to become aware of the business and to develop a use for what it has to offer, as the next example illustrates:

■ *Artie Benson and his family had seen a new type of store selling mill-end fabric remnants become very successful in a short time in Phoenix, Arizona. Since he was soon to retire as a Honeywell systems analyst and had always wanted his own business, he discussed with the family the idea of starting a similar store in some other area where none existed. Because his wife had relatives in Seattle and they had heard it was a pleasant city, they checked and learned that it had no such store, and then chose it as their site for their new venture. After locating and remodeling a building in a business district dominated largely by industrial supply houses, they opened their new remnant store in February 1974. Sales, however, were very slow to come. People were not familiar with such a store or how to use it, the location was not one which women normally visited for other shopping, and the owners themselves were unknown in the community. For a year and a half the company went on losing money. Traffic was too low. But gradually it began rising as a few customers tried the store, found a way to use it to their advantage, and told their friends about it. By the end of the second year, it had passed breakeven and steadily continued to move further into the black.*

Pricing, quality of service, decor, and promotions also can play important parts in building storefront sales, and it may take a while and some experimentation to find an effective combination for a particular enterprise. Coupled with the fact that margins in retailing tend to be low, it can be very hard for a thinly financed store to hold out long enough to reach profitability. Even so, the financing needed for retail selling can be considerably less than that needed for manufacturing, because in retailing the entrepreneur need not invest in fixed equipment, accounts receivable, or raw materials and in-process inventory to generate sales.

Trade Shows, Exhibitions, and Fairs

There are over nine thousand trade shows per year in the United States at which exhibitors and attendees spend around $9 billion. Most exhibitors are established companies, not entrepreneurs, but some entrepreneurs develop their first sales momentum through display at such shows.

Five alternative purposes for putting the product or service of a new venture on display at a show can be (1) to make sales directly, (2) to get prospective customer names for later follow-up, (3) to recruit dealers, agents, or wholesalers who may want to help sell what the venture offers, (4) to get reactions to a prototype so it can be further refined, and (5) simply to display the name of the venture and enhance its visibility. Attending shows, whether as a displayer or not, can also help keep the entrepreneur abreast of what other companies in his or her industry are doing.

It is important to know which of these purposes applies, because attending a show takes time, and presenting a display costs both time and money. Companies experienced at such shows perform such calculations as the number of contacts made per dollar of cost times the number of sales per contact. They find that some shows, some displays, and some operating procedures work better than others. Such calculations suggested that it cost $178 in 1981 to make a contact by direct selling versus $68 to get one through a trade show and that it took 5.1 sales calls to make a close versus 0.8 calls following up trade show leads.[17] Another survey in 1982 estimated costs of $137 in person versus $57 at a show[18] and yet another in 1987 put the figures at $229 for a sales call versus $107 at a show.[19] One entrepreneur who organized raft trips, for instance, commented that "It costs me $500 to exhibit at a two-day show in Los Angeles. A typical show can generate $30,000 to $40,000 in new business."[20]

Once some potential shows are identified, more detailed information about them, including expected audience, types of space available, and prices for that space, can be obtained by writing to the shows. Other companies that exhibited at previous shows can also be asked how effective they found those particular shows to be, and they can be asked for advice about how best to prepare for and take advantage of selling opportunities at the show. Some people experienced with shows recommend contacting selected prospective buyers in advance to invite them to visit the company's booth. A list of people who attended the show can often be obtained afterward for further follow-up sales literature or sales calls.

During the show, it should be possible to meet not only buyers, but also potential sales agents and other companies in parallel lines of business who may be able to help the new company sell its products. To do this, however, it will be necessary to gain their attention by designing an effective display, sales presentation, literature, and other possible "gimmicks," such as samples, acts, souvenirs, and so forth. Visiting other shows and taking note of the sorts of things done can be an effective way to get ideas. In any major city, and many smaller ones as well, shows are held at the local convention center. By paying a visit to the center, it should be possible for the would-be entrepreneur to obtain admission to one or two of them to see what they are like, how they work, and what kinds of display approaches can be effective.

Referring to a list of trade shows,[21] E. Joseph Cossman observed:

[17]Susan Buchsbaum and Mark K. Metzger, "Show and Sell," *Inc.* (May 1984), p. 66.
[18]Jacqueline Michaud, "Using Trade Shows to Build Sales," *In Business* (January-February 1982), p. 37.
[19]Jay Pridmore, "Another Niche, Another Show," *Venture* (January 1987), p. 38.
[20]Echo M. Garrett, "Please, Take My Card," *Venture* (September 1988), p. 16.
[21]*Exhibits Schedule*, Bill Communications, P.O. Box 3078, Southeastern, PA 19398.

Just reading the list of these 35,000 scheduled shows can stimulate many ideas on how to promote your product. Although our Spud Gun was basically a toy, we exhibited it at food shows, sporting goods shows, premium shows, housewares shows—as well as the more pertinent toy shows. Each show opened up a new market for our product.

However, merely exhibiting at a trade show does not insure success for your item. We discovered that at least 50 percent of our success in trade shows depended upon work done before the show . . . work in which mail order practices are utilized to the fullest.[22]

Experimentation and experience will teach entrepreneurs how to make the most of shows, as well as the following suggestions:[23]

- Do not waste time on people who are unlikely to produce desired business results. Qualify prospects.
- Giveaways can attract many people who do not buy.
- Do not be overly wordy in backdrop displays.
- Product demonstrations are particularly effective.
- Set measurable objectives and measure results.
- Repeated exposure is needed to get results.
- Tie in advance publicity and follow-up calls and letters.
- Negotiate insofar as possible for a prominent location on the show floor.
- Be different from other exhibitors.
- Ask the show in advance for a complete list of costs.
- Hire professional help to design a booth.
- Ask your trade association for literature on trade show advice.[24]

PERSONAL SELLING

Although some enterprises are able to sell through advertising, most cannot begin that way. Instead, the founding entrepreneur has to go out on the street, call on prospective purchasers, and obtain initial orders personally. Most of the examples already described and others that follow demonstrate this. Customers and a host of potential intermediaries need to be contacted.

Personal selling for a new enterprise often begins with customers of the entrepreneur's former employer (something the employer does not always appreciate). In the following example, the entrepreneur appears to have felt almost obliged to do this because of the poor performance of his employer:

■ *"I'd go in to see them and I'd be met by the damnest blast you ever heard. Every time there was something wrong. A needed delivery hadn't come through, or parts were delivered that weren't up to specs, or even sometimes they weren't even the right parts at*

[22]Cossman, *How I Made $1,000,000 in Mail Order*, p. 119.

[23]Joanne Kelleher, "Tips for Trade Shows," *Inc.* (October 1981), p. 152; Cossman, *How I Made $1,000,000 in Mail Order*, p. 120; and Michaud, "Using Trade Shows to Build Sales," p. 37 (this last article also lists other sources of trade show information).

[24]Deborah M. Burek, *Encyclopedia of Associations* (Detroit, MI: Gale Research, 1991).

all. I'd scurry around trying to make adjustments, but it was no good. These men, they were absolutely dependent on Lacey as a source of supply, and they couldn't help feeling that because I was their personal friend I was letting them down.

"I began feeling them out, asking them what they thought. This was tricky because these buyers, they were supposed to be maintaining good relations with Lacey. And then I was actually employed by Lacey. I was on salary there and I couldn't appear to be disloyal. It slowly became clear to me that some of them, some of the big ones, were ripe to make a switch if they could be assured of a reliable supplier."

Having his customers lined up from this personal selling, this entrepreneur spent several months planning a start-up, estimating needs in terms of capital and people, deciding whom to approach to obtain the financing and to staff the company, seeking out facilities, and obtaining a building lease. Then he called a meeting of all the interested parties in a hotel room and laid out his plans to the group, displaying an organization chart and pointing out the role of each participant. "This was strictly a one-shot proposition," he recalled. "I wasn't going to get a second chance. If Lacey got wind of it, they'd move against me immediately. A few promotions and a few promises and they could queer my whole proposition."

As it turned out, his proposition was accepted and the new company which had been inspired by the entrepreneur's sales calls on customers began.

This company, like the two engineering start-ups described earlier, knew just who the customers would be when the business began. In common with many other start-ups as well was this close link with customers of the entrepreneur's prior employer, and many entrepreneurs manage to serve those customers without any objection from prior employers. This knowledge of customers and their needs may be the most important asset an entrepreneur possesses in starting a company, and it may be why so many companies are started by former salespeople or by engineers who also are often in a good position to appreciate customers' needs because their job is to develop products for satisfying those needs. Perhaps a moral from this observation for the would-be entrepreneur is to take stock of which types of prospective customers and their needs he or she is most familiar with and work toward a venture from that. If the link is not very close, perhaps because the entrepreneur does not work directly with customers, then it may be advisable to work out a personal strategy for breaking out of that situation, either through a change of job or activities or through cultivation of avocations or after-hours activities that will make the linkage closer.

But it is not just what the entrepreneur knows about customers from personal contact that is important, it is often also what potential customers know about the entrepreneur that makes them willing to deal with him or her, as illustrated by the following example:

■ *William T. Harrold started studying radio technology in high school because his friends were taking the course. This led to wiring jobs for the student theatrical productions and audio systems for the musical groups. Then railroad and aircraft drafting and wiring design, then finally a shop of his own installing intercom systems. Wartime and the suggestion of a friend found him a job in the radiation laboratory at MIT, which provided more training and much practical experience in design of radar systems. His plan for after the war was to return to Seattle and, with a friend as his partner, install radar in ferry boats, but management of the ferries was not inclined to install any such new thing at the time.*

So the two men offered their services to Boeing, which began giving them orders for pulse generators and other electronic instruments. These orders ceased in 1948 due to sales cutbacks at Boeing, and his partners left to study for a Ph.D. But now a utility approached him with a request that he design and build for them a device for locating breaks in electrical cables. The device was not new, patents had long since run out on it, but the utility could not find any available at the time, and through others in the electronics business had heard this entrepreneur might be able to build them one. For a modest fee of $1,000 he made the unit and again his company was out of work.

He closed the shop and moved from Seattle to Los Angeles where a former associate from MIT had offered him a job. While on this new job, the utility company contacted him again with a request for more break locaters. He made these in his garage, then he moved back to Seattle, intending to form a company to make more.

Before he could do this, however, another former friend had obtained an electronics consulting contract and needed help. Two such contracts later, the entrepreneur took a full-time job with the second of their consulting customers. Again, however, he was receiving orders for break locaters, which he was building in his home garage. The volume of orders for these products continued to grow, and after a year in his new job, two years after returning to Seattle, he left the job to do what he had come back to do, work full-time for his own enterprise making break locaters.

If the entrepreneur is not already known to prospective customers, then canvassing may be required. One example was the entrepreneur mentioned earlier who began selling stereo sets door-to-door. Another was a man who started up in the window glass business by seeking customers through visiting construction sites and asking if any windows were needed. In each case, the entrepreneur narrowed his territory some, the first by choosing his neighborhoods as those most likely to buy, and the glazier by selecting particular construction sites.

The next two examples involve MBA students from the University of Washington who developed consumer products and started their sales campaigns by talking to store managers. The first found his sales somewhat disappointing. The second was so successful that upon graduation he went full-time with his own resultant company.

■ *He made some large wooden name plaques with raised letters for people's homes. After making up some samples, he went to the Yellow Pages and made a list of interior decorators, whom he then visited with the samples. Several let him put them on display in their offices. When someone wanted one, the decorator would phone in an order or drop a card. Few sales resulted. The same approach was tried with small craft and gift shops, and the response was better. Next, he planned to expand his line to include large wooden letters and numbers with which people could make their own plaques and also could nail on their house fronts. He also planned to offer them to hardware stores. This approach worked somewhat better, but not well enough to make a full-time business of it.*

■ *Bob Howard and two classmates came up with the idea of making a powdered mix that could be used with wine to make hot-spiced wine for an after-ski drink. In the kitchen they mixed up a batch of the wine, put it in a thermos, and took it around to stores, pouring samples for the managers and asking if they would put such a product on the shelves. They immediately received orders, plus the advice to sell the packages for no* *more than $0.99, so they were able to go to a contract packaging company and have the product prepared with enough orders in hand to guarantee sale of the first production run.*

What caused the difference between the outcomes? Apparently it lay in the products themselves. By personal selling, both entrepreneurs were able to get their products tried. But the second one continued to sell well enough for stores to continue to reorder, while the first did not. It is, of course, possible that the first entrepreneur missed some clues during his sales efforts that might have guided him to modify his product better so that it would sell or perhaps even ideas for some product he could have made, but that cannot be known. What does seem clear is that there was no "magic" or mysterious superior sales ability associated with getting those first orders. It was simply a matter of making the rounds and talking about the product with people who could help the selling process along and had something to gain by doing so.

The importance of simply getting out and making the calls to sell was illustrated by the early experience of another entrepreneur, Richard Heckmann. Later in his career, he took over two companies and was highly successful in sales. The first was Radair, a company in which he and some others invested and then took over when it got into trouble. Under Heckmann's management, sales rose from $200,000 to over $1.5 million in a little over one year. It subsequently failed, but not for lack of sales. The other was a medical equipment company that he took over for essentially no money after it had lost money for nineteen straight years. He boosted sales approximately fivefold within two years and sold out the year after that for around $1.5 million. The following is an earlier lesson that had led to this sales performance:

■ *During college Heckmann answered a want-ad for a part-time job selling Fuller brushes. The sales trainer who accompanied him the first day told him that one out of ten calls would, on the average, land a sale. But his own first day and a half landed him nothing but disappointment. He was ready to quit but decided to try one more call. To his surprise the man who answered the next door bought $80 worth of brushes. Swept by a wave of gratification, he drew two philosophical conclusions about personal selling. The first was that, provided the product was basically satisfactory to at least some customers, "if you make enough calls you will find somebody who will buy." The second was that "every time someone says 'no' to your sales presentation, you should rejoice, because you are now one person closer to a sale."*

The specific people or places to call on for sales depends on the product or service. In two previous cases, which involved consumer products, the contact points were store managers. They could also have been buyers for larger chains or wholesalers if the objective had been to reach more distant sales territories. If the products had been industrial ones, then retail stores would have been unlikely prospects for sales. Industrial supply houses might have fit, depending upon the product, or industrial wholesalers might have been people to call on, but presumably only after the entrepreneur had personally called on some industrial end-users and had enough sales to show supply houses or wholesalers that the product was worth carrying. If the industrial product were expensive enough, then the company might not only start by selling direct but might continue that way, as in the following case:

■ *The Pacific Northwest Branch Sales Manager for a large computer company became frustrated by the fact that he could rise no further in the firm he worked for without leaving the Seattle area. After looking without success for a company to buy, he decided to form one of his own to sell and lease minicomputers to small firms. Through personal contacts he lined up two partners for capital. At his employer he found another salesman eager to work with him on the new enterprise.*

Two major remaining problems required personal selling. The first was to obtain a product line. He identified a company in southern California which had just announced a minicomputer ready for market. Visiting the company he received a cool reception and a rejection of his request to form a new dealership. After several more visits and presentation of his business plan he finally persuaded that company to sell him a franchise for $5,000.

The remaining problem was to find customers. His former employer had sold larger scale systems which did not compete directly with his new product line, but he wanted insofar as possible to avoid competing for the same customers. To generate a new list of prospects, he combed the Yellow Pages *and manufacturers' directories for his territory and bought lists from Contacts Influential. His most important source, however, was through other computer salespeople of the area who carried noncompeting lines but knew the market. Dun and Bradstreet data giving statistics on individual firms were also purchased to target particularly likely prospects.*

Now he had to find a way to persuade prospects to buy from his new and unproven firm a new and unproven minicomputer from the California company. The main arguments he used to do this, aside from performance features, price, warranty, and delivery service, were providing satisfactory installations of computers plus the business reputations of his partners, which were strong, particularly because one of them had personally undertaken to make up losses of a company he had been involved with from his own funds. With these arguments and personal "pavement pounding," he was able to line up more sales in the first four months of operation than he had projected for the first year of his new company.

The important common thread of these examples is the need for the entrepreneur to obtain sales orders personally in starting many businesses. It is more comfortable to have the customer initiate the sale, but this cannot be counted on. The entrepreneur will have to force himself or herself to go out and seek orders. This is an uncomfortable experience for most. Professional salespeople find it helpful to count the number of people they approach per day as a measure of whether they are giving the personal selling job what it requires to be successful. A would-be entrepreneur might do well to impose needed self-discipline by keeping score the same way and making that score as high as possible. A preliminary form that may be helpful in planning for the crucial element of obtaining first sales orders is shown in Exhibit 7–2. Books on personal selling are numerous and offer other helpful ideas.

EXHIBIT 7–2　Planning First Sales

	By Founder	By Other	Prospects Approached	Contacts/ Prospect	Order Amount
Sale #1	————	———	————	————	———
Sale #2	————	———	————	————	———
Repeat Order #1	————	———	————	————	———
Repeat Order #2	————	———	————	————	———
Follow-Up Orders					
Week 1	————	———	————	————	———
Week 2	————	———	————	————	———
Week 3	————	———	————	————	———
Week 4	————	———	————	————	———
Month 2	————	———	————	————	———
Month 3	————	———	————	————	———

Direct to End Users

Methods of selling directly to end users include door-to-door sales, party plan selling, and sales seminars to which potential customers are invited, a method used by Bruce Milne (see Chapter 1). Another method is physical demonstration. This may be incorporated as part of the personal sales call, or it may be presented on selected sites open to more public viewing. The following entrepreneur began by demonstrating in a place where he knew he would have a captive audience, a barber shop, and then went on from there:

■　*Floyd Fleming had been a high school shop teacher and then had built a construction business from which he had retired when he happened to read a* Seattle Times *article describing a new "keg" bottle just introduced by the Heidelberger beer company. The article concluded with the statement that "hobbyists are trying with little or no success to make glassware out of it." "That was just enough challenge to intrigue me," Mr. Fleming commented, "so I really went at the problem of trying to cut the neck off that bottle to make mugs. I even dropped golf for a while to work on it. After about four weeks I had a solution."*

His solution consisted of a small framework of aluminum rods fastened end-to-end so as to hold a glass cutter against the neck of a bottle. As the bottle was rotated, the cutter would neatly scribe a ring around the neck. Tapping on the inside of the bottle against the position of this ring then cracked the glass so the neck neatly broke off to leave a "keg-shaped" glass.

"Then I went to the local barber shop," he said, "and showed it to the guys there. The barber said he wanted one, and that was about all I needed. I made up a few more and went to a shopping center. I didn't have nerve to demonstrate it at a store in my own home town where I'd been a school teacher and a businessman. It is embarrassing to take

your baby out and show it like that. I went to a shopping center which I thought was out of my neighborhood where I wouldn't run into any of my friends. I took along a little table and went over and talked to the grocery store man. He said I could set up and see what would happen.

"So I set up my table there and started cutting bottles. People would look at the cutter, but they didn't buy very many . . . just said they might come back. I sold three or four, and it was kind of fun, so then I went down and tried a store in another area. It wasn't a center, just a bunch of shops, all sort of unrelated to each other. I set up again, and sold a few more. One of the people who bought them was a man who said he wanted to make tunnels out of the bottle necks.

"Then I went to the fair and set up a booth, and there I sold quite a few. People just seem to love to spend money at demonstration booths in the fair."

From these beginnings Floyd Fleming expanded to other sales channels, including Sears and other chains and soon had a business shipping millions of bottle cutters.

To Commercial Customers

Sales to commercial customers have already been illustrated in connection with bid sales and response to customer requests. Commercial customers, such as original equipment makers, normally have purchasing agents and offices where salespeople are received. As with the other contact points, an advance phone call can be helpful for determining the location and best time to visit.

To Intermediaries

There are a great variety of intermediaries in the national distribution system who form another class of customers to be approached through personal selling, generally by the entrepreneur. Through them he or she can hope to obtain large volume orders, perhaps starting with samples and small orders first, and then building up as the product begins to justify itself.

Buyers for intermediary firms can be tremendously helpful in sizing up a product, because they make their living selecting ones that sell and rejecting those that do not. Their advice can be sought before the entrepreneur makes a substantial commitment to such things as product development, tooling, advertising, and inventory. If it passes the buyers' judgment in early stages, then the odds of being able to land orders from the buyers later on are much higher.

Some indication of the variety of intermediaries can be seen in Exhibit 7–3.

Several of these channel elements are usually used in combination, and the number of combinations is almost limitless. At each intermediary, there will be some sort of discount or commission, depending upon the degree of contribution that intermediary is supposed to make to the selling process. Some alternative breakdowns follow:

List price	$100.00	$100.00
Retailer discount	50.00	33.00
Wholesaler discount	5.00	10.05
Commissioned agent	2.93	2.59
Manufacturer	41.85	51.73

EXHIBIT 7-3   Some Types of Intermediaries

Retailers	Premium distributors
Brokers	Associations
Dealers	Truck jobbers
Chains	Converters
Warehousers	Manufacturers' representatives
Value added retailers	Commission (consignment) merchants
Commissioned agents	Street peddlers
Export management companies	Freight forwarders
Auctioneers	Leasing companies
Rack merchandisers	Rental companies
Drop shippers	Telephone marketing firms
Catalog companies	Video marketing firms
Post exchanges	Fulfillment companies
Cooperatives	Original equipment makers (OEMs)
Resident buyers	

In the breakdown on the left, the retailer is getting 50 percent off retail price, the wholesaler "50 and 10," or 50 percent plus another 10 percent off retail, and the agent is getting 7 percent commission on the manufacturer's price. In the second, the retailer is getting 33 percent off retail, the wholesaler 15 percent of wholesale price, and the agent 5 percent of the manufacturer's price.

Discount and commission practices vary by industry. For instance, book-stores customarily buy at 50 percent off retail price on trade books and only 20 percent off retail on textbooks. Hence, textbooks are not seen on the shelves of most bookstores, only those serving campuses. But the stores have the right to return to publishers any textbooks they do not sell, and they also do not need to stock as much variety. Hence, their inventory costs and their risks are lower, which justifies operation on the smaller 20 percent discount. The discount structure on the product or service of a new business must necessarily depend on (1) what channels are used for getting it to customers, (2) what services those channels provide to this particular company, (3) what the customary practices are in that particular industry, and (4) what the entrepreneur can negotiate through personal selling with the intermediary.

Independent Retailers.   There are three points of contact for selling through retail stores: owners, managers, and buyers. Sometimes the first two are the same, as in the following example:

■ *Daniel Feld had worked in marketing for thirteen years when, in 1986, he got the idea of trying to enter the fast-growing $3.8 billion potato chip market. Proposing to sell "kettle" chips, which are prepared in small batches with hand-stirred slow cooking, he approached David Sneddon, co-owner of Fairway, a well-regarded grocery retailer. Sneddon made no promises but offered encouragement and recommended distributors. Sneddon was predisposed to favor local producers because, he said, "The smaller producer has better quality* *control and better service. They are willing to do more than the big guy, and their products are usually fresher, better quality and better value."*

Coincidentally, Sneddon had been disappointed by what he saw as a drop in quality of the kettle potato chip brand he currently carried when the company producing it was acquired by Anhaeuser-Busch. Samples of Feld's new brand arrived shortly, Sneddon tasted them and gave Feld his first order. Referral by Sneddon to distributors further helped. By telling them Fairway was stocking his brand, Feld found that some of them were willing to try it too.[25]

Independent stores usually buy through the local manager or owner. Talking to many of them helps to cross-check answers and obtain contrasting views.

■ *Gary Gabrel had been playing a board game with friends adapted from the Japanese "Go" and decided it might be the basis for creating a business. After contacting major game companies, he found no interest. Nevertheless, in 1978 he gave his game a name, Pente, filed for a copyright, and made 200 sets. With a small amount of cash from family plus a small bank loan, he made a down payment on a van and went on the road.*

He made contact with owners of gift stores and clubs and buyers for local department stores, demonstrating the game to them, to reporters, and to anyone else who might buy. He also displayed it at craft fairs. He later recalled that "a good few days was selling $500 to $600 of the game. That was enough to keep me going for two or three weeks."

Sales gradually grew in strength as the game began to catch on in Oklahoma City clubs, and write-ups appeared in Oklahoma magazine and newspapers. He added magazine advertisements and a board of directors who could make contacts at larger stores. As sales were developing, he introduced improvements in design and packaging to make the game distinctive and justify a higher price than other board games like Monopoly. The number of sets sold reached 100,000 in 1976, 300,000 in 1979, and by 1984 were close to 1 million per year.[26]

In the following case, the entrepreneur lined up a retail outlet as his customer, then he fell back on personal selling when that customer dropped his line:

■ *In the late 1950s, a Seattle entrepreneur invented the idea of fusing rubber-lined canisters for tumbling rocks in lapidary work. He made arrangements with a local lapidary shop to sell the products, which he and his son manufactured at home in their spare time. A disagreement arose with the retailer, who dropped their line, leaving them with about 100 tumblers unsold in their basement. Meanwhile, the entrepreneur had been inventing other products and had developed a utility tray which he thought deserved more attention than the rock tumblers. However, he needed capital to manufacture the trays, and to raise this he and his son went out calling on lapidary shops to cash in the inventory of tumblers. This they found fairly easy to do, but the result was that they received more orders for the tumblers, which propelled them further into manufacture of that product rather than the trays. Eventually, this manufacturing load reached a point where they both had to work at it full-time. The entrepreneur invented still other lapidary products and a thriving manufacturing enterprise developed in that field which they eventually sold out to a major national corporation.*

[25]Andrea Chapin, "Cashing in Your Chips," *Venture* (October 1988), p. 82.
[26]Curtis Hartman, "Playing by the Rules," *Inc.* (July 1983), p. 79.

To find retail store buyers and to meet with them are unfamiliar experiences for most people, but they are relatively easy to do. One approach is simply to call any retail store and request the buying office phone number. Other stores work through central buying offices. These offices maintain regular hours for receiving salespeople. The entrepreneur can enter the waiting room and wait for his or her turn to be ushered in to see the buyer. During the wait, it is generally easy to strike up conversations with other salespeople. That in itself can be a good way to learn about how the sales channels operate.

Department Stores.   Larger stores usually have more formal specialized purchasing offices than smaller independent stores. The following example describes the case of an ex-lawyer who went into the toy business through approaching department store buyers:

> *I decided my model cars should have nationwide distribution and proceeded to contact the toy buyers of the four largest department stores in the country. Contacting the toy buyers was a very interesting experience. I travelled to all four and I got the same story from all of them. They were very conservative. One placed an order for only five dozen of these cars. I flew down to see the buyers at the next two and got the same story and figured that the whole thing was a fizzle. I was talking to the toy buyer at Picks. I was attempting to sell him on this car and explained to him that I could ship him the new model car on the day of introduction of the new models. He left me in the office for a few moments and came back with a little wooden automobile. He said, "Now what do you think of this?" I told him that I wouldn't give a dime for the piece of junk. He said that he thought the same thing all along; that it was a cruddy looking thing but that it was one of the largest-selling items Picks had. He told me that he had been stung so many times from these wrong decisions that he couldn't possibly give me a bigger order until he could see what was really taking place.*
>
> *I came back home very dejected. I felt that I could deliver on the auto account but it wasn't enough to make a real going business. I was ready to sell the whole thing out to somebody who could do something with it and complete the auto account. I didn't want to go back into law; I didn't have much interest in it because of the picayunish things that go on in law which I can't stand. I moped about for a couple of days and finally I made up my mind to call Bart Pick on the phone direct. I told Bart Pick my problem and described the car to him and mentioned the story I had gotten from his buyer. Mr. Pick told me to come to see him in a couple of weeks. It turned out that all the presidents of all the Picks operations in the four major cities and the other stores of Picks were at the meeting plus all their chief buyers. I was told this was the first time in the history of the company that all the presidents were brought together on a toy-buying meeting. They looked at the models that I had brought with me and immediately placed an order for some 5,000 of these cars. I came home with a purchase order and started production.*
>
> *There is a buying service for most of the commodities in New York City that keeps track of sales of certain items, spot checkers and so on. This buying service reported that on opening day the sales of these car items were really a hot thing. Lo and behold, within weeks I had orders for millions of these cars. I couldn't deliver them, but we worked day and night and finally got them out. From that point on I was really in business.*[27]

[27]Norman R. Smith, The Entrepreneur and His Firm (East Lansing, MI: Bureau of Business and Economic Research, Michigan State University, 1967), p. 50.

The entrepreneur can anticipate that the buyer will ask such questions as: How does this product work? How much will it sell for in various order quantities? How will it be packaged and displayed? How soon can delivery be made? What assurance is there that the new company will be able to keep its delivery commitments? What will be the policy on products returned by customers? If servicing or parts are needed, how can they be obtained? What guarantees are provided, and how are they backed up? What testing has been done on the product? What other stores have handled it and what has been their experience? Is the product expected to be modified or changed in the near future? What variations in design, color, construction, and so forth, are possible?

Although it is easier to ask these questions than to answer them, they will have to be faced sooner or later. Talking with a buyer in advance can be a helpful way to determine what the key questions are likely to be. The buyer may have had a prior experience with similar products from others. For example, he or she may be able to tell what the most effective price target will be, what kind of packaging would be preferred by stores, what features to add or remove, and so forth. One buyer should not be taken as representative of all, however, either in terms of how to succeed or in terms of a rejection.

Chain Stores. Chain stores may be local, regional, or national. Smaller chains may have single buying offices that cover their whole range of merchandise. Large chains, such as Sears and Penneys, have buying offices in only one or a few major cities. Moreover, buyers within these buying offices specialize in only certain types of products. The buyer for a given type of product may or may not be in a local buying office, and travel may be needed to see the right buyer. Chains such as Sears also have brochures on how their buying systems operate.

■ *A California entrepreneur developed a bumper rack for carrying bicycles on the back of station wagons which could fold down to allow opening the tailgate. Through personal visits to chain store purchasing offices he was able to sell it to a major national store chain provided he could demonstrate the capability to produce it. This he did by locating several manufacturers willing to bid on the production work. He accepted the lowest bid, which came from a manufacturer in a city roughly 85 miles from his home.*

With orders in hand from the chain, he contracted with the manufacturer to produce and deliver the racks. When the scheduled delivery date passed without delivery, he called to ask the reason why and was told by the manufacturer that there were some production problems which should be solved shortly holding up the work. Further delays and similar excuses followed. Finally, he made a serious investigation of the problem and found that the manufacturer was producing the units at a high rate, as fast as he could. But he was selling them himself through other channels. He dropped that producer and contracted with another to fill the orders. Luckily, he was fast enough to keep the chain store account.

■ *A Northwest inventor, Terry Copstead, came up with the idea of putting helium in aerosol cans for use in filling toy balloons. Through a manufacturer's representative he arranged space to display his "Helium Park Pak" at the New York Toy Fair, alongside Whamo Industries' Hula Hoop. Whamo took an interest in his product and bought the rights. However, six months later they changed their mind because of scheduling prob-*

lems for release of the products and gave the rights back to the inventor. Meanwhile, the inventor had set up to make the product, so now he had to find sales channels for it. He used a total marketing budget of $200 to print and mail postcards describing the product and price schedule. From Dun and Bradstreet he obtained a list of major stores to whom he mailed the cards. The first and largest order he received came from J.C. Penney. Other national accounts, he said, more or less automatically followed: "All those sales for the price of a postcard."

Catalog and Specialty Retailers.   As we saw in Exhibit 7–3, there are other types of retail distribution companies, such as premium sellers (company calendars, prizes, buying inducements), post exchange stores of the military, and catalog sellers that make products available to their membership. Other channels for retail sales come along with credit card statements. Each of these channels has a buyer to be contacted directly if the company wants to use that channel for selling its product. Sometimes trade show display is a way to reach them, and at other times direct personal cold calling may be best.

Associations can be viewed as contact points for defined market segments. There are, according to Gale Research, over 30,000 associations in the United States, including over 5,000 professional and trade associations.[28] If it can arrange to sell through one of these, a venture can focus sharply on easy-to-contact customers, who consider their dealer, the association, instantly credible and about whom considerable information may be available. Adopting this channel quickly improved the sales fortunes of the following enterprise:

■ *Menlo Corporation of Santa Clara had raised $4.5 million in venture capital to develop and market a PC software package helpful for tapping into Dialog, a library of journals and research reports. Retailers were recruited, but few people bought the product. Those few turned out to be librarians, and when the company, with all but $500,000 of its capital gone, noticed this it modified the product to fit librarians better. It also mounted a campaign to sign up library associations to sell, offering them the usual 30 percent to 40 percent discount if they became retailers or alternatively, if they preferred to have Menlo handle inventory and billing, a 20 percent discount as agents.[29]*

Wholesalers and Jobbers.   Wholesalers come in all types and sizes (see Exhibit 7–3). Appropriate ones can be sought out by asking retailers how to handle the type of product the entrepreneur wishes to sell. Usually, however, wholesalers neither push to sell products nor take on new products for which retail outlets have not yet been established. The advantages of giving wholesalers a discount off the retail price are that when sales begin they will maintain a warehouse to stock an inventory of the product for retailers' convenience in ordering and they will take care of credit to retailers, so the producer does not have to worry about collecting.

A wholesaler may agree to take on a new product, but unfortunately that does not assure sales success, because sales can still bog down at a subsequent stage in the channel, as happened with the following start-up's product:

[28]Burek, *Encyclopedia of Associations*, p. 1.
[29]Sabin Russell, "Marketing by Association," *Venture* (November 1985), p. 131.

■ *In the late 1960s during a recession in the aerospace industry, an unemployed aerospace engineer decided to apply his engineering talents to the development of a better toy glider. He had always used scale models in his engineering research and application of the same principles to toys seemed a logical direction to move.*

He began by commissioning a $1,500 systematic study of the toy industry over the preceding fifteen years, analyzing the fraction devoted to flying toys and the ages and interests of children within that product area. He determined what appeared to be the appropriate price ranges and was encouraged to learn that the market for flying toys appeared to have been very stable. Less encouraging was the finding that the particular concept he had in mind, a very slow flying toy glider, did not seem especially tuned to any inclinations of children. If anything, they seemed to prefer toys that were fast, violent, and noisy. By now, however, he had done considerable design work on such a product, including theoretical analyses, laboratory simulations of the glider's aerodynamic features, and testing of prototypes, and he was gratified with the technical results. With a partner he invested in tooling, brochures, packaging design, and finally inventory to put his product on the market.

He then approached a small toy jobber. No sooner had he displayed his new product to this wholesaler than the man immediately gave him his first order, for two gross (24 dozen) gliders. Encouraged, he continued production and approached other wholesalers. Sales to these, however, came much harder, and all of them ceased when it turned out that the wholesalers themselves had trouble getting retailers to put the product on the shelves because the retailers found the customer interest in them was weak.

The company attempted to develop a variety of other flying toys, but these too failed to catch on. Eventually, four years after its inception, the company was shut down and its equipment and residual inventory sold at auction.

The most likely kind of distributor for a start-up may be a distributor that is itself a start-up, as illustrated by the following case:

■ *In February 1981 Barry Rava and Mike Fischer initiated a wholesale electronics firm with $30,000 from personal savings and a silent partner. Achieving breakeven was encumbered by the need to recruit lines, rent warehouse space, and invest in an initial inventory. In seeking products to carry, they found themselves only one of 1,800 electronics distributors, 2 percent of which essentially monopolized over 75 percent of all business booked. Their strategy was to avoid competition with majors by seeking lines that were less well-known and specialized to smaller markets. Finding economical warehouse space and persuading suppliers to advance them credit, they managed to get started, and in their first six months shipped $65,000 worth of products and landed orders for another $55,000 beyond that.[30]*

ENGAGING OTHERS TO SELL

Once founders have "primed the pump" on sales, the venture can consider developing a force of salespeople to expand volume. A manufacturing company may start with founders, progress to independent agents, and ultimately begin taking over the strongest territories with salaried sales employees. A mail order firm may

[30]Richard Bambrick, "How Distributor Start-Ups Compete," *Venture* (October 1981), p. 66.

simply hire order takers rather than salespeople and spend its marketing money on advertising. A retail store may add salesclerks.

Commissioned Agents

■ *The JUGS company of Tulatin, Oregon, got started by purchasing patent rights on a baseball pitching machine. Sales have been developed largely through engaging retired coaches as representatives.*[31]

The approach requiring the least commitment by the venture is the engagement of salespeople on straight commission. It may not be easy to find people willing to risk their income entirely on sales of the new company's product. But manufacturers' representatives who carry other lines may view the new company's offering as a complementary product and be willing to take it on, and particularly in distant regions where the company may not be able to afford to send its own people, they may be a good choice.

A good way to find commissioned agents is to look at advertisements by established firms with similar but complementary products and contact the representatives they use. Displaying the company's product at a trade show is another likely way to find agents interested in taking it on. For party plan selling systems, the best way to recruit may be simply to have a party and selectively sign up attendees. As is often the case with necessities, the best time to look for representatives is probably before the venture needs them.

The fact that representatives receive no commission unless they produce sales does not mean they are free, however, and the fact that they normally operate on thirty-day cancellable contracts does not mean that taking them on is risk-free. They may receive commissions that would have come to the company without their efforts and hence constitute an added cost. In addition, there are the costs of training, literature, samples, accompanying them on sales during early stages, following up leads they generate, and interacting with them, all of which add up. Because agents usually work at selling only those products that produce the most commissions with the least work, which tend to be products they have been selling before, the new company is usually at a considerable disadvantage in appealing for their efforts.

Sales Employees

More controllable than commissioned agents are salespeople the company hires on its payroll. There are countless books about how to hire, train, motivate, compensate, and manage them, usually in an established and ongoing rather than a start-up venture. Because they get paid whether or not they succeed in selling, it is especially important that careful attention be given to the use of salespeople. Selection of the most appropriate people requires care and effort. Estimates should

---

[31]"Ball Throwing Machines Make a Big Hit," *In Business* (June 1984), p. 12.

be made in advance about the number of calls each will make per day and per prospect, the frequency with which sales will likely close, the amount that will have to be spent on training, support materials, and travel, and the number of prospects that will be available for contact. Techniques for economizing, such as using telephones to check out leads in advance and the use of mail for follow-up to save time, should be considered. For a discussion of this subject in connection with new ventures, White's *The Entrepreneur's Manual* is an especially good source.[32]

Dealers

If the company's product is strong enough to justify outlets of its own, then it may make sense to establish dealers, who display its logo and stock its merchandise. The dealer then obtains a franchise, possibly for its willingness to sign up or as part of an exchange involving training and other help from the venture in return for a fee and/or commission. New ventures usually lack the market power or financial resources to create dealer networks initially.

Foreign Markets

Sales in foreign markets are rarely part of the initial start-up. At a later point, the company may find contacts abroad who want to order from it and possibly even representatives abroad who want to carry its line. Alternatively, the enterprise may seek out foreign sales channels through the use of a domestic export management company or through leads easily obtained from the U.S. government, which seeks to assist companies wanting to sell abroad. At the outset, however, such activities are not likely to be of major concern. The more immediate task is to get the company up and running with at least some domestic sales.

COMBINING SALES ELEMENTS

The different ways of initiating sales in a venture are not mutually exclusive and may work best in combinations. Making proposals and personal calls, advertising, attending trade shows, and seeking publicity for what the venture produces can all be done at the same time. Sometimes experimentation is needed to find the right channel. An example was Chopper Industries of Easton, Pennsylvania, which was started to produce and sell a patented ax design. "Initial efforts at selling the ax through direct mail were relatively unsuccessful," *Venture* reported, "but when the company began selling it through stores such as J.C. Penney, sales soared."[33]

At other times a channel that works well initially has to be changed later on. Thus *Inc.* reported that "Ron and Pep Simek of Tombstone Pizza found that the way to regain lost control of their product was to replace distributorships with their

[32]Richard M. White, Jr., *The Entrepreneur's Manual* (Radnor, PA: Chilton, 1977).
[33]Udayan Gupta, "The Special Problems of 'Adolescent' Firms," *Venture* (January 1981), p. 52.

own sales force."[34] A more dramatic example was the evolution of channels that produced ComputerLand:

■   *IMS, a company described earlier in connection with advertising, began with a product to help extend the capabilities of a limited purpose Wang computer for auto dealers. It was sold through direct personal presentations to groups of dealers. Unfortunately, it had technical problems.*

   Next, the company tried adapting an early microcomputer, and it wound up offering copies of the computer through advertising for mail orders.

   As the number of these orders grew, the company began getting calls from people who wanted to buy computers in quantity at discount for resale, and the company developed a network of dealers.

   It was also approached by John Martin, a man who had previously operated slot car tracks, sold cars, worked for an employment agency and then started his own employment agency. Martin expanded his agency to a chain of eleven outlets through franchising, only to see it then decline to five. The owner of a computer store called Martin to ask for help based on his experience in franchising. Martin, in turn, became interested in franchising computer stores and proposed that approach to IMS and was hired by IMS to develop a chain of franchised stores to sell its computers and those of other companies as well. IMS, as it turned out, failed. But the stores were set up under a separate corporation, which became ComputerLand with sales by 1988 of over $1.7 billion.[35]

Thus, sales for a new venture can come about in many possible ways and combinations of ways. Developing a greater awareness of the variety possible and practicing with elements of it should help an entrepreneur acquire greater virtuosity in creating a selling combination that will work best for his or her particular enterprise.

PLANNING QUESTIONS

The following questions are intended to stimulate thought about what should be considered in moving ahead with a venture. Which questions best apply can vary among entrepreneurs and ventures, as can the order in which they should be considered, the priority that should be placed on them, and which of them should be answered in a written plan.

Getting Customer Orders

- Who will place the first order, and what chain of events will bring it about?
- Where and how will the follow-up orders come from?
- Should repeat orders be expected? Why or why not?
- Can some specific customers and the amounts they can be expected to buy each month be listed?

---

[34]Sara Delano, "Rolling in Dough," *Inc.* (November 1982), p. 67.

[35]Johnathan Littman, *Once Upon a Time in ComputerLand* (Los Angeles: Price Sloan, 1987) (emphasis added).

- What will be the overall dimensions of the selling effort in terms of people and budgets?

Responding to Customers

- How is it made easy for customers to locate the company?
- How will prices, discounts, shipping charges, service support, and any "extras" compare to what competitors offer?
- Will any buy under contract, and if so, on what terms?

Advertising

- How much do competitors spend on advertising, and how will the venture's budget compare?
- What steps will be taken to obtain free advertising, such as newspaper articles?
- What will be done to assess the dollar effectiveness of advertising?

The Shop

- How important will walk-in traffic be?
- How easy will it be for customers to get to the venture's facilities? Will parking be adequate?
- What will prevent facilities and displays from looking amateurish?

Personal Selling

- How will each sale be "closed" and by whom?
- How much will the selling effort cost per contact and per sale?
- How will performance be monitored and managed to maximize productivity per expense dollar?
- What training of employees, distributors, dealers, and customers will be needed, and how will it be done?

Selling Through Channels

- What alternative channels were considered for distribution? Which were selected and why?
- What inducements will be offered to those channels, and how do they compare to what competitors offer?
- What priorities apply to the various selling inducements and promotional activities planned?
- How hard will it be for competitors to combat them?
- How much will the average sale cost be in worker-hours, dollars, and elapsed time?
- How might the channels used be expected to evolve over time?
- What will be the trade-offs involved in the changes and what will justify them?
- How broad will the venture's sales territory be and how will it be extended over time?

POSSIBLE MILESTONES FOR A PLANNING TIME LINE

The most suitable milestones for a time line for a particular venture must be a function of the individual case. These that follow are intended to help stimulate thought about them.

- Competitive features defined
- Competitive grid laid out
- Market interviews begun and ended
- Initial price established
- First order obtained
- First follow-up order obtained
- First sales target achieved
- Breakeven sales level achieved

Chapter 8

STARTING OPERATIONS

INTRODUCTION

The *operations* of a company can be viewed as a collection of human habits combined with physical resources. It involves setting up the resources, engaging employees and aligning them to their work, connecting with customers and suppliers to stimulate the needed flow of inputs and outputs, and learning the leadership role of the particular enterprise as it emerges. Arranging for an initial location, negotiating written and/or informal contracts, deciding what to make and what to buy, and getting the work of the business underway all need attention, often at once. Studying and thinking about this process in advance can help reduce the strain, chaos, and cost of this phase of the company's development.

The elements needed to start operations vary enormously among ventures. At the simple end of the spectrum are enterprises that can operate from the dining room table, basement, or garage. Newsletters, information services, small handicrafts, answering services, and small-scale investment counseling are examples. At the other extreme are start-ups that require expensive facilities and large amounts of initial capital.

There are numerous pitfalls to avoid in setting up operations, including

- Running out of time or resources
- Making inappropriate facilities commitments
- Accepting uneconomical or otherwise ineffective deals with suppliers
- Employing incompetent people

- Mismanaging production so as to waste money and/or produce inadequate quality for customers
- Falling behind competitors on product or service improvement

This chapter concentrates on ways to avoid such problems, which are associated mainly with production. The next chapter considers ways to avoid still other problems associated with the paperwork aspects of setting up a business.

The Entrepreneur's Action Decisions

Start-up activities usually begin as a trickle that expands into a torrent. Trade-offs must be struck between such things as saving time at the expense of money, saving immediate cash versus paying more long run, and taking actions in advance to avoid a crush later versus waiting until it is clearer just how they should be done. Choices are constantly being made, often on the run as developments unfold and reveal needs for new actions and further choices. Here are some of the actions involved in starting Apple Computer:

■ *Steve Jobs personally approached the Byte Shop in Mountain View and to his amazement received an order for nearly $25,000 to buy fifty computers. When the first bank he approached for working capital turned him down he figured other banks would as well and instead offered to swap shares in the company for parts at a former employer, and received another rejection. Other parts distributors also turned him down, but he kept trying and finally one agreed to sell him $20,000 worth of parts, enough for 100 computers, on thirty days credit.*

With no money Jobs and Wozniak could not rent space and so began assembly on Wozniak's dining room table. When Wozniak's wife objected to this, they moved to a spare bedroom in the house of Jobs's parents, and then to their garage, where his father put up plasterboard, installed lights and a phone line, and built for the two a "burn in" box to test circuit boards under heat lights.

Jobs's sister, Patty, was hired at a dollar per board to do assembly work. (Watching TV at the same time, she sometimes put components in backwards.) Jobs also rented a post office box and hired an answering service to give the venture a businesslike front. A former college friend was hired to come in once a week and keep the books. Jobs's mother still did laundry in the "plant," took phone messages from the answering service and served coffee to visiting salespeople.

Eventually, the company could not continue to develop in this bootstrap manner and Jobs was able to bring in an investor, Mike Markkula. These two and Wozniak developed a business plan, hired an experienced manager, and Apple grew into a more conventional form.[1]

The first resources upon which a company draws are the time and energy of the founder or founding team, and it is easy to overlook in planning that this element is limited, even when evenings, weekends, and the extra effort an individual can put forth when inspired under the excitement and pressure of start-up are considered. Choices must be made about what to work on: selling, plant opera-

---

[1]Lee Butcher, *Accidental Millionaire* (New York: Paragon House, 1989).

tions, further refinement of the product or service, lining up financing, or attending to employee recruiting or government regulations. Meetings are needed with suppliers, bankers, attorneys, accountants, and other advisers. If there are other partners, then time and attention must be applied to coordinating with them, but this should be balanced by the partners' own contributions to the start-up work.

Books and articles on time management for entrepreneurs suggest activities such as setting personal goals, preparing time budgets, and analyzing how time is spent and how it could better be spent.[2] But there has been little systematic study of how entrepreneurs actually do spend their time and none on how they do it during start-up in particular. A survey of *Venture* readers found that over half worked more than fifty-five hours per week, but it was not specified how much of that time was spent on starting companies.[3]

Entrepreneurs spend time finding out how things are different than they expected and then figure out how to adapt to the difference. There is often a need for adaptation to new discoveries, unexpected problems, and new opportunities that develop down "side streets" as the venture moves forward. A danger amid this swirl is that the entrepreneur may try to do too much personally, rather than delegate tasks to partners or others, and as a result may end up handling tasks badly or not at all.

Setting priorities can be one way of managing time. In the following company, strategy centered around production—doing a better job of putting out the work correctly, on time, and at a competitive price:

■ *Two men working in the plating shop of a Seattle manufacturing company learned that another large nearby manufacturer which, unlike their employer, bought its plating work from outside suppliers rather than doing the work itself, had become dissatisfied with service from those suppliers. One of the two approached the manufacturer and asked whether he could get the plating work if he formed a new company to perform it. Although no promise was forthcoming, he gathered the answer would be affirmative if he did a good job.*

On faith that it would work out, the two men mortgaged their houses and each raised $15,000 to start a new plating shop. For three months they worked on lists of equipment the shop would require, gauging sizes and capacities to be sure they would handle the pieces and volume expected from their first account and beyond that allow them to accommodate other customers as well. For some items they would have to pay cash, including the boiler, tanks, installation, and modification of a building. That would use up $22,000 of their seed capital.

Other equipment could be bought on time, and to arrange that one of the men flew to San Francisco where he checked over the used equipment market and arranged terms with one of the dealers. He bought $20,000 worth of equipment with no down payment and installments scheduled to begin only after the shop commenced operation. To arrange those terms he had to show suppliers a plan for starting operations, including a timetable describing in detail how the shop could be set up and ready to start producing plating work within two months upon receipt of the equipment.

[2]"Save Hours and Dollars Through Time Management," *In Business* (November-December 1982), p. 57.
[3]Echo M. Garrett, "Time Is Money, So How Do You Spend It?," *Venture* (August 1988), p. 8.

Meanwhile, the other partner was scouting for possible sites. Seattle was found to be an undesirable site because of its tax structure and restrictions, including a requirement that the company employ a boiler engineer to fire the boilers, something which could be done by automatic machinery. An old vegetable shed was found outside the city and lease terms were negotiated for five years, long enough to justify installation and remodeling work needed to set up the facilities. The lease also included an option to buy, so that if the company succeeded it might never have to move.

By building their own tanks and installing much of the other equipment themselves, the two men saved money and were able to keep the setup work on schedule. Often this meant putting in very long days, but two months later the shop was ready to run. A brief checkout period followed, during which they ran time studies to make sure that prices could be set in the narrow range needed for survival, high enough to assure some profit, but not above the competition.

Returning to their prospective customer, the large manufacturer, they now were able to obtain a small order to start. When that work proved satisfactory larger orders quickly followed, and behind those orders from other customers as well. Within thirty days of startup the company was in the black, where it remained.

These two men concentrated their time on setting up production, the central purpose of the business. The majority of the financial resources were also applied to this goal, going for plant and equipment to make production possible. Alternatively, they could have applied more effort to seeking out other prospective customers, looking for cheaper or more capital, or trying out other strategies such as becoming middlemen in the plating business rather than producers. But they chose production, concentrated their resources on that, and succeeded.

Had production not been the central activity, an entirely different arrangement of priorities for their startup time and other resources could have been appropriate, as in the following case, where development and sale of a new proprietary product were the main objectives:

■ *In August 1976 a Seattle hardware store manager took note of the fact that several customers had made requests for a product he did not have. They wanted to be able to put out bait for garden slugs without danger that their pets could eat it. He took this problem to a nursery store manager, who said he had received such requests for years but had never done more than inform customers there was no product available to solve the problem. As the two began discussing potential solutions, the nursery manager suggesting ideas and the hardware manager sketching them out, it occurred to them that they might, by starting a company to produce slug-traps, be able to augment their modest salaries.*

Several approaches to the problem were considered but rejected. A throw-away design with built-in bait would have the advantage of not having to be cleaned of dead slugs for re-use. Premeasured packets of bait would have a much larger volume market than simply adding existing forms of bait to an empty trap. But competition for the bait market itself was fierce, and entering it would not only be hard but might pose substantial product liability insurance expenses as well. The design began to settle into the form of a cup based upon a spike which could be driven into the ground and covered with a lid which would permit slugs but not pets and birds to enter and eat the bait.

As the design concept became firmer, they considered how to protect it and contacted a patent lawyer. A patent search costing $70 turned up several slug trap patents dating from 1898 to 1967, but it appeared none had been actively used in nearly a decade. Efforts on new patent claims were begun. Deciding on a first run of 5,000 units, the *partners committed $2,500 to make a plastic injection mold. Contacting several molding companies they obtained production bids, then accepted the lowest they found, which was $30 for setup plus 51 cents per unit. After searching for suitable packages, they found a bargain in boxes made for another product which had not sold well, and they had labels printed for 17 cents each.*

Visiting the managers of other stores in the chain for which they worked, the partners now lined up initial orders for 1,000 units. Evenings and weekends they assembled, boxed, and made deliveries. To their great disappointment, the boxes which they were able to place on the store shelves simply sat there. Store customers weren't buying.

Then an unanticipated break occurred. The local TV host of a program on horticulture visited the nursery managed by one of the partners. Seizing the chance to show and explain his new trap, the partner persuaded his visitor to display it on his show as the "new product of the week." In the week that followed this show, all 1,000 units sold out.

Borrowing on their homes, the partners now ordered production of another 4,000 units and more boxes and labels. Now it seemed appropriate to line up distribution channels, so they contacted the wholesaler who serviced their employer, and he agreed to stock carry the product. Another mention on the TV show, and soon there were more orders. An accountant was hired to set up books and the two men began to plan for the next season, including professional advertising, new tooling, bank financing, and a development strategy to broaden their line which was now showing a profit. A buyout offer came from a large firm. The partners turned it down.

Another tactic helpful in arranging priorities and planning the flow of events is the preparation of a time line with dates or a Gantt chart of events showing start and completion dates for various tasks. A flow or "Pert" chart may be used for working out still more details. In the example appearing in Figure 8–1, the Pert chart shows both the flow diagram of parallel events in the start-up and the start and completion dates (above and below each task).

PREMISES

Exhibit 8–1 lists some variables concerning location that may be important, depending upon the nature of the particular start-up. Information on these dimensions can be systematically gathered but must be qualified according to a time frame. Usually it will be based upon the past, but for the start-up it will be both the present and future that are relevant. For instance, starting a new high technology company where other similar companies are locating may not matter to the start-up immediately, but as the company and surrounding industry grow they may generate a labor pool and ancillary industries that later help them all.

Decisions about which location variables matter most and in what ways can depend on many aspects of the particular venture, such as the type of product or service it will produce, who its prospective customers are and how they will buy, what the venture will make versus buy, as well as what space is available; how much it will cost in rent, construction and taxes; and what the founders consider most personally practical and appealing. Exhibit 8–2 shows how the type of business affects location choices.

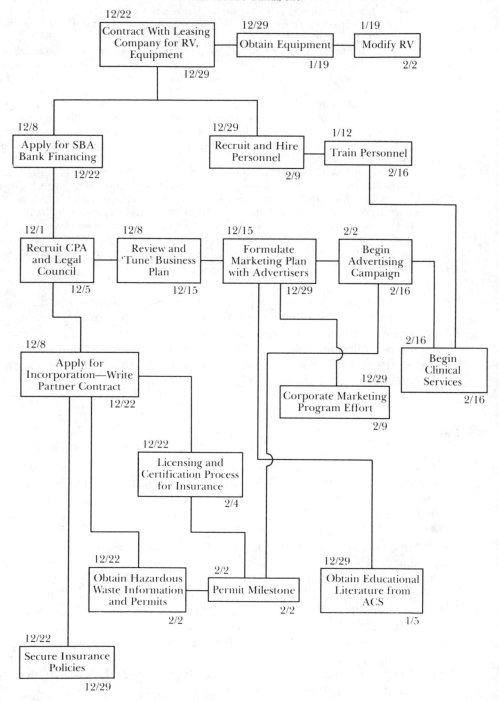

FIGURE 8–1   Pert Chart for a Start-Up

EXHIBIT 8-1   Location Variables

- Proximity to (number of) customers' homes or businesses
- Density of foot traffic
- Type of other businesses nearby
- Nearby labor force (salary levels, skills, education levels, work ethic) or people with special expertise
- Labor costs and union impacts
- Living costs
- Available facilities for the company to occupy
- Proximity to suppliers, labs, universities
- Capital available in the area
- Capability of the area to attract desired people (quality of life)
- Commercial and housing rental rates and/or purchase prices
- Convenience for employees
- Local taxes, fees, and restrictions, versus assistance available
- Housing costs
- State personal and business taxes
- Alternatives available for expansion
- Presence of relevant infrastructure (airport hub versus feeder, suppliers, equipment, shipping connections, university resources and quality, TV downlink (receiving system that passes the signal along to TV monitors), and appropriately experienced professionals)
- Availability of state and local governmental assistance[4]
- Security from crime[5]

EXHIBIT 8-2   Type of Business and Preferred Location Characteristics

---

1. *Retailing*—Convenience to customers is crucial. Good parking may trade off against heavy foot traffic and high visibility to the desired customers.
2. *Service*—Food and personal service businesses have similar requirements to retailing. For some other types, such as plumbing, construction, glass repair, or tree spraying, the location may be anywhere in town, although access for truck deliveries may be necessary.
3. *Proprietary Manufacturing*—If selling to local markets, then locate in same city as customers. If selling more widely, then freight costs in and out, availability of appropriate labor skills, and wage rates are vital considerations.
4. *Custom Manufacturing*—This has the same needs as proprietary manufacturing, except that closeness to potential customers should be emphasized even more.
5. *Wholesaling*—Locate in the town where a majority of the company's sales are made, but any part of town will do.

---

[4]"1986 Plant Directory," *Venture* (October 1986), p. 86; also "Directory of Incentives for Business Investment" (Washington, DC: Urban Institute Press, 1986).

[5]Mary Ann Stangil, "Seven Steps to Security," *In Business* (March-April 1982), p. 40.

Retail and Service Locations

Retail and service firms are, of course, needed in all areas, and the location issue eventually comes down to which sections of town and which street. Within a given city, some types of locations to consider for retail or service firms, together with their pros and cons, include the following:

- *Major streets* — Advantages are heavy auto traffic, high visibility, and ease of finding. Disadvantages may be high rent, poor parking, safety concerns, and distance from customers' homes or jobs.
- *Side streets* — Advantage is lower rent. Disadvantages are the same for major streets.
- *Downtown* — Advantages are similar to those for major streets, especially proximity to office workers and foot traffic. Disadvantages are similar to those for major streets.
- *Shopping centers* — Advantages are good parking, well-identified clientele, and predictable traffic. Disadvantages may be high rent, fees, and restrictions.
- *Industrial districts* — Advantages may be low restrictions, ample space, and well-identified clientele. A disadvantage may be limited density of traffic and particularly of shoppers.

Getting the right combination can be easy for some types of businesses, such as real estate agencies, or other paperwork-only enterprises. The problem of where to locate lends itself well to systematic analysis, as was done by the following entrepreneurs:

■ *The partners of Wordplay, a new West Hollywood word-processing business, first listed the general types of customers they wanted, then worked from addresses in the phone book to mark their locations on a map, using red for lawyers, green for insurance companies, and blue for film studios. After studying the resultant patterns, they drove through areas with highest dot densities to find potential sites and chose the most promising.*[6]

A particularly critical parameter for retail and service firms in picking location is the ratio of rent to expected sales. Information about typical ratios by line of business is available through several publications.[7] Demographic information for communities is usually available from the chamber of commerce, economic development office, and metropolitan newspaper advertising departments.

Two techniques that may help in selecting a site are first to look at many possible locations, both by riding around seeking empty buildings and by checking advertisements and talking with real estate agents. Second, develop a checklist of what items are important to the business and extend that list as the examination of possible sites generates additional ideas. Sufficient parking space for both employees and customers; presence of appropriate traffic; visibility; accessibility for

---

[6]Gregory and Patricia Kishel, "Choosing a Business Location," *In Business* (January-February 1983), p. 30.

[7]Three such sources are *Annual Statement Studies,* Robert Morris Associates, Philadelphia National Bank Building, Philadelphia, PA 19107; *Key Business Ratios,* 99 Church Street, New York, NY 10007; and *Expenses in Retail Business,* National Cash Register, Dayton, OH 45409.

goods to be moved in and out; permission to make needed alterations and put up a suitable sign; presence of needed hot water, heating, air-conditioning, other ventilation and electrical outlets; burglary protection; compliance with fire and health codes; and the capability to operate without producing unacceptable air pollution, other waste, or stains should all be checked, as well as simple things such as who is responsible for fixing doors, windows, and any roof leaks.

Elegance

How fancy the facilities for the start-up need to be also depends on the nature of the business. People shopping for a luxury car or fine furniture might be less likely to buy in a shabby showroom. A customer for precision finishing of expensive parts should care about the cleanliness of a shop bidding for the work and about the quality and condition of the machines that do the work. Someone hiring a high-priced law or accounting firm might be put off by cheap furniture in the waiting room or worn carpet in the offices. There are times that expensive facilities make sense.

Even if a good front is not necessary to impress customers, it may be important to employees. Professionals with substantial investment in education, such as engineers and scientists, may be incensed by surroundings that they consider incommensurate with their investment in money and time for career preparation.

When there is no clear business need for a higher-priced location, the cheapest facilities may be best. Many successful entrepreneurs refer back with sentimental pride to the adventure of starting in accommodations that were ramshackle, unheated, cramped, drafty, dark, and lacking in amenities. Conversely, there have been many unsuccessful firms that began in first-class facilities leased or even built with the hollow hope that architectural form would give a substance of prosperity, when in fact all it provided was cash drain causing the business to sink.

Manufacturing Space

Reflecting on what sort of space to obtain for a manufacturing start-up, Robert Morrison, who built the company that made plastic car bodies for Studebaker's Avanti and Chevrolet's Corvette observed that, "Probably the best advice I can give the new entrepreneur is, do not get stuck with an inadequate and inefficient building, but do not take on the costs of the building you will eventually need until you have an established profitable operation."[8] He offered detailed lists of desired features for plants and buildings, including such things as access, drainage, neighbors, restrooms, electrical requirements, expansion possibilities, and lease or purchase terms.

---

[8]Robert S. Morrison, *Handbook for Manufacturing Entrepreneurs* (Cleveland: Western Reserve Press, 1973), p. 88.

For some start-ups, the way to economize on location is to begin at home. In 1984, *In Business* reported that there were 10 million home-based businesses in the United States. A letter to the editor of the same magazine described the adventure of starting operations at home, then moving on to commercial quarters. Cheryl McBride created a venture making dolls. She recalled:

■ *Predictably, production of hand-poured, -sanded, and -painted pieces took far longer than I pre-judged, and soon I was under the table in a sea of orders. Also, many of the larger stores were slow to pay accounts, yet wanted to reorder. Dolls gradually crept into the house from the garage-converted studio ("ours is the only house where ornaments have price tags"). Visiting our home for a choice of dolls, buyers would grab one of our personal collection and try to purchase it.*

Exasperated by the chaos, my husband—John McBride—took a six-month leave of absence from his restaurant manager's position to manage me. First he dragged me out from under the table, and nagged unmercifully until I caught up with the orders. Next he arranged net/30 terms from all the doll supply companies that I had been purchasing from on a COD basis. He followed this with a tougher stance on the long overdue accounts.

Within four months, "Dollsville Dolls" was running smoothly. John took over all the heavy work, learning to pour the liquid porcelain into the plaster of Paris molds that are taken directly from the antique dolls. He also taught himself to assemble the dolls, with sufficient speed to get a "production" underway. Accompanying me to dollshows, throughout California, he gradually became absorbed by the doll business that he had up to now been extremely disinterested in. However, confined in the "garage" with little interaction with our clients was not fulfilling enough for the gregarious, ambitious Englishman, and when a tiny store became vacant ("overnight" as the best stores are rented thus in Palm Springs) John and I chewed nails for the 24 hours allotted to us by the landlord, in which to make up our minds . . . and signed a two-year lease.

The store, which was just on the outskirts of the "exclusive" walking area of Palm Canyon drive, was graced with a delightful 20′-window, and a 30′ depth (the landlord called it a 700 square-footer!) and at the almost unheard-of-on Palm Canyon drive—rent of $550 per month, including "water and trash," we McBrides felt it was well worth the exercise, if only to get the looky-loos out of our home. (The English are noted for being very particular about their privacy!) As a bonus, the previous tenants had completely pegboarded the entire store, with an extra pegboard partition running the entire width of the store, floor to ceiling—and it had carpet. Checking the local paper, John found a store-fixture sale, and purchased an eight-foot run of white cubing, originally used in a knitted wool display, for $50, two 6′ glass-fronted jewelry display cases for the same cost, and two glass-shelved gondolas for $75 each. We were in business![10]

An example described earlier showed how the builders of the first Tucker automobile used Mrs. Tucker's kitchen and stove to heat and assemble cylinder liners.[11] All that mattered was that the liners work properly, not the environment of their production. The variety of humble accommodations used by some familiar start-ups is shown in the following list.

[9]"Home-based Businesses at an All-Time High," *In Business* (February 1984), p. 4.
[10]"When It's Time to Leave Home," *In Business* (June 1984), p. 18.
[11]Charles T. Pearson, *The Indomitable Tin Goose* (New York: Pocket Books, 1960), p. 134.

First Locations of Some Well-Known Start-Ups

> *Abandoned mill* — Custom Silicon, Solar Vision[12]
> *Apartment spare bedroom* — ASK Computer
> *Basement apartment to room over garage, to milk shed* — Polaroid[13]
> *Bread factory* — Ventrex Laboratories[14]
> *Dry goods store* — L.L. Bean[15]
> *Employer's office to storefront* — Johnson Publishing[16]
> *Garage* — Everest & Jennings, Frederick Seal, Hewlett-Packard, Nike, Televideo, Medtronic, Printronix, Donzis Research[17]
> *Kitchen* — Burgmaster Turret Drills[18]
> *Kitchen table* — New England Farm Bulletin[19]
> *Old woolen mill* — Digital Equipment Corporation[20]
> *Prune-drying shed* — Rolm[21]
> *Synagogue* — Data-Ease[22]

The physical layout of an office and shop is an important consideration during the selection of a building. A rough rule of thumb is that the space per employee should probably be around 100 square feet. Wiring, ventilation, lighting, utilities, burglar and fire alarms, partitioning, special equipment such as loading docks or overhead cranes, interior decoration, and possibly outside decoration and landscaping are all aspects that may need attention, possibly with the help of experts. Longer-term as well as immediate needs must be estimated in planning.[23] It may make sense to lease more space than presently needed and temporarily sublease part of it.[24]

In some areas and for some types of businesses, an incubator may be a suitable first location. John Kennedy, president of a start-up in Northwestern University's incubator, said:

> ■ *Incubators provide the environment, both physical and psychological, for early-growth companies to survive past the initial stages of start-up. The affiliation of this incubator with Northwestern University is especially important to us, because we have access to some of the best marketing and management expertise in the country. And, be-*

---

[12]Bill Logan, "First Places That Work," *Venture* (December 1984), p. 92.

[13]Peter Wensberg, *Land's Polaroid* (Boston: Houghton Mifflin, 1987), p. 26.

[14]Logan, "First Places That Work," p. 92.

[15]M. R. Montgomery, *In Search of L. L. Bean* (New York: New American Library, 1985), p. 19.

[16]John H. Johnson, *Succeeding Against the Odds* (New York: Warner Books, 1989), p. 134.

[17]Leslie Schultz, "A Good Garage Is Hard to Find," *Inc.* (April 1983), p. 91.

[18]Max Holland, *When the Machine Stopped* (Boston: Harvard Business School Press, 1989), p. 11.

[19]Nancy Frazier, "Thriving at Home," *In Business* (March-April 1982), p. 37.

[20]George Rifkin and George Harrar, *The Ultimate Entrepreneur* (Chicago: Contemporary Books, 1988), p. 26.

[21]Schultz, "A Good Garage Is Hard to Find," p. 91.

[22]Logan, "First Places That Work," p. 92.

[23]Marita Thomas, "Facilities Planning," *Inc.* (September 1984), p. 111.

[24]Cathy Hedgecock, "Office Space, Planning Ahead," *Venture* (March 1984), p. 42.

cause the fee for space is far below average, we're able to put our money where it'll do the most good—into the development of the company and new products.[25]

Geography

Metropolitan areas are best for most start-ups. There are larger populations for products and services. The ancillary industries, transportation, and other infrastructures are more complete for manufacturing ventures.

Rural areas have serious disadvantages for high technology start-ups, such as the unavailability of supplier representatives, fewer airline flights, lack of bankers experienced with growing businesses, few other entrepreneurs with whom to exchange experiences, limited understanding of industry by local townspeople, unavailability of specialists, and limited labor pools.

Nevertheless, some entrepreneurs start there, usually for reasons of personal preference.[26] Some software firms have prospered in nonmetropolitan areas and so have some manufacturing enterprises, as illustrated by the following enterprise of Colleen King:

■ *In the sun-cooked California desert town of Victorville, she and other housewives began "stuffing" printed circuit boards on a piece rate basis for electronics manufacturers. At less than a penny per component in 1979, the work wasn't very profitable, but she was interested in anything she could do at home in addition to keeping the books for her husband's two shoestores that would be more profitable than the needlepoint she had been doing.*

The work was simple, just bend back the wires on each component, poke them through the right holes on the board, solder them in place and clip off the extra lengths of wire end. But she found that in addition she was able to distinguish her work by finishing it both more neatly than others did and more precisely on time. Consequently, her orders grew and soon moved from the kitchen to the living room where by 1981 a dozen other women and her husband joined her in the work.

She dropped price as far as 40 percent below competitors, orders grew, and more space was needed. She rented 600 square feet of commercial space in late 1982, then 4,400 in 1983 and 10,000 in 1984 as the number of employees grew to 75. In 1985 the company, now incorporated as King High Tech, occupied 85,000 square feet and had additional offices in Salt Lake City and on the San Francisco peninsula, where it had become a zero defects award winning supplier for Apple Computer. By the end of 1985 there was another factory in Provo, Utah, and employment was ranging around 500 people serving over 150 customers as a subcontract assembly company still shipping all orders within 24 to 48 hours.[27]

Choosing an overseas location during start-up is relatively rare for U.S. ventures, but sometimes happens.

---

[25]Barbara Quinn, "Plant Site Directory 1987," *Venture* (October 1987), p. 89.
[26]William Mueller, "Beyond Blue Highways," *Venture* (August 1988), p. 40.
[27]Ellen Hoffs, "King of the Desert," *California Business* (December 1985), p. 37.

■ *In 1974 Amin Khoury and John Martin started production of plastic containers to contain blood and other medical fluids in El Salvador. Appealing features of the country included a new international airport, new major hotel and new telephone system. Workers, Khoury said, were "conscientious, loyal and easily trainable," and even when revolution followed there was hardly any disruption of production in their new company, Delmed.*[28]

Advice about setting up such an operation can be obtained from consultants, trade offices of foreign countries, and particularly other entrepreneurs with similar types of businesses or who have sourced from the particular countries being considered. Even big companies may be able to offer guidance. In the example just mentioned, the entrepreneurs patterned their overseas arrangement in El Salvador after what a larger company, Baxter Travenol, had done in another country, Puerto Rico.

Real Estate Deals

At the early stages of start-up, there will probably be a priority on flexibility, because of the uncertainty about just how fast and how far the venture will go. This priority will favor leasing or renting on a short-term basis. If and when it becomes clear that real estate needs can be foreseen on a longer-term basis, there will be questions about whether it is better to buy or to lease and from whom. Both purchasing and leasing can be legally tricky.

One author has suggested the following ten rules for purchasing:

1. Include all details in the first paper you sign. Do not assume it will be a preliminary agreement.
2. Watch out for the "standard contract" ploy. There is no such thing. Have a lawyer examine it, then modify it as appropriate.
3. Consider alternatives, such as an option or lease with option to buy, to outright purchase.
4. Have the legal owner, not a stand-in, sign the document in person. Have a lawyer check if this is not done.
5. Be sure the document contains a full legal description, not just an address.
6. List all fixtures, such as counters, air-conditioning, and shelves, that are to be included.
7. Stipulate prompt delivery of premises and penalties due for delinquency.
8. Look into possible restrictions, ordinances, codes, rights of way, and so on and have an escape clause in case any may interfere with operation of the business.
9. Include contingency cancellation rights if any vital conditions, such as financing, do not come through.
10. Get warranties in writing for any promises the seller makes.[29]

Leasing, rather than buying, calls for similar precautions, plus some others. If the space is offered as a sublease, for instance, and the landlord defaults, the

---

[28]Thomas Gibson, "When Overseas Plants Make More Sense," *Venture* (August 1982), p. 82.
[29]Fred Steingold, "Ten Rules for Buying Real Estate," *Inc.* (August 1981), p. 87.

sublease tenants may be evicted. Also, there can be hidden fees for such things as cleaning.[30] Rent may not be very negotiable, but length and renewability may be more important anyway. To gain concessions from the landlord, a tenant can offer to fix up the space and install fixtures for free that the landlord will eventually own. The tenant can also offer to include an escalator clause tied to operating costs that can make the landlord more secure. That is probably better than tying rent to performance of the business.

Unfamiliar terms such as *loss factor* (difference between rentable and useable space) and *workletter* (value of standard accoutrements in the property) may catch a new renter unawares. It can help in these negotiations for the tenant to work through an agent whom he or she has selected and who will consequently serve as an advocate. Additional guidelines can easily be found in publications discussing leases.[31]

It is also possible to combine buying and leasing by setting up a separate corporation to own the plant and equipment and having one or more of the founders own and lease them to the start-up. Whether to do so turns on a variety of facts concerning liquidity, tax, interest, and depreciation rates, plus many other concerns.[32] Making sure the deal is sensible for both the company and the investors, even though the investors may own both, can be a challenge.[33] Expert help can readily be found among commercial real estate agents, space and facilities planning consultants, architects, and interior designers.

EQUIPMENT

To the extent that the venture chooses to make rather than buy what it sells, it will likely need equipment. Finding, acquiring, and setting it up are all tasks that can be done economically and effectively. It may be worth the price to obtain experienced help on some aspects.

Economizing Cash

There are five ways to obtain equipment: buy new, lease, buy used, borrow, or fabricate. The last choice for many ventures, because of its high cost, is to buy new equipment, whether through purchase, lease, or purchase and lease back. However, both buying used or creating homemade equipment take specialized knowhow, which the entrepreneur may or may not possess. It may be acquired through taking on partners or hiring specialists. It is most important that the equipment work well competitively. The second most important concern is that it be as economical as possible.

---

[30]Michelle Bekey, "Sharing Office Space," *Venture* (September 1983), p. 35.
[31]Kishel, "Choosing a Business Location," p. 31.
[32]Marita Thomas, "Facilities Planning," *Inc.* (September 1984), p. 111.
[33]Thomas E. Selck, "Should You Be Your Own Landlord?," *Inc.* (March 1980), p. 56.

Sharing

The new company may also be able to utilize the equipment of another company on a time-sharing, capacity-sharing, or space-sharing basis, as illustrated by the following examples:

- *When Leslie Williams, a West Los Angeles entrepreneur, needed to use a large drill press for some work, he asked around and learned that the father of one of his son's friends happened to have a large antique drill press in his garage. Although it dated from World War I and lacked a motor, he borrowed the machine, set it up and did the necessary work. Several weeks later, the job finished, he returned the press, including the motor he had installed as a return of the favor.*

- *Al Adler, a Seattle entrepreneur, wanted to enter the rotational plastic molding business when he learned that there was a shortage of capability for molding difficult-to-process polycarbonate plastics by that method in his area. What he needed was a molding machine. New ones were expensive and had long delivery lead times. But through a raw material supplier of plastics he learned of a machine possessed by a local company which wanted to sell it. It turned out the company only used the machine once per year for a limited run of one product made from polyethylene and had no interest in entering polycarbonate molding. Adler negotiated an arrangement whereby he would buy the machine on contract and leave it where it was, renting the immediate area of the plant where it sat. He also arranged to perform the once-per-year polyethylene molding work on contract, so the former machine owner became his first customer.*

- *Rather than rent a whole office and shop in its start-up period, the Traffic and Safety Control Corporation of Seattle shared with a construction firm. As a further economy, both firms shared the services of a single receptionist, secretary, bookkeeper who also helped out with shipping, billing, and collecting.*

- *John H. Johnson (see Chapter 7) obtained the first sales for his publishing company through sending a subscription letter using the addressing machine of his employer to potential customers. He further recalled how he obtained premises and equipment to produce his product,* Negro Digest, *as follows:*

  "Before sending this letter, I took the precaution of securing my first office and mailing address. One of my supervisors, Earl Dickerson, had a private law office and a law library in a private section of the Supreme building. I asked if I could use a corner of the law library, which contained old books and was seldom used. He said okay, and I moved a desk into the corner of the office, which was on the second floor of the Supreme building but had another entrance and another address, 3507 South Parkway.

  "This was the first address of what was then called Negro Digest Publishing Company. From June to November, I worked downstairs in the insurance company in the day and climbed the stairs at night to work on the magazine. One day in the summer of 1942 a man came and painted letters on the frosty glass door—Negro Digest Publishing Company—and every letter was music to my soul.

  "It was from this office that I sent letters to twenty thousand persons asking for prepublication subscriptions. Three thousand persons—an unusually high percentage—responded, sending $6,000.

  "While all this was going on, I drafted and sent out letters asking for the right to publish certain stories and articles that had appeared in Black newspapers and White magazines and periodicals. My wife, who was a social worker by day, helped at night. So did Jay Jackson, a brilliant artist and cartoonist who worked for the Chicago Defender,

and Ben Burns, a White free-lance writer I'd met when we both worked on the Earl Dickerson campaign.

"By October, there was only one remaining hurdle: finding a printing press and persuading the owner of the press to extend credit until the magazines were printed and sold. Here, once again, Supreme came to the rescue. One of my duties at Supreme was running the multilith machine and dealing with Progress Printing Company, which printed material for the insurance company. When I went to the printer's office and told him that 'we' were thinking about publishing a magazine, he assumed that I was talking about the insurance company when I was really talking about myself. Since he assumed that the magazine was either owned or backed by the insurance company, he started working without worrying about how I was going to pay him.[34]

Capital-conserving arrangements such as these usually require a certain amount of creative scheming plus personal contacts to be able to ferret out the opportunities. Both of these advantages can be cultivated through becoming aware of potential needs in advance and deliberately being on the alert to notice unused assets, develop acquaintances who will also notice them, and think of ways to bring these assets into play so as to benefit both parties.

Home-Built Facilities

Making do with what happens to be available is a widespread tradition among entrepreneurs. When needed equipment is not available, or is expensive, there may be an option of building what is needed out of purchased parts or even out of junk. Bill Kirchner can recall how the K-2 Corporation began and became the nation's largest ski producer with presses he made himself.

The decision to work up home-built facilities is not always clear or easy. Ready-made equipment may be available, and presumably the "bugs" have been worked out of it by prior users. Turn-key facilities (already completely set up) that are ready to run are sometimes available, as are suppliers who design and construct new special-purpose production machinery.

Used Equipment

Many successful entrepreneurs can tell one or more stories about how they acquired used equipment at a fraction of its original cost and found it as effective as new. Auctions are a common source of such acquisitions, and they are announced in the classified section of any city newspaper. It can be both instructive and energizing to attend a few company liquidation auctions to see how such selling is done and what kinds of deals can be made (as well as to see how unsuccessful companies can end up). Auctions can also be tricky places to buy; some advance study may help prevent mistakes. Other sources of used equipment include equipment dealers, classified advertisements, and acquaintances in business who know what equipment is around and available.

[34]John H. Johnson with Lerone Bennett, Jr., *Succeeding Against All Odds* (New York: Warner Books, 1989), p. 119.

Expert Help.   Other people may be able to help in obtaining equipment at bargain prices, as Debbi Fields discovered in setting up her first cookie shop:

■ *After searching, she had found a location in the Stanford Barn. But it did not "feel totally right." When a friend called her about an old market being converted to an arcade in Palo Alto she felt differently and took it.*

She needed a commercial baking oven next, but was completely unfamiliar with such equipment. She tried "used equipment" sections of classified ads, restaurant supply houses, whose prices were too high, and bankruptcy auctions, where she felt at a serious disadvantage relative to other buyers who seemed more expert. Searching through a used-equipment warehouse she encountered a man who apparently did not work there but asked if she wanted help. When he claimed to understand commercial baking, she said, "I'll pay you to tell me what I should buy, to help me buy it, and to look it over and make sure it works."

Together, they attended auctions until they found an oven the man said would be appropriate. He helped her move it with a rented trailer. "Then he found a place in San Francisco where I got the sinks," she continued. "In that way, I assembled about two thousand dollars' worth of equipment. I found a cabinetmaker to build the storage cabinets I needed.

"I couldn't have done it without all the people who pitched in to help. Whether they got paid or not they gave freely of themselves. Since that time I've spoken with many women and men who have opened their own businesses and again and again they say the same thing: it's amazing how people show up to help you."[35]

Setting Up Shop

What is required to prepare for opening the doors depends on the business and the facilities that happen to be available. For some ventures, such as insurance sales or tax advising, little more than a desk and a file cabinet may be needed. A manufacturing company may require special rooms for clean work or painting, special mounting and power hookups for machines, or special effluent cleanup equipment. A service business such as plumbing may require storage space for parts, and a middleman operation such as wholesaling or retailing may require display areas, and so forth. Generally, it is fairly easy to anticipate such needs by looking at similar firms.

When the business is a simple one, one person may be able to set up the shop personally:

■ *After ten years working as an appliance salesman in a small store, he quit when the owner "became too difficult to work for." For the next ten years he sold furniture and appliances in a large department store, where again he became tired of his job and longed for something new. When he learned that the man for whom he had formerly worked in the small store was going out of the appliance business and intended to use his building in another way, the salesman began to think about starting a store of his own. His former employer's store was the only independent appliance store within a three-mile metropolitan radius, and across the street there was a building recently vacated.*

[35]Debbi Fields and Alan Furst, *One Smart Cookie* (New York: Simon & Schuster, 1987), p. 73.

His first step was to check with distributors of the appliances sold by his former employer. He was concerned that if they would not sell to his new store it would mean both that he would have to carry other lines he did not think well of and also that those suppliers would be open to selling to other competitors who might develop in his area. To his relief he found that they remembered him from before and would be glad to service his account.

Next, he investigated the vacant building and learned that the owner preferred to sell rather than lease it and would not be willing to pay for renovation. This was a shock, because the thought of buying a building in addition to investing in inventory had never occurred to him. But he had an appraiser examine the building, and when the appraiser said, upon hearing the asking price, "Arnie, you just found $10,000," he began to figure seriously how he could purchase that as well. After two sleepless nights he decided to buy. He and his wife took out a second mortgage on their home to cover the down payment, renovation, and working capital.

He also quit his job at the department store to tackle the full-time task of repairing, remodelling, and setting up the business. At this point the full impact of what he had taken on hit home and he began to have second thoughts. The building was a dismal mess. His paychecks stopped and bills started to arrive. His banker had told him when he took out the loan that it was probably an unwise move. Even his barber had told him it would never work. The licensed public accountant who had helped him set up books and obtain city permits had been non-committal.

But now there was no choice. He began moving equipment he had bought from his former employer's store across the street, including a delivery truck, hand trucks, and office equipment. He arranged with the phone company to keep the same phone number along with the name of the other firm but change the address in the book. He went to work on the inside of the store, doing much of the carpentry himself to save money.

He almost panicked in the middle of this process when the first shipment of 30 major appliances was suddenly unloaded in the middle of the store parking lot. Hiring a man to help with the uncrating, he moved it into the unfinished store as evening approached.

The second thoughts remained even as the store was opened for business. Nobody bought anything the first day. But on the second day someone did, and then others followed and the business quickly took on momentum. Soon another salesman had to be hired, recruited from the department store where the entrepreneur had worked. New lines were added with additional inventory financed from profits, and the store steadily grew in profitability.

When a business performs well, it is easy to overlook the many problems that had to be solved to get it going. In the previous case, outsiders would be unlikely to perceive the soul-searching and misgivings the entrepreneur experienced in setting up shop or the work that was involved. Some factors worked well together in this situation, including an available name and location that happened to suit customers of the area who were willing to support the new enterprise.

Expert Help.   If the entrepreneur lacks prior experience in the business, some other person familiar with the industry may be able to help set it up. The next entrepreneur first looked at a franchise for help, then he decided instead to hire an expert, even though the business was a simple one:

■   *After graduating with a business degree from college, an eastern Washington man went to work with a public accounting firm as an auditor. He was disappointed by a performance appraisal which said he did not exhibit the kind of enthusiasm the firm wanted.*

Two other auditing jobs later, he began to consider a business of his own. One which stuck in his mind was a pipe shop he had seen during a visit to Seattle. He liked the products and the friendly, relaxed atmosphere of the business. The shop happened to be a franchise and during his visit the shop was managed by a man who specialized in opening for the franchisor.

Because he had no idea how to start or run such a business, the auditor investigated the possibility of buying a franchise for his home town in eastern Washington, but he concluded that the $70,000 franchise fee was more than he could justify. So he set the idea aside.

Two years later at work the auditor met an engineer who was a pipe collector and the idea of a business resurfaced. This man had a pipe collection worth $10,000 and had become familiar with suppliers in the business and how it worked. The two discussed possibilities of opening a shop and decided to become partners. The auditor began looking for space to rent, but nothing suitable was found and the two decided to give up on the idea.

Then one of the contacts the auditor had made during his search for space told him of a storefront that had become available. His interest rekindled, he now negotiated with a banker for a $15,000 loan to get started. By persuading a relative to cosign the note he arranged for the money. But the problem of how to set up and run the business remained.

The auditor went looking for the man he had met earlier in the Seattle shop. This man said he would be glad to help the auditor get started. For a very modest fee plus room and board in the auditor's house, the man traveled to eastern Washington and went to work. He told the auditor what inventory to order, introduced him to suppliers and told him how to get the right quality and develop good working relationships. More important, he ran the shop for two months and demonstrated effective ways of dealing with customers — what to tell them and how to close sales. Breakeven was achieved within a week and the store remained in the black thereafter.

DEALING WITH SUPPLIERS

Regardless of how much value the entrepreneur decides to add in-house, as opposed to buying outside, there will still be the need for purchasing from outside suppliers, even if only telephone service and office supplies. L.L. Bean, for example, needed help from a supplier to make his first product, the Maine Hunting Boot, suitable for the market:

■ *He had made prototypes himself by stitching leather uppers to rubber overshoe bottoms. But the bottoms were shaped to fit over shoes, not feet. Consequently, he borrowed $400 from his brother in 1913 to order fabrication of lowers by U.S. Rubber in Boston. But the money was not enough to pay for tooling, so he had to raise more and negotiate a compromise with the rubber company to become his supplier. From that time until the 1960's Bean was U.S. Rubber's largest "rubbers" customer.[36]*

Buying from a supplier is vastly different from walking into a store and buying retail. The customer, particularly if a start-up, is no longer "king." In comparison to other customers of the supplier, the start-up will often be a naive

---

[36]Montgomery, *In Search of L.L. Bean*, p. 22.

small purchaser, and one of dubious credit and future buying ability. Hence, the start-up may receive low priority and may encounter problems, as the next example illustrates:

■ *In early 1977 two women began exploring the possibility of setting up a store to sell hand–silk-screened fabrics for interior decoration. One had held several secretarial positions, while the other had worked as a drugstore clerk in addition to a variety of community volunteer activities. Several possible business ideas were considered and each had problems. With the fabric the problem seemed to be how to obtain material. The nearest supplier was over 200 miles away and was finding sales for all he could produce without selling to the proposed new store. The two women took a trip to visit his plant and persuaded the man to become their supplier.*

Space for the store was found by visiting other stores and "asking around." At a sporting goods store they found a proprietor who was planning to move, contacted his landlord, and arranged to take over the lease. They also read a book on how to start a business and attempted to follow its advice to work out financial forecasts. Presenting these to a banker with a request for a loan, they were told that they had forgotten to include repayment of the loan principal in their cash flow. This was corrected, and paperwork was processed to obtain a city business license, a state registration and tax number for retailing, and a federal I.D. number. They figured they could set up accounting books later.

Orders were placed for inventory with the silk-screen company and other decorator item suppliers. All required payment in advance. Some items arrived promptly; others took longer, as much as six months. On their main product, the silk-screen material, they found delivery times ranged from one to six weeks on some items, while others failed to arrive for months. "What can we do about it?," the partners asked. "They refuse to sell unless we pay in advance. So we pay and then they have our money and seem to feel they can take as long as they want to deliver. Others send us things that arrive damaged. We have to negotiate with them on that and about who is going to pay for the return freight. Meanwhile, we have the damaged goods sitting here taking up space and tying up the money we paid for them at the same time."

The main benefit for its founders of this venture may have been education. The two women liked the product but had no commercial experience with it. Their store was too small to seriously interest suppliers, and the suppliers themselves were apparently not sophisticated enough to have developed smooth ways of working with customers. Had the women been familiar with this industry, they would likely have known that and been able either to work out better contracts with suppliers in advance or else avoid the headaches by not trying such a business. Even experienced entrepreneurs, however, can run into new problems with suppliers, as related in the following experience:

■ *When my company decided to broaden its line of wood-burning stoves, we took our drawings to a small metals manufacturer. He studied the plans and within a few days we agreed on price, quantity, and delivery dates. He became intensely interested as well as enthusiastic about the wood-stove business.*

Much to our chagrin, he failed to deliver our stoves on the targeted date—he had simply lied to get our order. When we finally got the first units, they had been made with cheaper material than our specs had called for. While we hassled with him on this issue, he tried to raise the price on the units to a point well above his bid. Finally, the whole project bogged down in recurring rounds of delayed delivery, faulty product, and incessant bickering over price.

The climax came when our conniving manufacturer decided to bypass us. He made an insignificant design change in our stoves and started selling them himself. He had lied to us, cheated us, and finally wound up stealing from us.[37]

One way to avoid such a distressing sequence is to check out the reputation of the supplier. Prior customers, competitors, and suppliers of the supplier, as well as bankers, may have information about the supplier's business practices.

Purchase Contracts

Even if a supplier checks out as honorable, another advisable precaution is to formulate a written contract, particularly if the purchase is exceptional and major. Unfortunately, however, even with contracts there will still be room for problems, as illustrated by the next example:

■ *In late 1973 a Vancouver, B.C., architect decided he had been doing well enough to afford something he had always wanted, his own ocean-going sailboat. He had long been interested in sailing, having spent college summers crewing in races and sailing on others' boats in the years since. This experience had given him ideas about the combination of features he would want for own boat. He began searching through magazines and marinas to find such a boat, but without success. He therefore commissioned a naval-architect to design one. Terms were $6,000 for the plans, $1,000 for the copyrighting, plus $700 for each additional boat built to the plans—conditions that are not unusual for such jobs. Preparation of the plans would take ten months. He now began searching for a yard to build the boat, first in Canada and the United States, then finding their prices high, in Europe and the Orient.*

He also began showing preliminary sketches of his design to other acquaintances in sailing circles, where he encountered more serious interest than he had expected. Some went so far as to ask if they could buy rights to the plans. This gave him the thought that perhaps he might be able to make such boats as a business. When the plans were finished in October 1974, he began asking around about possible partners and through referral met a man who said he would like to share the business and work on selling. But there was no written agreement.

Construction prices seemed best in Taiwan, so the architect traveled there to meet a builder. After several days of negotiations the two seemed to be in agreement. The architect wrote up a one-page agreement providing $8,000 for the completed hull mold, $4,500 for the deck mold, and $58,000 each for two boats, all in U.S. currency. The agreement also made the architect the U.S. agent for the Taiwan builder so long as he sold at least three boats per year. The Taiwanese builder signed the contract but the architect did not, instead bringing it back home for his partner to sign. When it came to committing money to the venture, however, the prospective partner balked, and the architect concluded he had been "just a sweet talker" all along. The two parted company, and the architect began seeking another partner.

Through his attorney he shortly met such a man who was willing to invest $25,000 for half the business, and an agreement to that effect was signed. The two also signed the Taiwan agreement in January 1975, plus agreements with their banks to provide letters of

[37]James R. Cook, *The Start-Up Entrepreneur* (New York: Harper & Row, 1986), p. 138.

credit in Taiwan to begin the work. The Taiwanese immediately responded with a promise to deliver the boats by December 1975.

For $5,000 an advertising agency was hired to prepare brochures and copy for magazine advertisements, which cost an additional $4,000. By mid-year, over two dozen serious inquiries had been received, and shortly thereafter the two partners traveled to Taiwan to check on construction. To their disappointment they found that the "builder" was in fact just a middleman and the yard with whom they had contracted had stopped work because it concluded the price was too low. Unfortunately, the contract did not include a deadline which could be used to force completion of the boat. The contract had also failed to provide that the architect's company could take possession of the molds. Not knowing how to press the issue in foreign courts, the two partners accepted the promise of the Taiwanese middleman that he would work things out on their original price.

Back home they shortly found first one and then a second customer all ready to buy. Contracts were signed with both which included a $20,000 deposit, refundable if the boat was not delivered, plus a letter of credit for the balance due from the buyer's bank upon delivery. The Taiwanese middleman then arrived to announce that he had found another yard to complete the boats on time and at the original price. A new contract with him was signed, this time including not only provisions for mold ownership and delivery timing, but also to have a marine inspector sent from Canada to provide full-time supervision until the boats were complete. Terms provided that half his pay would come from the partners and the other half from the Taiwanese, and also that beyond the first two boats the price would rise from $58,000 to $65,000. The business continued.

One lesson from this experience is that it pays to be careful in writing contracts so as not to omit any important provisions. Learning about the terms of prior contracts through conversations with others who have used them, through looking at other contracts, and through consultation with an appropriately experienced attorney can help. A second lesson is that dealing with foreign suppliers can introduce cultural problems into the relationship. In this case the unwritten promises of the Taiwanese middleman proved as important or more so than the written contract. Contracts are further discussed in the next chapter.

HIRING

Some founders can set up operations with little or no permanent help, but if they lack special skills or simply do not have enough time to perform all the required work, there will be a need to hire other employees. These may at first come from among family and perhaps friends, but the odds that the talents of those particular individuals will happen to be just what the company needs may be somewhat slim. Former coworkers will likely be a better fit if the new business is an outgrowth of the entrepreneur's job. Drawing employees from a former employer, however, must be done with care to avoid legal problems. Negotiating with the employer ahead of time and reaching an amicable settlement if possible can be worth the effort.[38]

[38]Joanmarie Kalter, "Staffing a Startup with Former Co-Workers," *Venture* (February 1982), p. 34.

Employees

The importance of obtaining the right kind of employees is illustrated by the following comments by Shepard on hiring to start a disco:

■ *It can't hurt to hire employees carefully, not only for the image they project but for their honesty. A lot of employees delight in devising clever ways to rip off the boss. In one classic instance, the owner of a hugely successful New York night spot couldn't fathom why he wasn't making as much money as he should. The spotters he hired reported that every cent was being properly rung up on the three cash registers. The owner still couldn't figure out the scam—until he realized he had only two cash registers: The bartenders had brought in a cash register of their own.*[39]

It may be possible to hire temporary workers for some tasks. Accountants, bookkeepers, secretaries, receptionists, salespeople, clerks, and even engineers, lab technicians, programmers, and some types of managers and executives can be hired from temporary agencies.[40] With such help, a start-up may be able to avoid some problems of recruiting, processing payroll paperwork, and covering fringe benefits such as life insurance and medical and dental care. But the costs of those benefits, plus a profit for the temporary employee company, will be included in the price paid for help. Managing the temporary employees will still be necessary, but problems of expanding and reducing workforce capacity may be easier to handle, because such workers are by definition temporary.

Questions that enter into the decision of using temporary help include whether the business will be long or short term, cyclical or seasonal, and whether the expertise will be needed permanently. How much control, flexibility, and personal selection are needed must also be considered, as must the impact on costs and cash flow. There may be implications for the morale in the new venture, as temporary people will not be likely to feel they are part of a team.

Finally, it can be important to determine how the temporary agency selects its employees, and whether it bonds them to avoid the risk of theft. Having temporary employees sign secrecy agreements may be wise if there is a risk of exposing proprietary information. Checking references and backgrounds, applying close supervision, and taking care with keys and valuable property are other possible precautions, not only with temporary but also permanent new employees.[41]

One entrepreneur who had gone through a series of unsatisfactory hiring experiences concluded that his main mistake had been hiring people for low costs rather than high performance:

■ *Just when I had the least money, I needed the strongest person, but I didn't realize it . . . I made the lowest-cost hire I could find. In fact, I did it over and over again.*

[39]William G. Shepard, Jr., "Disco Fever," *Venture* (June 1979), p. 43.
[40]Ansi Vallens, "Temporary Help," *Venture* (July 1986), p. 120.
[41]"Using Temps With Care," *Venture* (August 1988), p. 75.

The problem with the cheap hire is that the costs are high, but you don't realize it because they're hidden. The incapable person eats up lots of management time. It goes in little chunks, so you don't see it happening.

But that's only the beginning of the hidden costs. What happens in the shop—in terms of ill will, problems, productivity that's lost—can stop you cold.[42]

Recruiting

Recruiting an effective team of people may do more than anything else to forestall such problems. Hiring the right people is not as tricky as selecting the right partners, because employees who do not work out can, unlike partners, be let go. Finding the right people may or may not be difficult, depending upon the special skills that they must possess. The next two cases may serve to illustrate. In the first, the search task proved insurmountable. In the second, it was not.

■ *An MBA student at the University of Washington thought he had a good idea for a new business when he sought to solve the problem of determining the value of his home possessions for buying homeowners' insurance. Why not, he thought, offer an appraisal service for other people who had this need. Then rather than having to go through all their furniture, appliances and other possessions, making an inventory, and attaching values themselves, they could simply hire it done by his service. He did a little market research by visiting an affluent neighborhood and going from door to door asking whether people would be interested. He found that many were already concerned about keeping their valuations up with inflation and were not sure what to do about it. They said they would be glad to have such a service and wondered what it would cost. Then came the barrier. He contacted some existing appraisal firms to ask about their charges and how they obtained appraisers. They told him they were very shorthanded and could not themselves find enough qualified appraisers to hire. The student concluded his enterprise would not work.*

■ *When Dave Ederer, a CPA, bought a heat treating company from one of his older clients who wanted to retire, he knew nothing whatever about how to perform heat treating. Therefore it was a somewhat alarming event when shortly after taking over the company his two top shop men left, one as a result of divorce proceedings and the other because of an arrest for some crime unrelated to the business. Ederer simply placed an advertisement in the newspaper classified asking for experienced heat treaters. Shortly he received a string of responses. He screened the applicants himself through interviews aimed at weeding out people he thought patently unqualified or with whom he did not think he would like to work. The others he sent back to the shop to be interviewed by the workers, who then selected people they were convinced knew what they needed to about heat treating and with whom they would like to work. This solved the problem to the satisfaction of all.*

Appropriate employees can be found by asking knowledgeable acquaintances and former coworkers, utilizing employment agencies, and even running classified advertisements. Competing with established companies that can offer higher pay and more fringe benefits can be hard. But new ventures have their advantages, as

---

[42]John C. Gardner, "I Paid Too Much by Hiring Too Cheap," *Inc.* (June 1979), p. 65.

Marshall Fitzgerald, whose start-up competed for technical talent with giants on the San Francisco peninsula observed:

■ *Good people are motivated as much by creative challenges, by a chance to learn and grow, as they are by paychecks. Here's where a small company actually has an advantage over a large organization. We can give a person a job and let him run with it.*[43]

One venture trying to compete for hard-to-get skills, however, found it had to offer competitive salaries; a bonus program; a health, dental, and vision program with a no-waiting period beginning on the first day of work; Christmas parties with $100–$400 per person gifts; a recreation program; moving allowances; housing reimbursements; generous life insurance; and free lessons in such things as aerobics, guitar, and English as a second language.[44]

References on work-force building offer advice on such issues as how to select a recruiter,[45] what to tell job candidates and what not to tell,[46] how to determine competitive pay scales,[47] how to make compensation motivational,[48] use of minimum wage,[49] evaluating employee performance,[50] anticipating invasion by unions,[51] and anticipating possible replacement of founders[52] and many other specialized topics. Most of them, however, concern post–start-up development of the enterprise.

Legalities

There are numerous governmental constraints associated with employing other people. It may be possible to work around them when the company is very small. For example, the company may get away with hiring the first one or two people as independent contractors or consultants rather than employees and thereby not have to deduct income tax withholding from their paychecks. Inspectors may be willing to educate the entrepreneur about safety violations, provided they are not too flagrant, and allow a chance to correct them without penalty. But if the company matures into a full-time enterprise for several people besides the owner(s), it will have to comply with a number of governmental hiring requirements, including the following:

[43]James Fawcette, "Money Alone Can't Buy Top Talent," *Inc.* (March 1981), p. 92.
[44]Craig R. Waters, "Recruit, Interview, Hire, Train," *Inc.* (May 1983), p. 82.
[45]James R. Arnold, "Executive Search," *Inc.* (November 1979), p. 108.
[46]David Diamond, "What to Tell Job Candidates," *Venture* (March 1984), p. 43.
[47]Nancy B. Tieken, "Are Your Salaries Competitive?," *Inc.* (June 1981), p. 84.
[48]Bruce G. Posner, "May the Force Be with You," *Inc.* (July 1987), p. 70.
[49]Michael Boehm, "Preserving a Social Covenant," *Inc.* (July 1987), p. 104.
[50]Berkeley Rice, "Evaluating Employees," *Venture* (September 1985), p. 33.
[51]Sabin Russell, "Living with Unions," *Venture* (February 1986), p. 33.
[52]Tom Richman, "Beyond the Start-Up Team," *Inc.* (December 1987), p. 53.

1. Minimum wage and the Equal Pay Act
2. Payroll deductions for taxes and Social Security
3. Labor laws if a union attempts to organize
4. Antidiscrimination hiring laws (race, sex, and age)
5. Workplace building codes (restrooms, etc.)
6. OSHA (safety) regulations

Both the local city hall and the U.S. Department of Labor can be contacted to get current literature on these rules and to answer questions. These rules cause few problems for most businesses. The entrepreneur can get by with a general familiarity, especially in the early stages. An hour or two of reading government literature should provide the needed information and alert the entrepreneur if more is needed.

PRODUCING

The first order for a product from what was to become Polaroid Corporation came from Eastman Kodak, for $10,000 worth of polarizing sheet from which to make camera filters. Edwin Land's partner, George Wheelright, described the preparation of the first delivery:

■ *"We were approaching, but had not yet achieved, a continuous sheet process. We had various ways of making larger areas than we have ever made before, but they were discontinuous, not a real manufacturing process. Then Land had a bright idea, and we all began working on it for days to try to get it running to fill the Kodak order. I came in the morning before Christmas. None of us of course had time to go out and buy presents, so I brought a quart of champagne to celebrate a little and then go out and do some shopping. I arrived about nine o'clock. The next time either Land or I took our clothes off at all was January eleventh. There is a lot of vague time in there that I don't remember well. The thing that I do remember was early one morning Andy Anderson and I were working on the jaws of the hydraulic press that was going to extrude the sheet. Din (Land) was on the floor sort of crying and working with something and not doing very well. He said, 'George, what is the matter? My wife has gone home and your wife has gone. Everyone has gone home and we're not getting anywhere.' I said rather crossly from the corner where I had myself propped up, because if I sat down I'd go to sleep, 'Do you suppose it has anything to do with the fact that we came in here on the twenty-fourth of December and it's now the eleventh of January? Neither of us has taken a shower in eighteen days.' Land said, 'My God, it's the eleventh of January! I've got to do my Christmas shopping. I should be home.' And I said, 'So should I.' But before we left the machine was running and we were making sheet."*

Land continued the story. "We packed the whole shipment in a small box, which we carefully wrapped around with black tape and sent to Eastman Kodak with a bill for five thousand dollars. They replied, 'We have received your precious package,' and the company was in business."[53]

---

[53]Peter Wensberg, *Land's Polaroid* (Boston: Houghton Mifflin, 1987), p. 44.

Paradoxical problems include not only that a company with profits and sales growth can fail, but also that too much capital can get a start-up in trouble as well. Seeq technology raised around $70 million in start-up capital between 1981 and 1985, which it "blew" on a fancy building, parties, contests, and celebrations. "We were always rewarding ourselves for things that didn't count," an employee recalled. "Every other week there was a champagne party for some weird thing — the Tandem computer came in today. Well what does that mean? It means you've got to start paying the lease on it." By May 1986, *Inc.* reported, the company had only $13,000 left in the bank. It had lost $4 million on sales of $8.5 million in its most recent quarter, and overhead was projected at $54 million on a sales projection of $30 million for the coming year. A new CEO slashed payroll and expenses, and by late 1987 the company moved into the black.[54]

Forestalling Problems

Sometimes problems simply cannot be solved as fast as they arise.

■ *Sanders Technology, set up to produce and sell word processing systems beginning with a large German contract, fell behind on product development. The German company was entitled to back out when delivery dates slipped, and did so. Expenses grew faster than revenues, a creditor demanded payment, and the company filed for Chapter Eleven bankruptcy.*[55]

Did this have to happen? Participants have different views. Among the possibilities is that the founders did not adequately think through what could go wrong and how to deal with it. Another is that the goals were not realistic and the company should not have begun. Still another, and perhaps most likely, is that by recruiting some additional talent and resources and guiding them with greater sensitivity to all participants as well as the technology, it could have made the grade.

The problems to be solved shift as the venture progresses through its start-up process and evolves into an ongoing business and then grows. The following company started with a "buy" approach, then it shifted to "make" as sales grew. This is a pattern many companies follow. But in this case expansion took place faster than management could keep up. At one point along this growth, management said it preferred flexibility over five-year plans and so did not make plans. What resulted was chaos.

■ *In the late sixties a Renton, Washington, print shop operator and several colleagues wanted a faster input device for giving commands to a phototypesetter. They undertook to develop an electronic keyboard with memory to replace the mechanical keyboards then*

---

[54]Edward O. Welles, "The Company Money Almost Killed," *Inc.* (November 1988), p. 46.
[55]Ronald Rosenberg, "Sanders Technology: What Went Wrong?," *Venture* (November 1980), p. 84.

available, worked up a prototype, and tried it. The best way to enter the business appeared to be to work with established manufacturers of typesetting machines, but negotiations with them failed to produce an arrangement the entrepreneurs liked, and they undertook to manufacture it on their own. Their target was to reach $7 million in sales, roughly half the national market, in 2½ years.

Arrangements were made with suppliers to produce various components and sub-assemblies accounting for roughly 90 percent of the production work. At the company one large room was used for incoming inspection of the subcontracted parts, assembly, testing, packaging, and shipping. Arranging with suppliers took a great deal of planning, negotiation, and coordinating, but the work got done, and production gradually rose to 30 units per month by the end of the second year in business.

Then the company undertook to shift over to its own manufacturing for a majority of the work and phase out most of the subcontracting. Output targets were raised from 30 to 300 per month to allow sales of $3.5 million per year. Another 16 model variations were also added to the product line. Workspace was expanded from the one big room to several additional rooms. Employees were rapidly hired on both permanent and temporary status. Production methods were changed from a batch process wherein each worked on one machine until it was completed to an assembly line with each employee adding parts until final testing at the end. Product problems, engineering problems, supply problems, and people problems followed. Employee turnover soared along with costs.

A production manager commented, "A month's production schedule would be changed several times by management during the month. The employee formerly responsible for 30 boards a month might be told to produce another 20. Then management would announce a change in the components on the board. The employee would wind up taking 10 days to modify and report on the boards he had just spent 20 days assembling and would be very happy, having produced only 20 boards that month."

Soon production was far behind sales and costs were far beyond budget. Consultants were hired, managers fired. The number of employees rose from 27 to 217 during 1971 alone. Six years later after a string of losses, a consultant was brought in who cut the number back from 280 to 130. Finally, in April 1979 the company filed for Chapter Eleven bankruptcy. In September 1979, now with 80 employees, the company was acquired by another on the East Coast.

Production was not the only failing of this company, but it was certainly a major one, which points up the importance of giving advance thought to the kinds of production problems that can arise, so that they will not complicate other aspects of the business and burden management more than necessary when there are other important things for management to do. Some potential problems to anticipate are as follows.

Production Problems to Anticipate

- Management does not know about problems.
- Costs exceed expectations.
- The product or service does not perform to standards.
- Delivery times are not met.
- Material is wasted.
- Disputes break out.
- Parts do not fit.
- Materials are not ordered in time.
- Defective materials are accepted.

- Purchases are made at prices that are too high.
- Supplier bills are not paid and supplies are cut off.
- Supplies do not match needs.
- Inventory becomes excessive or obsolete.
- Customers do not pay on time or at all.
- Customers pay, but the money does not arrive.
- The account at the bank is overdrawn.
- Orders that cannot be delivered are accepted.
- The venture cannot find or hire people it needs.
- Bad reports about the venture circulate.
- The bank refuses to give or extend credit.
- Customer leads are not properly pursued.
- Key employees quit.
- Improvement opportunities are missed.
- Costly tools or materials disappear.
- Production machinery breaks.
- Employees arrive late, leave early, do not work.
- Timing is wrong for advertising or other events.
- Promises are misunderstood or broken.
- The venture is upstaged by competitor(s).
- Tax payments become delinquent.
- A supplier sues for payment of an overdue bill.

Notwithstanding attempts to anticipate them, many problems simply cannot be solved in advance but must be dealt with as they arise, usually by the founder in the early stages of a venture. Bob Flaherty had the following experience in his financial publishing venture:

■ *I always imagined that in running a company the major part of your job was business policy over the long term. I took the short-term tasks of turning out the product for granted. But I learned there is no long term unless you survive each day. It's exactly the minute details that no one touches that can cause the most problems.*[56]

Flaherty tried three printers before his production problems were solved. First, there was an older man who printed with hot type in what looked like a garage. Then he tried a low bidder with a computerized cold-type system, but the result was a higher bill and more errors. Finally, he engaged a new printer with magazine experience who proved more satisfactory. But then there were problems with mailing delays, and so forth.

Advancing Quality

Taking extra steps to produce exceptional quality is a common feature of many companies able to earn higher returns on investment than their competitors in the same industries. This appears true both in larger companies that make up a

[56]Peggy Finston, "Rewriting an Old Story," *Inc.* (February 1984), p. 53.

data base of three thousand businesses studied by the Strategic Planning Institute (PIMS)[57] and in smaller ones, such as California's King High Tech, which assembles printed circuit boards;[58] Pennsylvania's Oberg Industries, an extraordinarily large and profitable tool and die shop;[59] or Florida's Burger Bug Killers, a cockroach extermination company able to charge the restaurants and hotels prices several times as high as its competitors because of its high-quality work.[60]

Producing is a very broad topic that has been barely scratched in this discussion. More than any other aspect of the business, it may tend to become complicated as the business grows and therefore deserves forethought in manufacturing start-ups. As "bugs" are brought under control, management's attention may shift to expansion of sales and raising capital. The attention of the technical side of the company may refocus on improving the existing line and developing the next one. Operations will become more concerned with filling orders and keeping costs in line.

As new people are added to the work force, they will create the need for more training, and they will likely discover new ways to do things, some better, some worse. Consequently, quality will continually be subjected to new attacks requiring attention. Because there may be a time lag between when the quality is compromised and when the mistake is discovered, and also because it is generally much cheaper to invest in avoiding rather than correcting mistakes, quality control should be planned for in advance and not relaxed as new opportunities develop. The best advice for maintaining quality is "don't relax."

Controlling Costs

Depending upon how rapidly the company starts to take off, the possibilities for letting money leak out of it can quickly increase. Too many people can be hired too fast. Too much material can be purchased. It is easy to lease a lot of equipment, vehicles, and even real estate. New employees can waste supplies trying to "get things right," long distance phoning can get out of hand, and myriad other waste avenues that beset mature companies may open quickly for the new one. One control to include is for the owner to insist on signing all checks personally or at least all those over a certain amount. Controls may also have to be placed on those authorized to order for the company on credit.

One entrepreneur in the financial publishing business, Bob Flaherty, recalled that economy was imposed upon him by investors who did not put up the million dollars he thought he needed:

[57]Buzzell and Gale, *The PIMS Principles* (New York: MacMillan, 1987).
[58]Hoffs, "King of the Desert."
[59]Donna Fenn, "The Lord of Discipline," *Inc.* (December 1985), p. 82.
[60]Tom Richman, "Getting the Bugs Out," *Inc.* (June 1984), p. 67.

■ *If I'd started out with my million, I'd probably be bankrupt by now," he recalled. Rather than renting an office he set up in the back room of a mutual fund. To save money on advertising, he swapped space with other publications. Instead of hiring writers, he bought articles from freelancers. His wife wrote for free. A friend wrote an article as a Christmas present. Novices more interested in having their work published than in being paid substantial amounts for it provided other articles at bargain rates. Teenagers and housewives were hired to help with mailings. For expert help, Flaherty looked for retired specialists. A postal worker was hired after hours to solve problems of zip codings and bagging to make delivery faster.*[61]

Arranging for financial controls at the outset not only saves the company money, but also helps to persuade others that it is a reliable party for investments or loans.

Preempting Competitors

It is important to consider speed and momentum as strategies to protect the company from being superceded (see Chapter 3). Competitors in most industries are constantly improving their products and services. The new company will have to be at least equal to the competition with what it initially offers, and quite possibly its competitive entry wedge will be at least partly based upon some extension of the technology of its line of business. If the new company does not keep advancing, its edge will be lost. From the outset, provision must be made in the company strategy to keep moving forward technologically.

Keeping a perspective on advance development while working out the "bugs" of the initial product or service may be difficult. It may seem that there is simply not enough time or money to go around on all the other things that need to be done and pursue advanced development as well, and for that reason it may be helpful to anticipate that need, along with all the others, in advance.

PLANNING QUESTIONS

The following questions are intended to stimulate thought about what should be considered in moving ahead with a venture. Which questions best apply can vary among entrepreneurs and ventures, as can the order in which they should be considered, the priority that should be placed on them, and which of them should be answered in a written plan.

Premises

- How much plant space must be committed to, and how was it chosen?
- What has been the historical use of these facilities, and how have they worked out for others?

[61]Finston, "Rewriting an Old Story," p. 53.

- Have parking and loading needs been arranged for?
- What are the logistical, communication, work-force, recruiting, and marketing advantages and disadvantages of the company's location relative to those of competitors?
- Will warehousing space or operations at different locations be required, and if so, how will it be set up and managed?

Equipment

- What equipment needs will the venture have, which of those will be for custom and which for standard equipment, and what alternatives were considered for economizing?
- How will any needed equipment be obtained, installed, and serviced?
- How will field servicing be handled, and what can be done if it develops problems?
- What special tooling will be needed, and what can be done to change capacity up or down with minimal loss?
- Have lighting, security, theft, and safety needs been anticipated?
- How will productive capacity compare to output needs at various stages in the company's future?

Suppliers

- What advantages and disadvantages in purchasing supplies will the venture have, and how important will those be?
- Who will be the principal suppliers, and what assurance is there that they will deliver on schedule?
- What can be done if much more or much less turns out to be needed?
- To what extent were competitive bids obtained in selecting suppliers, and how did they differ?
- What leverage will the venture be able to apply for obtaining priority with suppliers?

Hiring

- Have employee needs been projected out for alternative growth patterns, including consideration of recruiting, training, and compensating?
- What special productive skills will the venture have compared to competitors, and how will it obtain them?
- How will the skills it commands and the price it must pay for them compare to competitors'?
- What will be required to keep up with them?
- Is there a prospect of unionization, and if so at what point in growth?
- How will the needed work force be located, recruited, trained, organized, managed, and compensated?

Producing

- What will be the specific steps required in producing, delivering, and servicing what the venture offers?
- How will quality be defined?
- Has a flow diagram of operations been prepared?
- How much will be done in-house, and what will be contracted out in the near term versus the long term?
- How will production planning, inventory control, and quality control be handled?

POSSIBLE MILESTONES FOR A PLANNING
TIME LINE

The most suitable milestones for a time line for a particular venture must be a function of the individual case. Those that follow are intended to help stimulate thought about them.

- Production process designed
- List of start-up steps made
- Gantt chart of steps made
- Pert chart of steps made
- Location selected
- Lease signed
- Equipment and supplies ordered
- Facilities ready for start-up
- Debugging accomplished and checked
- First delivery made

Chapter 9

START-UP
PAPERWORK

INTRODUCTION

Most entrepreneurs would wish it were different, but the need for paperwork and systems to take care of it usually begins before a new company does and grows progressively with it. First there may be notes and correspondence in connection with the development of the product or service. Data on costs will have to be obtained, and there will be computations, financial forecasts, and budgets to file. Industry supplier data, contracts, and other legal documents and data on the industry, prospective employees, and other important contacts will have to be added and available when needed.

An entrepreneur's initial inclination may be to pile all the data in a heap or a box, but this method costs additional effort later when it can less easily be spared. It is better to design an orderly and effective paperwork system from the start, with enough flexibility to accommodate later modifications.

Some aspects of the business call for their own special paperwork. Designing, prototyping, and planning generate worksheets that may continue to be used for reference. Protecting ideas requires not only records, but also appropriate witnessing and filings with the government to obtain patents, trademarks, and copyrights. Marketing campaigns require brochure mailing lists, customer records, price lists, commission schedules, order forms, invoices, receipts, and sometimes contracts with sales agents. Teaming calls for written agreements between partners or, in the case of corporations, the filing of articles and bylaws, followed by regular corporate minutes and periodic reports to the government. Internal operations may require any number of additional forms for controlling the flow of work, controlling and recording quality, maintaining plant and equipment, purchasing raw materials, and keeping track of employees, as well as property records and lease arrangements. Despite the large number, none is frivolous or irrelevant.

The following examples illustrate situations in which paperwork could become important:

- The entrepreneur has been working to develop the enterprise and has come quite a way but now finds it would be desirable to bring a certain person in as a partner. As a basis for determining how much time and money the partner should expect to contribute for what share of the business, the entrepreneur would like to show a tabulation of what he or she has contributed to bring the business this far.
- The entrepreneur has been spending his or her savings all year to develop the product or service, and sales have started. Now April 15 is approaching, and it is time to file for income taxes. Some of the money can be recovered if records are available to verify deductions on the tax form.
- The company has just begun operations when a government inspector appears who wants to see certain permits that are required to operate this type of business.
- Customer orders are beginning to pour in, and the company needs more cash for purchases and payroll. The banker says that prospects for a loan are good, but the bank wants to see records of performance to date and projections that show just how big a loan will be needed and what sources of anticipated income will be available to repay it.
- The company's product or service has been on the market for a short time when competitors begin to spring up. They begin to offer reduced prices to break into the market. How far can the company cut its prices to match them without losing money?
- Just as the company is getting started, a founder whose technical skills are highly important to the development of the product or service dies. What insurance should the company have to help recruit a replacement?

Despite the importance of good records in situations such as these, there is a natural tendency to avoid this facet of the business. After all, records and paperwork do not develop a product or service; they take time and money away from creative design and production as well. Nor do they sell the product; instead, they take energy away from working with potential customers. They cost money, when every cent may be important to save. So it is natural to try to minimize such "red tape" as much as possible. It may be possible to avoid it entirely, at least temporarily. If the company never really gets started, then there will be no need for it. But even then there would be value in some records. A $1,000 expense, for instance, may bring $300 back in tax savings. If the company does get started, then the need is inevitable, especially if government permission is needed to operate.

At the same time, it is vital to restrain overhead costs. A horror story to be avoided was described by Buskirk in which the application of $1.5 million in seed money for a venture to develop new video learning systems was applied as follows:

Consultant fees	$415,000
Research expenses	285,000
Legal fees	230,000
Management salaries	210,000

Accounting fees	160,000
Rent	65,000
Prototyping	55,000
Office	45,000
Marketing	15,000
Remainder for working capital	20,000

At this point there had been no sales. The real "work" of doing business was mainly in research, prototype development, and marketing, which together totaled $355,000 or only one-third of what had been spent.[1] Most had gone to various forms of overhead, particularly consulting, legal and accounting fees.

PAPER HURDLES

Permissions

For some very simple and small enterprises, housepainting, for example, very little paperwork will ever be needed. For others that develop more complex products and grow in employment, paperwork will be simple initially, but it will increase in complexity as the company takes on momentum. In still other lines of work, such as setting up a new foundry or chemical processing plant, the initial paperwork may be crucial because without it the government may not permit the company to begin operations at all.

A general list of federal and Washington state industry regulations appears in Exhibit 9–1. This list was taken from a booklet entitled *Starting a Business in Washington State*. Similar booklets are available in other states and many large cities, typically from the Department of Commerce. The information in these books can help the entrepreneur anticipate how much red tape will be involved in starting a particular type of business. Care should be taken to note requirements from all three levels of government. In addition to federal and state areas of concern noted in Exhibit 9–1, for instance, a company starting in Seattle would need to worry about a city business license, city taxes, county licenses for some types of activity, and a county property and inventory tax. An example form for obtaining a city business license appears in Figure 9–1. A call to city hall can quickly provide the needed information. For federal requirements, a booklet entitled *The Regulatory and Paperwork Maze: A Guide for Small Business,* which is published by the Small Business Administration, may be the best place to start.

Many entrepreneurs begin without worrying about most of these governmental requirements, and often no serious problems result. At other times, careful attention to them can be crucial. A *Venture* article commented that in starting a

---

[1]Richard H. Buskirk, "The Dangers of Overcapitalization in the Start Up Stage." P. 425 in Karl H. Vesper, *Frontiers of Entrepreneurship Research, 1982* (Wellesley, MA: Babson Center for Entrepreneurial Studies, 1982).

EXHIBIT 9–1   List of Needed Licenses and Areas of Permission

---

Business legal form papers
Sale of securities
Out-of-state corporation transaction authorization
U.S. Department of Internal Revenue requirements
U.S. Social Security Administration requirements
U.S. Department of Labor requirements
State Department of Revenue requirements
State Department of Labor and Industries requirements
State Department of Employment Security requirements and assistance
City business licenses
State professional or occupational licenses
State Department of Ecology permits
Water resource and pollution control
Solid waste management
Air quality control
U.S. Environmental Protection Agency requirements
Shorelines management permits
Building permits
State Agriculture Department requirements
U.S. Army Corps of Engineers requirements
Import/export business requirements
Department of Fisheries requirements
Liquor Control Board requirements
Mining permits
Septic tank permits
Requirements for insurance and health care businesses
Requirements for banks, savings and loans, credit unions
Requirements for common carriers
Sale of franchises
Sale of camp club sites
Registration for sale of real estate
Registration for land development
Tax number
Financing (permission to use others' money)

---

disco, "the necessary permits can run to a dozen in some states; many a grand opening has been torpedoed because one was neglected."[2]

In some lines of work, failure to get clearance can terminate the business. Serving liquor without an appropriate license is rarely possible for long. Competitors see to that. Building in conflict with zoning ordinances can also provoke a crackdown. Garage start-ups are common, but they usually cannot go far before running afoul of residential zoning regulations. These typically allow a business to operate in a home so long as it is incidental to the residential use of the house, does not have outside displays of merchandise or signs, makes most of what is sold by the business at the home, and does not generate an unusual

---

[2]William G. Shepherd, Jr., "Disco Fever," *Venture* (June 1979), p. 43.

FEE $1.00

FILE THIS COPY WITH COMPTROLLER

ORIGINAL

CITY OF SEATTLE — COMPTROLLER'S DEPARTMENT
DIVISION OF LICENSES AND STANDARDS
101 SEATTLE MUNICIPAL BUILDING — 583-2950

APPLICATION FOR BUSINESS LICENSE

(A filing fee of $1.00 must accompany this application)
ORDINANCE No. 72630 AS AMENDED

PLEASE PRINT OR TYPE   PLEASE PRINT OR TYPE

To Be Issued to _____

Trade Name _____

Business Address _____
                              (Number and Street)   (Post Office)   (Zone)

Residence Address _____
                                                                                                                (Residence Phone)

Kind of Business in Detail _____
                                              (Be sure to fill in. Designate whether Retail, Wholesale, etc.)

Opening Date of Business in Seattle (Important) _____

State Whether Individual, Partnership, or Corporation _____

If Partnership List Partners. If Corporation List Officers, Giving Title, Residence Address and Phone Number of Each.

_____

_____

_____

Business Was Formerly Operated by _____ Bus. Lic. No. _____

Whose Present Address Is _____ Phone No. _____

Did You Take Over: Entire Business ☐   Portion Thereof ☐

Have You Ever Had a Seattle Business License? _____ Business License No. Was: _____

Remarks: _____

_____

Name and address of parent company _____

BE SURE ALL INFORMATION IS COMPLETE. If additional space is needed, attach supplementary sheets of this size. If business is conducted in more than one location within the City of Seattle, please list your business locations on bottom of this sheet. There is no charge for additional business licenses for branch locations.

Do the premises upon which the proposed business is to be conducted,

conform to requirements of the Zoning Ordinance? _____

BUSINESS LOCATIONS IN SEATTLE.
LIST BELOW ADDRESS OF EACH OFFICE, STORE, PLANT, OR WAREHOUSE IN WHICH STOCK IS MAINTAINED.

STREET ADDRESS	LICENSES ISSUED	FEE	RECEIPT NO.		CHECK BELOW	
				PLATE		OFFICE
				LICENSE		MAIL
				MASTER CD.		CLERK
				ADDRESS CD.		FIELD
				TR. NAME CD.		DATE

DO NOT USE THIS SPACE

Date _____   Signature of Licensee _____

Title _____
                                          (Owner, Partner or Corporation Officer)

Business Phone _____

BLT-101   2-70

FIGURE 9-1 Application for a city of Seattle business license.

amount of traffic. That last requirement can be troublesome if success brings customers or large delivery trucks too often, making people along the street more likely to complain.[3]

Starting a trucking firm without appropriate ICC permits cannot be done, nor can a radio station be started without permission from the FCC, and so forth. Testing requirements of the FDA are so stringent and expensive that few new companies have been formed to produce new proprietary drugs in many years. Salmon ranching, where fish are released to the wild and recaptured when they return to spawn—a successful industry in some other countries such as Japan and Russia—has to date been an economic failure in the United States because new companies have found themselves faced with red tape preventing them from operating efficiently, even after they waded through a great deal of other red tape to get permits to operate at all.

Private permissions are sometimes needed in addition to governmental ones, making paperwork hurdles still higher, as illustrated by the following enterprise to set up an excursion railroad near Lake Tahoe. Dr. Robert Keller issued a series of progress reports to backers of the venture, telling about problems of getting started and actions being taken to solve them. Here are some brief excerpts from his reports:

■   *"July, 1968. Our interest in South Lake Tahoe as a site for the railroad dates all the way back to the time a group of us decided to go on our own with a steam-operated, narrow gauge excursion railroad. Reasons include intense tourist activity here, the fact that the activity is well spread out over the week, and the scenery. The first actual exploration of the area for a good site was in 1966.*

"In April, 1967, a group of us made an elaborate presentation to the United States Forest Service to negotiate for terminals and routes on USFS land. The Service made no formal response to our presentation and did nothing in the way of continuing the discussions. We decided another approach would be necessary.

"In December, 1967, we contacted the Trimont Land Company, a subsidiary of Fiberboard Corp., developing a 25,000 acre holding. On April 17, we made a formal presentation, were complimented on it, and a good discussion followed with indication of serious Trimont interest. But a takeover battle developed between Fiberboard and Tenneco which held up Trimont, so we decided to dredge up an alternative as 'encouragement.' The alternative turned out to be the real thing.

"In May I called all Tahoe realtors with half-page ads in the phone book which led to connections with an old and influential family. Contacts were arranged with all property owners along a four-mile route. On June 22 I resigned at Hewlett Packard, and one partner offered to provide some financial support.

"This month's work included obtaining assessor's maps to verify land holdings, meetings with the Tahoe City Planner, presentations to civic groups and officials, informing the press, negotiating for some properties, beginning formulation of the corporate structure and 'pre-incorporation subscription agreements,' and investigation of insurance needs.

"We have one major problem. This may be serious or not, ruinous or not, or worth worrying about or not, depending on one's attitude and who he has talked to last. The

[3]Nancy Frazier, "Thriving at Home," *In Business* (March-April 1982), p. 36.

problem is that the supervisor of the El Dorado National Forest, Mr. Irwin Bosworth, has indicated in a letter to John Williams that the Forest Service is 'unalterably opposed' to the project. Locally, people say that this is the traditional way for the Forest Service to do business.

"*August 1968. At their meeting of August 1 the City Council unanimously approved preparation of a resolution favoring development of the railroad. Engineering practicality has also been established.*

"*Our first embarrassment with respect to property negotiations occurred when we found we had confused the meadow land owned by Wm. Ledbetter with that owned by Alva Barton. We hope an arrangement can be worked out with Miss Barton, who is Mr. Ledbetter's aunt.*

"*One of our most important meetings this month was with Mr. Irwin Bosworth. We have been promised a letter which will explain the Forest Service position. Negotiations for railroad equipment were carried on with Early West Park Railways and the D&GRW RR Co. Attempts to obtain track from L.B. Foster, railway supplies merchants, were not successful.*

"*September 1968. Summary — This has been a month made up of about equal parts of frustration, excitement and success, and it has about killed Keller. The frustration concerned one chunk of right-of-way, one steam locomotive, and communications with one property owner. The successes involved one chunk of right-of-way, a collection of locomotive parts and freight cars, and financial support for the project.*

"*The locomotive was one on display at a Hawaiian plantation. We learned of it Saturday evening Sept. 14. A child had fallen and been injured while playing on it, and the plantation management consequently wanted to get rid of the engine and was planning to cut it up Monday morning. Jay, chief procurer for the railroad, was willing to acquire it if we could guarantee backing. Since John Greco had earlier expressed interest in buying 'something with a boiler on it' we had several rounds of phone calls between him, Jay, and I, eventually reaching a satisfactory arrangement. Jay left Sunday morning for Hawaii, but unfortunately the Bishop Museum, official State Museum of Hawaii, had gotten into the act. We got the bad news Monday night.*"

Reports in this vein continued through the December report, which announced receipt of a Forest Service memo stating " . . . we would not support or oppose a project of this nature on private land in the Lake Tahoe Basin." Others announced approval by city and county planning offices, the regional planning agency, Division of Highways, a water district, property owners, other sources of railroad cars and equipment. An old diesel truck was bought for moving cars and approval for hauling was obtained from the ICC. The June, 1969 report announced "Keller decided on the 11th that he could operate the truck on the basis of engineering theory, experience with sports cars and gall, and found out that this was almost true." Eventually, all the permits were obtained, the locomotive was set up and run, and the enterprise began business. From that one Keller went on to a series of other excursion railroad adventures.

In this example, the entrepreneur had to rely on himself for getting things done. He could not ask a secretary to find out where land-holding information was filed and to obtain it because there was no secretary. He had to think about what kind of insurance was needed, what public and private agencies had to be contacted, when and for what to obtain an attorney, whether and where to buy a used diesel truck for hauling railroad cars, and where various facilities for the railroad such as fuel and water supplies, parking lots, tracks, and trash cans should be located. Meanwhile at home he was designing a special trailer to haul the cars, putting out the newsletter to partners, and in his garage overhauling running gear for the train by himself. The variety of tasks was tremendous, and the sole responsibility for the initiative and follow-through were on him alone.

The timing of events in Keller's start-up service were governed to a large extent by others. He and his partners could establish contacts and ask for decisions, for example, on permission for right of way, but then they had to wait for others to decide. Because there were so many contacts to be made, priorities had to be established, but often the significance of a given sequence choice became apparent only after the choice was made. For example, one contact might lead to another that could not reasonably have been foreseen. The total length of the sequence was longer than it would have been if there had been more Kellers working simultaneously, but because some contacting had to be done in sequence and some decisions were outside the partners' control, the path was inevitably a fairly long one no matter how many partners operated.

By choosing this particular venture, the entrepreneur had to be able to "hold his breath" both economically and psychologically for a long time. Dr. Keller's own concern about this showed up in his report dated December 1968:

■ *One item of some concern, everything being pretty close to wound up, is employment for Keller between the end of January and commencement of construction. Any suggestions will be appreciated.*

Some entrepreneurs cannot hold on long enough for permissions to come through. One Seattle area entrepreneur found that he had to close down his new restaurant because it could not break even on meals without liquor, and he ran out of time and resources to get a liquor license.

Prohibitions

Some kinds of ventures are permitted by the government even though the use of what they make is illegal (e.g., selling kits for brewing beer at home in Washington state). In other lines of activity, ventures are illegal even though the product and its use are not. For example, the government is inconsistent about permitting home textile work.[4] The U.S. Department of Labor lifted a forty-one-year-old ban in 1981, but it was overruled by a federal appeals court.[5] However, the 1938 Fair Labor Standards Act was invoked by the Labor Department against a Nebraska entrepreneur because the act "prohibits the home embroidery of clothing when the company does not manufacture the apparel."[6]

Sometimes government prohibitions are imposed not by law but by the bureaucracy. A dramatic example was the case of two inventors, introduced earlier in the discussion of patents (see Chapter 3), who were attempting to start an electronics business:

[4]"Home-Based Business," *In Business* (February 1984), p. 16.
[5]"Home-Based Business," *In Business* (June 1984), p. 19.
[6]William Mueller, "Beyond Blue Highways," *Venture* (August 1988), p. 42.

■ *Carl Nicolai and Bill Wright had come up with some new ideas in communication technology which they believed could be the basis of a whole series of new products. When they visited venture capitalists looking for development capital, they were turned down but told that their chances would be better if they had a working prototype and patent protection. So they went to work on a product prototype.*

The application they chose to pursue was that of a "voice scrambler." This was a device which could be plugged into a radio, telephone line, or tape recorder to transform voice sounds into a hiss which was unintelligible except to someone who possessed a decoding unit that would transform the hiss back into voice sounds. Thus messages could be protected from eavesdropping and information on tapes could be made inaccessible to everyone except a person with the appropriate decoder. Such devices were just coming onto the market, but whereas a police unit selling for $2,500 and requiring a $6,000 base station could only transform into 18 codes, the unit designed by Nicolai and Wright could accept thousands of codes and might sell for as little as $200.

Believing this should be a viable product, they applied for a patent on the technology and waited to hear from the patent office. Instead, they were shocked to receive a letter from the National Security Agency telling them that their technology had been classified secret by the U.S. government and telling them they could not use it without government permission under penalty of up to two years in jail, a $10,000 fine, and abandonment of the patent.

"It seems," Carl Nicolai said, "that if your patent falls into certain categories, which we suspect are computer generated, it triggers a review by the military and intelligence agencies, and they have the option to classify it, which is what happened to us.

"We started talking to people asking advice about what to do, and began to learn that there were only a few routes open to us. One would have been to just sit back and accept it. But we didn't want to do that. Another might have been to go to work for the government, as perhaps many people do. But we didn't want to be bought off like that.

"Still another would be to make an appeal of the secrecy order through channels the government considers appropriate. We met a man who tried this. He developed a device for monitoring railroad cars, an identification system which could determine the identity of any car by sending a beam against it. Wham, he got hit with a secrecy order on the device.

"So he started appealing it and went all the way up to the Secretary of the Treasury. They just told him, too bad. This went on for something like seven years, with him trying to work step by step through the channels, and finally after all that time they gave him a clearance. But by then his competitors, who had not filed for patents and had therefore not been hit with secrecy orders, had eaten him alive and it was too late for him to get into the market. Now he is trying to sue the government to recover damages for the loss.

"Finally, there was the alternative of mounting a counteroffensive against the government, and that is what we did. We engaged a public relations man who went to work on it and got results. We wrote to senators like Magnuson and Percy. The PR man got articles on us in publications like Science *and got us onto John Chancellor's TV news show. At one time we managed to be the number four most important story on the Associated Press news service.*

"The PR man also went to Washington D.C. and walked into the lion's den, the National Security Agency itself, put up with body searches and all the rest, to plead our case. If you are combating the federal bureaucracy you just about have to have somebody in the capital. When you are way out on the West Coast trying to deal with bureaucrats back there who can fine you, jail you, and play various games with you that take your time and burn up all your money on legal bills, it is very helpful to have someone back there who will walk into their office as soon as they come down on you and ask what they think they are doing.

"Then he goes to your congressman's office and says, 'Hey, do you know what the government here is doing to your constituents?' And then the congressman calls the bureaucrat's boss and asks what is going on over there in the bureau. That gets results.

"One of the best tools we learned about was the Freedom of Information Act. It turns out that if you file a freedom of information request asking about what they are doing to you and what the legal basis for that action is, they have to answer you within 15 days or you can immediately file suit. The idea of this from our point of view was to make it very expensive and troublesome for them to pick on us. If they can see it will cut deeply into their budget to do it, they are more inclined to think twice about whether it is really worthwhile to go after you.

"That is what we did, and it worked. Right after all the publicity started coming out we got another letter from them saying they had reconsidered the matter and decided to give us a rescinding order. Notice, they did it by another order. It wasn't just a letter telling us we could go our own way. They had to tell us they were giving us an order.

"Now we are authorized to make scramblers for use on the marine, aviation, and public safety channels. We think the biggest market would clearly be on the citizen's band, but the FCC for some reason tells us that it is illegal for people to keep their conversations quiet with scramblers on CB. Why this is we don't know. I guess people in the government just really like to govern. Anyway, it could be that they don't have a legal basis for that, but we can't bother with fighting it now.

"One thing we have decided is that we certainly won't go after any more patents on the products we plan to develop. That way at least we can't get hit with secrecy orders."

It should also be noted that government prohibitions sometimes work in favor of entrepreneurs. Market opportunities in consulting and even new hardware are sometimes created by passage of new laws concerning such things as safety and pollution. Real estate opportunities can be opened up by changes in zoning laws. Even antitrust laws can sometimes be very helpful to new ventures, as will be illustrated later in connection with legal disagreements.

Requirements

It can be hard or impossible in regulated industries to escape extensive paperwork and other requirements. To start an insurance company, for instance, according to Bekey:

> State laws mandate minimum start-up capital, averaging around $1 million, although a company planning to write only specialized coverage, such as plate-glass insurance, might be started for less. In addition, some states require set-aside sums based on projected costs of doing business during the first few years to cover claims and salaries as well as a surplus to cover possible heavy losses.
>
> Start-ups must file applications detailing articles and bylaws, biographies of officers and principal stockholders, and information on what kinds of coverage the company plans to write and how the plans will be written. The firm's plans for raising start-up capital and financial projections for a given period of time (usually three to five years) are also required. State insurance commissions also closely monitor investments and operations, especially during the first few years.[7]

[7]Michelle Bekey, "The Big Bucks Insurance Game," *Venture* (September 1980), p. 52.

For other lines of business, regulatory constraints are looser, and entrepreneurs are able either to ignore government requirements (except for taxes) or to find ways of working with them. A few small business operators suggested the following:

■ A store manager said, *"when my inventory gets extra large at Christmastime, I call the fire chief and tell him all the boxes are piled in a corner carefully with a no-smoking notice by them. He tells me that is all his people would be looking for anyway, and I don't get an inspection."*

■ A metal fabricator submitted the low bid on a city job but ran into difficulty on one of the forms in a thick stack which had to be filled out. *"It was the pink one which deals with affirmative action,"* the businessman recalled, *"and we didn't fill it out. The city wanted us to complete it so they could give us the job, because they knew the one other firm that bid was not competent. I asked if their own office had fully complied with affirmative action. They laughed. I said we would complete the form when their office was in compliance. We got the job without the form."*

■ In the fall of 1963 a man working as an installer for a Seattle cable television company visited an outlying town and noticed that its TV reception, where there was no cable, was quite poor. He knocked on several doors and found residents who were receptive to the idea of renting cable. Using his car as collateral, he borrowed $1,000 from the bank, bought some used cable TV equipment and by the fall of 1964 had 17 subscribers. Six months later the local city hall learned about his system and informed him he had to have a franchise. He made application, and after another six months, doing business all the while, received it. Then the phone company learned he was using their poles for his lines. He negotiated a lease with them. From there he expanded to more customers and other cities.

■ The opening day of Debbi Fields's first cookie shop began with a government inspection which she recalled: *"The first person who showed up was the health inspector, Bernie Tom. We had met many times before and I knew he was a nice man, always kind, always reassuring. He had coached me until I understood the health department rules and regulations and what compliance actually meant. He seemed to think that it was his job to help me meet the codes and get the approvals, and he was never suspicious or hostile. Once I understood the health standards, they actually made lots of sense, and I wanted to do the right thing. That morning he made sure the sneeze-guard (a sheet of glass between the customer and the product) was properly in place, and wished me luck."*[8]

It is generally desirable to accommodate to government constraints, as in these examples. Unfortunately, at other times, it may not work.

Taxes

One governmental requirement that can have a crucial and direct impact upon cash flow and therefore on the capability of the venture to survive and grow is tax obligations. Roger Melen of Cromemco (see Chapter 5) observed that "cash

---

[8]Debbi Fields and Alan Furst, *One Smart Cookie* (New York: Simon & Schuster, 1987), p. 77.

flow can kill faster than profits can cure, and running out of cash is the greatest threat to a small company."[9] He sought to minimize cash drain not only by keeping an outside job and taking no cash from the start-up, but also by the following legal tax moves:

- Taking, on the books, the maximum salary allowable by IRS rules as an expense deduction, to reduce reported earnings and corresponding taxes for the company
- Adopting the fastest allowable depreciation schedules on company equipment to maximize that as an expense deduction
- Paying employee bonuses in stock through an Employee Stock Option Plan (ESOP) by having the company "buy" stock from its treasury, which was a tax-deductible expense, then selling it to a profit-sharing trust, which let the company keep the cash

If the prospective venture is to be small and low profit, then tax considerations are correspondingly small. State and local taxes for such firms are routine matters, and the federal income taxes can be left as part of the entrepreneur's personal income picture. However, if the venture is to become large, then the tax consequences of early decisions, such as whether, when, and how to incorporate, can be expensive matters. Then economizing such taxes and attracting capital by designing the enterprise to include tax advantages for investors become important. The entrepreneur needs some knowledge of the tax considerations that may be important, as well as tax advisers, accountants, and/or lawyers who are up-to-date tax specialists.

The entrepreneur cannot hope to know all about the important tax issues personally: First, to learn that information would take all the time available and leave none for the rest of the start-up job; and second, the tax laws constantly change, and information the entrepreneur might learn for start-up would soon be out-of-date unless he or she continued to study taxes instead of working on the enterprise.

The first objective with taxes must be to comply with federal, state, and local laws and avoid legal trouble. An illustrative list, using San Diego, California, as an example, appears in Exhibit 9–2. Sources of information include the federal Internal Revenue Service, which publishes a free booklet, Publication 344, entitled *Tax Guide for Small Businesses*, state departments of revenue, and, for local taxes, city hall.

Legal Business Form. The legal form chosen for the business has an important bearing on federal taxes. If the venture is not incorporated, then income taxes are paid by the owner or owners at regular individual income tax rates. This can be an advantage if the business is losing money, because the proprietor or partners can then deduct the business losses against other income. It is even possible to distribute the losses unevenly, if for example one partner claims the real estate and its depreciation as his or her share of the partnership. Those expenses can be taken

---

[9]Robert A. Mamis, "Cromemco's Never Taken a Dime from Anyone," *Inc.* (November 1981), p. 117.

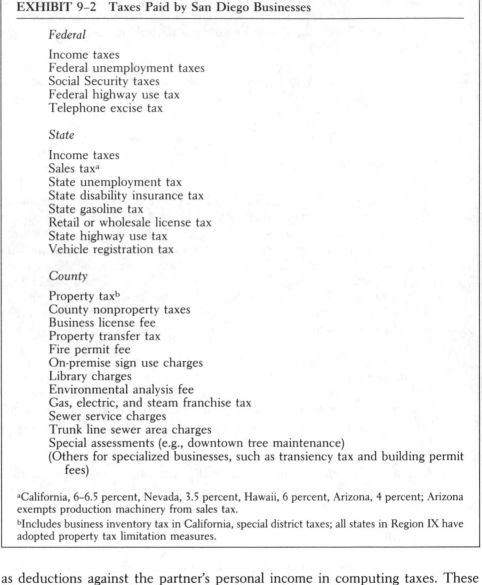

EXHIBIT 9–2   Taxes Paid by San Diego Businesses

Federal

Income taxes
Federal unemployment taxes
Social Security taxes
Federal highway use tax
Telephone excise tax

State

Income taxes
Sales tax[a]
State unemployment tax
State disability insurance tax
State gasoline tax
Retail or wholesale license tax
State highway use tax
Vehicle registration tax

County

Property tax[b]
County nonproperty taxes
Business license fee
Property transfer tax
Fire permit fee
On-premise sign use charges
Library charges
Environmental analysis fee
Gas, electric, and steam franchise tax
Sewer service charges
Trunk line sewer area charges
Special assessments (e.g., downtown tree maintenance)
(Others for specialized businesses, such as transiency tax and building permit
    fees)

[a]California, 6–6.5 percent, Nevada, 3.5 percent, Hawaii, 6 percent, Arizona, 4 percent; Arizona
exempts production machinery from sales tax.
[b]Includes business inventory tax in California, special district taxes; all states in Region IX have
adopted property tax limitation measures.

as deductions against the partner's personal income in computing taxes. These features of loss-flow through and unevenness are sometimes used to advantage in raising capital from wealthy people who welcome the tax deductions. To protect them from personal liabilities, such partnerships are normally cast in "limited" (Ltd) form. If the business is incorporated, this direct flow through feature can be retained by forming a "Subchapter S" corporation, which also retains the liability protection of the corporation for its owners.

If the entrepreneur is operating the business as the sole proprietor, tax information can be filed on the Schedule C form that comes in the individual tax information book from the Internal Revenue Service. The individual's Social Security number serves as the taxpayer identification number on Form 1040. For partnerships and corporations, other tax filing forms, such as Form 1065 for partnership income or Form 1120 for corporation income, are required. In addition to the individual's Social Security Number, an Employer Identification Number (EIN), which can be obtained by filing form SS-4 with the Internal Revenue Service, is required.

It is often desirable for a new company to start out with Subchapter S status because investors can deduct the early losses though they will have to pay the personal income tax rates on any profits. That rate starts at 15 percent and rises to 28 percent at profits of $30,000. When the venture moves into the black, it can choose a shift to regular C corporation status, which has a tax rate of 15 percent on the first $50,000 of taxable income that jumps to 25 percent on the next $25,000 and 34 percent above that. Any dividends paid out, however, will be subject to personal income tax and thus be doubly taxed. But a C corporation can carry losses forward and backward, whereas an S corporation cannot.

There can be other reasons to shift a corporation from S to C status. An S corporation is limited to thirty-five shareholders, none of whom can be another corporation, a trust, an estate, or a foreigner. Only one class of shares, common stock, is allowed in a Sub S corporation. Some group benefits such as deductible medical benefits, life insurance, and deferred compensation are denied to Sub S corporations. Its tax year cannot begin on any month, which sometimes gains cost advantages in hiring accounting firms, as can a C corporation, but must coincide with the calendar year. Once the shift from S to C is made, however, it cannot be reversed for another five years.[10]

The trouble with a C corporation is that it is difficult for investors to get cash out without being taxed a second time on the company profit. If the entrepreneur tries to pull money out as additional salary, the IRS may declare it excessive and impose more taxes. If the money is allowed to pile up in the business as either cash or securities, the IRS will apply a surtax of 28 percent on everything above $150,000 for a service business or above $250,000 for other types of businesses. The best hope may be to either sell off the business at that point to someone who can find a good business use for the money or apply the money to further development of the company. Buying a building is one remedy. Others are investing in expanding sales, acquiring another business, and setting up reserves for contingencies such as liability claims or repaying debt.

With a C corporation, it is important to have the stock classified as Section 1244 stock at the outset. Then investors can deduct any capital losses on that stock (although they hope there will not be any) against their personal income. Otherwise, they could only credit such losses against capital gains. This can be done in conjunction with a Subchapter S corporation, but some other things cannot without nullifying the effect of such a corporation. During the first year, it is

---

[10]Douglas H. Forde, "The Trouble with S Corporations," *Inc.* (May 1987), p. 141.

advisable to deduct all the organizational expenses and all the R&D expenses and to set up a bad debt reserve, all of which reduce the profit on which the company is taxed.

These are only a few main points for entrepreneurs to consider regarding the taxation of start-ups, they are by no means all. Tax angles can become much more subtle and complicated, as illustrated by the following situations:

■ *An inventor had developed and patented a new product for which there appeared to be a promising market. He formed a corporation to protect himself from personal liability and then transferred his patent to the corporation. Then he started selling licenses for use of the invention to others. The result was that because the only source of income to his corporation was from license fees, the corporation was declared to be a "personal holding company," which subjected it to extraordinarily high tax charges. If he had simply given 20 percent of his stock to his relatives, he could have cut his tax bill in half.*

■ *Another inventor did bring in other investors for 50 percent of the stock in a corporation which he formed to develop a new product. The investors put up all the money, and he agreed to provide his services in return for the 50 percent of stock which he retained. Immediately he became liable for taxes on the stock he received because the capital from the other investors made it worth money, whereas the agreement for his services was not so viewed. Had he instead formed the corporation owning 100 percent of the stock himself, which he took in return for drawings and other property of his own transferred to that corporation, then he could have sold stock to the other investors without incurring a tax burden.*

■ *Two entrepreneurs formed a corporation. One transferred some of his personal property to the corporation in return for stock. The other paid in cash for a five-year note. In recognition of this loan the second man received stock. Because of this sequence and the fact that the first man now held less than 80 percent of the stock, the second man now had to pay tax on the stock he received. If the second man had received some stock for his cash, it could have been a tax-free transfer.*

The point of these examples is not to show everything that can go wrong if tax angles are not properly anticipated, but rather how easy it is to make mistakes if tax rules are not carefully considered. Advice at the right time from a lawyer or accountant expert in taxes could easily ward off such problems. At the very least, it should preclude giving the government an excuse to make trouble over taxes, as illustrated by the following cases, first at state and then the federal levels:

■ *Three years after start-up, a small machine shop in Washington was audited by the state and billed $8,000 for past due state sales taxes. It had been determined that some customers of the shop, who had told the shop that parts made for them would be resold by them, had actually not resold those parts but had used them in their own activities. Had they resold the parts, it would have been all right that they had not been charged sales tax by the machine shop. But because they used the parts instead, the shop should have charged them the tax and remitted it to the state.*

The entrepreneur decided to fight the case. He produced purchase orders which showed the customers had stated they planned to resell the goods. For two years his battle continued, by which time, he said, the state had backed down to $500 as its demand. But *the entrepreneur decided to fight further. "I called a local politician who was up for reelection and explained the case," he said. "Two days later a man from the tax office came by, fell all over himself apologizing for the mistake they had made and told me they were dropping it."*

■ *The owner of a small Washington state timber company recounted that he was asked to meet with a state revenue agent who claimed that more state taxes were due on certain shipments of lumber marked F.O.B. the owner's plant and pickup by the customer's truck. The owner said this would include use by the customer of a common carrier. The agent said it had to be a truck owned by the customer and labeled with his name. The owner went to his lawyer, fought the case, and won.*

Shortly thereafter a federal Internal Revenue Service agent showed up at his plant to do an audit. "This guy told me he would help himself to whatever files he wanted and I told him that wasn't the way it would be. I said he would have to request the file he wanted, and then I would get it and I would have someone stay right with him to make sure nothing was removed from or added to it." The agent left and several weeks later returned to say it would be done the owner's way.

For five years, the entrepreneur said, an agent visited periodically on this basis, and then one day announced that another $118,000 was due to the government. "One thing he questioned was a ten-day trip to the East Coast costing $1,800," the owner recalled. "I told him I could prove that $170,000 in sales orders resulted from it. Then he asked if that was so, how come I charged $75 to personal expenses. I told him I did do some personal things, like get a haircut and shoeshine and maybe even bought a magazine."

Many hours of negotiations and verification of records followed after which the case was settled for $27,000.

It is much to the entrepreneur's advantage to head off problems of this sort before they ever arise, and some precautions include (1) calling the Internal Revenue Service and city hall with a request that they send current information about business taxes, (2) reading the general information and learning some of the main terms and tax angles, and (3) having plans reviewed by a lawyer and/or accountant who *specializes* in business taxes to learn whether anything important has been overlooked. It can be very expensive to visit such people looking for a general education on tax matters. It is more economical to read first, work up plans, and then get reactions on specific issues.

OTHER LEGAL ASPECTS

Throughout the preceding chapters, numerous topics requiring legal knowledge and intervention have repeatedly cropped up. Patent, trademark, and/or copyright protection is often an early issue. Forming the corporation or partnership, working out financing terms with investors or lenders, making arrangements with sales agents or distributors, and working out leases and employment agreements are others. In each case, there is the option of trying to work out the legal aspects personally. That can save cash, but it costs time and if incompetently done it can lead to serious problems. There is no complete assurance that incompetence will be avoided by using a lawyer, but if the lawyer is carefully chosen, the odds of ending up with legal problems can be greatly diminished.

Getting a Lawyer

Exhibit 9–3 provides a list of areas in which lawyers may help forestall legal problems and deal with them in the event that they do arise. These areas include written work such as drafting contracts, making court appearances, and also some less legalistic activities, such as reviewing business plans or introducing the entrepreneur to other helpful business contacts. The most common uses of attorneys, according to a 1982 *Inc.* survey, were for contracts and agreements, personal needs of top management, incorporation, lawsuits, real estate, and insurance issues. Over time, use for all these purposes increased, lawsuits the most.[11]

One risk is that the same lawyer whose caution will guide the client away from dangers will also impose overconservative and negative thinking that squelches legitimate opportunities. Thus, there are two types of mistakes that may follow from poor legal advice: those that allow the client to get into trouble and those that cause the client to miss good opportunities. The first typically remains invisible until it is too late and the trouble has already arrived. The latter may never

---

EXHIBIT 9–3   Areas Where Lawyers Can Help

1. Giving advice and asking questions to forestall both personal and business problems
2. Developing and processing patent applications and later litigation
3. Arranging introductions to helpful business contacts
4. Forming and filing the corporate papers
5. Guiding initial stockholders' meeting, elections, and procedures
6. Selecting corporate name and issuing stock to founders
7. Determining distribution of equity; setting up options
8. Drafting employment contracts and nondisclosure and noncompetition agreements
9. Setting up pension, profit sharing, stock option, and employee ownership plans
10. Finding potential investors
11. Preventing violation of securities laws
12. Drafting or reviewing leases
13. Drafting or reviewing purchasing agreements
14. Assisting in buy-sell and other negotiations
15. Checking insurance contracts for adequacy
16. Handling lawsuits
17. Licensing
18. Reviewing leases and rental agreements
19. Advising on taxes
20. Helping with governmental applications and reports

---

[11]Bradford W. Ketchum, Jr., "You and Your Attorney," *Inc.* (June 1982), p. 51.

reveal itself at all. Both must be headed off in advance by selecting the lawyer most likely to do a good job.

The best criterion for selecting the right lawyer for the right job is proven experience and performance in similar jobs. The way to find one is by asking around. Other entrepreneurs, bankers, and accountants are particularly likely sources. A source of information that can be found in the library is Martindale and Hubble's *Law Directory*, which tells which attorneys have which specialties, where they went to school, and to some extent what reputations they have.[12] People who simply select lawyers from the *Yellow Pages* or limit their search to friends, neighbors, and relatives tend to make poor choices. Attorneys sometimes do not acknowledge the areas they are not equipped to handle, keeping open their option to fee split. But the client then does not know who is doing the work.

Entrepreneurs may be deterred from shopping around for a lawyer because of a fear of having to pay high fees. Lawyers charge for their time. The entrepreneur can state that the purpose of an initial interview is not to obtain advice but rather to become acquainted and to learn what the charges will be and when they will begin. A lawyer will usually be willing to talk for a short time under those conditions and will also be willing to tell when charging will begin. At that point the client can either continue the discussion or leave without being charged. When the charges do start, they typically range upward from $100 per hour for an experienced lawyer.

An entrepreneur must also choose between a large law firm or a small one. Large firms contain many specialists to draw upon as well as established names and many high-level business contacts. The disadvantage of the large firm is that it may only assign junior people to work on the cases of a small client. They will say these people are backed up by senior people in the firm who will make sure things turn out all right. But how can the client know? And if junior people are just as good, why aren't they assigned to the large clients rather than the small ones?

A smaller law firm, on the other hand, will more likely bring the entrepreneur into direct working contact with senior people. To compensate for the lack of specialists, a generalist in the smaller firm may argue that he or she has a broader perspective and will be in a better position to determine what specialists will be needed and brought in from other firms—a common practice. For these reasons, many experienced entrepreneurs prefer to deal with smaller firms that are experienced with corporate legal work and have good reputations. Young lawyers just starting out usually charge substantially lower rates, but they can produce costly mistakes and oversights.

Most important is the individual with whom the entrepreneur will be dealing. Is it the same lawyer the entrepreneur met at the first interview, or will another be substituted once the law firm is engaged? Will that individual be available when needed? How fast or slow will his or her service be? (Law firms are notorious for

[12]Martindale-Hubbell Staff, *Martindale-Hubbell Law Directory* (1991).

taking days or weeks to type out a simple "boilerplate" document (standard printed form) and get it back to the client.) Will the individual be congenial to work with? Does he or she have the kind of legal mind that only sees reasons something cannot be done, or does he or she go further to suggest ways around legal obstacles to move ahead? Will that lawyer represent the venture well and enhance its image when he or she is identified to others as counsel for the venture? Will the lawyer likely develop a real interest and dedication to the success of the venture, judging from the experiences of other clients?

Helpful as lawyers are, however, the entrepreneur must retain responsibility for final decision making. To do this well, he or she will have to acquire some understanding of the law as it pertains to each problem that arises. The expensive way to do this is to be tutored by the attorney. It is more economical to read about the law and attempt to work the problem out as far as possible before checking with the attorney. Legal costs can also be controlled by requiring thorough periodic reporting of legal charges and reviewing them for possible errors or double billings. Lawyers can be delimited to spend only so much time on a given problem, and they can be asked to forecast what costs will be before proceeding.

Agreements

Many aspects of a new venture can be explored tentatively, and major commitments can be backed away from if it looks as if it will not work out. Prototype experimentation can often be done in a home shop for only the cost of parts and materials. Analysis of the market can be done with interviews that cost only time. Tentative discussions can be conducted with potential partners and backers. Plans can be conjured up and analyzed from any number of points of view, exploring the implications of different assumptions without making a firm commitment to any of them. If adequate profits do not appear certain enough to materialize, these plans can be scrapped with the only losses being the entrepreneur's time and the paper it took to write the plans out. Even the expense of having formed a corporation can easily be shrugged off with its termination.

But when contracts are signed that all changes. Now there is a definite commitment, and it usually involves a substantial amount of money. The money may be for payments under a rental agreement, expenses to a subcontract manufacturer to produce the first units, or to a supplier for initial inventory. Or a promise may have been made to a customer assuring delivery of the product or service the company is to produce. Once that promise is put in the form of a firm contract, the company is committed to it and must either deliver or else very likely go under, taking part of the entrepreneur's reputation and possibly much of his or her resources with it.

A start-up company can be particularly vulnerable to disagreement over deals. Someone who would not dream of holding back on fulfilling a contract with the government or a long-established company might feel differently about living up to promises to a new enterprise, which may not be around long or have strong resources to enforce the deal.

■ *A young company developed software to go with the new product of a manufacturer. Immediately after delivery of the software, however, the manufacturer's product was rendered obsolete by the new product of one of the manufacturer's competitors. The manufacturer refused to pay for the software. The young software developer sued for breach of contract but went bankrupt before the suit was settled.*[13]

What could the software developer have done? Maybe nothing, if the buyer was powerful enough. Or maybe he could have bargained for a better contract initially. Advance or partial payments would have helped. Promissory notes or an escrow account by the buyer might have helped even more.

Experience can be the most expensive teacher about such possibilities. Counsel from other entrepreneurs or attorneys may be more economical, and so may some study. The Uniform Commercial Code (UCC) is the law that governs such transactions in the United States. Ultimately, however, courts decide how to interpret it, as illustrated in the following case:

■ *In April and again in August, 1969, the two brothers named Cox contracted with a bowling equipment dealer for delivery and installation of equipment to build a new bowling alley. Neither contract specified a completion date. By September 4 most of the equipment was in, but didn't work right. Two days later, before being notified of this, the equipment dealer died. The Coxes complained to the executrix of the dealer's estate, but she did not immediately respond, so they hired others help to fix the alleys. Later, she sent help too, but the Coxes turned it away. She sued for full payment and the Coxes countersued for damages due to delay of being able to open their alley. The court decided against the Coxes, saying they owed payment for the equipment. Then an appeals court reversed the decision. Issues were whether the UCC applied to a combination of goods and services (it does, but not to services alone), whether the Coxes had sufficiently notified the dealer's estate that delivering inoperative equipment was a breach of contract (it was), and whether the dealer's estate had abandoned them when it did not respond to their complaint more quickly (it had).*[14]

This illustrates how legal relationships can become complex, even on simple things such as buying and selling services between firms. It also stresses the need for care in making contracts and for engaging attorneys to help with major contracts.

The best way to utilize a lawyer in negotiating agreements has been the subject of considerable debate, as Lipper points out.[15] Letting an attorney negotiate gives the entrepreneur a chance to second-guess a deal. But if one party brings a lawyer in, the other is likely to also. Then there will the cost of two, and lawyers are notorious for finding ways to create complications that they must then be paid to solve. It probably makes sense to have an attorney review any written agree-

[13]Miles Stuchin, "When It's Time to Be Paid," *Venture* (September 1982), p. 14.
[14]Raymond D. Watts and Neal L. Thomas, "The Binding Boundaries of Contracts," *In Business* (March-April 1982), p. 51.
[15]Arthur Lipper III, *Venture's Financing and Investing in Private Companies* (Chicago: Probus Publishing, 1988), p. 168.

ment, because whoever writes it will tend to build into it the best terms from his or her own point of view. But it also makes sense to negotiate directly without attorneys first and then charge attorneys with the task of making whatever is agreed to legal and binding on paper.

Disagreements

Start-ups are less likely to be sued and thus to need *defense* than established businesses, partly because they have had less time and fewer encounters with anyone to be sued about and partly because their lack of wealth makes them relatively unattractive targets. Unfortunately, they are also less able to afford powerful legal help and therefore more likely to lose in case of suit. If a suit does arise, the rule again is to seek a lawyer who is experienced and successful in the specialty that fits the occasion. The lawyer will help in deciding whether there is insurance coverage, how to handle records and information, and whether to seek a settlement out of court.[16]

Ventures can also take the *offense* and initiate lawsuits if they believe they are illegally injured by established companies.

■ *Two men began in their spare time to look for foreign products on which they might obtain U.S. importing and distribution rights. One such product was a Korean-manufactured racketball. Taking it to some professional players for testing, they found it to be fully up to domestic performance specifications, although its price was considerably lower. They signed on a professional to endorse the product and made application to have the ball certified for tournament play.*

They had trouble obtaining the certification, and indirectly they were informed that a large domestic ball manufacturer had put pressure on the tournament associations not to grant it. Without certification, professionals would not want to practice with the balls, coaches would not use it, and consequently many others would also not want to use it.

Sales were disappointing and the import venture failed. The founders discussed their problems with a law firm, which offered to sue, for a percentage of any award, the large ball manufacturer and one of the associations for violation of the Sherman Antitrust Act, a law that awards triple damages to injured parties. The case settled out of court.

This last case illustrates how government prohibitions can work in favor of an entrepreneur.

INSURANCE

Protection against many types of calamities, including some kinds of lawsuits, can be purchased in the form of insurance. Product liability insurance was mentioned earlier in connection with product development. This is only one of several to consider in start-up, even before doing business or signing a lease. Who, for

[16]Andrea Sachs, "When You Are Sued," *Venture* (August 1984), p. 35.

example, will be responsible for damage to rented property? Will the landlord's insurance cover any damage done by customers of the business? If it does, but the new business causes the premium rates to rise, who is responsible for paying the increased costs? Is there a need for boiler insurance, and if so, who should pay for that? It is possible to pay for insurance and not be protected by it, as happened in the following case:

■ *The landlord had an insurance policy on the building and the tenant paid the premiums. A fire struck, and the landlord asked for payment from the insurance company. He got the payment, but then the insurance company sued the tenant company and collected because the policy did not protect the tenant.*

An entrepreneur unfamiliar with such technical details amid the myriad other tasks of getting a company started should seek advice from people who know about insurance, such as general insurance brokers, trade associations in the company's line of business, other entrepreneurs in the same field, insurance consultants, and attorneys. All but the last two will probably provide information without charge. It may be most economical to begin with the former and then decide whether to pay for additional counsel.

Types of Coverage

Some types of insurance to consider include the following:

1. Product liability insurance
2. Liability insurance on the company's location
3. Liability protection for retired owner[17]
4. Casualty insurance
5. Fire, storm, and flood insurance
6. Demolition coverage
7. Rent insurance
8. Glass insurance
9. Earthquake insurance
10. Computer coverage
11. Loss of income or business interruption insurance
12. Vehicle coverage
13. Crime (including theft) insurance
14. Errors and omissions insurance
15. Fidelity bonding
16. Worker's compensation
17. Unemployment insurance
18. Group health coverage
19. Disability coverage
    a. For employees
    b. For owners (may include income replacement and/or business overhead during disability)

[17]"Liability Policies for Retired Owners," *Inc.* (October 1982), p. 31.

20. Life insurance
    a. For employees (group coverage)
    b. For executives (key person insurance)
    c. To cover buy-sell agreements
    d. To cover mortgages and loans
    e. For deferred compensation

It is not obvious from the names of the different types of insurance just what they do. For instance, fidelity bonding may reimburse a temporary help service if its employees make off with its clients' goods or cash. Errors and omissions insurance can, under certain circumstances, cover theft of proprietary information.[18] Key person life insurance (decreasing term is particularly inexpensive) can help assure prospective investors or lenders that they will recover their money if something happens to the entrepreneur or other irreplaceable people in the venture. Business interruption coverage makes up for income lost if the business is interrupted by a disaster, possibly including the failure of a supplier. Extra expenses is a cheaper variation for a business whose interruption is quickly correctable.[19] It covers extra costs of the quick correction but not income lost. Some types of coverage, such as worker's compensation and unemployment insurance, may be governed by both federal and state laws and agencies.

There are "package" deals from large insurance companies that contain combinations of coverage, much like homeowners' insurance does.[20] However, it is important to analyze each element of coverage separately to make sure it makes sense, is adequate, and is appropriately economical. Cross-checks can be made through obtaining additional opinions from other companies and insurance consultants. Some are better qualified than others. The designations CLU (Certified Life Underwriter) and ChFC (Certified Financial Consultant) denote extensive training.

Not all these types of insurance are needed at company inception. Some are eliminated if there is no leased space. Others do not apply until there are employees or partners. The planning process can schedule when they will come into play; then, when they are needed, it will not be necessary to spend much time worrying about them. They can be put in force according to a prearranged schedule with the company's insurance broker.

ACCOUNTING

The need for accounting begins as soon as money leaves or enters the enterprise. Even if it is only to track expenses in developing a prototype or buying information, some record-keeping arrangement is needed. The company may work its

[18]Doreen Mangan, "Using Temps With Care," *Venture* (August 1988), p. 75.
[19]Sid Kane, "Business Interruption Insurance," *Venture* (March 1984), p. 41.
[20]James P. Roscow, "Insuring for Growth and Safety," *Venture* (October 1986), p. 65.

bookkeeping system up slowly as needs dictate or start out with a full-blown system set up by a CPA. Most new companies do the former, which is adequate provided that the system keeps up with needs, rather than falling behind and having to catch up in response to expensive problems.

Purposes

In choosing a first accounting system, trade-offs will include the costs in both cash and founders' time versus purposes of the system, which include

- Governmentally required tax reporting
- Raising capital
- Controlling expenditures
- Reporting
- Analyzing company performance
- Valuing the venture for merger, sell-off, or inheritance

Each purpose imposes particular requirements on the accounting system, and designing it to satisfy them all can become complex.

Taxes.   Keeping track of tax-deductible expenses, even before the venture is really started, may be the predominant initial purpose for the accounting system. The main basis for tax savings will be deduction of business expenses. Virtually all costs associated with the development of the business can be deducted as business expenses, including materials and subcontract work on prototypes; business phone calls and travel by car or carrier; office utilities; professional fees from lawyers, accountants, and consultants; and entertainment and promotion expenses associated with developing the business. Also deductible are automobile mileage or costs, costs of attending conventions, and some kinds of educational programs.

The easiest way to keep track of expenses is to pay by check or charge card and to save stubs and receipts so they can be tallied up later. Every receipt has a value in tax savings. Out-of-pocket expenses can also be noted on a pocket calendar, to record the date, amount, and purpose of each.

If any equipment is bought for the new company, it should immediately be set up on a depreciation schedule for tax deductions. Allowable depreciation rates depend on the kind of property. There are three basic options for computing depreciation. The straight-line method calculates the annual deduction by dividing the number of years the equipment should last into the cost of the equipment. The declining balance method, which can only be used for equipment lasting three or more years, applies a fixed percentage each year (up to double the straight-line percentage) to the depreciated value left from the prior year until salvage value is reached. It offers an extra fast write-off in the first couple of years, then slower ones after that.

The third method, called sum-of-digits, is a bit more complicated and offers still faster write-off early with a slowdown later. The Internal Revenue Service provides information on how to perform these calculations and also a table indicating what life spans are acceptable for different types of equipment. The entrepreneur's decision must be whether it is advantageous to write off quickly, as it would be if the company were to attain profitability early, or to wait until later for the write-off, as might be preferable if a few years of losses are expected to follow start-up.

From time to time, it is also possible to claim an investment tax credit on new equipment bought for use in the business. The rules on this and other tax computations change. So if the amounts involved become large, it will be advisable to engage an accountant with tax expertise to make the most of the current regulations. Until such an adviser is engaged, the best rule is to document and date all expenditures so they can later be figured into income computations and deducted.

One early decision that can have important tax consequences is the choice of tax year. Unless the corporation is Subchapter S, any month can be chosen to end the first year, regardless of when it begins, but after that it needs to stay either on a twelve-month basis ending always with that month or else on an accounting period of 52 or 53 weeks chosen to end on the same day of the week each year. The choice matters both for the sake of first-year tax calculations and because it can be hard to change later.

Another early accounting decision with long-run tax implications is whether to use a cash or an accrual method of accounting or some combination of the two. The cash method is simpler and has the advantage of deferring income, because sales are not noted when they are billed but rather later when they are collected. Expenses are charged against income as soon as they are paid, and it may be possible to charge off the labor that goes into making products that way too, rather than accumulating it as part of inventory. Thus, income can be slowed on the books and expenses speeded up to result in lower apparent profits for tax purposes.

However, there are limitations with this method as well. Some things cannot be immediately expensed out. For instance, equipment must be depreciated over time rather than being charged as an expense when paid for. From a management point of view, the cash basis can give an unrealistic picture of what is happening because it initially tends to understate sales and overstate expenses.

Tax accounting purposes and management accounting purposes are often different. For example, tax computations allow carry-forward and carry-back of losses that do not reflect operating performance; tax depreciation may be less realistic than management analysis calls for; and management may find it useful to make corrections for inflation that tax computations cannot recognize. Hence, there may at times be valid reasons for keeping tax entries that are different from managerial accounting entries.

Control.   Setting up a suitable accounting system is the first of three needed links in a chain. The second is to enter data on an up-to-date basis, and the third is to make good use of the information they provide. Studies of business failures have found high correlation with inadequate accounting, though whether as a cause or an effect can be hard to discern.[21] It is possible to find many small companies with poor bookkeeping systems that manage to continue and even thrive. Some small firm owners are not eager to have their books reveal too clearly just how high their profits really are, because that could increase their taxes. One entrepreneur commented:

■ *We're not too careful about taking inventory. I just make an estimate, and if the tax collector wants to argue that I should be paying more inventory tax, why then he can go out there into the shop and count it himself. So far he hasn't.*

This man's system worked largely because he was close to the business. It was small and intuitively he had a good idea of what the real figures were. If the business were larger or he were less in touch with it, a loose system would leave him open to losses from inefficiencies or pilferage that might not show up in the books before a great deal of money had been lost.

Many other cases can be found, as illustrated by the next example, where an appropriately designed system enables the venture to anticipate and seize opportunities that might otherwise be missed:

■ *An agricultural implement dealer, with a small construction equipment business as a sideline, noticed a dollar-volume shift in his business toward newly developed light construction equipment. With that information he began a study that resulted in a large scale shift of resources to the new field. Subsequently, in the face of a declining agricultural industry, his business quadrupled as a result of rapid growth in the construction equipment area.*

If the venture is to manufacture products with many parts, attention should be given at the outset to the possibility of computer coding and tracking inventory. As early as 1983, *Venture* reported that 90 percent of venture capital-backed start-ups utilized formal materials resource planning (MRP) systems.[22] Although such a system may not be essential at the start when production is simple, it becomes more important as the number of parts and products grows. The danger of beginning without it is that employees will develop their own noncomputerized ways of tracking parts and will then have trouble un-learning them when computerization becomes essential.

Raising Capital. Any bankers or venture capitalists approached for financing will want to see reliable financial statements, as in the following situation described by an MBA graduate who went to work as the business manager of a small company:

[21]William M. Hoad and Peter Rosko, *Management Factors Contributing to the Success and Failure of New Small Manufacturers* (Ann Arbor, MI: Bureau of Business Research, University of Michigan, 1964).

[22]G. Thomas Gibson, "Inventory Planning," *Venture* (August 1983), p. 25.

■ *When I arrived on the scene in October the company was facing a rapid sales growth from its very small beginnings, and it needed venture capital fast to take advantage of those sales. The owner had employed a bookkeeper, but she did not know double entry bookkeeping. The bank, where he had pushed his borrowing to the limit, had persuaded him to bring in a public accounting firm to set up books four months earlier in July. They had worked up a chart of accounts and books and had made opening entries, which they had to estimate, since the owner did not want to pay them for more than that. His other concession had been to buy a book on accounting for the bookkeeper, but she had not yet been able to read it because things at the office were so hectic. She was operating out of a checkbook and a few single entry books, but the double entry system was a blank for the four months since the opening entries had been made.*

The venture capitalists we approached wanted not only up-to-date statements, but audited ones as well before they would give the company any money. We worked day and night for several weeks while I learned the things about accounting that I needed to know beyond the MBA course to really run books and the bookkeeper kept things running as usual in addition to giving me what I needed for starting a real system. We finally got it sorted out, produced some statements with audited balance sheets (the income statement could not be audited, since that would have required an additional opening audit the prior year) and got the venture capital. But we missed some business opportunities during this catch-up crunch, and the bookkeeper collapsed with pneumonia when it was over. The audit also cost the owner extra because of the overtime pressure on the CPA firm and the messy condition of the original records.

In contrast, another entrepreneur who brought in an accounting firm from the outset paid more money sooner for his accounting system, but he avoided such headaches later on. He described what prompted him to do so:

■ *My investor was putting up the money with the understanding that I would do the work, we would share the stock, and he would be repaid in cash. So I could not afford casual bookkeeping. I had a first-class accounting firm come in and set up the books as well as provide us with audited statements right from the day we opened up a bank account to begin the company.*

If a company ever plans to issue stock publicly, then depending upon the size and type of that offering, it may need audited statements beforehand. For some types of offerings, audited statements *from the venture's inception* will be required.

Reporting.   If the company plans to do work for the government, there may be record and reporting requirements imposed by that work. They can depend upon whether the work is to be charged on a time and materials, cost plus fixed fee, or fixed-price basis.

Shareholders are also entitled to financial reports. If they become anxious because the reports are late, incomplete, or inaccurate, they may begin pestering management, which consumes time and is distracting, or even file lawsuits that could destroy the company.

As the company grows, obviously the accounting system will be a key to making effective management decisions. At some point in the company's life, the accounting records may be needed for establishing value for estate purposes or to sell out.

Alternatives in Accounting Systems

Accounting systems evolve over time as different purposes arise for them, the number of transactions increases, and tasks in the venture become more specialized. The sort of system to begin with depends on how much is at stake, how massive and complex the start-up is, and how fast it is expected to change. For most ventures, the best way to start is with as simple a system as possible. The following are some forms through which the system may evolve:

Tax Records Only. Tax accounting records are an inescapable need of any venture. The federal form needed for this purpose is most likely the Schedule C for personal taxes, the partnership Form 1065, or the Corporation Return Form 1120.[23] These include accruals for depreciation and inventory; therefore, as soon as there is any equipment or inventory, more than a checkbook is required for bookkeeping. State requirements may include inventory, sales, and other records and should be determined at the outset by asking local authorities for instructions.

Store-Bought Books. Stationery stores normally carry various types of ledgers, registers, receipt pads, and looseleaf forms. Bookstores can offer handbooks, manuals, and textbooks on how to set up and run accounting systems.

Bank Help on Payroll. As soon as the company employs other people, accounting becomes more complicated. There must be deductions for the employees' income taxes and Social Security. In addition, the company must set aside amounts for state requirements such as unemployment and industrial insurance. Periodically, these other amounts must be paid to the government. If the company provides health care, life insurance, and retirement benefits, other deductions must be made for those.

To handle the routine of such payroll deductions and prepare paychecks for employees, many banks offer services to relieve small firms. Because it is so important that this be done in a timely, legal, and accurate manner, this service can be helpful as soon as the venture engages one or more employees beyond the founder.

Pegboard Systems. For transactions that require posting more than one entry (noting a withdrawal from inventory and at the same time posting the amount to accounts receivable, for example), there are pegboard systems for simultaneously overlaying the various forms to carbon-copy entries on the proper lines of each. These can be bought at stationers or ordered directly from manufacturers of the systems, such as Safeguard Business Systems.[24] The latter, who make their profits from resupplying the forms, will be glad to help set up the system.

Microcomputer Software. The problems of assuring that all the required entries are made and making the totals for various accounts add up correctly can

[23]*Tax Guide for Small Business* (Washington, DC: U.S. Government Printing Office).
[24]Safeguard Business Systems, 455 Maryland Drive, Fort Washington, PA 19034.

be greatly relieved by computerizing the process. Software stores offer many microcomputer programs for handling classes of accounts, such as inventory systems and accounts receivable systems, as well as comprehensive systems that combine the handling of different types of accounts.[25]

Service Bureau Help.   Rather than buying a computer, selecting software, and setting up its own system, the venture can contract out the processing of accounts to a service bureau that may offer greater computer power to handle a more complex set of accounts more comprehensively. This can reduce capital outlay requirements of the venture as well as provide continuity should there be a turnover of bookkeeping employees in the venture.

System Evolution

The accounting system may start with any of the previous alternatives and then incorporate any or all of the others. In the early stages of planning and prototyping, it may not make sense to set up a permanent system because the venture may be abandoned and any effort put into setting up an accounting system would be wasted. Receipts should be kept, however, for tax purposes.

As the likelihood of putting a product or service on the market increases, a longer-term accounting commitment should be considered. The bigger the start-up investment, the more formal the accounting system probably should be and vice versa. For starting small, a checkbook plus a few pads of forms purchased from a business stationery store can form a minimal starting point. The forms can have the company name printed on the top, or the entrepreneur can do it with a rubber stamp, and would include receipt forms, purchase order forms (very helpful in obtaining purchase discounts), invoices, and other shipping forms (if the company sends goods out), as well as the business letterhead and business cards. Business checkbooks are available in which the stubs include a set of columns for breaking expenses into different categories. Most of these forms will need to include carbons so the company can keep a copy of each, and a file drawer should be set up for accumulating these copies in some orderly way.

As soon as this is done and transactions start, a system should almost automatically evolve. For example, the company will write out a purchase order to get some supplies. A copy of that will be kept by the entrepreneur. When the supplies arrive, that copy will represent something that has not only been on order, but has now arrived. This may call for moving it to a different file folder, to separate it from orders that have not yet arrived. That next folder will thus include a new account payable to which the incoming invoice and then the bill from the supplier may be stapled. When a check is written out and sent to pay for it, the purchase order will change status and perhaps be moved to another folder again, because it is now no longer an account payable, and so forth. This kind of paper shuffling may seem tedious to someone who wants to get out, make sales, produce goods, and interact with the world, but by doing it systematically many headaches can be avoided later.

---

[25]Larry Reibstein, "Accounting Software," *Venture* (August 1984), p. 36.

As the business begins to take on more momentum, it will need more than a checkbook and files. It should then set up a book (accountants call them journals, registers, or ledgers) or section of a book for each of the following:

1. Cash receipts
2. Cash disbursements
3. Accounts payable
4. Accounts receivable
5. Sales
6. Payroll
7. Equipment and depreciation
8. General journal for other accounts
9. General ledger for summarizing all accounts

Each business must determine the account categories that may become useful. The earlier and more completely this is done, the less modification and readjustment will be needed later. The aim should be not to set up tiny accounts of no value in analysis, but enough breakdown to be meaningful. A helpful guide in defining accounts is the *Portfolio of Accounting Systems* published by Prentice Hall. Prepared by members of the National Society of Public Accountants, this book includes nearly 600 forms and diagrams, some filled out as examples. Other examples and helpful tricks may be available through a trade association closely related to the company's line of work.

How inventory is handled will depend on whether the company is on a cash or accrual basis, as discussed earlier. Either way, this will tend to be a particularly sticky part of the accounting system to work out, because in any business handling or manufacturing goods, there will be items added and removed on a daily basis. Discrepancies tend to be introduced not only by errors in keeping track of these shifts, but also from such things as breakage, scrap, and pilferage. Therefore, it is periodically necessary to count and price everything in the inventory and make a correcting entry in the books.

It may be simplest to begin with single entry bookkeeping, working from a checkbook register and keeping bills and invoices in folders. But if the venture takes hold and starts to grow, a double entry system will soon be appropriate. Both types are available in the alternative forms previously listed. When to change systems is a decision for which professional help may be worth the cost.

Even with such help, however, problems can still arise as illustrated by the next example, in which the company attempted to shift from a less formal system into one suited to a larger-size operation and got in trouble along the way:

■ *From its inception the company had determined work-in-process by pricing out items in the line according to their levels of completion. Their CPA said this method would become increasingly cumbersome as the company grew and urged that a more automatic procedure for computing these costs from expenditures be adopted. With the aid of this firm such a system was installed. A few months after it was started, the president began to get the feeling that something was wrong. Profits were increasing, which was encouraging, but the work-in-process figure seemed to be getting very high. The firm was indeed growing, and shortly found it needed a larger plant. During the move a physical inventory was taken and work-in-process was found to be vastly lower than stated by the books, because with the new system certain overtime expenditures that did not truly increase its value had been attributed to it. What had shown up as a profit for the year turned out to be a substantial loss from which the company had considerable difficulty recovering.*

Two suggestions to avoid such troubles are for management to be sure it understands the accounting system and to choose professional accounting help with care.

Accountants

In recruiting accounting help, it is a good idea to shop around. Asking other entrepreneurs whom they use and what they have learned over time should be particularly helpful. A CPA should be good at designing and setting up an accounting system and then later in formulating budgets, evaluating performance against them, preparing statements, minimizing taxes, hiring and directing employed bookkeepers in the company, performing audits, and even finding and arranging financing.

For keeping the books, it will probably be more economical to hire a full- or part-time bookkeeper, possibly a retired accountant. The more that person does, the less time should be required from a higher-priced CPA.

Periodic audits by a CPA can help in coping with tax collectors and in preventing disputes among shareholders. They can also help reassure bankers and/ or investors from whom capital is desired, and in getting legal permission to sell stock publicly. They can also be expensive, particularly if the books are not well set up and maintained.

The cost of utilizing accounting firms tends to scale up with the size of the venture. A 1984 *In Business* survey of small firm owners found that average fees paid by firms with sales of less than $100,000 per year were $400 annually, while firms with sales between $100,000 and $1 million averaged $2,000, and those with sales over $1 million averaged $6,000. In the last category, the lowest figure was $1,500 for tax preparation and year-end statements only. For all respondents, the average annual cost was $2,780 and the median was $1,000. The majority (85 percent) of small firms utilized independent rather than national accounting firms.[26]

RECORDS

There can be a natural tendency to avoid careful record keeping, not only in accounting but other aspects of the venture as well. After all, records and paperwork do not develop a product or service; they take time away from creative design and production. Nor do they sell it; instead, they take energy away from working with potential customers. They cost money, contrary to the start-up's need to save

[26]"How Good Is Your Accountant?," *In Business* (September-October 1984), p. 37.

every cent possible. So it is natural to try to minimize such red tape. If the company does get started, however, then the need for records is inevitable, especially if government permission is needed to operate.

Which records to maintain, how long to keep them, and how to classify and store them can be categorized several different ways:

By Line of Business

It is easy to imagine why record needs in an insurance agency would be different from those in a grocery store. It is not so easy to see the extent of the record needs in the myriad other types of potential start-ups, which details are most important, and how they can best be handled. The best sources of information about these special needs are (1) owners of companies already operating in those lines of business, (2) books and pamphlets describing how to start and operate such firms, and (3) trade associations for the particular lines of business.

By Federal Government Agency

Federal record requirements also vary with line of business. Some major ones that apply to all industries are those of the IRS (employees' withholding, Social Security taxes, and federal unemployment taxes), the Department of Labor (wage and hour reporting, occupational health and safety records), the Equal Employment Opportunity Commission (employer information report), and the Bureau of the Census (employer identification number census form).[27] Each of these agencies publishes booklets of its requirements that can be obtained by calling or writing. In addition, the Small Business Administration has two very large volumes, one entitled *Guide to Record Retention Requirements for Small Business,* and the other the *Catalog of Federal Paperwork Requirements by Industry Group.*

By State and Local Government Agency

Examples within this category appeared in Exhibit 9–1. They vary with locale and can best be investigated by contacting (1) state and local chamber of commerce offices, (2) other entrepreneurs in similar lines of business, and (3) local lawyers and accountants. For further illustration, a checklist for federal tax filing requirements appears in Table 9–1.

By Business Function

Each area within the business may have need of records to guide and tune its performance. Incorporation papers and minutes must be filed.[28] Accounting records for taxes will not likely help as much with cost control as will additional records designed for that purpose. If the company is a manufacturer, it will need records of drawings, specifications, quality control, and servicing for its own

[27]Raymond D. Watts and Neal L. Thomas, "The Paperwork Chase," *In Business* (Autumn 1981), p. 43.
[28]Bernard Kamoroff, "Filing Your Business Records," *In Business* (May-June 1990), p. 52.

TABLE 9-1   Federal Business Tax Forms

YOU MAY BE LIABLE FOR	IF YOU ARE	USE FORM	DUE ON OR BEFORE
Income Tax	Sole proprietor	Schedule C (Form 1040)	Same day as Form 1040
	Individual who is a partner or S corporation shareholder	1040	15th day of 4th month after end of tax year
	Corporation	1120 or 1120-A	15th day of 3rd month after end of tax year
	S Corporation	1120S	15th day of 3rd month after end of tax year
Self-employment tax	Sole proprietor, or individual who is a partner	Schedule SE (Form 1040)	Same day as Form 1040
Estimated tax	Sole proprietor, or individual who is a partner or S corporation shareholder	1040-ES	15th day of 4th, 6th, and 9th months of tax year, and 15th day of 1st month after the end of tax year
	Corporation	1120-W	15th day of 4th, 6th, 9th, and 12th months of tax year
Annual return of income	Partnership	1065	15th day of 4th month after end of tax year
Social security (FICA) tax and the withholding of income tax	Sole proprietor, corporation, S corporation, or partnership	941	4-30, 7-31, 10-31, and 1-31
		8109 (to make deposits)	See Chapter 33
Providing information on social security (FICA) tax and the withholding of income tax	Sole proprietor, corporation, S corporation, or partnership	W-2 (to employee)	1-31
		W-2 and W-3 (to the Social Security Administration)	Last day of February
Federal unemployment (FUTA) tax	Sole proprietor, corporation, S corporation, or partnership	940-EZ or 940	1-31
		8109 (to make deposits)	4-30, 7-31, 10-31, and 1-31, but only if the liability for unpaid tax is more than $100
Information returns for payments to nonemployees and transactions with other persons	Sole proprietor, corporation, S corporation, or partnership	See Chapter 36	Forms 1099 – to the recipient by 1-31 and to the Internal Revenue Service by 2-28 Other forms – see Chapter 36
Excise taxes	Sole proprietor, corporation, S corporation, or partnership	See Chapter 35	See the instructions to the forms

Source: Internal Revenue Service.

products as well as maintenance records on plant and equipment. Whether in manufacturing or not, the company will need records of purchases and customers. If it has employees, the company will find it useful to keep not only the governmentally required records, but also a file of leads on prospective talent it may need in the future.

At the outset, it will be a simple matter to keep such records. Most of them will not be needed right away, and there will not be many in total, so that finding them will be easy. These can be arguments for postponing thought about which records are most needed and how they can best be filed. With experience, it will become easier to figure out what sort of system will work best.

The problem with this approach is that it may postpone the sorting-out process to a time when there are so many other things to be done that the entrepreneur cannot afford to stop and set up the better system when it is truly needed. So there is also a good argument for setting up record management systems early and revising them gradually as further needs come into view.

PLANNING QUESTIONS

The following questions are intended to stimulate thought about what should be considered in moving ahead with a venture. Which questions best apply can vary among entrepreneurs and ventures, as can the order in which they should be considered, the priority that should be placed on them, and which of them should be answered in a written plan.

Permissions

- What government permits will the venture need, and when will it have them?
- What are the latest points in development of the venture when it is safe to obtain each of them?
- Has a lawyer checked zoning requirements, permits, licenses, leases, and other contracts?
- What penalties will be risked if they are not obtained soon enough?

Requirements

- What reports or inspections will be required to operate the venture, and what will it cost to deal with them?
- Is the venture's line of activity likely to be outlawed or regulated out of existence at any foreseeable time?
- Is there potential for changing prohibitions or zoning rules to the advantage of this venture or others?
- What legislation, if any, might be introduced that could materially affect the venture's competitive position?
- What state, local, as well as federal taxes will the venture have to pay?
- How will compliance with tax requirements be assured?

Contracts

- Has the venture been set up as a separate corporation or formal partnership? What are key provisions of either?
- What is the actual or planned date and time of incorporation?

- What, if any, plans are there for change in this structure?
- If so, what special provisions are included in the arrangement that might be of concern to a new investor?
- Are any assets of the venture, including rights to ideas, encumbered legally, and if so, how?

Legal Help

- What are the qualifications of the law firms to be retained by the venture and of the particular individuals in those firms who will be handling the venture's affairs?
- What provisions have been made in the budget for audits and legal counsel to contend with possible lawsuits?
- What warranties will be provided with what the company offers, and what liabilities could they reasonably impose on the company?
- What legal opinions have been given on them by what law firm(s)?
- What special contracts or permissions with other companies or individuals will be required or are in hand?
- What employment contract provisions will be needed to preserve secrets and retain key skills?
- What potential lawsuits, if any, can be foreseen? Have professional opinions been obtained on insurance needs of the business?

Insurance

- What forms of life insurance on which people are in place or contemplated?
- What other insurance coverage, such as directors liability insurance, may be needed, how much will it cost, and has it been included in the venture's budget?
- Will there be safeguards against unauthorized spending and embezzlement?

Accounting

- Have formal books been established, or when will they be?
- Who will keep them up-to-date?
- Who is or will be the company's auditor?
- How will the company's accounting system be expanded over time if the venture grows?
- Has an accountant been asked to review the expected type of accounting system to be used, and how will it evolve over time?
- What auditing of the company's books has been done so far, and what is contemplated?
- What reports will management and investors receive, and by when?
- How will delinquent accounts be defined and handled?

Records

- What sort of filing and record-keeping requirements will become important and when? How will they be arranged for?

POSSIBLE MILESTONES FOR A PLANNING TIME LINE

The most suitable milestones for a time line for a particular venture must be a function of the individual case. Those that follow are intended to help stimulate thought about them.

- Incorporation or partnership agreement formalized
- Business license obtained
- Any needed permits obtained
- Lease signed
- Insurance policies in force
- First contract signed
- First audit completed

Chapter 10

VENTURE PLANS

INTRODUCTION

Venture planning has been the subject of countless "how to" publications but relatively little systematic study. Rockey found that entrepreneurs often visualize in advance the characteristics of their ventures and the steps in their creation.[1] Professional investors and lenders, however, require more than simply oral descriptions of mental visions. They want to see written plans before committing resources to ventures. However, plans are necessary but not sufficient for getting capital.

At the same time, plans can be helpful for other purposes than raising capital (see Chapter 1). A study by Bracker, for instance, found that small entrepreneurial firms that used "structured strategic planning were statistically more effective with regard to industry-specific financial performance" than those that did not.[2]

This chapter examines venture planning from several perspectives, including the sort of planning entrepreneurs actually do, alternative purposes for planning, and different planning methods. In so doing, it will draw upon and pull together material from earlier chapters.

---

[1]Edward H. Rockey, "Envisioning New Business: How Entrepreneurs Perceive the Benefits of Visualization." P. 344 in Robert Ronstadt, John A. Hornaday, Rein Peterson, and Karl H. Vesper, *Frontiers of Entrepreneurship Research, 1986* (Wellesley, MA: Babson Center for Entrepreneurial Studies, 1986).

[2]Jeffrey S. Bracker, "Planning and Financial Performance Among Small Entrepreneurial Firms" (Tempe: Arizona State University, Department of Management, March 1983), p. 8.

What Entrepreneurs Actually Do

The example of Bruce Milne and his software start-up (see Chapter 1) illustrates the approach many entrepreneurs take to written planning. He sketched out a simple budget and a few rough notes when he first started; he worked up a more formal written plan only when it was needed for raising money. Subsequently, the venture repeatedly ran out of capital, and the plan was successively revised to raise more. In hindsight, Bruce felt that earlier and more systematic planning would likely have helped his company develop better, although it nevertheless was a substantial success, not only as a software innovator, but also in terms of both market and financial performance.

Some companies start with extensive formal plans, as illustrated by Stephen Vallender, a member of the founding team of Celerity Computer, who recalled:

■ *We completely planned, right down to the unit level, when to bring in each piece. And we had recovery plans to get back on track in case something went wrong.*[3]

Another company that did substantial systematic planning at an early stage and subsequently prospered greatly was Apple Computer. As *Inc.* reported in early 1979:

■ *A lot of small company managers talk about planning for fast growth. Professors and consultants preach the need for it. Apple Computer Inc. does it. "We've been running Apple like a $100-million company from the word go," says A. C. (Mike) Markkula, 35-year-old chairman and 20 percent owner of the two-year-old, privately held maker of personal computers.*[4]

The plans of some other fairly well-known companies have even appeared in print.[5]

However, even though some entrepreneurs believe that formal planning at start-up is vital to their success, a majority of entrepreneurs do not begin with formal plans, even those who start high-growth companies, including Apple Computer at its earliest stage when Steve Jobs and Steve Wozniak were working alone.[6] In a 1985 survey of "Inc 500" companies, Shuman et al. found that of 244 respondents, about half (50.7 percent) began without formal plans.[7] In another study of 150 Minnesota start-ups, most of them service firms, Egge found that

[3]Ira Sager, "When Haste Doesn't Make Waste," *Venture* (July 1986), p. 116.

[4]Norman Sklarewitz, "Born to Grow," *Inc.* (April 1979), p. 52.

[5]For instance, plans for Shopsmith, *Venture* magazine, and Storage Technology appear in Joseph R. Mancuso, *How to Write a Winning Business Plan* (Englewood Cliffs, NJ: Prentice Hall Press, 1985), p. 187. Ironically, the first two of these subsequently failed (*Venture* failed in October 1990).

[6]Lee Butcher, *The Accidental Millionaire* (New York: Paragon House, 1989).

[7]Jeffrey C. Shuman, Gerald Sussman, and John J. Shaw, "Business Plans and the Start-Up of Rapid Growth Companies." P. 294 in John A. Hornaday, Edward B. Shils, Jeffry A. Timmons, and Karl H. Vesper, *Frontiers of Entrepreneurship Research, 1985* (Wellesley, MA: Babson Center for Entrepreneurial Studies, 1985).

although 71 percent had prepared written business plans, only 38 percent had done so as early as three months after start-up. Thus it appears that although many entrepreneurs do prepare written plans, a majority of entrepreneurs do not do so in anticipation of start-up, but rather some time after.

Often, it is when there is a need for help from outside, perhaps to recruit a partner or apply for a bank loan, that some sort of written business plan will be prepared—the minimum needed, perhaps only a cash budget, to satisfy the request. If the venture is to be highly complex and require major investment, there may be need for a more extensive written plan, but most ventures do not encounter such a need, particularly in their early stages.

Certainly, there must be some thought given to what lies ahead. Even more than that is the need for new information, the kind that comes from talking to potential customers, technical experts, prospective partners, employees, suppliers, landlords, governmental agencies, and various professionals, not from plan writing. Without information from these sources, planning can be worse than useless because its factual foundation will be incomplete or flawed. To get the information, however, takes time, just as planning does. When a choice must be made between getting more useful information versus processing the available information to create a formal plan, the better decision will often be to pursue information.

Inc. magazine found conflicting views about formal planning among successful company founders. It drew the following observations from a computer company entrepreneur, one with an MBA at that:

■ *"You don't need a plan for a hundred person company," says Scott McNealy, chief executive officer of Sun Microsystems. His co-founders wrote the founding plan and he read it over. But he hasn't referred to it since. The key, he says, is knowing "in your gut" what cash flow is like, how expenses are running in relation to sales. In a start-up, things change too quickly for any plan. "You basically throw out all assumptions every three weeks."*

For some ventures, formal planning may be essential at the outset, whereas for others the need may not come until later, as Bob Cashman, the CEO of Pacific Envelope, Inc., in Anaheim, California, observed:

■ *If you're doing all the driving, you may not need much of a map. But as soon as you begin to delegate authority, you need to show people where you're going.*[10]

Among the examples examined by *Inc.*, a plan was usually developed but it was incorrect, mostly in projecting sales; the company did not make much use of it;

[8]Karl Egge, "Expectations vs. Reality Among Founders of Recent Start-Ups." P. 322 in Neil C. Churchilo, John A. Hornaday, Bruce A. Kirchhoff, O.J. Krasner and Karl H. Vesper, *Frontiers of Entrepreneurship Research*, 1987 (Wellesley, Babson Center for Entrepreneurship Studies, 1987).

[9]Erik Larson, "The Best-Laid Plans," *Inc.* (February 1987) p. 60.

[10]Bruce G. Posner, "Real Entrepreneurs Don't Plan," *Inc.* (November 1985), p. 130.

and the document could no longer be found. However, some well-qualified venturers favored formal planning.

■ *Bill Foster, the founder of a prosperous computer company, Stratus, referred to his start-up plan as "something we took very seriously. Our first year of sales, in '82, we were behind plan and we were really concerned; I'm convinced that if the original plan had had a lower goal, we would have achieved less." He also said that if the goal had been set $50 million higher, "I don't think we would have made $125 million, but I bet we would have done more than $75 million."*[11]

Venture Goals

Formulating plans is partly a process of mental "playing around" to explore what might be possible, and partly one of seeking ways to achieve conscious goals. These two ways of thinking generally work together, the first suggesting what alternative goals might be possible, and the second indicating obstacles that further thought might find ways to overcome. The general activity is one of search, between the desired and the possible, and between the general and the specific. It is important to recognize these distinctions, because although planning can drift around within the desired and the general, the action must ultimately be possible and specific. Tomio Moriguchi, who developed a family grocery into a successful chain of Asian variety stores, commented:

■ *Most people go into business with a general idea of what they want to do but without the specific details of how to do it. They have goals like "wanting to be a millionaire." Later, you find that your major preoccupation is simply to provide the best product at the best possible price in order to reach that goal.*

Several levels of goal specifications are appropriate. One level concerns what business the company is really in (or what it is really good at, and in what ways that competence can be employed) and whether it should be redesigned in major ways. Other levels deal with what percentage gross margin the company should achieve, how many dollars of profit it should produce, what percentage of market it should capture, how much cash it should generate, and what rate of labor turnover would be tolerable. At yet another level are questions such as whether to make or buy, how much to keep in inventory, how much to charge, whether to hire a direct salesperson, how much output to expect per employee, and what fringe benefits to offer.

A paragon of high-level goal setting appears to be Dr. George Hatsopolous of Thermo Electron Corporation. Over thirty-three years, he managed to build sales from zero to $600 million without having a single employee leave to start a rival company:

[11]Erik Larson, "The Best-Laid Plans," *Inc.* (February 1987), p. 60.

■ *I would have a company that had a certain core technology, then look around to identify what needs existed, and try to invent things that met those needs.*[12] *... My idea was a broad-based technology company that would work simultaneously on lots of ideas that were risky but, if any one of them worked out, would be profitable.*[13]

The *Inc.* articles in which this quote appears go on to say that all he asks in choosing which ideas to pursue is that the potential market be large and that the engineers at Thermo Electron be better equipped than anyone else to develop the product or service.

A starkly contrasting overall goal statement is that of a restaurant, The Palomino, "A Euro-Seattle Bistro," which reads in part as follows:

■ *You've seen me before, but can't quite remember when. Milan? Rome? Nice? Perhaps Manhattan? Sort of a blend of the old and new world. ... I'm no kid's place—a world away from trendy "here today, gone tomorrow" places. ... I'm a Mediterranean adventure making an important "Northwest" statement.*[14]

From either statement, different as they are, it is fairly easy to imagine how other levels of goals and planning decisions might follow in selecting people, choosing facilities, and pursuing customers.

All levels of goals are important. If higher-level goals are effective, more mistakes can be tolerated on lower levels without sinking the company. But it is only lower-level actions that can achieve the higher aims. Marilyn Kyd believed her decision with a partner to start an employment agency was a good one but that they chose the wrong town and wrong office location within it, failed to anticipate delays in opening the office, and made lease commitments based on an overestimated rate of expansion and underestimated level of needed advertising. In hindsight, she concluded: "Our miscalculations were the result of planning so poor we might be tempted, were it not true, to call it unbelievable."[15]

Another author tells about an entrepreneur whose sales failed to materialize because he neglected to apply his effort according to a logical plan:

■ *Every day was a new day for Mr. Jones and he would rush on, in an attempt to solve whatever problems had arisen. One larger customer offered more potential business than any other, and yet Mr. Jones had managed to call on him only twice during the year. On the other hand, a small customer, who represented a small potential sales volume, received more than fifty visits because he had problems and asked for assistance.*[16]

---

[12]Bruce G. Posner, "The Thinking Man's CEO," *Inc.* (November 1988), p. 29.

[13]Tom Richman, "The Master Entrepreneur," *Inc.* (January 1990), p. 47.

[14]Taken from an advertising flyer for The Palomino.

[15]Marilyn Kyd, "The Little Business That Failed," *Venture* (December 1986), p. 112.

[16]Albert J. Kelley, "Planning for the New Enterprise." P. 102 in Clifford M. Baumback and Joseph R. Mancuso, *Entrepreneurship and New Venture Management* (Englewood Cliffs, NJ: Prentice Hall, 1975).

Clear goals should help prevent this sort of myopic groping by making clearer what is important and what is not as a basis for making better day-to-day decisions about how to apply money and effort. Then when a customer wants a product or service from the company, a salesperson drops in with merchandise to sell, civic groups such as the chamber of commerce make requests for contributions, employees ask for different working arrangements, or the entrepreneur develops personal preferences about office redecoration, a company car or vacation, the requests can be tested against company goals. Will granting the request serve appropriate goals or not? If not, should the proposal be rejected, or should the goals be changed instead? Either may apply, as later examples will illustrate. Flexibility can be crucially important.

Some alterations in direction can be made to seek out what will work best and can be imposed by management. At other times, management can run into forces from outside that require it simply to respond with flexibility in order to survive. After studying performance patterns of literally millions of companies, Dr. David Birch described implications for maintaining flexibility in his own enterprise, Cognetics, as follows:

■ *My understanding of growth-company instability has affected how I run my company. For one thing, that awareness has given me comfort—because I understand there's nothing pathological about my own company's tendency toward instability. Plus, I've been prepared for it. . . . All of us at Cognetics share a kind of knowledge; we've all studied the companies in our database and seen what the fast growers go through—their extreme and threatening ups and downs. That's made us much more inclined to allow room for mistakes so that the bottoms don't kill us. We know they're coming, so we've built in cushions rather than going for the most rapid growth we could.*[17]

Another fact that Birch observed from his studies was that although a few start-ups are able to grow fast, most grow slowly and so must in planning regard larger size as a long-term, if ever, goal.[18]

TAKING INCREMENTAL ACTION

There are many ventures in which planning can be handled adequately in the entrepreneur's head and need not be done in a formal written sense, at least not at the outset, and if the venture does not grow large, even for the long term.

Step-by-Step May Work

If the first steps in creating the venture can be minimal and do not require large commitments, if the range of possible outcomes is very large, and/or if the entrepreneur, because of these uncertainties, possibly coupled with his or her own

[17]David L. Birch, "Managing in the New Economy," *Inc.* (April 1990), p. 33.
[18]David L. Birch, "Live Fast, Die Young," *Inc.* (August 1988), p. 23.

inexperience, really cannot plan very well except by going ahead on a small scale to learn what will happen, then advance formal planning is not only uncalled for but could actually stifle the venture by becoming a substitute for action. In Chapter 2, the development of a prototype was illustrated by the experience of Walter Meyer, a laid-off aerospace worker who developed a fireplace-insert stove. Here another look at that experience shows the contrasting choices he faced between working on development of a plan versus working on the prototype and the venture itself.

■   *His "fireplace range," he supposed, might be salable through fireplace shops and possibly also through direct advertising and even appliance stores. His income at the time was zero. His savings were modest and dwindling. If this product was not going to work out, he figured he should get on with job hunting.*

At this point, Mr. Meyer could have sat down with paper and pencil and gone through all sorts of planning motions. He could have taken his sketches of the device and estimated the steel and labor costs to build it. He could have gone to the library and looked up information on the store industry, read about fuel costs and trends. From the Manufacturers Directory he could have learned about how many competitors were in the stove business, and from the Yellow Pages he could have listed stores selling fireplace equipment. By looking at prices of existing fireplace products and at the estimated costs of his own, he could have projected a sales price and estimated some sort of volume and expenses to come up with operating statement projections. He could have listed the shop equipment needed to make the product, estimated figures for inventory and receivables and worked out balance sheet forecasts. Then all this could have been written out with explanations of the assumptions and elaborations of details in the format of an elegant venture plan. But action, not planning, was what this situation called for.

Mr. Meyer's first action was to buy some materials and build a prototype, which he installed in the family fireplace and tested. He was pleasantly surprised to find that the baking chamber not only worked but threw a great amount of heat out into the room. As he worked with the prototype and mulled its design over in his mind he kept getting ideas for improvements. Trying glass for the firebox doors he found that the fire inside was pleasant to watch, that the glass did not crack from the heat, and that air sucked in at the top of the doors tended to sweep down across the inside face of the doors on its way into the fire, bathing the doors in clean air and keeping the smoke away so the doors did not become clouded with soot.

How much could the product be made for? He visited some sheet metal shops, showed them his drawings and prototype and obtained estimates. How much could it sell for? He visited fireplace shops to price other fireplace units and to discuss his own new product with the proprietors. How could he protect the novel features of his design? He visited a patent attorney for an opinion. What other things should he concern himself with and how should he proceed? He asked other people, an engineering friend, a professor who specialized in small business, an executive friend in the broadcasting business. Meanwhile, he kept refining the prototype, finding ways to make it work easier, install it better, improve its appearance, and reduce costs. He obtained bids for making 12 units, $105 each from one shop and $78 each from another shop for delivery in six weeks.

What would it sell for? If he paid $78 and sold it for $150, Mr. Meyer figured he would be close to a 50 percent gross margin. Visiting a fireplace shop he told the owner, "I can let you have it for $150." The owner replied, "then I would have to sell it for around $230." As the discussion concluded, the shop owner offered to display a unit if he could take it on consignment. Mr. Meyer said he would deliver the unit shortly.

Planning in the sense of thinking through what lay ahead, imagining options and weighing them, puzzling out solutions to problems, and deciding upon courses of action was certainly going on in Mr. Meyer's mind. But there was no planning in the formal written sense. Nor would it have helped this venture at this stage. There was not enough information at hand with which to plan except as it was brought in through moving the enterprise forward; building the prototypes; and talking with prospective suppliers, customers, and advisers. Taking action was probably harder than planning would have been; contacting all those strangers who might resent the intrusion on their time, might scoff at the venture, or even worse might somehow prove that it was doomed, might refuse to provide the information or assistance asked of them. But Mr. Meyer could not afford the luxury of sitting back with pencil and paper. He needed income.

Inexperience — An Early Handicap

A major problem with planning in advance of a venture, as opposed to further downstream, is that the entrepreneur may not yet know enough about what the particular venture involves to be able to plan it well. It may be necessary simply to move ahead and learn from mistakes. Dan Bricklin, the Harvard MBA who, with MIT student Bob Frankston, created Visicalc and started Software Arts, Inc., undertook his subsequent venture, Software Garden, Inc. and recalled what he learned from his first venture and how he applied it in his second:

■   *When we started Software Arts, we had no idea what was what. The industry hadn't been around long enough to see a product life cycle. We had no models for a software company, so we operated on the book-publishing model, which turned out to be wrong. We thought we could just develop new products and sell them — without realizing that different organizations were needed for different types of products. We didn't appreciate that the overhead appropriate for one product might be totally inappropriate for another. So there was a lot of waste. I could see it in my company, and I saw it even more when I did consulting for Lotus. It wasn't purposeful. People just didn't understand what was necessary and what wasn't. . . .*

   I wanted to do something different at Software Garden. I wanted to take a minimalist approach, to be lean and mean. I wanted to constantly throttle back and ask, How can I minimize the number of people I need? . . .

   I make midcourse corrections all the time. I've had my heart set on certain things about a product and then done total about-faces based on arguments from three or four test sites. At first, I've resisted. I've said "No, no, no." But the people doing the testing have convinced me, and I've been able to turn the whole organization around because we were just two or three people.[19]

Importance of New Information

To the extent that early stage venture planning represents only the reprocessing of information already possessed by the entrepreneur, it may not be very helpful. The importance of learning new information can easily be seen in almost any start-up. A particularly vivid example is that of Octavia Randolph during her start-up of a new company to produce and distribute snack foods made from Caribbean fruits:

[19]Dan Bricklin, "My Company, Myself," *Inc.* (July 1989), p. 35.

■ *Here is a woman for whom the past two years have amounted to a crash course in the art of starting up. In that time she has made hundreds of cold calls, hung out in grocery stores to watch how merchandise moves, and tapped the talents of people who know more about the food business than she does. She had studied everything from the economy of the Caribbean Basin to the placement of bar codes on soft drink labels.*[20]

To raise outside capital, she also needed a plan, a written one at that. But it is the information that was essential, and much of it had to be new. Trying to plan without it might have had some degree of educational value, but for starting the venture, it would have wasted time.

Need for Flexibility

Obsolescence is inevitable to some degree in a plan, and for that reason it may have to be regarded as only a short-term guide subject to major revision. It is sometimes much more important to emphasize flexibility. How ventures may need to change strategy dramatically is illustrated by the experience of two entrepreneurs who formed a new air freight company, Skyway Freight:

■ *Bob Baker and Jim Watson, the partners in running this enterprise, started out together as consultants turning around a freight company that had gone into Chapter XI bankruptcy. How they did it is not stated, but suffice to note it turned around. Management must have made a difference.*

After working for a freight company, Baker and Watson started their own company to carry air freight. Fed Ex was three years old at the time, and the strategy of these two men was to provide customers with a schedule of progressively slower delivery times from Fed Ex's overnight service, at correspondingly lower rates. Their cost-cutting angle was to use the cargo holds of passenger airliners which were largely empty on late-night flights. Sounded like a good idea.

But, in that form, it was not. Shippers, it turned out, did not want to hear about slower delivery times. In the first four months of selling this new service, the two men managed to lose $200,000. This was two-thirds of the total capital they had raised from seven investors to get started.

So they experimented. They stopped bringing up the matter of lengthened delivery times, and instead just emphasized lower price to the shippers. Then the service began to sell, at least enough to break even. But the new company still had a lot more improving to do.

One day while they were selling in the New York garment district to suppliers of buttons, collars and laces, a light went on. As they described it they tended to find themselves there selling to shippers who were "guys smoking short, unattractive cigars." These shippers sometimes asked how much would be kicked back to them if they put in good words on behalf of Watson and Baker's freight company with customers to whom their products were shipped.

Suddenly, Baker and Watson realized that Skyway was selling to the wrong end of the chain. They should be selling to the receivers of these products, rather than to the cigar-smoking shippers.

[20]Edward O. Welles, "Educating Octavia," *Inc.* (June 1989), p. 84.

> When they pursued that approach, still another discovery cropped up. It turned out that receivers were not as much interested in how fast delivery occurred as they were in knowing the time of arrival and being able to schedule it.
>
> So now Skyway began to offer a different service, one that would tell receivers just where their supplies were along the route at any time, and when they would arrive.
>
> Next, the two men began to focus on customers that had the largest volumes of incoming air freight, rather than selling to whomever they could. This let them concentrate on better serving a smaller number of receivers.
>
> And for those receivers they added yet another service. If a receiver would specify to its suppliers that their freight company, Skyway, should be the only one used for air deliveries, Baker and Watson would audit for that customer all its incoming invoices to make sure that the lowest shipping rates for the needed delivery times were being provided. If a supplier used another carrier against the customer's instructions to use Skyway exclusively, and if the other carrier charged more than the best Skyway could do, then the supplier would be dunned the difference in rate for violating instructions. This gave Skyway a nice monopoly with some receivers, while at the same time it helped receivers control their incoming freight costs. Baker and Watson had found the core of a profitable new game.
>
> The article observes that "Baker and Watson no longer think of Skyway as being in the air freight business. Rather it is part of the customer's inventory management system, providing just in time delivery of production materials." At last, a winning strategy. And next, they began to analyze ways of providing surface as well as air delivery.[21]

Clearly, this evolution in strategy included some dramatic departures from the company's original conception. Moreover, it is also clear that they had to be discovered by taking action initiatives and responding to new information. No original plan could have foreseen them.

SELECTIVE PLANNING

Because plans are costly in terms of time to develop and are bound to be somewhat limited and blind anyway, there is good reason to concentrate on developing only those aspects that are most likely to be needed and helpful.

Predicting Sales

One selective planning option is to develop a forecast of sales. If financial forecasts are needed, then sales estimates must be done. Also, if estimation must be made of the breakeven point to cover fixed expenses, or of profits to justify return on investment in something that cannot be reconverted into cash, such as investment in special tooling or in advertising, then sales estimates must be made.

Forecasting sales into a future where the evolution of selling methods, markets, and even what the company has to sell are likely to shift and change may not be easy. There are basically three approaches: *top down, bottom up,* and *parallel extrapolation.*

---

[21]Tom Richman, "Pressure Point Marketing," *Inc.* (May 1984), p. 149.

In the top down approach, broad estimates are made of the total potential market and then some sort of share is estimated as a percentage of that total that the new company should be able to obtain. The total market figures that apply to different industries and geographical areas can sometimes be learned from published statistics found in the library, sometimes from trade associations in that line of work, and at other times have to be estimated by someone, or better yet several people, with extensive experience in the industry.

In the bottom up approach, an estimate is made on a finely broken-down basis, customer by customer if possible, of each sale the company should be able to make. These separate small estimates are then added together to give an estimate of total sales. Generally, this approach involves more work but produces more accurate results than a top down estimate.

In the third approach, parallel or trend extrapolation, the estimate is based upon prior experience of a similar company, product, or market with the presumption that the new company's sales will run on a parallel path, tilted perhaps by some innovations the new company plans to introduce and qualified for the fact that the company starts without the advantage of the momentum that the prior company had. If such precedent exists, and if those doing the extrapolating are familiar with it, this can be a very good method. But the new company is often too different to assume it will run parallel. To back up any approach, it may be possible to use methods of market research to gather data from the prospective market, usually through either interviews or questionnaires, as discussed in earlier chapters.

Many new companies begin quite small, so they are able to test out the market on a small basis and expand only as fast as the market justifies. In a sense, they themselves become the vehicles of market research. Hence, it may be possible to minimize effort spent on sales forecasting and concentrate instead on steps designed to maximize flexibility, start the company small, and use it to test the capacity of the market.

Projecting Sequences

Either as an alternative to the question of what the venture should be able to sell or as a consequence of the answer, another avenue of planning is to chart the sequence of steps that must be taken to establish operations and accomplish delivery. Yet another alternative is to map out such sequences for only selective areas deemed to be most critical for the start-up.

Sequence planning begins with anticipation of events and arranging them into some sort of order that will cause the desired events to happen. If the sequence is fairly simple and straightforward, as in the case of Walter Meyer, described earlier, then it can be worked out in the entrepreneur's head from step-to-step as the venture progresses. Mr. Meyer had to contend with a six-week time delay introduced by his supplier, but this was not hard to remember and other fairly simple events in the start-up, such as arranging printing of advertising brochures, continuing product development work, talking to prospective dealers, and thinking out how to arrange for installation in customers' homes could be worked out while awaiting delivery.

But variations on his venture can easily be imagined that would encourage a more formal sort of planning in which the sequence of events should be written down. One would be if he were going to collaborate with one or more partners, especially at different geographical locations. Such a written plan would help to avoid overlap or conflict of activities, or worse yet, omissions of the type wherein both partners look at each other and say, "but I thought you would take care of that." Another circumstance calling for more formal listing of steps to be taken would be if setting up the company were complicated by such things as requirements for certification, lead times in obtaining permits or equipment, or recruiting to get personnel who might have to move from another part of the country.

Large firms are accustomed to planning out such details in both routine and new lines of activity. Application of this discipline to a new independent venture is illustrated by the actions of a former executive, Mary Anne Jackson, an MBA and CPA with eight years of financial experience with Beatrice Companies. She was fired in April 1986 as part of restructuring after a leveraged buyout and decided to start her own firm. In addition to seeking job offers and possible acquisitions, she looked for business ideas. One approach was to take a mental tour of supermarket shelves looking for slow-moving areas and thinking of what could be added. The idea she chose was to develop pouch-packaged microwaveable meals for young people. The venture she set up to exploit the idea was My Own Meals (MOM). *Inc.* senior writer, Tom Richman, described how she planned the start-up sequence:

■ *Once she committed herself to My Own Meals in November, 1986, she broke the start-up into its separate but often related processes. There were, she figured, about twenty of them: setting up an office, developing a product, creating a sales plan, finding a producer, and so on. Next, one by one, she listed the steps comprising each process and the time each would require. Then, beginning with the last step in each process—the date by which she would, for instance, have to have printed boxes available at the product manufacturer's plant—she and Martin worked backward to the first step. That told her, in the case of packaging again, she had to begin interviewing designers. Finally, she and Martin plotted the time chart. The payoff? Every morning when they came into the office they knew exactly what had to happen, what had to get done to keep each part of the start-up on track. They knew what was late and, if they needed to steal some time from somewhere, they knew what task could slip without seriously jeopardizing the process.*

It ought not to surprise anyone that the first production run was made in March—within budget.[22]

The next example singles out manufacturing planning in particular. Part of a sequence-mapping conversation in a trailer manufacturing venture follows. The aim was to get a fairly sizable company started in a short time, and several people would have to coordinate efforts to bring it off.

[22]Tom Richman, "The New American Start-up," *Inc.* (September 1988), p. 64.

■ *Trailer manufacturing was nothing technologically new and the plant manager had prior experience in it. Production facilities for the company had already been largely lined up through acquisition at auction of another failed trailer company. The failure had been in part due to a major sales decline in the industry as a whole resulting from the Arab oil embargo, which had caused many trailer companies to fold, and partly due to lack of capital which caused many purchasing and operating inefficiencies. Now that many trailer companies had quit the field, however, demand seemed to be bouncing back faster than supply, and the entrepreneur who had bought the equipment and taken over the plant lease of the defunct company was well supplied with capital.*

The following excerpts were from a conversation between the entrepreneur (E) and his new plant manager (M).

■ E: *If we move into the plant on September 1 and start setting up to make trailers, how long will it be until we have one trailer complete?*

M: *It will probably take us six to eight weeks at the very least. One big problem will be to get delivery on some of the plumbing and electrical parts. We'll be lucky if we can get all the parts in six weeks.*

E: *Will we need to hire someone for purchasing? It seems like raw material costs as a percent of selling price are awfully high in this industry compared to other industries. So it will be important to profits for us to get the best prices we can on purchasing.*

M: *Right. We'll need a good person for purchasing. I'll be able to train them some, but they'll need to set up a good system for keeping records on suppliers and their prices. We should hire that one right at the start.*

E: *How soon can you get the plant itself set up? Will there be any problem there?*

M: *I don't think it'll be much of a problem. I've already figured out a layout for the machinery and production flow. We'll need some code approvals from the city, but I can take care of those. We should hire two people to help me right away, then add the others at the end of September to start production. We'll need two welders, four people making sides. . . .*

E: *So then we can have complete trailers starting to come out the door by the first week of November.*

M: *Right, which means we should have at least two weeks of sales orders in hand by then. So we should start visiting possible dealers right now and deciding what kinds of features and deals they will buy. The company I was with before used to invite all the dealers and their families in for a show of the new models, and that seemed to work pretty well, so maybe we should try that after we're going.*

Sequence planning is not often a process of starting at one point in time and working steadily through to a later point, but rather of figuring out things that need to be done and then trying to fit them together, working backward and forward to get them to mesh. The ordered result often comes from a rather disorderly hunting and adjusting process.

It can be helpful to use some graphical tools in laying out the sequence. A blackboard has the virtue of erasability as items are adjusted and refitted. Another method is to write important tasks on 3 × 5 cards and lay them out on a large poster board which has a time scale with dates on it. Using different colored pens in marking the cards can be a way to keep track of which tasks are which person's responsibility, and different color cards themselves can be handy for sorting out marketing versus production versus financial areas, and so forth. Eventually, the array of cards laid out in sequence, or the blackboard layout, can be transferred to paper so copies can be made for everyone concerned, who can then translate the overall agreed-upon sequence into steps of action to carry out his or her responsibilities.

Gantt and Pert charts with Critical Path Method (CPM) analysis have also been suggested by Dean as useful in managing start-up ventures,[23] though no widespread venture use, except in construction projects, has yet appeared.

Forecasting Cash Flow

When potential sales and production costs have been estimated, it should become possible to sketch out financial forecasts as (1) breakeven computations, (2) *pro forma* income statements, (3) corresponding balance sheets, and most important, (4) cash flow forecasts. Ideally, these should be created for different levels of success: high, worst case, and most likely. Methods were discussed in Chapter 5.

Forecasts may initially take the form of estimated sales margins. If those look promising, then some possible sales volumes and associated expenses might be guessed. Either algebraic calculations or plotting a graph of sales level versus sales minus expenses will then reveal breakeven. An advantage of graphing is that it will easily allow examination of nonlinear patterns.

If the rough breakeven looks at all feasible, then a consideration of investment would be required to allow a comparison with the level of potential profit through computation of ROI. For comparison, the ROI of money in the bank typically ranges around 3 to 8 percent. The ROI usually sought by venture capitalists ranges from 30 to 50 percent. So perhaps an ROI above 20 percent, after allowing salary for the entrepreneur, might be a reasonable range. If estimates appear to be in that range, then more detailed financial estimation is needed, followed by cross-checking assumptions behind the figures. A computer spreadsheet can be tremendously helpful in spinning out these numbers. But the entrepreneur must make the estimates on which they all depend. (See also pp. 147–152.)

All this calculation might come before attempting to write a plan. In the case of the previously mentioned trailer company, a guess was made about how many trailers could be sold and put out the door each month during the first twelve months, then during the second through fifth years by year. Later, these figures would be refined to monthly for the first two years and quarterly for the other

[23]Burton V. Dean, "The Project Management Approach in the 'Systematic Management' of Innovative Start-Up Firms," *Journal of Business Venturing*, 1 (no. 2) (Spring 1986).

three. Other corrections would be added for the specific models and prices of individual trailers expected to be sold and for expected inflationary price changes. But in the preliminary forecast, these adjustments could be ignored.

Once the sales figures are laid out by month, other figures can be estimated. How many people would have to be working in the plant to put out that number of trailers each month? A listing was made for several possible levels of production. Each job implied a certain level of skill, which would cost a certain amount per hour to hire in the labor market. From these figures, it was possible to estimate labor costs by month to match the sales and production forecast. To cross-check how reasonable these labor figures were, a comparison was made with labor cost as percent of sales in the trailer-making industry generally.

The general industry figures also gave material cost percentages that could be used in the forecast for a first approximation of material expenditures. Later, this rough estimate would be cross-checked by making a list of all materials needed to build each model of trailer and pricing the lists out to get totals.

Now the remaining expenses of the profit and loss statement were listed and estimated. Because this too was only a first rough estimate, it was assumed that many figures, such as shop supplies, would stay roughly constant throughout the year, although in fact they would vary. Refinements could easily be made later, and the first estimates served mainly to make sure no major problems or cash needs were being overlooked.

Turning next to the balance sheet, estimates were made of the equipment that would have to be bought to get started. This gave a fixed asset entry for the statements. Guesses were made about how much inventory would have to be kept on hand for production (at least one month's materials in advance) and how fast receivables could be collected and payables would have to be paid. Applying these estimates to the income statement figures for sales, labor, and materials gave approximate figures for inventory, receivables, and payables. Thus, an approximate prediction for the balance sheet began to take shape. By simply copying the format of any conventional manufacturing balance sheet and filling in these numbers, a *pro forma* estimate could be created.

As the figures were filled in and the profit and loss figures were added to the net worth section, a gap between the asset total and the liability total appeared — the amount indicated the money necessary to make the totals balance. This crucial figure was much of the reason for generating the balance sheet in the first place. If the company could not come up with this amount from some debt or equity source, it simply could not buy the materials needed to operate and would have to cut back or shut down altogether. Because this number was so important, the forecast was reiterated with different assumptions as to the receivables collection period and payables payment period to see how it would change. To clarify further how the cash needs might change, a cash flow statement was prepared by month and reconciled with cash needs seen in the balance sheets.

This was all still a first approximation. In a more detailed reexamination, possible variations in all the assumptions would have to be explored as to their impact on the outside cash needs of the company.

For a more spectacular start-up, Digital Equipment Corporation, Roberts recounted how financial forecasts were prepared to persuade Georges Doriot's venture capital firm, American Research and Development Corporation (AR&D), to provide the initial capital:

■ *Ken Olsen and Harlan Anderson were told by AR&D that their plan showed promise but needed the addition of financial forecasts. Olsen recalled taking an economics course from which he still had the text. A section on economics told about balance sheets and income statements using as an example a fictitious company, "Pepto Glitter Inc." The two copied its statements, changing the company name and numbers and resubmitted their plan. Later they were told by AR&D that it was one of the most sophisticated business plans the venture capital firm had ever seen.*[24]

This approach of scaling numbers from others' financial statements also worked for another computer company, Stratus, in raising venture capital. How closely the venture capitalists looked at the statements or questioned the assumptions behind them was not reported for either case.

How much to rely on luck versus systematic calculation in preparing financial forecasts may be decided in part by the entrepreneur's level of comfort with gambling on vague guesses, the amount of time available to generate the numbers, the level of sophistication investors can be expected to apply, and the entrepreneur's familiarity and comfort with spreadsheeting and details of the type of business to be created.

One purpose of these forecasts may be to raise capital. More important, however, may be the need to avoid cash crises by anticipating needs in time to manage the individual elements of the company's balance sheet in order to avoid financial problems.

Forestalling Problems

The kinds of problems that can arise in a new venture have been noted in previous chapters. On average, ventures do not seem to turn out as well as entrepreneurs expect. From a sample of 150 start-up entrepreneurs, Egge reported that

- 48 percent failed to achieve expected first-year revenues.
- 53 percent found they needed more capital than originally estimated.
- 53 percent underestimated the time needed to process payroll and tax paperwork or time spent in recruiting and training.
- 55 percent failed to become as successful as they expected with their ventures.
- 63 percent found progress was slower than expected.
- 74 percent ended up with a lower personal standard of living from the venture than they expected.[25]

---

[24]Edward B. Roberts, "Business Planning in the Start-Up High-Technology Enterprise." P. 115 in John A. Hornaday, Jeffry A. Timmons, and Karl H. Vesper, *Frontiers of Entrepreneurship Research, 1983* (Wellesley, MA: Babson Center for Entrepreneurial Studies, 1983).

[25]Egge, "Expectations vs. Reality Among Founders of Recent Start-Ups." P. 322 in Churchill et al., *Frontiers of Entrepreneurship Research, 1987*.

Those who wrote business plans were less likely to have shortfalls in revenues, to underestimate the importance of record keeping, to underestimate the competition. The unhappiest entrepreneurs appeared to be those who had made what they considered to be mistakes of being unprepared or running out of capital. Those who had utilized help from others in their planning had less of a tendency to judge themselves as less successful than they had expected to be. Although Egge was careful to note limitations of his small sample, the results appear to support the use of written plans prepared with help from others.

Much of what will happen when a venture starts up will be fairly predictable by either routine, plan, or precedent. One entrepreneur who felt that the main concerns of his venture were probably typical of most described them as follows:

■ *For about a year we did work 80 hours a week. During this period we were only interested in three things (I expect these will become your interest too). The first was that we all listened for the telephone and dove for it as soon as it rang in case it was an order coming in. The second was that we all worked like mad to get the order out the door. The third was that each morning we all dived for the mailbox to see if there was a letter with a check in it. Basically these are the three things one lives for in the early months. Nothing else matters. In our case it worked.*[26]

Although a "wait-and-see" approach worked in this instance, there have been many others in which it has not. It can be helpful to guess about potential problems ahead and plan possible responses. By considering possible cash shortages in advance, for example, the entrepreneur may be able to line up emergency sources so he or she will not have to drop everything else in the business at a crucial moment to go capital hunting. Other concerns include the possibility of the company's source of supply being cut off and customer dissatisfaction and subsequent need for compensation. If some key people leave the company in its start-up phase, how could they be replaced? If strong competition develops, should the venture be sold out or would some other defensive course of action be better?

It can be particularly helpful to plan for problems that require long lead times to solve. Having cash available when needed is one such problem, but there can be many others. For instance, it can require weeks to construct special tooling, obtain delivery of needed equipment or materials, find and train certain types of skilled personnel, work out "bugs" in a new product or obtain certification, such as UL approval. In the following example, a young entrepreneur failed to start soon enough on working problems out with city hall:

■ *He had worked in several eating places and taverns during college and graduate school and thereby learned the business. During the last year of his business studies, he decided to start a restaurant of his own in a shopping center which had recently undergone major renovation and had space available. There were two other restaurants doing well near the center, but none in it. The entrepreneur arranged for space in the center to enter*

[26]David S. Watkins, *Founding Your Own Business* (Manchester, England: Manchester Business School R&D Unit, 1972), p. 11.

competition with them, figuring that with a comparable menu and prices, plus a location which offered better parking and was more central to the traffic pattern, he would have a substantial advantage. Through family and friends he raised capital to augment his own savings, had an architect work out the decor, while he himself designed the menu, recruited the help and ordered the supplies. He had noted that the other two restaurants served liquor and he had seen before that a license was needed to be able to sell it, but he didn't give the matter much thought, instead working problems out as they arose. Shortly before he was ready to open he approached city hall to apply for a liquor license. But he had not anticipated all the delays that were involved. Opening day came and there was no license. The new restaurant consequently operated at a loss as the young entrepreneur struggled with red tape compounded by political problems, opposition of the other restaurants, and the uneasy feeling that somebody was kicking back something someplace and preventing him from getting anywhere. After a few weeks of scrambling after the license unsuccessfully, he ran out of working capital and had to abandon the venture.

Working out a plan in advance might not have made this venture succeed, but it might have pointed up the license problem more clearly so that solving it could have begun sooner. Had it still proven unsolvable, at least the venture could have been abandoned earlier and with fewer losses.

It would be ideal to think through each function and budget line of the future business, to ask "What can go wrong there?," and to formulate plans to prevent the problem and responses if it occurs. There may be several potential problems associated with each item. The objective, however, is not to list as many problems as possible, but rather to identify those that pose the greatest threats and then to concentrate on sketching out possible solutions to them.

Although each venture is unique, there do seem to be some broad patterns of likely problems. From responses of seventy-three venture capitalists, each of whom had dealt with many ventures, Ruhnka and Young gathered that at the earliest stage of funding, inability to complete a workable prototype, insufficiency of market, delays in development, and excessive production costs were the greatest risks. At later stages, limitations of managerial competence and running out of cash most often seemed to become more severe.[27]

Product development problems often begin with difficulty in working out engineering solutions to technical impasses, start to show in schedule slippages, and finally take their toll in consumption of more money than was expected. Technical delays can crop up at all stages, from preliminary design through production, field test, and later customer use. Methods for anticipating potential technical problems were developed to their highest art in the space program and introduced new systematic analytical procedures such as *fault tree analysis* and *failure mode analysis* during the 1960s. Basic to all these methods, however, was simply the process of trying to guess what could go wrong, what could be done to reduce the likelihood of such events, what could be done to minimize their impact, and what action could be taken if they went wrong after launch.

[27]John C. Ruhnka and John E. Young, "A Venture Capital Model of the Development Process for New Ventures," *Journal of Business Venturing,* 2 (no. 2) (Spring 1987), 167.

Some general types of preparation an entrepreneur might consider in planning to avoid technical problems might include

1. Preconsidering how much money and effort to spend before giving up if the technical problems become intractable
2. Identifying in advance the most likely danger signals that such problems may be arising
3. Identifying possible sources of help in advance that can be turned to if and when those signals occur
4. Considering the impact of such technical problems on the rest of the company's plans

Notwithstanding such forethought, however, each technical problem must be treated on its own, as illustrated by the following incident recalled by Burton McMurtry, a Menlo Park, California, venture capitalist. This episode could have ended like many technical projects, as a write-off after throwing much good money in after bad, but instead, after talking it out, it turned around and went well:

■ *I was sitting with the president of the company 7:30 in the evening, and he looked across the table at me and said, "Burt, we've really made a mistake." I said, "What do you mean we've made a mistake?" He said, "This company is just never going to happen. We're not going to be able to make that machine work. And if we could make it work, nobody is going to buy it at the price we'd have to charge. The costs are 2¹/₂ times what we projected. It's just a mistake."*

I didn't respond right away, so I got up and walked back into the lab. One of the young engineers was sitting there and said, "You know, Burt, you just can't schedule this kind of work." I said, "Bruce, what do you mean you can't schedule this kind of work?" He said, "Well, this creative design work, you just can't say it's going to be done at this time and have it done then." I said, "Oh, Bruce, a good engineer is a guy who knows what to do and how to get it done at a certain time with the right amount of money." We discussed it a while, and then he said, "You know, Burt, this project has gone so much better than any I've ever worked on before."

There was only one door to the building or I think I'd have used the other one. But I had to go back out past the president. So I talked with the president some more and we began to see that maybe it wasn't a disaster after all. In fact it wasn't and the company became a profitable investment.

Once a venture is past the new product development stage, the threat that sales will fail to materialize as hoped can occur and can have many causes: Discounts are unattractive to distributors, or all the right distributors are already tied up with other companies; customers do not understand why they should buy, or are already committed to something else; the advertising is not convincing, or it is not reaching enough potential customers; the product or service is not sufficiently new or improved, or the timing is somehow wrong. Somewhat less serious are causes associated with insufficient selling effort on the part of the new company. In that case, the effort can often be stepped up either by reallocating efforts, by seeking more capital and assistance, or simply by trying harder. Another example of McMurtry's is illustrative:

■ *This business started out with a very incomplete team, four guys who wanted so badly to get into business that they didn't care what business they entered. They had probably the* *worst business plan I've ever seen, a plan to attack three different markets with five products simultaneously. There was nobody on the team with real marketing, financial or management experience, but they were strong characters and, remarkably, they persuaded someone to put up seed capital. There was at least one strong leader in the group, inexperienced but with a good business head, and there was some good engineering strength in the group. A prototype was demonstrated in October of 1969, and they then set out to raise $600,000 to go into production. It took until March, 1970, to get the money, but they did.*

Then they had a delay in getting orders. The marketing vice president was the personal best friend of the president, his former college roommate. But he seemed to lack a sense of urgency. By August, 1970, the financial projections showed that the company had about a month and a half of cash left, and although the product worked alright the orders were totally insufficient. I was sitting in a meeting of the partners and the president pointed out that we were going to lose the whole company in just a couple of months unless something changed. Then he announced that he was going to move his friend out of marketing and do the job himself. It was remarkable, because he had no experience in marketing at all. But the president got out and brought in orders. I could have told him a thousand reasons why it couldn't be done and why he in particular couldn't do it, but he did. A month later the company shipped $200,000 worth of products and it has been in the black ever since.

Running out of money is, as noted earlier, a type of problem for which advance planning is more straightforward. It tends to arise, moreover, when the company does either too badly or too well. If the company does badly, it may run out of cash because costs are too high, sales are too low, collections are too slow, creditors press for early collections, or combinations of these and other problems. If the company does too well, it will need more cash to support more accounts receivable, carry more inventory, buy more equipment, acquire more space, and so forth. Precautions that can be considered in advance are (1) setting up an accounting system that will predict financial problems as early as possible, (2) considering where to cut back or change policy if things go badly, (3) building a "pad" into the budget to allow for surprises, (4) working out whom to approach for more money if it is needed, and (5) considering what actions to take if it cannot be obtained.

Managerial limitations and other "people problems" in a venture can sometimes be forestalled by choosing partners and making appropriate agreements with them that anticipate potential future divergence (see Chapter 4). Becoming familiar with potential sources of employees, especially those with critical skills needed by the company, and formulating a procedure for obtaining them when they are needed can be an important part of planning, something that might have helped particularly in the following venture:

■ *Kaleidoscope, a new mail order firm put out its first gift catalog in 1974, hit sales of $1.9 million the following year, then went to $16 million by 1978. How could it have foreseen that it would then go bankrupt due to a combination of incompetent order handling, bugs in a new computer system, and a shortfall in capital?*

For still other enterprises such as the following, failure may be inevitable due to outside events beyond control of the entrepreneurs that cannot be reasonably discerned at start-up:

■ *Vector Graphic in March 1981 was one of the fast rising companies of the new microcomputer industry. However, it was based upon the CP/M operating system. How could its founders have seen that IBM PC would shortly rise to prominence based on the MS-DOS system and put Vector out of business?*[28]

■ *By 1984 Federal Express had become a $1.2 billion dollar success against the competition of long-established delivery companies. It then undertook to create another new enterprise by applying over $100 million to introduce Zap Mail. Certainly there were detailed plans, financial forecasts, and professionally developed facets of design features in the new service, which turned out to be a complete failure when widespread fax machines eliminated any need for it. How should better planning have forestalled the loss?*

Though failure may not be foreseeable, there can still be value in planning when to cut the venture off before failure becomes catastrophic, thereby at least minimizing losses:

■ *After the magazine* Psychology Today *was introduced in the early 1960s, and became a great success, its founders decided to start another,* Careers Today, *which would focus on people's jobs and work patterns. After a few issues,* Careers Today *abruptly ceased. Sales had not developed as rapidly as planned and the founders decided to minimize losses by terminating publication.*

In this case, the magazine founders were able to cut off the venture before it broke them. Had there not been a plan, it might have been easier for them to ignore the departure from expectations, to "kid themselves" about how things were going, and thereby to continue to lose money longer, possibly even ending up in court in bankruptcy as did another 1960s' magazine attempt, *Innovation Magazine*, which went broke and had its carcass picked clean by bankruptcy lawyers and accountants over the next several years.

FORMAL WRITTEN PLANS

Sometimes selective planning is not enough, and a full written plan is needed. Such a plan certainly does not guarantee success. Every year thousands of them are turned down by venture capitalists. Many ventures that do go ahead on the basis of formal plans also fail. But those entrepreneurs who plan carefully are more likely to succeed than those who do not, if the judgment of bankers and venture capitalists experienced in backing many ventures is any guide. An entrepreneur must weigh the time and money cost of planning against the prospect of lowering risk, discovering better sequences for taking action, and finding life easier thanks to better foresight. In that context, spending some time on a plan may look like a good bargain.

[28]Susan Benner, "Next Stop Wall Street," *Inc.* (March 1981), p. 37.

The role of a written plan in helping a partnership survive was emphasized by Stephen Thomas, whose injunction to "put it in writing" was noted in Chapter 4. He observed:

■ *Writing everything out will allow you to encounter and solve many of your problems before they jeopardize your company or destroy your friendships. Once you get going you should continue to plan on paper. A record of your agreements on goals, policies and procedures protects the company in general and the partners in particular. If you have agreed to limit spending on a particular marketing target and the marketing partner exceeds the limit with no results, a reprimand is in order.*[29]

When Formal Planning Is Required

Some circumstances in which the development of full written business plans may be worth the cost in time, effort, and possibly cash include the following:

1. Major financial or personal commitment from others is required. The lenders, investors, partners, and key employees who are being asked to leave other good jobs to join the venture will want to see just how their contribution is going to be applied, what results it can be expected to produce, why those results are likely to happen, what kinds of profits are possible, as well as how and when they will be able to cash in (or out).
2. The entrepreneur wants to maximize potential success and/or minimize chances of failure. Written planning can be a careful way of thinking through many possible problems and their solutions. As the venture goes into motion, the written plan can also provide benchmarks against which to check progress and make corrections. Particularly if the venture is novel or even just new to the entrepreneur, the plan can help provide a testing scenario to which others can react and give counsel. Unfortunately, the difficulty of planning, novelty, and complexity of the venture and the importance and value of planning all tend to scale up together.
3. A sizable start-up team must work together and coordinate activities. The written plan can serve as a guide for routine parts of the project and free up minds and communication channels to concentrate on important exceptions and unforeseeable developments.
4. The venture is routine. Planning should then be easy and the time and effort required will be small. The plan can be used for fine-tuning to make the start-up process smooth, free of unpleasant surprises, and more comfortable. For people experienced in that particular type of enterprise, the plan may not be essential. But if there are members of the start-up who are new to the business, a plan may be instructive.

How much time and money to spend on the plan and how to go about creating it are other questions. Planning does exact a price in time, effort, and often money, and if too much is spent on it or if it is done badly, the value may be much less than this cost. An example of a business plan to raise money for the start-up of Priam, which turned out to be a very successful computer disk drive company, appears in Appendix B.

---

[29]Stephen G. Thomas, "Why Partnerships Break Up," *Inc.* (July 1981), p. 67.

Planning as Prospectus Formulation

Notwithstanding other possible benefits, the reason most venture plans are written is to raise capital from people outside the business. (The second most common reason is probably for academic course requirements.) Some alternative audiences among capital sources include the following:

1. *Bankers*—Loan proposals have been discussed in an earlier chapter. Of paramount importance are the financial projections, particularly the repayment schedule and collateral.
2. *Public Investors*—Legal requirements for different types of offering circulars can be learned from the Securities and Exchange Commission and from lawyers. Examples of others' prospectuses can be seen at the SEC and brokerage firms. Of paramount importance is full disclosure of risks and potential problems.
3. *Private Investors*—The degree of formality and elaboration may vary among individuals, particularly depending on their relationship with the entrepreneur and venture. What is most important can vary considerably from one investor to another.
4. *Venture Capitalists*—Venture capitalists are not constrained by legal requirements but may be very demanding in terms of detail required and ease of assessment. Of prime importance are upside potential, the multiple investors can hope to achieve, and the size of investment needed to produce that multiple.

The last of these, venture capitalists, are probably the most useful target at whom to aim the plan because they are experienced both in assessing business plans and in helping work on the ventures themselves to achieve their maximum upside potential. At the same time, they are probably most demanding in terms of plan quality, and plans written for them can usually be adapted to other audiences either directly or by eliminating parts.

What Capitalists Want. The plan should provide validity, realism, truthfulness, and full disclosure. The odds that the prospectus will succeed in raising the money are extremely low. Venture capitalists have noted, for instance, that out of every 200 propositions they receive, there will be around 25 worth full reading, perhaps 10 worth full investigation, and one or two worth investing in. Moreover, out of those they do invest in, about 25 percent will be total failures, 50 percent marginal survivals, and only 5 percent highly worthwhile. So the prospectus is far from being any assurance that either financing or venture success will follow. Without a prospectus, however, the odds of raising venture capital are virtually zero. So the prospectus can have a purpose, and to serve that purpose best, it should be drafted with care.

Money-raising plans need not necessarily be elaborate. There always seem to be alleged ventures that received financial support from "back of the envelope" notes or a few handwritten pages. But these are the exceptions. Usually, formal business plans are carefully thought-out documents, systematically presented, and represent a substantial time investment. Some experienced venture investors commented on what they look for in plans:

■ *"Many of us read business plans," said Arthur Lipper, owner of a New York investment firm and investor in many ventures, "hundreds each year, by glancing quickly at the summary and quickly reviewing the five-year projections. If the business concept seems at all reasonable* and *if the five-year projections are of sufficient magnitude to be interesting to me, and appear reasonable in relationship to the various elements, then, and only then, do I think about reading the entire thing. This may be a little like reading a murder mystery by looking at the last chapter first. I want to know what 'happened' and then go through the drill of reading to see (1) how it happened and (2) if it was a reasonable conclusion to reach based upon the facts presented.*"[30]

■ *"The ideal proposal," said venture capitalist Fred Adler, "has a business plan and a market analysis, with a full explanation of how and why the plan will work. It discusses the problems — every company has problems — and tells how they will be overcome. The plan should also contain an evaluation of the competition and show how and why the product and the plan have the competitive edge. A proposal should be an analytical business plan, not a sales pitch."*[31]

■ *"For us the most important thing is the cover letter," according to Steven J. Gilbert, managing general partner of Chemical Venture Partners, a venture capital fund in New York. "Were you referred by someone we know?"*[32]

■ *"The trouble [in the venture capital industry] is that the conventional 'business plan' can become not only a lie — but a long and detailed lie. And, when spiffed up, a high-tech business plan can look glorious to the rookie 'vulture capitalist' who, armed with a fresh Ivy-League MBA, has carefully documented and cataloged the ingredients of the next Apple or Tandem. The trouble is that the would-be imitation entrepreneur has also read the same articles and glory tales in the same magazines. Advice abounds on how to raise bigger and better start-up funds, with several do-it-yourself, fill-in-the-blank business plan formats. And, of course, if the first 'vulture' doesn't like your numbers, a quick tweak can produce the desired results in a blink."*[33]

The time of those reading the plan is important, and the plan should be as direct and to the point as possible.

What Capitalists Do Not Like to See. A way to make the plan more concise and direct is to leave out the items venture capitalists do not like to see. These include:

- *Length for Its Own Sake* — The body of the plan should be no longer than twenty-five to thirty pages maximum. Appendices should be kept down to only those most needed. Inclusion of whole articles or brochures is usually less effective than including only highly selective excerpts or depictions and giving references to the rest.
- *Irrelevant Information* — Unless the information is a direct part of the logic, it should be left out. General references usually are not helpful.
- *Self-Adulation* — The writing style should avoid self-congratulatory words and phrases such as "our excellent," "the fine experience of the management team," "the great promise of this venture," and so forth. It is better instead to give facts and, if it exists,

---

[30]Arthur Lipper III, *Venture's Financing and Investing in Private Companies* (Chicago: Probus Publishing, 1988), p. 130.

[31]Burton W. Teague, "Venture Capital, Who Gets It and Why," *Inc.* (June 1980), p. 70.

[32]Warren Strugatch, "Wooing That Crucial Business Plan Reader," *Venture* (May 1988), p. 80.

[33]"What Companies Are Saying About Venture Capital," *Inc.* (November 1984), p. 14.

the evidence from which such judgments can be deduced by the reader. Evidence of a good customer relationship, for instance, can be a copy of a purchase order or letter of intent. Evidence of management competence can be the list of prior jobs and accomplishments on the founders' resumes. Evidence that the product or service can be expected to work properly may consist of a working prototype or description of the success of another company with something similar. Models, photographs, copies of patents, or other documentation can all help replace self-glorifying adjectives with more convincing facts.

- *Bad Writing*—Having others review the plan and help improve its writing and presentation can be helpful.
- *Professional Jobbing Out*—Turning formulation of the plan over to someone hired to do it completely undermines the credibility of the entrepreneur, who is supposed to be the one who conceives the plan and understands it best.
- *Reliance on Written Document Alone*—Personal introductions and personal presentations to go with the plan can be even more important than the written plan itself. The plan, however, can provide the basis for these too.
- *Terms for the Deal*—Venture capitalists consider this their realm of expertise and believe it is their prerogative to propose the terms.

Outline

Despite the many articles and books that have been written about how to prepare business plans,[34] many plans are not well-written. A review by Roberts of twenty business plans submitted to venture capitalists revealed that

- 30 percent failed to include a specific business strategy.
- 40 percent of the teams lacked marketing experience, and marketing was generally the business area least fully developed.
- 55 percent failed to discuss technical idea protection.
- 75 percent failed to identify details of the competition.
- 10 percent included no financial projections at all, and another 15 percent left out balance sheet projections; 80 percent failed to provide adequate details of the financial projections.
- The more plan deficiencies, the lower the odds of gaining support from venture capitalists.[35]

The plan should include some fairly obvious mechanical details. Even if it is only for the entrepreneur's own benefit and not to be read by others, which is

---

[34]*Business Planning Guide* (Portsmouth, NH: Upstart Publishing, 1981); Robert V. Delaney Jr. and Robert Howell, *How to Prepare an Effective Business Plan* (New York: Amacom, 1986); Donald M. Dible, *Up Your Own Organization* (Santa Clara, CA: Entrepreneur Press, 1971); Lee A. Eckert, J.D. Ryan, and Robert J. Ray, *An Entrepreneur's Plan* (New York: Harcourt Brace Jovanovich, 1985); Gary S. Lynn, *From Concept to Market* (New York: Wiley, 1989); Joseph R. Mancuso, *How to Write a Winning Business Plan* (Englewood Cliffs, NJ: Prentice Hall Press, 1985); Stanley R. Rich and David Gumpert, *Business Plans that Win $$$* (New York: Harper & Row, 1985); W. Keith Schilit, *Entrepreneur's Guide To Preparing a Winning Business Plan* (Englewood Cliffs, NJ: Prentice Hall, 1990); Phil Shragge, *Starting a Business from Scratch* (Edmonton: Northern Alberta Institute of Technology, 1985); John A. White and Jerry F. White, *The Entrepreneur's Master Planning Guide* (Englewood Cliffs, NJ: Prentice Hall, 1983).

[35]Edward B. Roberts, "Business Planning in the Start-Up High-Technology Enterprise." P. 107 in Hornaday et al., *Frontiers of Entrepreneurship Research*, 1983.

unlikely, there should be an introductory summary, a table of contents with page numbers, and clear section headings, which will help make it easier to read, return to, and work with. It may also help to use declarative sentences for section headings, sentences that summarize a main point of the section. The sections themselves should begin with clear but brief descriptions of what the venture will deliver to customers, what its main competitive advantage will be, what its present status is, what it will seek to become, and what needs to be done next. After that can come sections providing fuller descriptions and supporting information.

A possible outline for this information follows. Other formats, illustrating that the appropriate order of topics can vary from one venture to another, appear in Appendix A.

I. INTRODUCTION
    1. Executive Summary
    2. Table of Contents
    3. Layout of the Plan
    4. Product or Service Description
II. VENTURE DESIGN
    5. Proposed Role of the Company
    6. Needs of the Venture
    7. Market and Sales Expectations
    8. Competitors' Relative Advantages and Disadvantages
    9. Technical Development to Be Done
    10. Production Scenario
    11. People and Organization
III. LONGER TERM
    12. Strategy for Staying Ahead Long Term
    13. Financial Projections
IV. SUPPORTING DETAILS
    14. Financial Assumption Statements
    15. Supporting Detail Appendices

An expanded outline might include the following elements, elaborated where appropriate by answers to selected planning questions that have been suggested in earlier chapters. (The plan of the Priam Corporation, a company that turned out to be very successful in the computer industry, appears in Appendix B).

I. INTRODUCTION
    1. *Executive Summary* presents the high points of the plan in one or two pages, using specific figures, dates, names, and descriptions as much as possible to tell
        a. What the company will do; what its product or service is
        b. The present stage of development
        c. How the selling will be done: direct or through what channels, and with what methods
        d. What the competitive advantage of the company will be; how the product or service will be superior to competitors'

     e. Who the key people in the company are: name, age, share of owner-ship, position, years of related experience, and what they will do

     f. Anticipated company size — sales, people, profits — one, two, and five years hence

     g. How much money will be needed by when

(The order of these items may be rearranged. The objective is to capture with facts, not generalities, the reader's interest.)

2. *Table of Contents* lists major sections with page numbers for both the sections and the appendices of the plan.

3. *Layout of the Plan* gives a one-paragraph reiteration of what the venture is about and what it needs, followed by a brief description of how the plan is organized and what sequence its reasoning will follow.

4. *Product or Service Description* includes what is special about it. The plan should make as clear as possible just what *new value* the venture will make available to potential customers. Pictures or sketches of the product, advertisements, equipment to be used, or other aspects of the enterprise can help add realism to the vision it entails. Another often helpful exhibit is a competitive product/service (value) grid, listing competitive products/services along one axis and features along another. Where possible it is better to use numbers (figures of merit) to describe levels of performance rather than just words. Examples often appear in motor magazines and *Consumer Reports*. (For possible additional material, refer to the questions at the end of Chapter 2.)

II. VENTURE DESIGN

5. *Proposed Role of the Company* in developing, producing, and/or selling this product or service, short and long term includes an explicit description of the company's strategy, possibly through a mission statement, and a brief indication of how it is supposed to work.

6. *Needs of the Venture* are those that must be obtained in order to be able to pursue these goals. These may include additional financing, recruiting of key people, obtaining certain licenses, customer or supplier contracts, government permissions, and so forth. They can be listed in order of priority with a brief description in this section and further elaboration elsewhere in the plan.

7. *Market and Sales Expectations* include *target customers* and why they should buy; the *total market,* how it is composed, segment by segment with profiles of typical target customers for each segment, and how its segments are changing; as well as the *sales plan* for reaching that market, how the first sale will be made (possibly described as a customer buying decision scenario, noting sales barriers and how they might be overcome) and how follow-up sales will be made, with a dated schedule. In addition to the product comparison grid previously noted, others that list market segments along one axis and features of the venture, its product/service and the strategy aimed at each segment along the other can also be helpful to display important information in compact and easy-to-grasp

form. A PERT diagram for promotion and the creation of sales channels, listing milestones, timing, and major costs can be a helpful display to include. (See the questions at the end of Chapters 2 and 7.)

As noted earlier, marketing was inadequately treated in the sample of plans submitted to venture capitalists who were studied by Roberts. Further emphasis on the need for attention to this area was added by other venture capitalists interviewed by Strugatch, who observed that "The marketing section often gets inadequate attention: It just isn't enough to plan to hire a marketing director in six months or to set up a regional marketing office in two years. Investors expect more. For starters they expect you'll scout out your competition—anticipating rivals not even at the starting gate—before they do."[36]

8. *Competitors' Relative Advantages and Disadvantages* for coping with what the venture will offer should be projected into the future. In addition to the comparison grids previously noted, others that list competitors along one axis and such features as their positions, strategies, strengths, and weaknesses along the other can also be helpful displays. (See the questions at the end of Chapters 1 and 2.)

9. *Technical Development to Be Done* to put the product ahead of the competition and keep it there includes time and costs. A PERT diagram for this development depicting milestones, timing, and major costs can be a helpful display. (See the questions at the end of Chapter 2.)

10. *Production Scenario* includes location, resources needed, where they will come from, and on what schedule production will commence. As with the development of sales channels and technical features, a PERT diagram can help in describing the plan for development of operations within the company. A time line with major milestones and a Gantt chart showing expected start and completion dates for them may also be helpful. It should make evident the main priorities and potential bottlenecks. Such techniques as failure mode analysis (the main ways things can go wrong) and fault tree analysis (the cascading of problems that can occur from a particular item going wrong) can help with examination of ways to cope with possible unfavorable contingencies. (See the questions at the end of Chapter 8.)

11. *People and Organization* includes those who will make up the founding team and subsequent work force, their qualifications, and how those are special compared to competitors. Specific prior experiences and accomplishments of key people and how those are relevant to competitive activities of the venture should be noted in the text with reference given to more detailed résumés attached as an appendix. Often an organization chart, or perhaps more than one showing different stages in the venture's development, as illustrated by the "prefunding" versus "operating" orga-

---

[36]Strugatch, "Wooing That Crucial Business Plan Reader," p. 80.

nization charts from one venture plan shown in Figures 10–1 and 10–2, will be helpful. (See the questions at the end of Chapters 4 and 8.)

III. LONGER TERM

12. *Strategy for Staying Ahead Long Term* is needed as competitors respond to the opportunity exploited by the venture. (See the questions at the end of Chapter 1.)

13. *Financial Projections* include *pro forma* income statements, balance sheets, and cash flow projections—monthly for the first two years, annually for three more. They should be detailed down to 5 percent or less on each total. It should be clear just how cash will be applied and how much could be recovered if the venture were to be liquidated at various stages. There should also be some form of sensitivity analysis that examines "what if variations" of important numbers in the forecasts. A breakeven chart, particularly one that includes expected dates for various levels of performance, can also be a helpful exhibit in this regard. Also helpful can be projecting financials at three levels—optimistic, worst reasonable case, and expected most likely. (See the questions at the end of Chapters 5 and 6.)

IV. SUPPORTING DETAILS

14. *Financial Assumption Statements* follow the financial statements and are tied to their most important numbers with footnotes telling how those numbers were derived.

15. *Supporting Detail Appendices* contain market information, technical specifications, and resumes of founders, displayed as appendices that are listed with page numbers in the table of contents and referenced in the text.

This list will fit some ventures but not others. Generally, the order of topics should start with whatever is most important. Sometimes that may be develop-

FIGURE 10–1 **Prefunding Organization Chart**

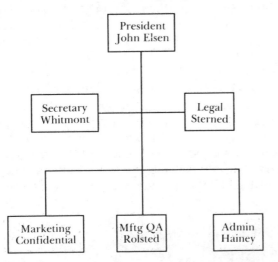

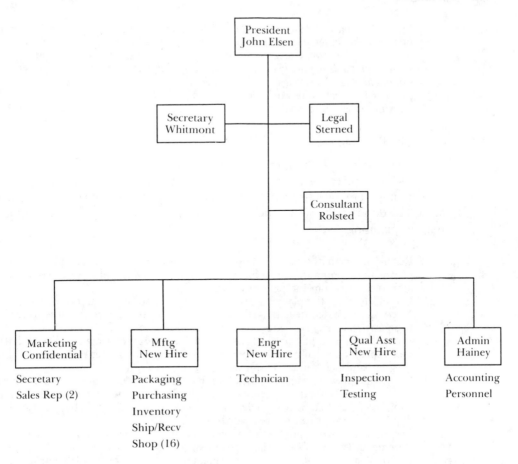

FIGURE 10–2   Operating Organization Chart

ment of certain technology. Other times it may be the nature of the customer and market segments or the recruiting of key personnel. It is up to the entrepreneur to anticipate what the reader will want most to know and to put that information forward as directly as possible.

It is helpful to include (1) as direct an entry as possible for each topic, (2) the use of graphical displays wherever they can convey more information more quickly and easily for the reader than words, (3) decimal numbering of sections, (4) use of declarative sentences for section headings where possible, and (5) consideration of options and alternate scenarios that will add to the venture's flexibility in responding to surprise developments. Against these many possible inclusions must be balanced the advantage of brevity. Tight wording, graphical displays, and the use of appendices for backup alternate views and supporting data can be ways of combining both.

Wherever possible the plan should be expressed in measurable terms. One experienced venture capitalist gave the following example.

■   *State what you will do in a way that can be measured. A proposal we worked on recently included the statement "In our initial marketing efforts, our principals will contact representative customer companies in each of our major market segments." This is so vague it probably applies to all new ventures and therefore says nothing. As reworked, the statement spelled out which segments would be covered, how many companies would be contacted in each, who would contact them, by when, and what results were expected. Backup material included a complete schedule for this critical marketing work.*[37]

The Planning Process

Planning is often fun, but if well done it is time-consuming and not necessarily an easy process, particularly if seeking out additional information is required. If planning were easy, it would probably not be very valuable, because it could always be done on the spot rather than in advance. The following suggestions may help in planning:

1. Regard any plan as tentative. This can make it easier to begin the process, because a plan is not a commitment. Expect to try different variations in developing the plan and to depart from the plan in executing it.
2. Do not delegate the planning process, either to another person or to a set of purely mechanical procedures. It is the process of thinking through the future of the company that may be more valuable than the plan itself.
3. Write the plan out; do not just think about it. Writing has a way of making thinking more specific and of exposing gaps and holes. It allows later reference for assessing progress and helps in communicating the plan to others.
4. Use hard data where possible. Much of the plan must be guesswork — the future sales, for instance. But other parts of it can and should be factual, such as material, equipment, and labor costs; advertising costs; and so forth. These may take some digging to get but can be well worth it.
5. Pretest the plan against written data. Such data include any plans or financial statements that may be available from similar companies and also the more generalized data on similar types of companies that may be available from Dun and Bradstreet ratios, Robert Morris Associates ratios, and trade association statistics.
6. Pretest the plan against knowledgeable individuals. These may include such "no cost" advisers as bankers, venture capitalists, and other entrepreneurs, as well as those who will charge for the service such as business consultants.
7. Build in controls to match the plan. The company's information and controls system should be designed to give early signals regarding the most critical problems and to indicate the degree to which the plan is working out.
8. Do not let the plan be a substitute for action.

A highly successful venture capitalist, Ben Rosen, observed of planning that

■   *It is a good discipline to get together the staffing requirements, specifics of the product plan, specifics of the marketing plan. It takes the idea and fleshes it out. But our decision to invest isn't based on the fleshing out. We're really investing in people.*[38]

[37]John P. Windle, "The Financial Proposal." P. 67 in William D. Putt, *How to Start Your Own Business* (Cambridge, MA: MIT Press, 1974).

[38]Erik Larson, "The Best-Laid Plans," *Inc.* (February 1987), p. 64.

Some aspects of planning have to be left as an art form rather than a science. In starting a disco, for instance, how to arrange the decor and lay out the facilities, what sort of talent to hire for playing records and for live performances, what sort of sound equipment to buy, what to serve and what to charge for it, how to deal with different types of customers, and how to order needed supplies are all areas where a "greenhorn" could go wrong. One solution can be to team up with a partner whose experience includes proven capability to handle those aspects. Another can be to hire selectively as each need arises.

In an established company where repetition, routine, and planning are more common, this heavy task could be performed by a team of experienced specialists. But in a new company it falls entirely on the entrepreneur, as illustrated by Rex Lindsay, a former production manager who started his own magnetic tape reel company on the San Francisco Peninsula:

■ *I had been used to an office with a staff, a secretary, the whole bit. So I went to my office and I began to plan. Now, let's see, I need the Industrial Engineering Department to set up the layout of the plant, and I'd better ask Production Planning and Scheduling to work out the production rates of all the machines and match them; better have the Purchasing Department start looking for material sources, and better get the Personnel Department writing out some manuals. Then I took a walk around the plant, which was an empty building with nothing in it, came back to my office and realized that I was all those departments, and if anything was going to be done I was the one who had to do it.*

There are some indications that ambitious effort in planning produces better results. A *Venture* survey, which drew 1,090 responses from small firms, 68 percent of which were five or fewer years old, found that those whose plans extended five or more years tended to have higher accuracy than those with shorter plans. Moreover, one respondent who reported accuracy to within 2 percent said his secret was "not quarterly revisions, but revisions that take a quarter to complete."[39]

PLANNING QUESTIONS

The following questions are intended to stimulate thought about what should be considered in moving ahead with a venture. Which questions best apply can vary among entrepreneurs and ventures, as can the order in which they should be considered, the priority that should be placed on them, and which of them should be answered in a written plan.

Sequences

- What would be optimistic, pessimistic, and most likely time lines for start-up actions and milestones?
- Is there a time window that this company must be started within?

---

[39]Nancy Madlin, "Sticking to Business Plans," *Venture* (April 1985), p. 25.

- What might make the venture too late to take advantage of it?
- What could be done to get around such a possible problem?
- What contingency options are available for responding to setbacks and minimizing downside losses?
- What will be the alarm system for signaling shortfalls in cash as far in advance as possible?
- What branches in a decision tree and/or PERT diagram are likely to be most influential?

Direct Action

- What steps are low enough in cost and high enough in learning value to justify taking them with little or no planning?

Selective Planning

- What, in order of priority, were reasons for the planning exercise?
- Has the planning been done in such a way as to fit those reasons?
- Was there an appropriate balance between obtaining new pertinent information and time spent on planning?
- Was help from others adequately sought in the planning process?
- After thinking through the plan, does it appear that the business should be entered boldly, cautiously, or not at this time?
- How well does the plan fit the aspirations and talents of the people who should carry it out?

Formal Plan Writing

- Have the founder(s) worked extensively on the plan themselves, not simply farmed it out to others?
- Is the presentation style appropriately suited to the needs of those who are supposed to read and use the plan?
- Have graphical depictions been included for those likely to find them helpful?
- What are the most vulnerable parts of the plan, and what should be done next about them?
- Does the plan include consideration of possible contingencies?
- Has a sensitivity analysis been run on financial forecasts of the plan?
- Have the people whose participation in the plan is important all read and commented on it?
- What are the expectations about how further revision of the plan will be accomplished and utilized in the future?
- How well do the different elements of the plan fit together?
- Are appropriate copies of literature, photos, or sketches of what the business is and what it sells attached?
- Can the length of the entire plan be kept under thirty pages?

POSSIBLE MILESTONES FOR A PLANNING TIME LINE

The milestones for the final plan can be developed by compiling those that were developed in earlier chapters. Some milestones for the planning process itself, which should not appear in the plan but may be helpful in developing it, are as follows:

- Prioritizing of plan contents
- Sections of plan completed
- Full draft prepared
- Review of draft by another knowledgeable party
- Successive revisions

Appendix A

OTHER BUSINESS PLAN OUTLINES

Microcomputer Rental Store

    I. Introduction
   II. Conceptual Plan
  III. Definition of Market
  IV. Product Scope
   V. Location
  VI. Cost Analysis
 VII. Staffing and Inventory
VIII. Projections
  IX. Conclusion

Motor Components Company

   I. Objectives, History
  II. Market and Pricing
 III. Production
 IV. Financial Analysis
  V. Organization and Future Plans
 VI. Appendices: Product Details, Contacts, Suppliers

Import Company

  I. Customer Profile
 II. Product
III. Suppliers
IV. Buyers
 V. Competitors

VI. Sales Forecasts
VII. Cost and Price
VIII. Shipping
IX. Paperwork Procedures
X. Financing

Engine Builder

I. Objectives
II. Product
III. Marketing
IV. Operations
V. Financial Plan
VI. Overall Strategy

Appendix B

BUSINESS PLAN EXAMPLE

SUMMARY BUSINESS PLAN

PRIAM CORPORATION

12 July 1978

CONTENTS

			Page
1	–	INTRODUCTION	3
2	–	FOUNDERS	4
3	–	MARKET	6
4	–	PRODUCT	9
5	–	COMPETITION	11
6	–	FINANCIALS	13

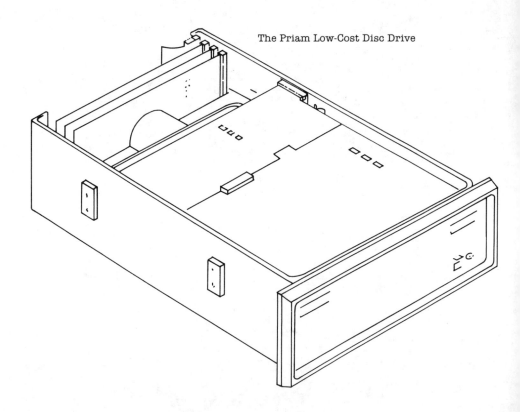

The Priam Low-Cost Disc Drive

1—INTRODUCTION

PRIAM, a California corporation, was founded to develop, manufacture, and market mass storage devices for small business computers, distributed processors, and word processors. The initial product is a low-cost disk drive based on a state-of-the-art Winchester technology.

Winchester disk technology was first introduced by IBM for its large systems due to the significantly lower cost, higher reliability, and higher capacity offered by this new technology. IBM shipped the first Winchester disk (IBM 3350) for the large S/370 systems in early 1976. PRIAM intends to rapidly bring this new 3350 technology to the small business computer market, thereby leap frogging competitors who are using non-Winchester technology or early versions of Winchester (i.e., IBM 3340).

The uniqueness of PRIAM is that this product will be the lowest possible cost 30–40 megabyte Winchester disk drive using a fast-access mechanism.

The market for low-cost Winchester disk drives under 50 megabytes is expected to explode over the next five years. Unit shipments will reach levels experienced by today's floppy disks. This explosion will be driven by small business computing, distributed processing, and word processing demands for reliable, low-cost mass storage. The fastest growth segment within these markets will be multiple-terminal systems, which demand fast disk access capability to satisfy multiple users running multiple programs that share on-line data bases.

Competition also senses this market opportunity and a variety of entrants are making plans or introducing products. Most entrants will find Winchester technology surprisingly difficult to design and manufacture efficiently. Shugart and CDC will be the toughest competitors. Shugart can be beaten on performance in multiple-terminal applications and matched in cost at the 30-megabyte capacity level. CDC can be beaten on cost. However, both companies have strong established market positions and product introduction leads that will need to be overcome by PRIAM's superior price-performance product.

The PRIAM strategy is to capitalize on the window that has opened as a result of the expected shift to Winchester disk technology. The high twin barriers to entry of the difficult technology and the heavy capital requirements will be overcome with a Winchester-experienced team and institutional-level financial backing. Product development will focus on achieving the low-cost design in a small, reliable package. Later product enhancements and additions will be aimed at building a disk product family. Financial leverage will be used during the launch since most successful OEM businesses generate cash after momentum has been achieved. Manufacturing rights may be sold in Europe or Japan in order to minimize dilution. PRIAM will sell its product direct to OEMs in the U.S., but will initially use distributors offshore. Selling expense will be minimized by focusing on OEMs rather than end users. Other overheads will also be minimized to allow more effective price competition. PRIAM will target on the multiple-terminal small business computer (SBC), clustered word processing, and distributed processing markets. Initially, one or two large OEMs will be targeted to get the PRIAM disk accepted in the industry. Only one standard product will be offered and variations/ options will be limited. The factory will be focused on that single product and costs will be driven down to achieve the low-cost position. Strong manufacturing controls will be emphasized to allow rapid but controlled growth. Time-phased investments will be made in automatic production equipment. Class 100 clean room conditions will be established to ensure superior product reliability.

Financing PRIAM will require an equity investment of $4.1 million during the first two years. The first round of financing will be $1.5 million. Other capital will be raised via an equipment lease line, a receivables line, and inventory advances.

The founders group is comprised of individuals who are uniquely qualified, through experience and training, to organize and manage a start up disk drive company and to design the products required.

PRESIDENT: William J. Schroeder

Industry-specific experience in disk drives. Also experience and training in general business and technology management.

1976–1978	MEMOREX CORPORATION Santa Clara, California

Manager of Product Planning. Responsible for equipment product planning. Initiated formal product management disciplines. Led new product effort from product concept to first production shipment. Presented MRX product strategy overview to numerous key accounts, helping to capture several significant orders. Prior to this assignment was responsible for strategic planning/acquisitions at the corporate level. Completed two acquisitions.

1972–1976	McKINSEY & COMPANY, INC. Los Angeles, California

Associate. Industrial marketing and business strategy projects, including the organizational work to implement changed strategies.

1964–1970	HONEYWELL, INC. Minneapolis, Minnesota

Senior Development Engineer (1968–70) Systems & Research Center. Managed digital avionics proposal efforts. Provided technical support to marketing. Was co-op engineer with Aerospace Division (1964–66).

1970–1972	HARVARD BUSINESS SCHOOL Boston, Massachusetts

MBA with High Distinction. Baker Scholar. Emphasis on finance and marketing.

1962–1968	MARQUETTE UNIVERSITY Milwaukee, Wisconsin

MSEE and BEE. Eta Kappa Nu, Bacon Foundation Fellowship, Engineering Service Key. Emphasis on digital control systems.

VICE PRESIDENT—ENGINEERING: Alonzo A. Wilson

Twenty-three years experience in development of disk storage subsystems through release to manufacturing. Co-founder of two disk start up operations.

1975–1978	MEMOREX CORPORATION Santa Clara, California

Program Manager—3650 Disk Subsystem. As program chief engineer had direct responsibility for hardware, software, and microcode development and release. As Program Manager also had start up responsibility for manufacturing, field engineering, product planning, test engineering, and quality assurance. Program was launched in March, 1976. First engineering-built hardware (still installed and on rent) was delivered to customers in March, 1977. First preproduction units were shipped in July and first production units in September, 1977. This version of the IBM 3350 will be the mainstay of MRX equipment revenues and profits during the late 1970's and early 1980's. Prior to this assignment was Director of New OEM File Development. Was responsible for first known application of Winchester technology (IBM 3340) to OEM disk product (MRX 601).

1973– DISK SYSTEMS CORPORATION (STC)
1975   Santa Clara, California

Director of Engineering.   One of three founders of the Storage Technology Corporation disk start up operation. Put STC in the disk drive business.

1971– TELEX DASD
1973   Santa Clara, California

Manager of Drive Development.   One of five IBM engineers recruited to start the Direct Access Storage Division for Telex.

1956– IBM CORPORATION
1971   San Jose, California

Senior Technical Engineer.   Wide range of product and technology development with increasing scope and responsibility. Participated in development of RAMAC 305, 1311, 2314, and 3330 products.

1954– SAN JOSE STATE UNIVERSITY
1956   San Jose, California

BSEE coursework.   Left due to sudden death in family.

VICE PRESIDENT—MARKETING: George Toor

Twenty years experience in marketing disk and tape storage subsystems worldwide. Co-founder of successful disk company.

1978–   PERSCI
Present Santa Monica, California

Vice President Marketing.   Joined with objective of establishing direct selling organization, restructuring rep organization, and defining market niche for this specialized product.

1969– WANGCO
1978   Los Angeles, California

Founder and Vice President Marketing.   Wrote first business plan before company was started in mid-1969. First product shipped mid-1970. Revenues reached $1.6 million in 1971 and grew at a 70% compound rate to $40 million in 1977. Established 160-person distribution and service organization. Developed domestic and international markets. Built customer base of several hundred accounts. Captured major business from Datapoint, Univac, IBM, Data 100, CMC, Ferranti, Olivetti, Sycor, Data General, Entrex, General Automation, Four Phase, Basic Four, Harris, Telefunken, Telemecanique.

1967– CAELUS
1969   Los Angeles, California

Regional Manager.   Established Southwest region.

1958– AMPEX
1967   Los Angeles, California

    Regional Sales Manager. Computer Products Division. Established Southwest region.

1948– UNIVERSITY OF MINNESOTA
1950   Minneapolis, Minnesota

    B.A. in Journalism. Previous coursework with USAF and USN (2 years) in engineering.

VICE PRESIDENT—MANUFACTURING: The Vice President—Engineering will act as the Vice President—Manufacturing during the first 3–6 months. He will be supported by the manufacturing engineering, test engineering, and material control managers. Several Vice President—Manufacturing candidates with Winchester process experience are under consideration.

VICE PRESIDENT—FINANCE: The President will act as the Vice President—Finance during the first 9–12 months. The successful candidate will have a strong control background and will have high-volume manufacturing experience.

TECHNICAL TEAM: This team is comprised of a group of top-rated disk drive and microprocessor engineers who are highly experienced in the technical task PRIAM needs to perform. These key individuals are briefly described below:

1. *Mgr. Mechanical:* Ph.D. from Stanford University, 1966. Also M.S. (1956) and B.S. (1953). In computer peripheral development and release to production since 1960. Designed disk drives for IBM, STC, Data 100, and MRX. Worked on both MRX 601 and MRX 3650. Five patents, six published papers.
2. *Mgr. Read-Write/Servo:* B.E.E. from U.S.C., 1955. Tau Beta Pi, Eta Kappa Nu. Disk drive electronics design with Telex, CDS, STC, GSI, and MRX. Worked on both MRX 601 and MRX 3650. Specialist in analog circuit design—both read/write and servo circuits.
3. *Mgr. Logic:* B.S.E.E., San Jose State. Currently working on M.S.E.E. Tau Beta Pi, Eta Kappa Nu. In-depth experience with digital circuit design, particularly microprocessor based. Processor designs with AMS, NSC, Singer Business Machines, and MRX—some disk related. Five patents, three published papers.

In addition, several other technical personnel have been informally approached and it is expected that a strong technical team can be quickly assembled.

3—MARKET

The rapidly growing small business computer (SBC) market is causing an explosion in demand for low-cost, high reliability disk drives. This exceptional market opportunity is described below in terms of SBC growth, the disk drive's role in this growth, resulting requirements for new disk products, and a sizing of the disk market.

SBC Growth

The demand for SBCs, distributed processing, and word processing has been fueled by declining costs, increasing reliability, and expanding software/applications. Thus, small business computers and minicomputers have become *the* EDP growth segments of the future.

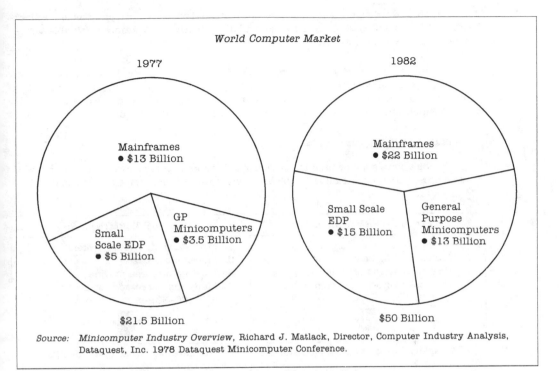

World Computer Market

1977

Mainframes
● $13 Billion

Small
Scale EDP
● $5 Billion

GP
Minicomputers
● $3.5 Billion

$21.5 Billion

1982

Mainframes
● $22 Billion

Small Scale
EDP
● $15 Billion

General
Purpose
Minicomputers
● $13 Billion

$50 Billion

Source: *Minicomputer Industry Overview*, Richard J. Matlack, Director, Computer Industry Analysis, Dataquest, Inc. 1978 Dataquest Minicomputer Conference.

Most SBC growth will take place in the multiple terminal segment, at the expense of growth in the single-terminal segment.

SBC CATEGORY	U.S. SBC MARKET ($ MILLIONS)				
	1975	*1977*	*1979*	*1982*	*1977–82 AAGR*
Single Terminal Systems	9,000 $320	13,500 $440	19,000 $500	28,000 $450	16% 0%
Multiple Terminal Systems	1,000 $60	3,500 $175	10,000 $485	29,000 $1,300	53% 49%
Source: Dataquest, Inc.: MCIS Volume II: February, 1978.					

Disk Drive SBC Role

The disk drive comprises the major component of SBC cost (30–40%), and will remain as such in the future for three reasons:

1. Electronics costs are declining more rapidly than electromechanical costs.
2. Demands for SBC mass storage capacity per system are continually increasing as software applications expand.
3. Alternative means of nonvolatile storage, e.g., bubble memory, are not expected to be cost competitive with moving head disk until the 1990's.

Moreover, since the disk drive is an electro-mechanical device, it is perceived as less reliable than the CPU or memory. SBC users are particularly sensitive to this since a valuable asset—business information—is stored on the disk.

Thus, a low-cost, highly-reliable disk drive of sufficient capacity for the small user (30–40 megabytes) would provide the best vehicle for the SBC or word processing manufacturer to significantly improve the price/performance of his system. This in turn explains why the low-cost Winchester disk is expected to be an explosive growth product.

Disk Drive Requirements

The disk drive's major function is to provide random-access mass storage for the SBC. The two different classes of SBCs, however, imply different disk drive requirements.

SINGLE-TERMINAL SBC	MULTIPLE-TERMINAL SBC
1. Single-tasked 2. Dedicated data base 3. Most data stored off line 4. Few disk accesses per second (e.g., 3)	1. Multi-tasked, virtual system 2. Shared data base 3. Most data stored on line 4. Many disk accesses per second (e.g., 20–30)
⬇	⬇
2–5 megabyte capacity at 100–300 msec access time	20–40 megabyte capacity at 35–60 msec access time

The winning multiple-terminal SBC disk drive will be the low-cost, high-reliability, fast-access entrant. It is PRIAM management's contention that the disk drive that can best meet the OEM's objectives will be a single-platter disk based on 3350 Winchester technology using a linear voice-coil access mechanism.

Market Size

The market for the low-cost disk drive based on Winchester technology is on the verge of a rapid expansion, lasting perhaps for 5 to 10 years. A recent sampling of a variety of industry experts indicates a market, in units, as is shown below:

LOW-COST WINCHESTER DISK MARKET (UNITS)						
1977	1978	1979	1980	1981	1982	1983
3000	10,000	30,000	70,000	130,000	200,000	270,000

PRIAM believes it can capture 10% of this market by 1983.

The PRIAM product is described in this section in terms of the basic product, planned options, product specifications, pricing and possible future product extensions.

Basic Drive

The basic drive product is design optimized around a single fixed disk using low-mass head, high-recording density technology. This latest "3350 Winchester" head/disk technology is the most cost effective and reliable technology available in the industry today.

1. *Reliable* because the low-mass heads "land" and "take off" on the lubricated disk surface and because the media is sealed from the outside environment, thereby eliminating head crashes. Moreover, the technology has been proven by "large-system drives" (e.g., IBM 3350, STC 8350, ISS 7350, MRX 3650) that are presently in high-volume production.
2. *Cost effective* because this high-volume production will drive down the cost of critical head/disk components and will allow PRIAM to capitalize on the technology investments already made by the IBM plug compatible disk drive industry. Cost effective also because it allows the most efficient bit-packing densities available today, and because it eliminates the need for complex head loading and cartridge insertion mechanisms. Finally, Winchester products require no preventive maintenance, and are therefore extremely cost effective on a "life cycle" basis.

The mechanics of the drive are a structurally rigid "unitized" base casting, a low-cost voice coil motor, four heads, a single disk, and a spindle and drive motor.

The electronics are functionally packaged on three printed circuit boards (read/write, servo and control logic). The control function will be performed by a microprocessor-based design that will simplify interface and servo requirements and will offer diagnostic capability in the drive itself.

A closed-loop, low-mass linear voice coil positioner is used for access speed and accuracy. The recorded servo tracks offer the advantage of a precisely controlled sector size, selectable from 256 bytes to 2048 bytes in 256 byte increments. Moreover, the separate access mechanism for each platter (there by virtue of the single-platter design) also minimizes arm contention and allows overlapping seeks in multiple-disk systems.

The electronic interface will be the defacto "industry standard" SMD interface. Other interfaces will also be available (e.g., the Shugart interface). The VFO/data separation functions will be provided at the interface. A unique standard feature of the PRIAM disk drive will be the ability to dynamically correct single-bit drop outs in the read data. This feature may be patentable.

Power required for the disk unit is standard 50 or 60 cycle AC power. An integrated power supply provides DC power to the drive. Use of a brushless DC motor for the spindle drive simplifies the spindle design and improves the reliability of the disk unit. The integrated power supply is expected to be capable of powering a "companion" floppy disk drive, a potential cost savings to the SBC manufacturer. (Note: Floppy disks are expected to be frequently packaged with Winchester disks in future SBCs as their manufacturers adopt the S/32, S/34, and Series 1 architecture introduced by IBM).

The direct labor and material cost of a fully configured PRIAM disk (including power supply and data separation) will be slightly less than $1000. The objective of the design and manufacturing engineering teams will be to further reduce this product cost.

Options

Limited options are planned to be offered along with the initial disk drive model.

1. *Formatter:* This option will furnish the necessary electronics to format all tracks on the disk drive with the correct sector data and to write the necessary inter-record gaps. Since this function ties closely to the CPU operation, most users will design their own formatter. However, the PRIAM formatter will be required by PRIAM to check out its own disk unit, will be useful for large OEMs to evaluate the PRIAM disk drive, and will be potentially attractive as a product offering for small OEMs and systems houses. The formatter will be a physically separate device. Later, an LSI floppy disk port will be added as an optional feature on the formatter.
2. *Packaging:* Several packaging aids will be offered including a front panel appearance option, a desk top mounting case, and 19" relay rack mounting hardware.

Product Specifications

The preliminary PRIAM product specifications are depicted below:

PRIAM MODEL 3350 PRODUCT SPECIFICATIONS	
Capacity (megabytes)	33.2
Cylinders	555
Track Capacity (bytes)	19,963
Cylinder Capacity (bytes)	59,904
Tracks Per Inch	480
Bits Per Inch	6,300
Data Transfer Rate (k bytes/sec)	889
RPM	2,660
Average Latency (msec)	11.2
Access Time	
Minimum (msec)	20
Average (msec)	50
Maximum (msec)	95
Power (watts)	200
MTBF (hours)	7,500
MTTR (hours)	0.5
Width (inches)	17
Height (inches)	7
Length (inches)	20

Pricing

The fully configured 33 megabyte unit, including power supply, will be offered on the terms depicted below.

PRIAM MODEL 3350 PRICING		
ANNUAL PURCHASE COMMITMENT (UNITS)		$/UNIT
1–4		3950
5–9		3450
10–19		3150
20–39		2850
40–99		2550
100–249		2350
over 249	Published	2150
a500–749	Not Published	2000
750–999		1900
1000–1499		1800
1500–1999		1750
2000–2499		1700
over 2499		1650

aExpected 4Q81 average selling price.

Note: Price reduced by $250–300 for special orders where power supply not included. Also, price reduced by $100 for special order 11MB unit, $50 for 22MB unit. These price-reducing options will not be published.

Future Enhancements

Potential follow-on products and product enhancements are summarized below:

1. *Model 4450:* Embed the servo tracks and increase capacity to 44.3 megabytes with only a slight production cost increase.
2. *Model 9035:* Incorporate 3350 double-density technology (probably available to independents in about 2 years) to double the Model 4450 disk capacity to 90 megabytes. Improve access time to 35 msec with lower-mass inertial components.
3. *Custom LSI:* Reduce electronics cost by implementing portions of the electronics with custom-designed large scale integrated circuits.

5—COMPETITION

Competition will be intense in the growing Winchester market, but many of those who announce Winchester products, or lay plans to develop such products, will not be successful in achieving efficient production of this difficult technology. The most serious competitors PRIAM will face in the low-end market will be Shugart and CDC.

1. *Shugart:* Announced in April, 1978, the SA 4000 "hard floppy," with production quantities available in 1979. This device, while gaining a great deal of attention due to its aggressive pricing ($1800 at 250 unit quantity for 29 megabytes, $1325 for 14 megabytes; power supply not included) has several serious drawbacks:

A. Uses stepper motor positioner, and thereby achieves only a slow 90-msec average access time. This will not allow Shugart to be a contender in the fast-growth multiple-terminal SBC market.

B. By virtue of the stepper motor, the SA 4000 positioning accuracy is limited, resulting in a relatively poor bit packing density (172 TPI, 5640 BPI) vis-a-vis the PRIAM drive (480 TPI, 6300 BPI). Steel band/capstan wearing could further degrade head positioning accuracy. Moreover, the SA 4000 cannot be upgraded in capacity when IBM doubles the density of its 3350, and is therefore a "dead end" technology.

C. Due to this poor bit packing density, the SA 4000 needs 2 disks and 8 heads to achieve 29 megabytes, vis-a-vis the PRIAM drive's 1 disk and 4 heads to achieve 33 megabytes. Thus, what the SA 4000 gains in cost by using open-loop stepper-motor servo techniques, it loses by using additional heads and disks.

D. Moreover, the SA 4000 requires a special "clock track," and a separate fixed head and read circuit for the clock track, since servo information is not available to select sector size. This adds further product cost.

Furthermore, the Shugart drive does not include a power supply, and Shugart expects that fully half its drives will be shipped with the $350 fixed-head option as a way of reducing the impact of its slow access time. These price/performance factors, coupled with the expected longer-term effects of the Shugart acquisition by Xerox, will prevent Shugart from achieving a major position in the multiple-terminal system segment. Shugart will, however, probably dominate the single-terminal segment.

2. *CDC:* Announced and shipped a 2-platter 3340 Winchester disk drive called the mini-modile (MMD). At $2500 for 12 megabytes and $2800 for 24 megabytes (250-unit pricing), the CDC 9730 MMD would not appear to be a long-term contender in the low-cost disk market were it not for CDC's strong market position. The drive does include an integrated power supply and offers a 40-msec access time. It can also be later upgraded in capacity. However, CDC's large size and OEM product proliferation will tend to make it a less responsive competitor than Shugart.

3. *Calcomp:* Formally announced and displayed their "Marksman" drive at the National Computer Conference (NCC). The "Marksman," a product basically similar to the SA 4000 in technology, drew a significant amount of attention at the show. The product was judged by most to be more impressive than the Shugart unit, which was also on display.

The "Marksman" is well packaged and leaves a good first impression. However, closer examination shows a fair amount of "rambling" electrical connections and components, especially those related to the AC induction motor and the brake. It would appear that there is a high exposure to AC noise due to the routing of cables and the spreading of components, e.g., the starting capacitor and brake switching components. Moreover, the specifications on the unit were changed one week before the show in two key areas:

A. *Bits per inch* on the unit were increased from 6300 to 7545. This 20% increase over current standard industry practice presents some exposure to read/write reliability and places an additional constraint on the head and disk. Calcomp attempted to compensate for this by reducing the disk speed to 2400 RPM, which is approximately 20% below the industry standard for their level of Winchester technology.

B. *Access times* were decreased from 92.5 ms average to 60 ms average and 162.5 ms maximum to 130 ms maximum (includes settling time). This 35% decrease in the average access time is very difficult to achieve with a stepper motor technology. At this rate of speed the stepper must be capable of moving at 1850 + steps per second. Whether or not Calcomp will be able to perform to specification with production hardware (vs "engineering-tuned" units) remains to be seen.

It appears that Calcomp made the last minute "spec" changes so that their unit would be more competitive with Shugart's unit. If they can perform to this specification, PRIAM would consider their unit the most competitive of any offering to date. However, it is significant that the project manager for this program resigned and left Calcomp early in June just prior to the NCC. This, coupled with their apparent operation at the design limits of the product, could cause a delay in their production release and shipment, now forecast for September.

*　*　*

The traditional suppliers to the low-end hard disk market (Pertec, Diablo, Wangco, Ampex, Caelus, Iomec—all of whom use obsolete 2314/15 cartridge technology) appear unable or unwilling to make the technology and manufacturing investments required to compete with Winchester products. Unless they do this, however, they will eventually lose their market positions.

<h2 style="text-align:center">6—FINANCIALS</h2>

The financial plan contemplates raising approximately $1.6 million for the first round as is shown below.

PROFORMA STATEMENT OF EQUITY OWNERSHIP			
OWNER CLASS	STOCK CLASS	SHARES	AMOUNT
Employees	Common	354,546	$ 177,363.92
	Preferred, Series A	4,546	17,638.48
Investors	Common	320,454	166,636.08
	Preferred, Series A	320,454	1,243,361.52
TOTAL		1,000,000	$1,605,000.00

These funds will allow PRIAM to design and validate its product, build and place several demonstrator units, prepare the production facility, and secure orders for preproduction evaluation units. This will take approximately one year. An additional $2.0–3.0 million in equity will be raised over the following year to reach cash breakeven. Three schedules that summarize the PRIAM financial forecast are included as Exhibits I through III.

13

Exhibit I

PRIAM
Proforma Income Statement

	FY 1979	FY 1980	FY 1981	FY 1982	FY 1983
NET SALES	φ	830	9,150	27,200	50,000
GROSS PROFIT	(200)	(295)	3,390	10,880	20,000
OPERATING COSTS					
Marketing	140	320	850	2,300	4,000
Engineering	610	725	815	1,470	2,750
Other	235	320	460	940	1,560
PBIT	(1,185)	(1,160)	1,265	6,170	11,690
INTEREST & EQUIPMENT LEASE EXPENSE	100	265	495	700	905
PBT	(1,285)	(1,925)	770	5,470	10,785
PAT	(1,285)	(1,925)	385	2,735	5,395
EXTRAORDINARY CREDIT (NOL)	φ	φ	320	1,130	φ
NET PAT	(1,285)	(1,925)	705	3,865	5,395
EQUIVALENT SHARES OUTSTANDING (000)	947	1,280	1,335	1,365	1,385
EPS (BEFORE CREDIT)	(1.35)	(1.50)	.29	2.00	3.90

Exhibit II

PRIAM
Proforma Balance Sheet

	FY 1979	FY 1980	FY 1981	FY 1982	FY 1983
ASSETS					
CASH	95	20	150	150	200
CURRENT ASSETS					
Accounts Receivable	φ	340	2,400	5,250	9,900
Inventory	30	420	2,000	4,300	7,500
Lease Escrows	100	100	20	40	40
FIXED ASSETS					
Leasehold Improvements	20	40	60	90	110
Equipment & Furniture	600	1,300	1,500	1,800	2,100
TOTAL ASSETS	845	2,220	6,130	11,630	19,850
LIABILITIES & EQUITY					
CURRENT LIABILITIES					
Accounts Payable	20	160	910	1,900	3,300
Accounts Receivable Line	φ	240	1,600	1,920	3,245
Inventory Line	φ	210	575	600	400
LONG-TERM LIABILITIES					
Lease Line	600	1,300	1,500	1,800	2,100
TOTAL LIABILITIES	620	1,910	4,585	6,220	9,045
EQUITY					
Paid-In Capital	1,550	3,560	4,090	4,090	4,090
Retained Earnings	(1,325)	(3,250)	(2,545)	1,320	6,715
NET EQUITY	225	310	1,545	5,410	10,805
TOTAL LIABILITIES & EQUITY	845	2,220	6,130	11,630	19,850

Exhibit III

PRIAM
Proforma Statement of Changes in Financial Position

	FY 1979	FY 1980	FY 1981	FY 1982	FY 1983
SOURCES OF FUNDS					
INCOME (LOSS) BEFORE EXTRAORDINARY CREDIT	(1,285)	(1,925)	385	2,735	5,395
EXTRAORDINARY CREDIT	ϕ	ϕ	320	1,130	ϕ
SALE OF CAPITAL STOCK					
Preferred	1,380	2,000	530	ϕ	ϕ
Common	130	10	ϕ	ϕ	ϕ
INCREASE IN CURRENT LIABILITIES					
Accounts Payable	20	140	750	990	1,400
A/R Line	ϕ	240	1,360	320	1,325
Inventory Line	ϕ	210	365	25	(200)
INCREASE IN EQUIPMENT LEASE LINE	600	700	200	300	300
TOTAL	845	1,375	3,910	5,500	8,220
USES OF FUNDS					
INCREASE IN CURRENT ASSETS					
Cash	95	(75)	130	ϕ	50
Accounts Receivable	ϕ	340	2,060	2,850	4,650
Inventory	30	390	1,580	2,300	3,200
Lease Escrows	100	ϕ	(80)	20	ϕ
INCREASE IN FIXED ASSETS					
Leasehold Improvements	20	20	20	30	20
Equipment & Furniture	600	700	200	300	300
TOTAL	845	1,375	3,910	5,500	8,220

AUTHOR INDEX

Alexander, Don, 164
Allen, Robert N., 157
Alsop, Stuart, II, 207
Andrews, Edmund L., 147, 170, 176, 184, 201
Armour, Lawrence A., 96
Arnold, James R., 265

Baker, Kenneth G., 32
Ballas, George C., 30, 39, 40, 146, 152, 178
Bambrick, Richard, 235
Barbieri, Richard, 184
Baty, Gordon B., 59, 128
Bekey, Michele, 201, 212, 254, 283
Benner, Susan, 169, 175, 330
Bennett, Lerone, Jr., 217, 256
Benton, Lee F., 194
Birch, David L., 12, 315
Birley, Sue, 35, 110
Boehm, Michael, 265
Bracker, Jeffrey S., 310
Bricklin, Dan, 317
Brown, Catherine, 111
Bruno, Albert V., 118, 128, 153, 174, 179, 189, 193, 194, 197
Buchsbaum, Susan, 222

Buckley, Jerry, 202
Burek, D., 234
Burek, Deborah M., 223
Buskirk, Richard H., 276
Butcher, Lee, 154, 242, 311
Buzzell, Robert D., 59, 270
Bygrave, William D., 176, 187, 191
Bylinsky, Gene, 46

Case, John, 1
Chandler, William R., 187
Chapin, Andrea, 231
Cherin, Antony, 188
Christy, Ron, 108
Colborne, Carmen, 111
Collins, Orvis, 60, 106, 117, 118, 123, 126, 134
Cook, James R., 261
Cossman, E. Joseph, 215, 223
Currier, Susan E., 44, 56

D'Amico, Marie, 202
Danco, Leon, 106, 107
Daniels, Judith, 110
Davis, Eileen, 169
Dean, Burton V., 323
Delaney, Robert V., Jr., 334

Delano, Sara, 238
Diamond, David, 265
Dible, Donald M., 49, 214, 334
Doherty, Edward, 195
Drossler, Richard A., 49
Duchesnau, Donald A., 142

Easton, Nina, 128
Eckert, Lee A., 334
Egge, Karl, 114, 312, 325

Farrell, Kevin, 197
Fast, Norman A., 188
Fawcette, James, 265
Feinberg, Andrew, 39, 41
Fenn, Donna, 270
Fields, Debbi, 219, 257, 284
Finston, Peggy, 269, 271
Forde, Douglas H., 287
Frazier, Nancy, 217, 251, 279
Freear, John, 173, 176, 177, 199
Fucini, Joseph J., 6, 7, 11, 12
Fucini, Suzy, 6, 7, 11, 12
Furst, Alan, 219, 257, 284

Galant, Debbie, 156, 203
Gale, Bradley, 59, 270
Gardner, John C., 264
Garr, Doug, 79, 80, 98
Garrett, Echo M., 222, 243
Gartner, William B., 117, 142
Gersten, Alan, 199
Gibson, G. Thomas, 187, 188, 190, 299
Gibson, Thomas, 253
Golder, Stanley C., 190
Goldstein, Nora, 195
Gorman, Michael, 193
Gould, Alan, 6
Greve, John W., 101
Gumpert, David, 334
Gumpert, David E., 108
Gupta, Anil K., 193, 198, 237
Gupta, Udayan, 185, 196

Halloran, Michael J., 194
Harrar, George, 187, 251
Hartmann, Curtis, 231
Hauck, Donald, 220
Hedgecock, Cathy, 113, 201, 251
Heldman, Victoria C., 71
Hergert, Michael, 188
Hillkirk, John, 41
Hills, Gerald E., 50

Hoad, William M., 299
Hoffs, Ellen, 252, 270
Hollas, David, 30, 39, 40, 146, 152, 178
Holman, Jonathan S., 105
Howell, John, 133
Howell, Robert, 334
Huerta, Loretta Kuklinsky, 196, 198
Hutchins, Dexter C., 212
Hutt, Roger, 114

Ioannou, Lori, 187, 196

Jacobson, Gary, 41
James, Ellen, 198, 218
Johnson, John H., 195, 217, 251, 256
Johnson, Steve, 195
Jones, Billy M., 108
Jubrak, Jim, 78
Juilland, Marie-Jeanne, 90, 114, 159, 185, 204

Kahn, Joseph P., 162
Kalter, Joanmarie, 262
Kamoroff, Bernard, 305
Kane, Sid, 199, 296
Kelleher, Joanne, 223
Kelley, Albert J., 314
Ketchum, Bradford W., Jr., 290
Khoylian, Roubina, 188, 192
King, Pamela J., 181
Kipling, Rudyard, 100
Kirk, Margaret, 114
Kishel, Gregory, 220, 248, 254
Kishel, Patricia, 220, 248, 254
Kotkin, Joel, 167
Koxma, Robert J., 198
Kulow, David M., 188, 192
Kyd, Marilyn, 314

Larsen, Erik, 312, 313, 340
Levering, Robert, 216
Lindorf, Dave, 202
Lipper, Arthur, III, 180, 182, 190, 293, 333
Little, Royal, 139, 140, 177
Littman, Johnathan, 238
Logan, William, 32, 179, 181, 251
Long, Richard, 117, 135
Lovejoy, Jesse Robert, 194
Lovinger, J. D., 192
Lynn, Gary S., 92, 334

MacMillan, Ian, 188, 189, 191, 192
Madlin, Nancy, 122, 341

Magnet, Myron, 31
Maier, John B., 191, 194
Maldin, Nancy, 58
Mamis, Robert A., 94, 145, 169, 178, 181, 285
Mancuso, Joseph R., 311, 334
Mangan, Doreen, 296
Manley, Marisa L., 77
Marquis, Donald G., 47
McElhaney, J., 71
McMullan, W. Ed., 45, 111, 117, 128, 135
McWethy, Andrew, 193
Metzger, Mark K., 222
Michaud, Jacqueline, 222
Middendorf, William H., 77
Milne, Bruce, 14
Molland, Max, 251
Montgomery, M. R., 251, 259
Moore, David G., 60, 106, 117, 118, 123, 126, 134
Moore, Norman H., 4, 101
Morita, Akio, 9, 12
Morrison, Robert S., 249
Mueller, William, 252, 281

Narashima, P. N. Subba, 189
Nicholas, Ted, 108

O'Neill, Michael F., 32
Obermeyer, Judith H., 95

Park, Robert, 92
Pavan, Sahgal, 199
Pearson, Charles T., 37, 42, 78, 250
Poindexter, J. B., 191
PosnerBruce G., 170, 180, 184, 192, 265, 312, 314
Post, Tom, 199
Pratt, Stanley E., 197
Pressman, David, 92
Pridmore, Jay, 157, 222
Putt, William D., 59, 127, 138

Quinn, Barbara, 252

Raffio, Ralph, 170
Ray, Robert J., 334
Rea, Robert H., 189
Reibstein, Larry, 302
Rice, Berkeley, 265
Rich, Stanley R., 334
Richman, Tom, 116, 145, 265, 270, 314, 319, 321

Ridgeway, James, 216
Rifkin, George, 251
Rifkin, Glenn, 187
Roberts, Edward B., 325, 334
Roberts, Hilyard V., 71
Robinson, Richard B., Jr., 190, 191
Rockey, Edward H., 36, 310
Roscow, James P., 195, 196, 296
Rosenberg, Ronald, 267
Rosko, Peter, 299
RothDavid, M., 215
Ruhnka, John C., 186, 327
Runde, Robert, 57
Russell, Sabin, 184, 196, 234, 265
Ryan, J. D., 334

Sachs, Andrea, 294
Sager, Ira, 311
Sahlman, William A., 193
Sangal, Pavan, 175
Sapienza, Harry J., 193
Schaden, Richard F., 71
Scherer, Ron, 198
Schilit, W. Keith, 334
Schragge, Phil, 334
Schroeder, Curtis, 185
Schultz, Leslie, 251
Schwartz, Robert G., 116
Seglin, Jeffrey L., 169
Selck, Thomas E., 254
Shaw, John J., 311
Shepard, William G., Jr., 157, 263, 277
Shils, Edward B., 35
Shuman, Jeffrey C., 311
Siegel, Robin, 189
Silver, A. David, 185, 201
Simer, Frank J., 114
Sklarewitz, Norman, 311
Smith, Norman R., 232
Springer, Robert M., Jr., 76
Stangil, Mary Ann, 247
Stata, Raymond S., 129
Steingold, Fred, 253
Stockwell, James I., 122
Strugatch, Warren, 333, 337
Stuckin, Miles, 293
Sugarman, Joseph, 48
Sussman, Gerald, 311
Sutton, David P., 199, 202

Tanner, Robert, 203
Tapp, Jay, 117, 135

Tarpley, Fred A., Jr., 116
Tarter, Jeffrey, 164, 219
Teach, Richard D., 116
Teague, Burton W., 197, 333
Thackray, John, 190
Thomas, Marita, 251, 254
Thomas, Neal L., 70, 72, 293, 305
Thomas, Stephen G., 133, 331
Thorpe, James F., 77
Tieken, Nancy B., 265
Timmons, Jeffry A., 26, 108, 130, 176, 187
Trombetta, William L., 75
Troop, Paul, 194
Tyebjee, Tyzoon T., 118, 128, 153, 174,
     179, 193, 194, 197

Udell, Gerald G., 32

Vallens, Ansi, 263
Van Hook, Barry L., 114
Verity, John, 198
Vesper, Karl H., 10
Vincent, Linda, 188

Walker, David A., 191, 194
Waters, Craig, 265
Watkins, David S., 326
Watts, Raymond D., 70, 72, 293, 305
Webster's, 2
Webster, Frederick A., 135
Welles, Edward O., 267, 318
Welsh, John A., 150
Wensberg, Peter, 251, 266
Wetzel, William E., Jr., 173, 177, 179, 181,
     199
White, Jerry F., 150, 334
White, John A., 334
White, Richard M., 237
Willis, Clint, 196
Wilson, Frank W., 101
Windle, John P., 340
Wolpert, Tom, 201

Young, John E., 186, 327
Yue, William, 188

ENTREPRENEUR INDEX

Adler, Al, 255
Adler, Fred, 333
Adler, Robert M., II, 214
Alexander, Arthur P., 59, 143
Altos, 21
Altschuler, John, 200
Amdahl, Gene, 31, 175
Anderson, Harlan, 187, 325
Au, Alex, 203

Baker, Bob, 318
Baldwin, Dwight, 11
Ballas, George C., 30, 39–41, 50, 87, 146, 152, 178
Barnes, Tracy, 139
Bean, L. L., 259
Bell, Alexander Graham, 90
Bennett, Bill, 44
Benson, Artie, 221
Birch, David, 315
Borden, Gail, 6
Bricklin, Dan, 207, 317
Bunnell, Bert, 44

Carlson, Chester, 41, 47
Carrol, Phil, 5

Carver, Bob, 35
Cashman, Bob, 312
Chandler, Laurie, 17–25
Cheever, John, 183
Cheiky, Charity, 57, 188
Cheiky, Michael, 57, 188
Citron, Robert A., 203
Coca Cola, 100
Copestead, Terry, 233
Cossman, E. Joseph, 215
Cox, 293

Daniel, Mann, Johnson, and Mendenhall, 132
Daniels, Judith, 110
Darby, S. Newman, 94
Der Torossian, Papken, 90
Dole, James, 8
Doriot, Georges, 325
Drake, Jim, 94
Drawbach, Daniel, 90
Duthie, Brian, 16–25

Edelman, Steve, 192
Ederer, Dave, 264
Egnew, James, 184

Eller, Joe C., 80
Ely, Carol, 169

Feld, Daniel, 230
Fields, Debbi, 219, 257, 284
Finnie, Robert, 56
Fischer, Mike, 235
Fitzgerald, Marshall, 265
Flaherty, Bob, 269, 270
Fleming, Floyd, 228
Ford, Henry, 105, 157
Forster, Harry, 127
Foster, Bill, 313
Frankston, Bob, 207, 317
Fuller, Buckminster, 32

Gabrel, Gary, 231
Garland, Harry, 145
Geist, Tom, 40
Gilbert, Steven J., 333
Glaze, Thomas, 79
Goldsmith, Dave, 56
Grady, Bill, 139

Haley, John, 105
Harar, Robert, 157
Harp, Lore, 169
Harrold, William T., 224
Hatsopolous, George, 313
Hauck, Donald, 220
Head, Howard, 3
Heckmann, Richard, 226
Hewlett, Bill, 47
Hoffman, Eliot, 128
Holman, Jonathan, 105
Howard, Bob, 53, 225
Hughes, Howard, 152
Humphrey, John, 53

Ibuka, Masaru, 9, 12

Jackson, Mary Ann, 321
Jensen, Rob, 5
Jobs, Steve, 152, 154, 242, 311
Johnson, Bud, 58
Johnson, Dick, 55
Johnson, John H., 217, 255

Kaiser, Henry, 4
Kaldenbach, Robert, 217
Kearns, Robert W., 78
Keller, Robert, 279–281
Kennedy, John, 251

Khoury, Amir, 253
King, Colleen, 252
Kirschner, Bill, 256
Knief, Alfred, 153
Kramer Brothers, 46
Kyd, Marilyn, 314

Land, Edwin, 89, 266
Lasater, Dan, 96
Lear, William, 152
Lewis, Milton, 210
Lieberman, Mike, 145
Lipper, Arthur, 332
Little, Arthur D., 39
Lucas, Kenneth, 203

Mann, Jim, 32
Markkula, Mike, 242, 311
Martin, John, 253
McBride, Cheryl, 250
McBride, John, 250
McDonnell Aircraft, 105
McNealy, Scott, 312
Melen, Roger, 145
Melohn, Tom, 116
Mennen, Gerhard, 11
Meyer, Walter, 39, 316
Michaels, Allen, 178
Milender, Sumner, 32
Milne, Bruce, 13–25, 96, 228, 311
Moore, John, 184
Moore, Norman H., 3, 101
Moriguchi, Tomio, 313
Morrison, Robert, 249
Morrow, George, 114, 216
Muller, Len, 209–211
My Own Meals, 321

Nicolai, Carl, 92, 282

Olmstead, James H., 203
Olsen, Ken, 187, 325
Otis, Elisha, 7

Papson, Vicky, 58
Paxton, Lowell, 218
Percy, Roger, 43, 93
Pierce, Charles, 163
Poure, Jim, 180

Radcliff, Barbara, 128
Randolph, Octavia, 317

Rava, Barry, 235
Rector, John, 139
Red, Beverly, 139
Rennie, John C., 212
Rich, Stan, 147
Rodgers, Bill, 162
Rollnick, William D., 178
Rosen, Ben, 340
Roth, Sanford, 98
Ruby, Sandy, 219

Schroeder, William, 189
Schweitzer, Hoyle, 94
Sender, Florence, 145
Shane, Michael, 54
Simek, Pep, 237
Simek, Tom, 237
Simons, Sam, 167
Sneddon, David, 230
Speer, Roy, 218
Stata, Ray, 129
Steele, Dave, 5
Steinway, Henry, 11
Stickney, Henry, 180
Stockwell, James, 122
Sugarman, Joe, 47–49
Sutherland, Steve, 55

Terry, Georgina, 35
Thalheimer, Richard, 105

Thomas, Stephen, 331
Thomas, Stephen G., 133
Townsend, Robert, 156
Tracht, Robert, 167
Tremulis, Alex, 37
Tucker, Preston, 37, 42, 77
Turek, Joseph J., 175
Twain, Mark, 84

Von Ohain, Hans, 38, 100

Warner, Ted, 210
Watson, Jim, 318
Weed Eater, 30
Wetzel, William, 180
Wheelright, George, 266
Whittle, Frank, 38, 100
Wiedemann, Rudi, 139
Williams, Leslie, 255
Wilson, Al, 189
Wilson, Kemmons, 115
Wozniak, Steve, 7, 152, 242, 311
Wright, Bill, 92, 282
Wurlitzer, Rudolph, 6
Wythes, Paul, 189

Yahn, Rob, 162

Zaffaroni, Alejandro, 45

ENTERPRISE INDEX

Accountants' Microsystems, 17–25
Accounting firm, 300
Adage, Inc., 122
Air Designs, 32
Aircraft radios, 208
Altair, 216
Amdahl Corporation, 31, 175
Apple Computer, 7, 8, 32, 152, 154, 242, 311
Appliance store, 257
Applied Medical, 200
Appraisal service, 264
AR&D, 325
Artificial arm, 177
ASK Computer, 251
Avon, 139

Baldwin Pianos, 11
Balloons, 139
Bar, 139
Bicycle, 208
Bicycle carrier, 233
Blood Containers, 253
Blowers, 139
Bonanza, 96
Bone healing monitor, 98

Bottle Cutter, 228
Bowling alley, 293
Break locators, 225
Burger Bug Killers, 270
Burgmaster, 251

Cable television, 284
Careers Today, 330
Carver Corporation, 36
Celerity Computer, 311
Cetus Corporation, 199
Chem-Tech Films, 199
Chopper Industries, 237
CMI, 134
Coca Cola, 82
Cognetics, 315
Columbia Engineers, 209–211
Commercial construction, 212
Compaq Computer, 214
Computerland, 238
Construction equipment, 299
Convergent Technologies, 178
Cookies, 219, 257, 284
Copy machine dealership, 170
Crystal Chemicals, 80
Custom Silicon, 251

Data Ease, 251
Dataword, 17
Dell Computer, 216
Department store, 220
Depth sounders, 120
Digital Equipment Corporation, 15, 187, 251, 325
Disco, 263
Dole, 8
Dollsville Dolls, 250
Donzis Research, 251
Door manufacturer, 72
Drugs, 184
Dump truck lift, 77
DuPont, 177

Ebony Magazine, 217
Edgewater Films, 199
Electronic Concepts, 83
Electronics, 139
Electronics wholesaler, 235
Engineering and architecture, 132
Engineering temporaries, 210
Environmental research, 213
Everest & Jennings, 251
Excursion railroad, 279–281

Fabric store, 221,
Fabrics store, 260
Farallon Industries, 3, 101
Federal Express, 330
Filmmaking, 156
Financial publishing, 269
Fireplace range, 316
Fish smoker, 208
Ford Motor, 78, 141, 177
Ford Pinto, 74
Formulated foods, 145
Frederick Seal, 251
Furniture manufacturing, 161
Furniture retailer, 48

General Instrument, 192
Gillette, 141
Goodyear, 139
Grumman, 73
Gun, 70

Hair rollers, 76
Heat treating shop, 264
Helium dispenser, 233
Helmet, 70
Hewlett-Packard, 139, 251

Hi-fi amplifier, 208
Hi-fi speakers, 208, 209
Hobby product, 208
Holiday Inns, 115
Holograph Corporation, 127
Home Shopping Network, 218
Hot spiced wine mix, 53
Houseboats, 5

IBM, 32, 169
Import-export, 167
Imported racketballs, 294
Imported wigs, blue jeans, 54
Imports, 220
IMS, 216, 238
Industrial chemicals, 143
Innovation Magazine, 330
Intrusion detector, 175
Ithaca Systems, 192

Jet engines, 100
Johnson Publishing, 217, 251, 255
Jugs, 236
Just Desserts, 128

K-2, 3, 256
Ki-Jack, 199
King High Tech, 252, 270
Kleidoscope, 329
Kodak, 89, 94, 141

L. L. Bean, 251, 259
Landlord, 295
Laundromat, 131
Leading Edge, 55
Lockheed Electra, 73

Machine shop, 288
Magazine, 157
Mail order, 48
Medtronic, 251
Menlo Corporation, 234
Mennen, 11
Metal fabricator, 284
Metamorphic Systems, 32
Microcomputers, 145
Microsoft, 17
Minicomputer sales, 227
MITS, 57, 213, 216
Model cars, 232
Monoclonal Antibodies, 79
Movie theater, 220
Multiplexing, 92
Muse Air, 199

Name plates, 225
Negro Digest, 217, 255
New England Farm Bulletin, 217, 251
Nike, 251
Nutritional supplements, 214

Oak Capital, 192
Oberg Industries, 270
Office machines, 157
Ohio Scientific, 57, 188
Otis Elevator, 7

Pacer Systems, 212
Pacific Envelope, 312
Palomino, 314
Papermaking machine, 70
Parking garage, 37
Pente, 231
Personal Software, 207
Pet Rock, 7
Photo enlarging, 209
Phototypesetter, 267
Pipe shop, 259
Plast molding, 255
Plating shop, 243
Polaroid, 89, 94, 251, 266
Ponderosa, 96
Potato chips, 230
Power Jets, Ltd., 38
Priam, 148, 189, 335
Printronix, 251
Proctor and Gamble, 141
Psychology Today, 330
Puffer, 44

Radair, 146, 226
Radius Corporation, 8
Raft trips, 222
Reactor control rods, 35
Restaurant, 36, 326
Retail store, 284
Riegel Textile, 71
Right Products, 32
Road grader guide, 118
Rock tumblers, 231
Rolm, 251
Running equipment store, 162

Sailboats, 261
Sales training, 53
Sanders Technology, 267
Savvy Magazine, 110
Sawhorse kits, 203
Screw machine products, 208

See Technology, 267
Sharper Image, 105
She's A Sport, Inc., 58
Shrunken heads, 209
Silicon Valley Group, 90
Singer, 139
Skyway Air Freight, 318
Slide projector, 46
Software Arts, 317
Software Gardem, 317
Solar Vision, 251
Solid waste disposal, 208
Sony, 9, 12
Southeastern Telecom, 105
Spacelabs, 203
Speedylube, 55, 57
Sperry-Rand, 83
Sports Information Database, 199
Spud Gun, 223
Spud guns, 215
Steinway Pianos, 11
Store chain, 184
Stratus Computer, 148, 313, 325
Sun Microsystems, 312
Survey stakes, 118
Sutter Hill Ventures, 189
Systec, 192

Tech Hi Fi, 219
Telephone information service, 8
Televideo, 251
Tentmaking, 184
Textron, 141
Thermo Electron, 313
Timber company, 289
Tombstone Pizza, 237
Toy glider, 235
Toys, 139
Trade show, 157
Traffic and Safety Control, 255
Trailer, 107
Trailer, camping, 126
Trailer, travel, 92, 130
Trailer manufacturer, 321, 322
Travel tour wholesaler, 154
Trilogy Corporation, 31
Tucker Auto, 37, 42, 77, 251
TV response, 43

United Sciences America, 214

Vacuum, 220 volt, 75
Vanguard, 190

Vaporizer, 72
Variety store, 313
Vector Graphic, 169, 330
Ventrex Laboratories, 251
Venture Capital Network, 180
Veterinarian, 52
VisiCalc, 207
Vitalec, Inc., 203
Voice scrambler, 282
Voice stress analyzer, 170

Weed Eater, 30, 39–41, 50, 87, 146, 152,
    178

Windsurfer International, 94
Wine mix, 225
Wordplay, 248
Wurlitzer, 6

Xerox, 41, 47
Yogurt, 56
Yoplait Yogurt, 44

Zero Stage Capital, 187

SUBJECT INDEX

Abstract design, 35
Accountant as director, 113
Accountants, 112, 304
Accounting, 23, 296–304
  cost of, 304
  evolution, 302
  ledgers, 303
  systems, 301
ACE, 108
Advertisements, 215
Advertising, 213–218
Advertising agencies, 112
Advisers, 113
Agreements, 292
AICPA, 21
ANSI, 71
ASTM, 70

Balance sheet forecast, 324
Bank, 24
Bank borrowing, 19, 160
Bank loan application, 166–167
Banker as director, 113
Bankers, 108, 332
Bankers, finding, 163–166
Bankruptcy, 114
Ben Franklin Partnership, 159

Best efforts, 202
Bids, 211
Boilerplate, 81
Books, store bought, 301
Bottom up forecasting, 320
Brainstorming, 8
Breadboard, 39, 73
Breakeven, 323
Bridge financing, 140

C corporation, 287
Capital, from customers, 157–159
Capital, raising, 299
Capital needs, 142–145, 148
  start-up, 175
Capital raising methods, 174
Cash flow, 147, 150–152, 285, 323–325
Cash, shortage of, 326
Cash requirements, 141
Catalog retailers, 234
Certification mark, 95
Chain stores, 233
ChFC, 296
Claim, insurance, 78
CLU, 296
Code of Federal Regulations, 71
Commerce Business Daily, 211

Commission practices, 230
Commissioned agents, 236
Common stock, 174
Communication, written, 74
Community development, 169
Competence, 10
Competition, preempting, 271
Concept clarification, 14
Confirming house, 156
Consequence chains, 5
Constraints, Government, 200
Consultants, 112
Contact approaches, 53–58
Contacts, 10, 110, 123, 255, 281
Contract development, 43
Contracts, 292
Control, accounting, 298
Copyrights, 95
Corporate veil, 80
Corporate Venture Capital, 196
Corporation, 121
Cost estimation, 324
Cost of going public, 198
Costs, controlling, 270
CPA, 304
CPE, 21
CPSC, 70
Cream skimming, 59
Creative thinking, 8
Credit cards, 156
CSPC, 70
Customer requests, 209

DBA, 107
Deal terms, 182–184, 193–194
Dealers, 236
Debugging, 43
Delays, 327
Demographic analysis, 51
Demographics, 248
Department stores, 232
Depth sounders, 120
Design
   defensive, 71
   production, 45–47
Design notebook, 90, 91
Design reviews, 74
Design stages, 32–34
Designing around, 68
Development corporations, 184
Directors, 113
Disagreements, 294
Disclaimer, 76
Dun and Bradstreet, 148

Egocentric evaluation, 50
Electronic media, 218
Employees, 22, 153
   recruiting, 264
Encyclopedia of Associations, 110
End users, 228
Engineering analysis, formal, 72
Engineering, reverse, 83
EPA, 70
Equipment, home built, 256
Equipment, used, 256
Equity, retaining, 138, 168
Equity, sharing, 115–134
Equity capital
   inside, 18
   outside, 19
ESOP, 285
Estimates, 41
Executive recruiting, 105
Expansion, geographical, 21
Experience, 35
Experimentation, 11
Expert help, 258
Expertise, 120
External team, 111–115

Facilities, 249
Factors, 169
Failure causes, 31
Failure mode analysis, 73, 327
Fair Labor Standards Act, 281
Fault tree analysis, 73, 327
FDA, 70
Feasibility, 31
FED, 70
Federal Regulations, Code Of, 71
Finance companies, 169
Financing, 13
Financing sources, 138
Financing stages, 140
Finder's fee, 180
Finding investors, 179
Firm underwriting, 202
First order sources, 208
First sales, 206
First stage financing, 140
Flexibility, 318
Forecasting, 319
Forecasting, financial, 147–152
Forecasts, 25
Forecasts, financial, 323
Formal surveys, 54
Founders' money, 152–154
Franchising, 170

Friendly lenders, 154
Friendly money, 18
FTS, 70
Full Registration, 201

Gale Research, 234
Gantt chart, 245
Gantt Charts, 323
General partner, 81
Goals, 315
Goals, venture, 313–315
Government, 108
Government customers, 212–213
Graphical tools, 323
Guarantee, 161–163, 182

Hazard analysis, 74
Help sources, 108
   low cost, 108–111
Help, temporary, 263–266
Hiring, 262
Holding period, 191
Home-based businesses, 250
Home-built, 255
Hours worked, 243

ICC, 70
Ideas, 41
Imitation, 16, 68, 84
   forestalling, 81–102
Impact wheels, 5
Implication trees, 5
Incorporation, 79–81
Incremental action, 315–319
Incubators, 251
Industrial revenue bonds, 170
Informal interviews, 53
Informal investors, 179–184
Information, 318
Infringement, 78
Institutional Venture Capital, 196
Instructions, product, 75
Insurance, 294
Insurance brokers, 78, 112
Insurance types, 294–296
Insurance, product liability, 77
Intellectual property, 78
Internal Revenue Service, 80, 289
Intra-state, 201
Investors
   corporate, 184
   foreign, 185
   private, 332
   public, 332

Job machine shop, 41
Jobbers, 234
Jury rig, 73
Jury rigs, 39

Lawyer, 111, 290–292
Lawyer as director, 113
Lawyer, patent, 84
Leasing, 169, 254
Legal aspects, 13
Legal costs, 80, 94, 106
Legal form, 285
Legal format, 107, 121
Liability, 16
Liability insurance, 78
Liability, product, 68–81
Licenses, 277–281
Litigation, 70
Loan terms, 168
Loans, starting with, 139
Location, 248–252
Loss factor, 254
Luck, 325

Magnuson-Moss, 76
Mail selling, 217
Make or buy, 143
Market comparisons, 50
Market pull, 47–49
Market research, 50–58
Mathematical analysis, 37
Mezzanine financing, 140
MIT Forum, 181
Mockups, 38
Models, 73
   computer, 38
Models, physical, 38
Momentum, competitive, 102

National Safety Council, 71
Negotiating, 293
Networks, 110
Networks, social, 180
NFIB, 139
Niche strategy, 49

Operations, starting, 22
Opportunities
   future, 4, 7
   ready, 4
Opportunity clues, 5–7
Opportunity prerequisites, 4
Opportunity signals, 9
Opportunity occurrence, 2–5

Organization chart, 338
OSHA, 70
Outside team, 111–115
Overhead, 275
Ownership, dividing, 128–131, 138

Packaging, 45
Paperwork, 23
Partners, 115
   finding, 121–123
   going without, 106
   selecting, 123–128
   silent, 177–179
   working, 153
Partners breakup, 134
Partners policies, 133
Partnership, 120
   limited, 81
   R&D, 20
Patent, 107
   preparation for, 89–95
   utility, 91
Patent claims, 84, 89
Patent cost, 92
Patent Gazette, 84, 87
Patent interference, 90
Patent lawyer, 92
Patent litigation cost, 94
Patent pending, 89
Patent witnesses, 90
Patents, 84
   defending, 94
   design, 84
   foreign, 90
   utility, 84
   value of, 89
Payroll deductions, 266
Payroll, bank help, 301
Pegboard systems, 301
Pencil and paper analysis, 36
People problems, 329
Permissions, 276–281
Permits, 277
Personal capabilities, 10
Personal preferences, 10
Personal savings, 152
Personal selling, 223–235
Personnel, 12
PERT chart, 245, 323
Philanthropy, 155
Pilot selling, 57
PIMS, 270
Pitfalls, operations, 241
Plan, worst, 328

Plan outline, 335, 344
Planning, 24–27
   cons of, 26
   informal, 15
   purposes of, 25
   selective, 319–330
Planning process, 340
Plans, formal, 311, 330–341
Plans, shortcomings of, 334
Portfolio of Accounting Systems, 303
Positioning, market, 49
Precedents
   design, 43
   role of, 34
Predicting sales, 319
Predicting sequences, 320
Preferred stock, 174, 178
Premises, 245
Pricing, 58–60
Primary data, 53
Private investors, 176, 181
Private placements, 177–185
Pro forma financials, 149
Problem anticipation, 73
Problem forestalling, 267–269, 325–330
Problems
   partner, 131–133
   technical, 328
Produceability, 31
Product liability, 69
Product, life stages, 71
Production, 12
Production problems, 268
Production specifications, 77
Profitability, 31, 60
Prohibitions, 281
Proposals, sales, 211
Proprietary, 21, 25
Proprietorship, 107, 121
Prospectus, 332
Protection, 16
Prototype, 41, 46, 73, 107, 125
Prototypes, 39
Public issue, selling, 202
Public offerings, 197–203
Publicity, free, 214
Purchasing, 12

Quality, 269

Real estate, 253
Records, 13, 275, 304–307
   tax, 301
Regulation D, 201

Regulatory constraints, 284
Reporting, 300
Requirements, government, 283
Resources, 10, 137
Retailers, 230–235
Return, venture capital, 190
Robert Morris, 148
ROI, 190, 323
Royalty, 182

S.R.I., 43
SAE, 70, 75
Sales, 12, 328
   development phases, 21
   seminar, 21
   start-up, 20
Sales call cost, 222
Sales intermediaries, 229
Savings, personal, 137
SBA, 108, 159
SBI, 109
SBIC, 186, 196
SBIR, 159
Schedule C, 286
SEC, 180, 201
Secondary data, 51, 52
Secrecy, 82–84
Secrecy agreement, 82
Secret, definition, 82
Section 1244 stock, 287
Seed capital, 181
Seed capital sources, 152–159
Seed financing, 19
Seed money, 140
Seed plus debt, 174
Seed stage capital, 176
Segmentation, market, 49, 51
Self underwriting, 202
Self-assessment, 126
Sequence, reading, 27
Sequence planning, 320
Service bureau, 302
Shareware, 59
Sharing equipment, 255
Sketches, 36
Small Business Administration, 108, 162
Software, accounting, 301
Sole ownership, 106
Solo takeoff, 104
Sounding boards, 112
Specialty retailers, 234
Splitoff, 184
Splitout, 170
Stages, capitalization, 176

Stakeholders, 153, 155–160
Start-up capital, 140, 176
State sales tax, 288
Stereolithography, 38
Storefront, 218–223
Styling, 45
Styling push, 49
Subchapter S, 210, 286
Supplier relationships, 22
Suppliers, 19, 108, 155, 259, 261
Surveying stakes, 119
Systematic searching, 8

Tax forms, 306
Tax help, 290
Taxes, 284, 287, 297, 298
Team
   grade-A, 189
   outside, 18
Teaming, 17
Teams, 115
Technology push, 47
Term sheet, 194
Testing, product, 73
Thinking through, 35
Thomas Register, 41, 96
Time, lack of, 115
Top down forecasting, 320
Trade associations, 70
Trade credit, 155
Trade Names Dictionary, 96
Trade Secrets, 78
Trade show display, 57
Trade shows, 221
Trademark, 95–98
   application, 97
   cost, 96
   nullification, 98
Trend extrapolation, 320

Underwriters Laboratories, 71
Uniform Commercial Code, 75, 293
Unique selling proposition, 49
Used equipment, 255

Value analysis, 101
Value engineering, 101
Venture capital, 176, 186–193
   choosing, 197
Venture capitalists, 332
Venture planning, 310
Venture plans, 24
Visualization, mental, 36

Warning labels, 77
Warnings, product, 75
Warranties
  implied, 76
  product, 75
Warrants, 184
Wholsalers, 234

Workability, 31
Workletter, 254
Worst case analysis, 74

Zero defect, 74
Zoning, 24